DANUVIUS

OESIA

BLACK SEA

CASPIAN SEA

Philippopolis

Sinope

THRACIA

ONIA

Philippi

Byzantium

salonica

BITHYNIA ET PONTUS

Nicaea

Ancyra

REGNUM
POLEMONIS

ARMENIA
MINOR

Pergamum

GALATIA

ASIA

Smyrna

Antioch

CAPPADOCIA

Athens

orinth

Ephesus

Lystra

Sparta

LYCIA

Tarsus

AEGEAN SEA

RHODES

Antioch

CILICIA
ET
SYRIA

Salamis

Damascus

CRETA

CYPRUS

Sidon

SEA

Tyre

Caesarea

Jerusalem

Alexandria

Gaza

NAICA

NABATAEA

Memphis

AEGYPTUS

ARABIAN GULF

NILUS

Thebae

Syene
(Elephantine)

CITIES AND TOWNS ●

PALESTINE
IN THE MACCABEAN PERIOD
(168-63 B.C.)

Sidon

Damascu

MEDITERRANEAN SEA

Tyre

Ptolemais

GALILEE

SEA OF
GALILE

Sepphoris

Strato's Tower

Scythopolis

Pella

SAMARIA

JORDAN

Gerasa

Joppa

Alexandrium

Jamnia

Modein

Philadelphi

Azotus

Jericho

Jerusalem

Hyrcania

Medeba

Ascalon

JUDEA

Hebron

Machaerus

Gaza

DEAD
SEA

KINGDOM OF ALEXANDER JANNAEUS ▨

FOURTH EDITION

UNDERSTANDING THE NEW TESTAMENT

HOWARD CLARK KEE

Boston University

Prentice-Hall, Inc., *Englewood Cliffs, New Jersey* 07632

Library of Congress Cataloging in Publication Data

KEE, HOWARD CLARK.
   Understanding the New Testament.

   Includes bibliographies and index.
   1. Bible.   N.T.—History of Biblical events.
2. Bible.   N.T.—Introductions.   I. Title.
BS2407.K37 1983   225.6′1   82-16482
ISBN   0-13-936591-5

Editorial/production supervision and
   interior design: Patricia V. Amoroso
Cover design: Karolina Harris
Manufacturing buyer: Harry P. Baisley

Printed in the United States of America

10   9   8   7

ISBN 0-13-936591-5

PRENTICE-HALL INTERNATIONAL, INC., *London*
PRENTICE-HALL OF AUSTRALIA PTY. LIMITED, *Sydney*
EDITORA PRENTICE-HALL DO BRASIL, LTDA., *Rio de Janeiro*
PRENTICE-HALL CANADA INC., *Toronto*
PRENTICE-HALL OF INDIA PRIVATE LIMITED, *New Delhi*
PRENTICE-HALL OF JAPAN, INC., *Tokyo*
PRENTICE-HALL OF SOUTHEAST ASIA PTE. LTD., *Singapore*
WHITEHALL BOOKS LIMITED, *Wellington, New Zealand*

Contents

iii

Preface to the Fourth Edition

Thirty years have passed since work began on the first edition of *Understanding the New Testament*. At the time of its initial publication, two aspects of the book were distinctive: (1) Most introductory works on the New Testament were content to sketch the origins of the individual books along chiefly literary lines. On the other hand, studies of Christian beginnings concentrated on either theological or historical development, but in either case, the specific New Testament writings and the circumstances of their origins were treated only in passing. The decision made in 1953 was to undertake all three tasks, weaving together literary, religious, and historical concerns. (2) At a time when a dominant theme in the approach to religion, including the study of Christian origins, was the individual's relationship to God, this introductory survey emphasized the community pattern of Christianity from its birth. Both these factors have been retained in the second (1965) and third (1973) editions.

In this edition, however, concern for community is intensified by concentration on the range of ways in which the early Christians found personal identity in a communal context. That fundamental social dimension is here treated explicitly in light of recent attention by biblical scholars to the bearing of sociological study on the history of the ancient world. Both sociology of knowledge and sociology of religion are now seen to be essential to the analysis of the shared world views that provide the coherence and the rallying-point for the rise of religious movements and for their subsequent development. For many decades biblical scholars have been speaking of the "life situation" in which religious tradition—including early Christian tradition—arose and was transmitted. But few have paused to analyze that life setting in detail. The methodological aspect of the present study, with its reliance on sociological insights, is traced in detail in Appendixes I and V of the present work: The first describes the concept of personal identity as it has developed in the field of sociology of knowledge, and is designated life-world, or world view. The other discusses from a sociological perspective the development of power structures. Other appendixes offer summaries of technical matters relating to sources and classification of the early Christian tradition.

The present edition, which has been largely rewritten, is the work of only one of the authors who shared in the earlier versions; to Franklin W. Young and Karlfried Froehlich, I want to express gratitude for their part in the earlier editions of this book. The Epilogue on the canon of the New Testament, however, has been written by Paul J. Achtemeier of Union Theological Seminary in Richmond, Virginia, whose recent research has demonstrated a special competence in this subject area. My gratitude is extended to him, as well as to colleagues and students at Boston University, whose challenges and comments have aided me in preparing the present edition. Its aim continues to be best expressed in the title: understanding a set of documents of unique significance in shaping our religious and cultural heritage.

HOWARD CLARK KEE

ACKNOWLEDGMENTS

The National Council of Churches of Christ in the United States of America, for permission to quote throughout this volume from the Revised Standard Version of the Bible, copyright 1942, 1952, and 1971 by the Division of Christian Education, NCCCUSA.

Harcourt Brace Jovanovich, for permission to reproduce my classification system for the Gospel tradition (Appendix II) and my reconstruction of the Q source, from my *Jesus in History* (2nd ed., 1977).

End-paper maps and all interior maps except *Jerusalem in the Time of Jesus* and *Ancient Rome* are based on maps in *The Westminster Historical Atlas to the Bible* (Revised Edition), edited by George Ernest Wright and Floyd Vivian Filson, copyright 1956 by W. L. Jenkins, copyright 1945 by The Westminster Press, and are used by permission. The map *Jerusalem in the Time of Jesus* is based on the map *Jerusalem in Second Temple Times* from the book *Jerusalem Revealed,* edited by Yigael Yadin, and is used by permission of the Israel Exploration Society and Yale University Press.

All photographs by Gordon N. Converse are from the books *Come See the Place* by Gordon N. Converse, Robert J. Bull, and B. Cobbey Crisler, © 1978 by Gordon N. Converse for photographs, by Robert J. Bull and B. Cobbey Crisler for text; and *Fishers of Men: The Way of the Apostles* by Gordon N. Converse, Robert J. Bull, and B. Cobbey Crisler, © 1980 by Gordon N. Converse for photographs, by Robert J. Bull and B. Cobbey Crisler for text. Both books published by Prentice-Hall, Inc., Englewood Cliffs, New Jersey 07632.

Cover art: *The Holy Trinity* by Albrecht Dürer, circa 1511, from *Symbols, Signs, and Signets* by Ernst Lehner, Dover Publications.

PART I

COMMUNITY AND IDENTITY

Introduction:

What Is
the New Testament?

As any reader of the New Testament will observe from the opening pages of the first book, the Gospel of Matthew, the writers of these documents insist on the continuity of Jesus with the figures of the Jewish Bible, or as Christians call it, the Old Testament. All the New Testament writers join in the claim that it is only in the events connected with Jesus that the prophecies of the Old Testament find fulfillment: the birth of Jesus, the place of his birth, the flight into Egypt, the return to Nazareth, the role of John the Baptist in preparing Jesus for his public ministry. The New Testament does not supplant the Old; rather, it claims to supplement it, and to bring its expectations to fruition. Jews, of course, have perceived the biblical tradition very differently: On what grounds do Christians base their claim to possess "the *New* Testament"?

As soon as we read through the New Testament for the first time, we are confronted by other specific questions. Why is the story of Jesus told four times over in the first four books? Why is it that none of the four agrees in

3

every detail? Sometimes the differences are minor, such as whether there were one or two donkeys ready for Jesus to ride into Jerusalem (Matt. 21:7; Mark 11:4). In other cases, the differences seem more important, such as whether the resurrected Jesus appeared to his followers in the vicinity of Jerusalem (Luke 24) or in his native Galilee (Matt. 28:16). Why was it thought necessary to include four gospels? And why is one of them, John, so different from the others in content, style, and sequence of events?

When we move beyond the Gospels to the Acts of the Apostles, the story of Jesus makes a transition into the account of the work of his followers and those commissioned to spread the news about him. The narrative begins in Jerusalem with expectations of universal outreach, but it ends in Rome on a note of some uncertainty about the fate of Paul and of the enterprise for which he risked his life. A careful reading of the opening part of the Acts shows an identity of literary style, and presumably of authorship, with one of the Gospels: Luke. But why did only one Gospel writer think it important to tell the next chapter in the story of the spread of Christianity?

To read beyond the Acts is to enter into a series of letters, addressed for the most part to specific churches in cities or regions, but including greetings, instructions, and even rebukes for individual members or workers. Some of the writings seem to have no specific intended readers, such as the Letter to the Ephesians and the Letter to the Hebrews. Some of these writings are so similar in content it is possible to infer that one was derived from the other— for example, Ephesians from Colossians; 2 Peter from Jude. One letter is purely personal and addressed to a single individual (Philemon). The last book in the collection we know as the New Testament calls itself an *apocalypse*—the Greek word prosaically translated as Revelation.

How did such a diversity of styles, content, intent, and size (from one page in length, 2 John, to about eighty pages, Acts) come to be assembled in a single collection? Scholarly analysis shows that the writings vary widely in style (from crude popular Greek with evident traces of Semitic speech, as in Mark, to polished literary style, as in Acts and Hebrews). Literary allusions range from misquotations of Hebrew prophets (Mark 1:2, corrected by Matthew) to excerpts from Greek poets (Acts 17) and the use of technical philosophical terminology (Heb. 1:3). Why was such a seemingly miscellaneous collection of writings brought together? On what principle was material selected for inclusion?

NEW TESTAMENT OR NEW COVENANT?

The first clue we have to how the New Testament came to be derives from the title given it in some ancient translations, in which the Greek word *diatheke* is translated as "covenant" rather than "testament." "Testament" is still used in legal terminology for the disposal of the goods of the dead, but "covenant" is also a term for a mutual contract, for a binding agreement between certain parties. The phrase "new covenant" has an important role in both the Old and New Testaments.

   In Jeremiah 31:31–33 the prophet announces that Yahweh, the God of Israel, is going to make a new covenant with his people, one different from the agreement by which he had brought them out of Egypt. His instructions will not be written on tablets of stone, as they were at Sinai, but "in their hearts"—that is, where they will directly affect each person's life. The relationship to God will be transformed, so that all his people will know him. The covenant relationship entered into between God and Abraham (Gen. 15:18), which was to endure in perpetuity for all Abraham's descendants (Gen. 17:7), is to be renewed and transformed, Jeremiah declared. And it will take place at some point in the future, about which he says simply, "the days are coming."

   Paul, however, uses the phrase "new covenant" in connection with the Christian community's celebration of Jesus's last meal with his disciples (1 Cor. 11:25). Jesus is reported in the Gospels to have said that the cup he shared "is the new covenant in my blood." But in the Gospel account, Jesus goes on, as Jeremiah does, to link that symbolic meal with the fulfillment of God's purpose for his people in the future: "Truly, I say to you, I shall not drink again of the fruit of the vine until that day when I drink it new in the Kingdom of God" (Mark 14:25). Running through the entire New Testament is the theme that Jesus is in some way the agent for the renewal of the covenant between God and his people. What does that imply about who Jesus is, and about those who claim to be the people of the new covenant?

   The New Testament writers agree that these are the central questions, even though they may differ in the specific answers they provide. Matthew reports Jesus as calling on his hearers to "fulfill the Law" (Matt. 5:17), while Paul declares Jesus Christ to be "the end of the Law" (Rom. 10:4). Yet both agree that he is God's agent for the renewal of his covenant with Abraham and his posterity (Matt. 1:1; 26:28; Gal. 3:6–29). Paul scorns human wisdom (1 Cor. 1:17–30), while the Letter to the Hebrews builds his case for Christianity by using concepts derived from Platonic philosophy. Plato contrasted earthly phenomena, which he regarded as transitory copies, with the heavenly eternal patterns of reality. The author of Hebrews declares that the Israelite worship of God was copied from the heavenly pattern shown to Moses on Sinai (Exod. 25:9). It was ordered to be repeated in the portable shrines of the wandering tribes, but Jesus's sacrifice was presented only once in the archetypal heavenly sanctuary itself (Heb. 9:23–26). Yet in spite of cultural differences, Paul and the author of this letter both see Jesus as the agent by which the new covenant is established. Elsewhere Paul asserts that faith is the sole criterion for admission to the covenant (Rom. 3:28), while the Letter of James insists that living faith must be supplemented by works (James 2:17). But both agree that the church is the new Israel (Rom. 11:26; James 1:1). Why are these questions of covenant participation and of fulfillment of an ancient tradition of such central importance for the writers of the New Testament?

   The explanation for the pervasive insistence on the continuity between the heritage of Israel and the Christian community, and for the diversity of ways in which that conviction is expressed in the New Testament writings, is not hard to discover. The basic conviction, in spite of all the ways of expressing it, is that Jesus is the agent of God through whom the new covenant has been brought about. The appealing prophecy of Jeremiah is seen to have been fulfilled through Jesus:

> Behold, the days are coming, says the Lord, when I will make a new covenant with the house of Israel and the house of Judah, not like the covenant which I made with their fathers . . . which they broke. . . . But this is the covenant which I will make with the house of Israel after those days, says the Lord: I will put my law within them, and I will write it upon their hearts; and I will be their God, and they shall be my people.
>
> —JER. 31:31–33

This passage is alluded to in various parts of the New Testament (for example, Mark 14:24; Luke 22:20; Matt. 26:28), and is quoted in full in Heb. 8:8–12. But its main point about a new covenant and a new kind of relationship with God pervades the New Testament. It is essential that this claim be documented by an appeal to prophecies and continuities with the faithful under the old covenant, as well as by evidence of the newness of what Christians think Jesus has brought.

If the central concept is the new covenant, the central figure is, of course, Jesus. Yet both Jesus and the covenant community will be perceived differently by those who come to faith from various backgrounds. Depending on whether converts to the new faith were reared in urban or rural settings, whether they were schooled in the Semitic-speaking Jewish tradition or among Greek-speaking Jews of cities such as Antioch or Alexandria, or whether they heard about Jesus in a situation that had no associations with Judaism, they would respond to the message in a different way. They would almost certainly incorporate into their way of expressing their new-found religious convictions and responsibilities features from their previous training and experience. Since Christianity spread across the Roman Empire with astonishing speed, it should not be in the least surprising that the collection of documents we call the New Testament would reflect all these circumstances and responses.

The Jesus movement, as we might expect from its grounding in the covenant idea, was a corporate rather than an individual affair. Christians discovered a new identity in the context of the new covenant community. Although all shared the conviction that Jesus was God's instrument through which the covenant was established, there were significant differences among them on a variety of subjects. Some stressed continuity with Judaism, especially in conformity to the ritual laws about food and circumcision. Others, who had never been part of the Jewish community, or who had been alienated from that tradition, were concerned with the moral rather than the ritual dimensions of the Jewish law. Some expressed their new-found faith in terms of the Greco-Roman culture in which they had been reared; others relied on the visionary hopes of what modern scholarship calls "Jewish apocalypticism," such as one finds in the Book of Daniel. We will see that the writers acknowledge sharp differences among those who identify themselves as followers of Jesus, as the

New People of God. We will analyze the various New Testament writings in such a way as to try to discover the spoken and unspoken assumptions about human need and divine aid, about evil and redemption, that operated in the various segments of the early Christian community in which these writings were produced.[1]

THE CONTEXT OF THE SEARCH FOR IDENTITY

Christianity set out to evangelize the world at a time of unprecedented political, social, and cultural change. In Rome, Augustus came to power ostensibly to restore the law and political process of the republic. The republic was the form of government in effect before Julius Caesar's seizure of power, which had led to a political struggle culminating in the murder of Caesar by his opponents. Roman society in the period of the republic was hierarchical: At the bottom were the slaves and subject peoples, devoid of personal rights or legal standing; social rank was based on wealth, with specific requirements in personal assets. One had to possess 250,000 denarii, for example, to be a senator. The total number of senators out of the estimated 50 million subjects of the empire has been figured at about 1/500 of 1 percent. Slaves who had been granted freedom, no matter how great their wealth, could not move up the social ladder. Rural people lived on the brink of disaster, victimized by absentee owners of the land they worked, by taxes, and by marauders who swept through their villages unchecked. In the cities, the rich and powerful lived in great houses, the poor in terrible slums. The rich set aside open space in the cities and provided public entertainment, often vying with one another in public benefactions. But the public baths, gardens, and theaters did little to ease the pain of poverty, and they merely aggravated the awareness of the gulf between the powerful rich and the hopeless poor.[2]

In an attempt to gain some kind of identity, city dwellers organized neighborhood associations. Craftsmen lived in clusters in sections of the cities (for example, the potters' quarters) and were organized politically as well as for parades, festivals, and community events. Others—especially those from distant lands transplanted to an unfamiliar city or town—sought to overcome their sense of alienation by joining with devotees of a deity, such as Dionysus or Isis. In commercial cities such as Ostia, Antioch, or Corinth, cult centers for dozens of nonlocal deities sprang up, attesting to the yearning for personal identity through joining with others of like conviction and commitment. Augustus's concentration of power in his own hands and his manipulation of the sociopolitical structure by giving his friends enough money to qualify for

[1] A brief sketch of the historical method employed in this book, drawing on models developed by sociologists (including the sociology of knowledge), is given in the Appendixes.

[2] The descriptions here and the statistics are drawn from Ramsay MacMullen, *Roman Social Relations* (New Haven, Conn.: Yale University Press, 1974).

equestrian or senatorial rank altered that structure in a way even the rich found disquieting. The imperial policy of sending into exile or demanding the suicide of those who opposed the ruling group produced profound anxiety. Even the wealthy began to seek solace in the worship of an exotic god or goddess, and many turned to magic as a way of guaranteeing protection for themselves against their enemies.

The official Jewish religious leadership, the priesthood, had become thoroughly secular, to the point that designation and confirmation of the High Priest was negotiated with the pagan rulers. The wealthy class in Palestine was indistinguishable in its way of life—villas, theaters, baths, gymnasia—from the rich of any pagan city of the empire. The people of the land of Israel were as exploited by absentee landlords as were the peasants of Italy or Egypt. At issue in the minds of faithful Jews were not only the future of their people and the criteria for participation in the covenant relationship with the God of Israel, but the reality of his power and the credibility of his covenant promises as well.

As Christianity spread across the Roman Empire, its message was heard in a variety of ways. The common factor was the search for identity, but the specific questions and aspirations of those who heard and responded to the story of Jesus were deeply affected by their cultural and social background. As any thoughtful person knows, once you have formulated a question, you have already influenced the answer. This was clearly evident in the range of ways in which the New Testament writers explained who Jesus was and what God's purpose through him was.

But it was not only the conceptual aspects of Christianity that were affected by the environment of the hearers. Equally diverse were the ways in which the early Christian communities themselves developed. Group leadership as well as group structure varied from place to place and from time to time. Some of the leaders relied on association with Jesus, some on personal charisma, some on divine revelation, some on wisdom, and others on proper ecclesiastical credentials. Similar variety is evident in the way in which the literature of the New Testament functioned, both among those for whom it was first written and then among subsequent generations. As we have noted, some of the writings were personal letters. Others seem to have been official declarations. Some were intended for a wide readership; others seem to have been written for the inner group only. We must therefore explore not only the literary forms employed by the New Testament writers, but also the functions these writings were meant to serve.

Because of the diversity of the social, economic, and cultural backgrounds of the early Christians, and because of the changing circumstances in which they lived, we can discern within the New Testament changes in their understanding of the world, of the problem of evil and what to do about it. Some writers are antagonistic toward contemporary culture; others want to use it for the Christian cause. Some despair and long for the end of the age; others see evidence of transforming progress. In this diversity of response to Christianity, there is no single line of evolutionary development. Running concurrently were very different strands, each claiming to be the true carrier of the Jesus tradition.

IS THE NEW TESTAMENT
HISTORICALLY RELIABLE?

Once it is acknowledged that there are differences of outlook within the New Testament and that there are discrepancies within the narrative accounts, many feel that the credibility of the New Testament as a historical document is compromised or even denied. Candor requires us to acknowledge, no matter what our point of view, that the New Testament writings record events that occurred at least a generation before they were written down. When we add to this the New Testament's own description of the disciples as illiterate (Acts 4:13), we must acknowledge that there was a crucial stage of oral transmission of the Jesus tradition before the Gospels were produced as we have them. The differences that are evident among them are in some cases not matters of great consequence—such as whether the family of Jesus lived originally in Bethlehem (Matt. 2) or whether they were only temporarily there, but resided in Nazareth (Luke 2). Nevertheless, a serious effort to understand the New Testament must come to terms with these differences and seek to account for them.

We must also call into question whether it is appropriate for us to impose our supposed standards of historical objectivity on documents like the New Testament, which were written not merely to provide information, but to persuade. As John 20:31 puts it, he has reported the story of Jesus's spectacular acts ("signs") in order "that you may believe that Jesus is the Christ, the Son of the living God." Clearly not all his readers are going to share his conclusions, but he is forthright in telling his readers his aims. And those aims are not objective reporting. Using the term in its root sense, of a means of propagating a point of view or belief, the New Testament is not objective history, but *propaganda.* But then history in any time and culture is always *event plus interpretation;* it is never merely objective, in the sense of lacking a framework of interpretation or point of view. What is required is to be aware of the writer's assumptions, the aims of the writing, what its vocabulary, style, and conceptual language presuppose.

The question then is not whether the study and analysis of the New Testament will involve critical judgments, but rather whether the critical process will be conscious, well-informed, and open-minded. "Critical study" does not mean to treat the New Testament negatively, but to approach it perceptively and analytically. The intent of critical study of the New Testament is not the undermining of confidence in its credibility or trustworthiness. It is rather to show the concrete historical setting into which Jesus came, and in which his followers lived and sought to spread his message. The legitimate aim of historical-critical work is to enable the student to enter more fully into the world of Jesus and the early Christians, sharing over the space of two millennia their world view,* their anxieties, their aspirations, their joys and responsibilities as they found themselves participants in the community of the new covenant.

---

* The technical sense in which *world view* and *life-world* are used in this book is explained in Appendix I.

HOW THE NEW TESTAMENT BECAME
THE SCRIPTURE OF THE CHURCH

So far we have been focusing on the diversities—literary, conceptual, contextual, cultural—within the New Testament writings. But we have not considered why these so-different documents came to be included in a single collection. That issue will be explored in detail in the Epilogue of this book, but it is important at the outset to recognize that the writers were addressing themselves to specific audiences and special aims. Only in the later stages of the production of the New Testament literature are there indications that the writings have begun to be collected and recognized as authoritative. For example, 2 Peter 3:14–16 refers to Paul's letters and speaks of them, along with other writings, as "scripture." Sometimes the acknowledgment of the authority of the writings is only implicit, as in the acceptance of Paul's letters as a paradigm for the later epistles of the New Testament. Well into the second century there was disagreement among Christians as to what should be considered authoritative, and therefore included on the official list of scripture, or *canon.* At the same time, other writings were being produced on the model of the earlier Gospels, letters, and Acts, as a way of supplementing the older works, or even of reworking material they contained. The Gospel of Thomas, for example, recasts the tradition in such a way as to alter fundamentally the early Christian teaching about the goodness of creation and the hope of the age to come.

Even before the canon was widely agreed upon in the form we now know, while its components were still in process of being grouped (as in the case of Paul's letters), there were powerful factors at work seeking to unify and harmonize the New Testament writings. In relation to the Gospels, for example, an Assyrian Christian named Tatian in the mid-second century combined all four of them into a single "Harmony," smoothing out differences. This has continued to have a profound influence on attitudes toward the Gospels, since it is still widely assumed that the four Gospels can be fitted together neatly, rather than recognizing that each is a document in its own right, with its own point of view and literary context. Our approach will take fully into account the historic factors of apostolic authority in the early Church and of the rise of the New Testament canon. But we will consider these forces toward unity and commonality even while we are analyzing the cultural factors that are evident in the diversity of the writings we know as the New Testament.

This book is organized into four main parts. In Part I we look analytically at the world in which Christianity arose to see what helped shape the response to the Christian story as it appears in personal faith and commitment, as well as in community structure and stance toward the world. In Part II we look at Jesus of Nazareth, the central figure of the New Testament and of Christianity, and we explore the ways in which his message was heard and responded to by his immediate followers and by those transformed through the testimony of these early Christian messengers. In Part III we examine how the movement Jesus launched, which was carried forward in his name, moved out from Judaism and Palestine into the wider Mediterranean culture, especially through the work of Paul.

The final section, Part IV, shows how the Church became more visible in Roman society, and hence more vulnerable; how it had to plan a strategy and develop an organization that would enable it to survive. We will see that Christians had no single answer to these problems but reacted to the crises in a variety of ways. Internally, we will note how the Christian community moved toward stability, searching for a consensus in faith and a unity in organization. Finally, we will observe how it was deemed necessary to draw limits as to what was or was not Christian faith and proper Christian behavior, as well as what did or did not belong in the New Testament.

In the introduction to each of the parts, we will point out what the central issues were in the minds of the community, as well as some of the central interpretive and historical questions for the modern reader. At the end of each section is an annotated list of books and other resources for further reading and exploration of the New Testament.

I

Quests for
Community and Identity
in the
Early Roman Empire

Every age is an age of transition, for the world never stands still. But in some ages the rate of change seems to speed up: Ideas move swiftly from place to place, the population shifts about restlessly, social classes become more mobile, loyalties are made and unmade overnight, and political and economic institutions are dramatically reshaped. Rapid changes of this sort always dislocate groups and individuals, creating an atmosphere of uneasiness or even of anxiety. Life seems to be open at both ends; the past seems to be crumbling, and the shape of the future has not yet become clear. Fascination with new developments breeds insecurity, and men and women cling uncertainly to the discredited beliefs of the past or grasp frantically at any new proposal that offers a solution to the perennial problems of life. It is as though some sinister hand had written across the face of the present: "Subject to change without notice."

Unsettled by the insecurity of such an age, people search for certainty. Some seek a more profound understanding of the nature of the universe and the ultimate meaning of life. Others may prefer to put their confidence in the appealing promises of would-be saviors, or in the secret formulas of those who purvey quick and easy answers. An age of transition is a flourishing time for religions and philosophies that promise security and for governments that promise stability. When the old patterns of society break up and men and women are set adrift in a hostile, unpredictable world, they seek security in some group that is bound together by common concerns and common aspirations. They search for true community—that is, for community of interest, for a common destiny, and for a sense of belonging.

It was in such an age of transition and searching that Jesus was born and that the movement that became Christianity had its origins. Superficially, the world in which Jesus was born and Christianity arose seemed to be stable and unified. All the civilized world was subject to a single sovereign power: the Roman emperor. In principle, the Roman territories were controlled by the Senate and the Roman people; in practice, they were dominated by the emperor and his military forces. According to the Gospel of Luke (Luke 2:1ff), it was during the reign of the first and in many ways the greatest of the Roman emperors, Octavian (27 B.C.–A.D. 14), that Jesus was born. Better known by his title, Caesar Augustus, it was from him that "a decree went out . . . that all the world should be enrolled," an effort by him to determine the number and the identity of his vast throng of subjects, for purposes of taxation and political control.

WAR AND PEACE:
FROM ALEXANDER TO AUGUSTUS

For the most part, the people of the subject nations and realms were not only willing to comply with the imperial decrees, but also grateful to the emperor for the stability he had established throughout his empire. He was acclaimed by many as a deliverer and savior. And he had indeed brought to an end the power struggle among the Roman leaders that had led to the murder of Julius Caesar in 44 B.C. He had driven the pirates from the seas, making them safe once more for travel and commerce. He had quelled Rome's enemies, some of whom had harassed its borders for decades. Above all, he had managed to create an atmosphere of peace and unity throughout the empire. On landing at ports, sailors gave thanks to Augustus that they had been able to sail unmolested by pirates. The Italian peasants, with their strong sense of morality, were profoundly grateful to Augustus for combating the immorality that had become rampant among the upper classes of Rome in the years before his rise.

The people of the empire acclaimed Augustus not merely as a human deliverer from conflict and struggle, but as a divine savior-king. Temples were

Augustus Caesar, whose name was actually Gaius Octavius, was given the title "Augustus" by the Roman Senate in gratitude for the peace and prosperity that he brought to the Roman lands. He was the first to be designated emperor. (*Fototeca Architettura e Topographia dell'Italia Antica*)

erected in his honor; sacrifices were made and incense was burned on the altars. In Palestine, for example, the puppet king Herod built Caesarea, an imposing seaport in honor of Augustus. From it one could see glistening on the distant Samaritan hills the white limestone columns of the Temple of Augustus, which stood at the west gate of the city Herod had built on the site of ancient Samaria and had named Sebaste (the Greek equivalent of Augustus). Although the Jews themselves did not pay divine honors to Augustus, most of the other Eastern peoples accepted him as divine, in keeping with their ancient tradition of regarding the king as a god. Augustus carefully avoided accepting the title of king, and even tried to preserve the fiction that he was no more than the leading citizen (*princeps*) among equals in the empire.

The worldwide acclaim given Augustus was not without precedent: In the fourth century before Christ a young Macedonian prince named Alexander had been hailed as a divine king in Egypt, in Asia Minor, and throughout much of western Asia. The military conquests of Alexander the Great, as he came to be called, were aided by the popular belief that he was a divine ruler before whom resistance would be useless and impious.

Although Augustus did not publicly seek divine honors as had Alexander the Great (356–323 B.C.), he benefited from Alexander's success in establishing himself in the minds of men from the Mediterranean basin to the borders of India as a divine king destined to unify the civilized world. Even the three centuries that intervened between the time of Alexander and that of Augustus had not tarnished the popular image of the divine ruler. So Augustus took on a familiar role when he set about extending the empire from the Nile to the Seine and from Gibraltar to Jerusalem.

Caesar Re-creates Alexander's One World

But Augustus inherited from Alexander more than the tradition of divine kingship; the atmosphere of outward peace and inner unrest that characterized the age of Augustus was a direct development of forces that had been set in motion in the time of Alexander.

Alexander's conquests had begun in Greece at a time when the city-states were in decline (336 B.C.). The weakening of the Greek social and political structure resulted in both military weakness and a breakdown in the sense of group loyalty that had reached its height in the golden age of the city-states. Although Alexander managed to build up an administrative unity among the Greek cities, he failed to create a common allegiance to himself to take the place of the old devotion to the city-states. In the eastern territories, however, where the tradition of divine kingship reached back for centuries, Alexander did succeed in winning great personal devotion from the conquered peoples.

A story arose that the tide along the coast of Asia-Minor had retreated at his coming to enable him to pass along a narrow beach between sea and cliff. Since there was an ancient legend that the sea would recede at this point to herald the coming of a world ruler, word of the event sped before him and prepared the way for his acceptance in the East as a divine king. Had

Alexander the Great on a
silver coin (tetradrachm)
minted during his reign.
(*James T. Stewart*)

Alexander lived, there is little doubt that he could have developed tremendous support and affection—even veneration—from the peoples he had conquered, for legends of his divinity had begun to flourish even during his brief
lifetime. But his efforts to create a politically unified world were cut short by
his death in 323 B.C.

Alexander's vision of one world stretched far beyond the political sphere,
however; he took with him a small army of scholars to record descriptions of
the peoples, customs, animals, plant life, and terrain he and his armies encountered. He had caught from his old teacher, Aristotle, a love of knowledge
and an insatiable curiosity about the world around him. And he shared Aristotle's conviction that Greek learning was superior to all other, and that it was
his responsibility to spread Greek culture wherever he went. This process of
"Greek-izing" the world became known as *Hellenizing*, since the Greeks called
their own land *Hellas* and themselves *Hellenes*. In their intensive efforts to dis-
seminate Greek culture, Alexander and his followers established Greek-style
cities as far east as the Indus Valley and as far north as the territory now included in the Central Asian states of the Soviet Union. Reports have come
down to us of petty monarchs in Central Asia who staged Greek tragedies as
entertainments for their courtiers. Alexander did not present himself to the
world as an innovator but as the conservator of the great traditions of the past,
both of Greece and of the East. The new element in his enterprise was that the
benefits of Hellenic culture were now to be available not merely to the peoples
of the Greek city-states, but to the whole inhabited world.

Yet Hellenization never succeeded in laying more than a thin veneer of
Greek culture over the Oriental parts of Alexander's realm, either during his
reign or after his death. The mass of the people in the subject lands remained
faithful to their native customs and ways of life. Among the aristocracy, however, there was a strong desire to ape the ways of the Greeks. The aristocrats
changed the names of their temples to honor local gods under new Greek
titles. They built gymnasia and hippodromes and theaters to provide a setting
for Greek-style entertainment. The upper classes even adopted Greek dress.
But most of the people in these conquered lands continued to live and amuse
themselves much as they had before Alexander began his conquests.

In one area of life, however, Hellenization had a profound and lasting
effect, for Greek was widely accepted as the common language of commerce
and international correspondence. Although people continued to speak their
native languages among themselves, Greek became the *lingua franca* of the Hel-

lenistic world. So readily did it gain acceptance that some colonies of expatriates—such as the Jews living in Alexandria—stopped using their native tongues altogether and spoke only Greek. The Alexandrian Jews finally had to translate their Hebrew Bible into Greek so that their own people could understand it. This translation, known as the Septuagint (i.e., seventy, since a Jewish legend claimed that seventy men had prepared independent translations that miraculously turned out to be identical), was widely used by Jews and was known to educated Gentiles throughout the world. It soon became the Bible of the Christians.

With Alexander's death, all appearances of political unity vanished. His generals vied with one another to gain power over their dead leader's domain, and conflict among them and their successors raged until the rise of Rome in the middle of the first century B.C. Only two relatively stable centers of power remained in the Hellenistic empires: one was Syria, where the Seleucids (successors of Seleucus, one of Alexander's generals) ruled, and the other was Egypt, where Ptolemy (another general) established the Ptolemaic dynasty. But in Asia Minor and Greece there was an unending series of wars and dynastic disputes until the Romans seized control.

In spite of the widespread disruption created by the continuing struggles, important centers of learning managed to grow up during the period between Alexander and Augustus. Athens had already begun to decline as the center of philosophical thought, although the Academy founded by Plato (427–347 B.C.) continued to exist until A.D. 529, eight centuries after his death. Tarsus, on the southern coast of Asia Minor, however, became an important university city. But most significant of all was Alexandria, the city Alexander had founded at the western edge of the Nile Delta as a center for commercial and cultural interchange between East and West. There Alexander had founded the Museum, by definition a shrine to the Muses, but in actuality a great library with more than half a million volumes, and a center of learning and research unparalleled in the ancient world. It was there that Euclid developed his principles of plane geometry, that Archimedes performed his famous experiments with water, and that Eratosthenes discovered the formula by which he was able to calculate the circumference of the earth.

At the eastern end of the Mediterranean Sea there was continual conflict between the Seleucids and the Ptolemies. As we shall see later, one victim of this conflict was the Jewish nation, situated as it was in the buffer zone between the two great centers of power. The Ptolemaic kingdom enjoyed a high degree of stability because of the great desert that protected it on three sides and because of the immense wealth it acquired, both through the agricultural produce of its own lush valley and through the luxuries that were shipped across it on the way from India to the Mediterranean cities. The Seleucids, on the other hand, had vast territories to the east over which they exercised only feeble control and beyond which lived powerful hostile tribes who constantly threatened to engulf them. Except for a century of relative independence, Palestine, from the time of Alexander until the coming of the Romans in 63 B.C., was subject to either Egypt or Syria, the one rich and indolent, and the other aggressive but insecure.

The Failure to Create Unity

In spite of the efforts of Alexander's successors to bring unity to their realms, they succeeded only in creating profound unrest. The simpler units of society, like the Greek city-states and the petty Eastern kingdoms, had been ruined by the military and cultural conquests of Alexander and his successors. And nothing had risen to fill the void. Merchants could no longer look ahead in the certainty that their business would continue as usual. Villagers never knew when a pillaging army might sweep through and leave them impoverished. The old worship of local gods had been disrupted by attempts to make all people worship universal deities, or at least to give new and unfamiliar names to the old ones. Politically, a person's allegiance to city or to petty prince was irreparably shaken; religiously, the world revealed by these widening horizons was too vast to be controlled by local gods.

In Rome itself even the most skeptical citizens felt it was important to maintain the elaborate rituals of the state cult, since they assumed that proper sacrifices to Rome's patron deities guaranteed the security of the Roman state. Any extraordinary event—ranging from a lightning bolt out of a clear sky to the birth of a deformed calf—was seen as a sign from the gods and called for careful investigation by the augurs, whose task it was to interpret the signs, and for propitiatory offerings to appease the gods and thus preserve the health of the state. Efforts to import into Rome more emotional and personal modes of worship (especially from the eastern Mediterranean) were resisted, but agreed to by the Roman authorities when it could be shown that the presence of a shrine to a particular deity was in the best interests of the state. Thus, the worship of the Great Mother was introduced at Rome from Asia Minor when it was determined that her coming would help bring an end to the Punic Wars at the close of the third century B.C. The goddess was welcomed at the mouth of the Tiber by distinguished Roman citizens and turned over to certain women who were in charge of maintaining the cult in her honor. Even though this precedent was established, there was great reluctance to allow the worship of foreign deities in Rome; and during the power struggle with Cleopatra, Augustus forbade the worship of Egyptian deities within a mile of the city limits.

The worship of foreign gods was enormously attractive to many Romans, however, and the Council of Fifteen which supervised religion in Rome was forced several times to expel the devotees of this or that Eastern deity. But the cult of Mithra, which was more concerned with personal devotion than public ceremony, was tolerated. Developed on the basis of Persian religion but with mystical elements added from other sources—the devotee passed through stages of initiation and thereby prepared his soul to move through the heavenly spheres on its ascent to the god of light—Mithraism was allowed to flourish, and became a favorite religion of the common people and the soldiers. Mithraic shrines have been uncovered in the heart of Rome and in its port of Ostia, as well as at the sites of Roman military outposts from the Taunus Range in Germany to the banks of the Thames. Almost as widespread were shrines of Isis, some of which still bear testimony to her healing and renewing powers.

The insistence on preserving the state cult in Rome in spite of the appeal of the Oriental cults should not be considered mere mindless conservatism; rather, it was believed to be essential for the welfare of the state and the identity of the Roman people. But as Rome became an empire of diverse peoples and cultures, it was impossible for its subjects to find their identity in Roman tradition or indeed to find any sense of belonging or of personal security in the vast world in which they were engulfed. The close-knit groups of worshippers, the promises of security in this life and the life to come, the sense of awe that the exotic rites provided combined to offer the sense of identity and certainty that all else lacked. Even the adherents of some of the Hellenistic philosophies, notably those who revived the teachings of the sixth-century B.C. mathematician-musician, Pythagoras, organized themselves into brotherhoods and constructed chapels for study and meditation. The spirit of the Neo-Pythagoreans was to be an important factor in the rapid development of ascetic and even monastic life among Christians of subsequent centuries.

Rome's contact with the religious philosophy of Greece and the gods of the East was an outcome of commercial and military operations in the eastern Mediterranean. For centuries, Romans had modestly busied themselves developing and safeguarding agriculture and commerce within the limits of the Italian peninsula. But in the process of extending their power over all of Italy, they came into conflict with the Phoenicians, who dominated the sea from their capital, Carthage, across the Mediterranean in North Africa. In the course of its long struggle with Carthage (264–146 B.C.), Rome gained control of the southern coast of France and Spain, and of the western Mediterranean. Only then was it ready to extend its power to the east.

Rome's sympathy with the democratic ideals of the Greek city-states moved it to aid Greece in the struggles during the early second century B.C. against the Macedonians and other Hellenistic kingdoms that were competing for the opportunity to absorb it. But Rome's motives in turning to the aid of Greece were not altogether unselfish, for commercial success in the West had led Romans to cast ambitious eyes toward the East. When a Seleucid ruler (Antiochus the Great) intervened to support Macedonia in an invasion of Greece, he was defeated by the Roman army and driven back into Syria (192–190 B.C.). Now Rome was in control of Greece, Illyria (modern Yugoslavia), and Asia Minor as far east as the Taurus Mountains. By treaty and military conquest, Roman expansion continued steadily for more than a century (200–63 B.C.), until at last Syria, including Palestine, became a Roman province. Egypt continued its independence under the Ptolemies, although Rome had to intervene in 168 B.C. to keep the Seleucids from taking over. The final round in Rome's battle for the East came in 30 B.C. when, following the defeat of Anthony by Octavian (Augustus) and the suicide of Cleopatra, Egypt too became a part of the Roman Empire. Augustus's victory was the crowning one. The Mediterranean had become a Roman lake; what began as a defense of democracy had ended in the establishment of the most powerful empire the world had ever seen.

The calm that fell after Augustus's destruction of his enemies brought peace to the empire but not peace of mind to its peoples. In the long struggle for power, the Roman ideals of democracy had been crushed. Public and private morality had declined appallingly in the presence of new wealth and power. The local Roman gods had been offered up on the altar of political expediency, for over and over again the Roman leaders had honored foreign gods in order to win the favor of subject peoples. The strict moral philosophy that the Roman ruling classes had borrowed from the Greeks had withered away. And, in spite of efforts to create a kind of universal religion by identifying the Greek and Roman gods with those, for example, of Egypt, people everywhere were left with no sense of religious certainty. Instead of worshiping the gods who were meant to keep things as they were, people searched for a religion that would deliver them from the evils of this world and provide a promise of new life in the next.

THE DECLINE OF PHILOSOPHY

Although the Greeks tried hard to spread their culture throughout the civilized world, the rich tradition of Greek philosophy degenerated on foreign soil. And even at home, the lofty heights of philosophy reached by Plato were never attained by any of his successors in the Academy.

The Decline of Platonism

In the golden age of Greek philosophy, Plato had taught that reality does not consist of specific, tangible objects or observable activities like houses, men, and good or evil deeds. Rather, reality consists of *the idea or universal pattern of any particular class of object.* For example, the *idea* of "house" exists independently of whether or not a particular house exists; the *idea* of "goodness" exists independently of whether or not people do in fact perform good deeds. These "ideas," Plato suggested, exist eternally; they are not concepts that exist only in human minds; they are the true and perfect realities of which the objects and actions we know in this world are only imperfect copies. Even though by the beginning of the Christian era philosophers who claimed to subscribe to Plato's thought had debased his system, his understanding of reality had an important influence on Christian thinking almost from the start.

The Appeal of Stoicism

The name Stoic was originally given to the philosophical school founded by Zeno (336–264 B.C.), who instead of giving his lectures in a hall, as did other teachers of the day, gathered his pupils around him in one of the colonnades or *stoas* adjoining the public marketplace of Athens. During Zeno's lifetime, and for centuries after his death, the Stoic way of life continued to attract a large following among both aristocrats and the common people. Perhaps the chief appeal of the great Stoic figures was their personal character and quality of mind, for they were earnest men of great moral integrity. Their outlook on life was one of quiet joy and serenity, and they accepted suffering and tragedy with calmness. Although their ascetic ways discouraged plea-

The agora at Athens was the marketplace and main gathering point of the city. The Acropolis is the hill on the right; the reconstructed portico known as the Stoa of Atallos is in the center; and the temple of Hephaestus, commonly but erroneously called "The Theseum" is the well-preserved building on the extreme left.   (*Courtesy of the American School of Classical Studies, Athens*)

sure-seekers from following them, their ability to discipline themselves appealed to many in an age when the moral standards of public officials and private individuals were notoriously low.

The Stoics rejected the Platonic belief that ideas exist independently of humans and of the physical universe, and affirmed instead that the real world is the world of material bodies acting and reacting upon one another. They believed that the universe is a single organism energized by a world-soul, just as a person is a body energized by a human soul. Soul itself is an extremely fine bodily substance that penetrates everything and is to be found in greater degree in humans, in lesser degree in animals and inanimate objects. This world-soul is Reason, an impersonal force that operates throughout the universe, shaping its destiny and bringing it to its predetermined goal. Then evil will be overcome and great happiness, unknown since the legendary past, will again prevail. True unity will be realized in the establishment of a great society of humankind. The world will be absorbed by God, who is all in all; a great conflagration will purge the universe, and a new cycle of the ages will begin.

Critics of the Stoics scoffed at the notion that the history of the world is the unfolding of a divine purpose, claiming instead that humans are free to make their own decisions on the basis of what serves their natural desires, and that there are, after all, no certainties in this world, only degrees of probability. In spite of critical attacks, Stoicism continued to exert a powerful influence into the Christian era. The two greatest figures in the later period of Stoic thought were Epictetus, a contemporary of Paul the Apostle, and Marcus Aurelius, the philosophizing Roman emperor of the second century A.D.

Epicurus's Vision of the Pleasant Life

A more sophisticated philosophy than Stoicism was that of Epicurus (341–270 B.C.), whose views were adopted by such outstanding Roman thinkers of the first century B.C. as Lucretius and the Latin poet Horace. Epicureanism never exercised a wide popular appeal, however, largely because it pictured the gods as far removed from the world and utterly indifferent to human affairs. Contrary to popular misconception, Epicureanism did not teach self-indulgence; rather, it taught peace of mind based on the conviction that the universe operates according to fixed laws over which humans have no control, and in which the gods have no interest. Its chief concern was to free people from anxieties over the terrors of hell, and from fear of the acts of capricious gods. Although the scientific treatises of the Epicureans (like Lucretius's *On the Nature of Things*) are filled with quaint and fascinating speculations on the natural world, their ethical and religious statements sound like commonplaces from the pen of some contemporary writer telling readers how to stop worrying, how to find inner peace, how to live bravely in the face of adversity, and so on.

The Hybrid Philosophies

None of these philosophies continued for long in a pure form. As the years passed, elements from all of them were merged into a kind of generalized religious philosophy, which became immensely popular among self-styled intellectuals during the last century B.C. and the first Christian century. To this philosophical mixture each of the philosophical schools contributed some facet of its thought. Stoicism provided its stress on reason, thereby permitting the hybrid philosophers to claim that they were essentially rational in their approach to truth. From Platonism came the yearning for a vision of the eternal world. But Platonism itself provided no mediators to bridge the gap between the finite world, known to human senses, and the eternal world. Accordingly, the popular philosophies developed hypotheses about ways of mediation through which humans might attain direct knowledge of the eternal. From Stoicism and Epicureanism came curiosity about the physical world; so the composite philosophy had its quasi-scientific interests as well.

One of the best known of the eclectics (i.e., a thinker who chooses what suits his fancy from a variety of philosophical systems) was Seneca (4 B.C.–A.D. 65), a chief adviser at the court of the Emperor Nero. Even though his basic viewpoint was a modified Stoicism, Seneca drew heavily on Plato and Epicurus and on anyone else whose moral teachings happened to appeal to him at the moment.

Perhaps the most prolific of the eclectic philosophers of the first Christian century was a Jew named Philo. Born into a prominent family among the nearly third of a million Jews of Alexandria, Philo distinguished himself in public affairs as leader of an embassy to the court of the Emperor Gaius Caligula (A.D. 37–41), and in intellectual circles as the first thinker to join together in thoroughgoing fashion rational philosophy and the revealed religion of the Jews.

Philo's voluminous writings consist chiefly of long treatises on the spiritual (philosophical) meaning of the narratives and laws included in the Hebrew Bible. For example, Abraham's journey from Ur in Mesopotamia to Hebron in Palestine is really not a narrative of ancient Semitic nomads, but a description of the spiritual journey of the seeker after truth, who moves from the world of the sense (Ur) to the place where he has a direct vision of God (the promised land of Palestine). By fanciful explanations of Old Testament stories, names, and numbers, Philo tried to show that the sacred books of the Old Testament were really saying the same things as the religious philosophers of his own day. Although we have no evidence that Philo's writings attracted a wide following among Gentiles, they do show how eager the Jews of the first century A.D. were to find in the Bible some knowledge of God that would be rationally defensible and that would at the same time provide an experience of God's living presence. In his interpretations of the Old Testament, Philo uses many of the commonplaces of Stoic and Platonic philosophy as they had come to be understood in his time.

Growing rapidly alongside these movements in philosophy, and at times overlapping them, were three other closely related approaches to the universe: astrology, magic, and speculative wisdom, which subsequently developed into Gnosticism.

EFFORTS TO CONTROL A HOSTILE UNIVERSE

Astrology developed in Mesopotamia, where for centuries people had observed and recorded the orderly movements of the stars and planets. At last they had come to the conclusion that the stars possessed power over human affairs, and that the particular configuration of the stars at the time of one's birth shaped one's destiny. To gain happiness in life, therefore, humans must try to understand and, if necessary, to placate the star spirits. Plato's belief that the stars were gods (*Timaeus,* section 40) had provided a link between astrological speculations and the Greek philosophical tradition. Other Hellenistic philosophers, by combining astrology with Greek mathematics, heightened the sense of order and precision with which the stars moved. As a result, people of the late Hellenic and early Roman periods grew apprehensive about the power of the stars, and more eager than ever to learn their secrets in order to gain the favor of the star spirits. Only in this way could humans guarantee that the fate ordained for them by the stars would be a happy one.

The urge to curry the favor of the gods and of the heavenly spirits was widespread and deep. It took many forms, ranging from the proliferation of magic formulas invoking clusters of deities and spirits to a more reasoned development of myths in which the divine names from many cultures were portrayed as belonging to a single deity. This phenomenon is known to historians of religion as *syncretism.* In the Greek Magical Papyri there are appeals to the Jewish names of God Adonai, Iao (Yahweh); to the Greek deities Psyche, Eros, Hermes, Zeus, Helios (the sun); to the Egyptian gods Osiris, Anubis, cat-faced Re, and Tais. One of the papyri (manuscripts written on material prepared from reeds) asserts that there are 365 gods, while others assume the identity of the god behind the multiple names. The magical texts are largely negative in the aim to ward off evil, or prophylactic against disease, demons, and enemies. They include recipes, prescriptions, and formulas which—properly performed—are automatically effective. The will of the gods is not a significant factor: all that matters is careful enactment of the rite or precise recitation of the formula.

In the *Metamorphoses* of Apuleius (second century A.D.), Isis identifies herself to Lucius by reciting the different names by which she is known to various ethnic groups—Mother of the Gods, Minerva, Venus, Diana, Ceres, Juno, Hecate—although her true name is that by which she is known among the Egyptians: Isis. As such she is both the guarantor of cosmic order and the personal benefactress of those in physical need or in mental anguish. Hers are words of profound sympathy and reassurance for the unfortunate hero, who has been transformed into an ass, a condition depicted as literal, but also clearly symbolic of alienation and despising of self:

> Behold I am come to take pity of thy fortune and tribulation; behold I
> am present to favor and aid thee; leave off thy sorrow, for behold the
> day of deliverance which is ordained by my providence.[1]

She goes on to assure him of her restoration of his true humanity, of her protection in this life, and of her preparing him a place in the life to come.

Two strands of religious thought and practice are linked with the figure of Isis: one is the mystery religions; the other is wisdom speculation. The mysteries promised direct, personal relationship with the gods. Wisdom offered a more intellectual way of understanding them. It is to the background and development of the mystery cults that we now turn.

THE SPREAD OF THE MYSTERY RELIGIONS

What is depicted in the *Metamorphoses* quoted above is the initiation of Lucius Apuleius into a mystery cult of the second century A.D., though the roots of

[1] Quoted from the Loeb Classical Library translation of Apuleius (by W. Adlington), in *Metamorphoses* (Cambridge, Mass.: Harvard University Press, 1915; reprinted 1977).

these mystery religions go back to a much earlier period. Specific evidence about them is scarce, precisely because the secrets of the cults were forbidden to be passed on to noninitiates. Through participation in religious dramas and other ceremonies, the initiates believed that they could share in the life of the gods. The myths on which the mysteries were based varied from country to country, but the basic intent and the general pattern were common to all. In most cases there is a wife (or mother) who grieves for her lost husband (or child). After a period of suffering, the son or daughter is restored to the mother—usually from the dead—and begins a new life. The early Christian offer of new life in Christ had obvious competition from the mysteries.

The Mystery of Osiris

In the Egyptian cults, the myth tells of Isis and her consort Osiris, a divine king of ancient Egypt. Osiris was seized by his enemies, killed, and dismembered, and Isis wandered over the earth searching for his body, burying each part as she found it. Part of Osiris's corpse was eaten by the fish in the Nile, which the Egyptians believed to flow into the underworld; as a result, Osiris became god of the underworld, where he ruled over the dead. While he was absent, nature languished and vegetation died (the fall of the Nile), but Isis enabled him to return to life and nature flourished (the flooding of the Nile). This agricultural cycle became linked with personal religious aspiration. As a result of the initiate's union with Osiris, the king of the dead, death holds no more fears and the person is assured of life beyond death. The dignity of the ritual, the splendor of the robes worn by the priests, and the awesomeness of the drama combined to give the worship of Isis and Osiris a tremendous appeal not only in Egypt, but in Rome and throughout the empire as well.

In the early second century A.D. Plutarch wrote a treatise, *On Isis and Osiris*. Originally a rationalist, Plutarch had moved to a type of mysticism. Influenced by the Persian religion, Zoroastrianism, he perceived the operation in the universe of two opposing powers, good and evil. In Plutarch's version of the Egyptian myth, Typhon is the power of evil, seeking to destroy the supreme beneficent deity, Osiris. Isis is the one who, through a combination of intellectual insight and ritual initiation, is able to bring the faithful to the highest being, which is Osiris, and thereby to enable them to share in eternal life and immortality. As the kindly mother figure, she appealed to the Romans, who responded with emotion to her compassion. Among the Greeks, she became the instrument of wisdom, and the crasser details of her myth were interpreted allegorically to give them rational appeal. As early as Hellenistic times she was portrayed in Egypt as a universal power, archetypal spouse and mother, omnipotent goddess, cosmic power, dispenser of life, mistress of the royal throne, and ruler of divine destiny. To the extent that she was the embodiment of divine order and the agent of natural law, she could readily be linked with the second of our Isis themes: intellectual speculation about wisdom, and especially the Stoic concept of natural law.

Discussion of this topic we defer until the next chapter, since its major

Dionysus, the god of wine, with a procession of his devotees. Fifth century B.C. vase. (*Metropolitan Museum of Art, Rogers Fund, 1907*)

impact on Christian origins was transmitted indirectly through the links between Isis and Jewish wisdom traditions.

Greek Mystic Saviors

DIONYSUS. Before Hellenistic times, other mystery cults had developed in Greece around the myth of Dionysus, the god of wine, and Demeter, the goddess of grain. Dionysus was the son of Zeus, the father of the gods, and was destroyed and devoured by the Titans. His heart, however, was snatched from them and given to Semele, one of the wives of Zeus, who bore another Dionysus to the father of the gods. Since the human race sprang from the Titans, the divine spark the Titans took in by eating Dionysus was also present in humans. Through mystical union with Dionysus, humans could purge the earthly aspect of their existence and, by rekindling the divine spark, enter more closely into the life of the gods. From the classical era of Greece down into the Roman period, union with Dionysus was sought by groups of people—especially women—who through night-long ceremonies and the drinking of wine entered into a state of frenzy in which the god allegedly appeared to them. A gruesome account of one such ecstasy is preserved in the *Bacchae,* by Euripides (ca. 485–406 B.C.), one of classical Greece's greatest dramatists.

According to this tragic drama, women devotees of Dionysus, seized with the frenzy[2] associated with the ceremonies in his honor, attacked and dismembered an animal they thought was threatening them, but which was in reality the son of the leader of the Bacchantes. Inscriptions found in Athens bear testimony to the existence of all-male Bacchic clubs, though among them wine drinking was supposed to be strictly regulated and orderly. Almost certainly Euripides's portrayal of these women as bloodthirsty is exaggerated, but groups of *maenads* did conduct solemn rites that included eating raw meat

---

[2] In Greek *bakchia,* from which root came the Latin name for the god, Bacchus.

as a way of sharing in the life of the god. The second century B.C. Latin historian Livy describes how Bacchic rites had spread rapidly through Rome until the worshippers numbered in the thousands, whereupon the Senate proscribed the ceremonies, denouncing the cult as a threat to military and civilian discipline. Many men and women were killed in the repressive governmental reaction, although most women, who had only minimal legal rights, were turned over to relatives to be punished (Livy, book xxxix, 8–19). In the imperial period, membership in clubs was elaborately organized for cultic functions to determine, for example, who carried what sacred objects in the processions.

DEMETER.   Among the cluster of myths that have survived is that of Demeter, in which she is pictured as the goddess of earth, whose daughter, Persephone, was stolen from her by the god of the underworld. In her grief, she neglects the earth, and all vegetation withers and dies. Through the intervention of other gods, Persephone is restored to her, but since Persephone has eaten food in the lower world she must return there for a part of each year. During the months of the year when mother and daughter are united, the earth rejoices and vegetation flourishes; but during the winter months Demeter mourns her lost child. While Demeter was searching for her daughter, she disguised herself as a child's nurse and stayed at Eleusis, a town about twelve miles from Athens. From early Greek times, a series of ceremonies was conducted here every year, beginning with a procession from Athens, and including the reenactment of the mourning of Demeter, the journey of Persephone into the underworld, and her joyous return.

Only the general outline of the Eleusinian and other mysteries is known, but we know they were attended by thousands every year from all over the civilized world. From the time of Caligula (A.D. 37–41), who granted permission for the worship of Isis to be carried on in Rome, to the initiation of Julian (A.D. 331–363) into the cult of Attis, the mysteries found support in high places in the empire.

The Origins and Appeal of the Mysteries

Scholars have offered various theories to account for the origin of the mysteries. The fact that one of the most important of the sacred objects displayed to the initiates at Eleusis was a stalk of grain suggests that the rites originated as a means of guaranteeing good grain crops. This conjecture may be confirmed by the way in which the sacred mystery dramas follow the pattern of recurrent death (sowing), mourning (the winter period when seeds are dormant), and life from the dead (growth and harvest). In one of the cultic liturgies, the priest shouted at the sky *Hu-eh* (meaning "rain"), and at the earth *Ku-eh* (meaning "bring forth"). As we noted, the myth of Isis was associated with the annual flooding of the Nile, which was the sole source of fertility for Egypt.

But it is obvious that by Hellenistic times the ceremonies had become far more than rituals performed to ensure good crops. The crops' cycle of life and death had become a symbol of the human cycle of life and death, and the intent of the mystery drama was to assure new life not for the crops, but for the worshippers. Some modern scholars have suggested that the visions of the gods and the journeys to the underworld were induced by a combination of autosuggestion and hallucinatory drugs mixed with ceremonial wine. But the appeal of the mysteries was far deeper and more significant. In an age when the future held so little promise, and when the old order had broken down, men and women turned with enthusiasm to these cults, with their secrets of life beyond death and their promises of immortality.

The mystery religions had another strong appeal: The initiates of each cult were united in a secret society for which the barriers of race and social standing were erased. All presented themselves to the deity on the same level, and through participation in the sacramental rites all were united into a fellowship that was to endure forever. That the mysteries were ridden with superstition, that the myths on which they were based were jumbled and contradictory, and that they provided no basis for social or individual morality seem to have mattered only to cynics and critical satirists. Slaves and freedmen, middle-class merchants and artisans, men and women of the upper classes—all flocked to the mystery cults in their search for security and for a sense of community in an age of uncertainty.

OTHER RELIGIOUS MOVEMENTS

Other religious movements of the Greco-Roman world were apparently more concerned with meeting individual needs than in creating community, although even these cults may have subtly changed in the direction of associations in the imperial period. Orphism is the name given by historians for a movement thought to have consisted of members of a community devoted to Orpheus, to whom ancient tradition assigned the roles of poet, oracle, healer, moral exhorter, and of one who entered the realm of the dead and returned. There is, however, no sure evidence of the existence of an Orphic community, but there is clear testimony that Orphic priests performed initiation rites, purifications, and healings. The knowledge of the rites, of love and healing formulas, was apparently transmitted within families by a hereditary priesthood. Perhaps there were during the Greek and Hellenistic periods certain followers of Dionysus who looked to Orpheus as the ground of their faith, but a widespread Orphic sect did not emerge.

Others looking for cures or solutions to specific needs turned to Asklepios, the god of healing honored throughout the Greek world, but especially in Epidauros in mainland Greece and in Pergamum on the coast of Asia Minor. Tablets affixed to the cult center at Epidauros claim to be testimonies of those whose needs Asklepios had met: the blind received sight, childless women became pregnant, and those long pregnant were delivered. The pilgrims who visited the shrine came infested with lice, leeches, and worms; they were suffering from growths, pus, abscesses, sores, ulcers, paralysis, headaches, baldness, embedded spear points, epilepsy, dropsy. All bear witness to Asklepios's healing powers; we do not know how many left Epidauros in the same condi-

Asklepios, the god of healing, restoring a patient while the concerned friends or family look on. (*Deutsches Archäologisches Institut, Athens*)

tion as that in which they arrived. The testimony from the shrine and from other ancient sources depicts the pilgrims gathering in the sacred enclosure and bedding down for the night, during which the god appeared among them in human form, or in the guise of the sacred snakes that symbolized Asklepios or of the sacred dogs that licked the wounds of the afflicted. In any case, the god appeared among them—an *epiphany*, as the Greeks called such a divine self-disclosure—and their needs were met by the compassionate Asklepios.

At Pergamum by the second century A.D., the Asklepion had become a kind of health resort, with members of the wealthy leisure class taking up residence for extended periods of time in the vicinity of the shrine, coming to have their ailments cured. The most verbose of Asklepios's devotees from this shrine—or at least the one whose lengthy testimonies have been most fully preserved—was one Aelius Aristides. A native of northern Asia Minor, he had traveled to Greece, Rome, and Egypt on religious quests but found relief for his bodily ailments, as well as a sense of direction and divine destiny in his role as rhetorician or public orator, through visions of Asklepios.

Like Orphism, there does not seem to have been an organized cult or sect, but the priests and attendants maintained the shrine and oversaw the rites and offerings that honored the god and served as instruments of his divine beneficence. Elsewhere in the Greek world, physicians seem to have called themselves Asklepiads and to have developed medical centers and schools in the god's name. Whether it was in miraculous cures (as at Epidauros), in overcoming illness and gaining a sense of purpose in life, or in effecting medical services, Asklepios was directly present to his followers in time of need.

Formal honor continued to be given to the Olympian gods and the official Roman deities: Zeus of Jupiter, Hera/Juno, Pallas Athena/Minerva,

Artemis/Diana, Aphrodite/Venus, Hermes/Mercury. But of increasing importance in a world where political order was being imposed at the cost of dislocation of the populace, shattering of social structures, and consequent personal anxiety was the god or goddess to whom personal access was possible, whose kindly acts were directly experienced, and who provided devotees with a sense of personal identity.

Ironically, the effort to create one world, begun by Alexander and achieved militarily by Augustus, had produced the opposite of what was intended. Because nations and peoples were melted together in a single vast empire, individuals felt lost in a universe beyond their comprehension or control. As an antidote to this depersonalization, the voluntary communities created by the religious cults and philosophizing sects offered new forms of identity and enabled their adherents to reappropriate old traditions in new ways. It was into this outwardly serene, inwardly anxious world that Christianity was launched.

2

The People of the Book and Their Destiny

Throughout the Roman world, from Rome to Babylon, there were members of a group whose identity was clear: the Jews. To the outsider there were impressive evidences of social cohesion, since Jews had a common history, a common set of sacred writings, common ritual and ceremonial obligations, and a famed religious capital, Jerusalem, at the center of which stood one of the architectural wonders of the world: the Temple of the God of Israel. There, Jews believed, God dwelt invisibly among his people. Large numbers of Jews had stayed on in Mesopotamia after the Persians in the sixth century B.C. permitted the Jews to return to their land. An entire quarter of the city was occupied by Jews in Alexandria. Even in smaller cities, such as Philippi in Macedonia, there were enough Jewish residents to warrant their gathering regularly to pray (Acts 16:13). In Rome, Jews were sufficiently visible to come to the attention of Claudius (A.D. 41–54), who brutally brought to an end an internal dispute within the Jewish community by expelling them all from the city. This incident, which is mentioned by the Roman biographer Suetonius in his *Lives of the Twelve Caesars,* had consequences for the spread of Christianity to which we return in Part III when we consider Paul's mission to the Gentile cities.

If from outside the Jews appeared to be unified, from within the community as a whole there were important and deeply divisive differences. At root, these revolved around the question of what it meant to be a Jew, a member of God's own people. Was biological descent from Abraham, and through him from one of Jacob's twelve sons, sufficient to guarantee participation? Or was it essential that, to be worthy of the name, a Jew must obey the Law of Moses? If so, must all of the law be obeyed? If not, which precepts were essential? Did Israel's existence require political autonomy? If so, how could Jews live under the dominance of a pagan power? Were the priests who cooperated with the Romans and were dependent on Gentile overlords for their posts fit leaders of Israel? And was the ceremonial life of the nation they led truly the worship of Israel's God? Was the truth of the Torah a unique revelation to Israel, and hence flatly incompatible with Gentile wisdom? Or was truth one, so that a synthesis was appropriate to unite the best of Gentile learning with the self-disclosure of Yahweh in the scriptures? Would conformity to pagan culture cause Jews to lose their special identity as the people of God?

These were pressing questions for Jews of the early Roman period, and the various answers offered to them were vigorously championed by different segments of Judaism. Christians shared these questions with Jews, although they offered different answers. Some Jews assumed that Israel could exist in integrity only as an autonomous political state. The issue was an old one, as we can infer from the Old Testament's report of the grave reluctance of the prophets and judges in ancient Israel to approve the transformation of the people from a federation of tribes into a monarchic state with Saul as king (Judg. 9; 1 Sam. 10–12).[1] In certain strands of the prophetic tradition, especially the book of Zechariah, leadership of the nation is shared between an anointed priest and an anointed king (Zech. 4–6). The same notion is implicit in the noncanonical Jewish document Testament of the Twelve Patriarchs, and in some Jewish documents dating from the first century A.D. and earlier that have recently been found in the Dead Sea caves, in which the messianic priest has precedence over the messianic king. But before examining in detail the range of responses to these questions about the nature and destiny of the people of Israel, we must trace the major features of Jewish history following the return from captivity in Babylon.

THE JEWISH COMMUNITY BEFORE CHRIST

The Return from Babylonian Exile

By the end of the fifth century B.C., Jerusalem had once again become the center of Jewish national and religious life, even though the Jews were the political subjects of Persia. Jews were free to develop their religious life and thought with little interference from the Persian authorities. Under the leadership of their High Priest, they developed into a small theocracy set within the confines of the Persian Empire.

When the Greeks under Alexander conquered Persia and its territories, the Jews, like most subjects, welcomed them as liberators. Following Alexander's death, in 323 B.C., Palestine, along with the rest of Syria, came under the rule of the Ptolemies, who secured control of the land and resisted incursions from the Seleucids to the north by means of elaborate fortification of cities along the coast and of rebuilt cities in the interior on both sides of the Jordan River. Soldiers from Greece, Macedonia, and Thrace were brought in to colonize the area. The economic pressure on the tiny land of the Jews was severe, with the result that thousands of young Jewish men signed up as mercenaries to fight for their Hellenistic rulers in Egypt, Asia Minor, and elsewhere. Thus the tendency of Jews resident in Palestine to resist Hellenization was offset by the presence of Hellenistic Gentiles and the impact of returning Hellenized Jewish soldiers.

Greek coins, Greek pottery, and especially the Greek language were widely used even during the Persian period and appear commonly in excavations of Hellenistic sites throughout the land. Commercial exploitation of the land and its people, especially for production of grain and olive oil, led to a gross gap between the wealthy—largely urban-based—and the wretched poor of the countryside. It was perhaps a coalition of the urban middle class, pro-

---

[1] The narrative as we have it in 1 Sam. is based on two sources, one of which celebrates Saul's being anointed as "prince," and the other which deplores Israel's having anyone but God as king (Cf. 1 Sam. 10:1 and 10:19, 12:19).

foundly offended by the secularization of the wealthy city dwellers and absentee landlords, with the pious and oppressed villagers that led to the revolt against the forced Hellenization of Jews under the Seleucids. The spearhead of this drive was Antiochus IV Epiphanes (175–164 B.C.).

His Seleucid predecessor, Antiochus III, had wrested control of Palestine from the Ptolemies in 201 B.C. with the encouragement and support of a segment of the Jewish populace of Jerusalem, and in turn he had freed imprisoned Jews, allowed exiles to return, and made decrees guaranteeing the sanctity of Jerusalem and its temple. But Antiochus IV quickly reversed the policy of toleration toward the Jews.

The Maccabean Revolt

Ancient and modern historians have offered many reasons for Antiochus IV's attack on the Jews. Among them was a very practical economic reason. For some time, the Seleucids had been hard pressed for funds not only to carry on their feud with the Ptolemies, but also to maintain control over their vast holdings in the East. One of their sources of revenue was the Jewish nation. In addition to increasing the taxes levied on the Jews, Antiochus decided to offer the office of High Priest to the highest bidder. He deposed the rightful High Priest, Onias, and in his place appointed a man named Jason, who offered large sums of money for the office and agreed to support Antiochus in the Hellenization of the Jewish nation. Antiochus, who fancied himself a true representative of Hellenistic culture, was eager to force this culture on all his subjects. It was this effort, in which Jason joined, that led to conflict between Antiochus and the Jews.

Jason built a gymnasium in the heart of Jerusalem in which young Jews, some of them from priestly families, exercised in the nude according to Greek custom. Some Jews even submitted to surgery to remove the distinctive marks of circumcision. These practices horrified many Jews, who regarded them as contrary to the law and in violation of their covenant with God. Conse-

Antiochus IV (Epiphanes) on a Greek coin. The reverse side carries the Greek words: Basileos Antiochou, Theou Epiphanous, Nikephorou—"(coinage) of King Antiochus, God Manifest, Bearer of Victory." The king represents himself as Zeus, seated on a throne, holding in his left hand a royal staff and in his right the figure of the goddess of victory, Nike, who holds in her hand the laurel wreath, symbol of victory. (*Courtesy of the American Numismatic Society*)

quently, a strong opposition party called the Hasidim (pious ones) arose in opposition to Jason and to the Jews who were sympathetic to Hellenization. The Hasidim fought against all efforts to adopt Greek ways, for to them these customs were inseparably bound up with the idolatry and immorality they associated with the Greek religion and way of life.

Antiochus finally realized he could not bend the Jews to his will until he had first destroyed their religion. So in 168 B.C. he issued an edict of proscription. Under penalty of death all Jews were forbidden to circumcise, to celebrate religious festivals, or to observe the Sabbath. He ordered all copies of the law to be destroyed, and anyone found in possession of it to be punished. Antiochus's men set up a Greek altar to Zeus in the Temple in Jerusalem, and sacrificed swine upon it. Heathen altars were erected throughout the land, and the Jews were compelled to worship heathen gods. To enforce his edict, Antiochus stationed troops throughout Israel.

Although the Jews who had favored Hellenization in the first place acceded to these demands, the stubborn Hasidim refused to comply. Finally, the Jews revolted under the leadership of a priest named Mattathias (from the Hasmon family—Hasmoneans), who came from the village of Modin. After killing a Jew who was in the act of sacrificing on a pagan altar, Mattathias fled with his five sons to the rugged hill country outside Jerusalem. There they gathered around them followers who were ready to fight the oppressors in the name of God and in defense of their right to live according to their law.

This action marked the beginning of the Maccabean Revolt, named for Judas Maccabeus, Mattathias's son, who assumed command of the forces when his father died. The Syrians were little disturbed by the uprising, for the Jews had no trained militia, no arms, and almost no financial backing. But Antiochus underestimated their religious zeal, their bravery, and their ingenuity. Since the Jews were greatly outnumbered and had only crude weapons, they turned to guerrilla tactics against the Syrians. After suffering a number of discouraging defeats, Judas and his men made a heroic effort and finally managed to win a peace treaty from Antiochus's general, Lysias. In December of 165 B.C., Judas entered the Temple in Jerusalem, cleansed it, and reestablished the traditional Jewish worship. To the present day, Jews commemorate this triumphant event in the festival of Hanukkah (Rededication), the Feast of Lights.

Now that religious liberty had been restored, many of the Hasidim were apparently ready to consider the revolt completed. But Judas and his followers carried on raids against the Ammonites and Idumeans, traditional enemies of the Jews, and led expeditions to Galilee and Gilead to rescue Jews who were suffering at the hands of Gentiles. The fact that the Syrians were still in control of strong fortifications in Judaea and in Jerusalem itself also must have made Judas reluctant to disband his forces. Furthermore, there was still an active Hellenizing party among the Jews that continued to seek the high priest's office and was quite ready to call upon the Seleucid king for assistance.

What had begun as a revolt for religious liberty now became a struggle for full political freedom carried on by the brothers of Judas after his death. Under the leadership of Simon (142–135 B.C.), the Jews took several strategic Syrian fortresses, including the Acra in Jerusalem, and gained virtual independence. The people acknowledged Simon's success by naming him the legitimate High Priest, even though he was not a member of a high priestly family. As the years passed, efforts were made to enlarge the boundaries of the kingdom, and the Hasmonean rule became more obviously political. John Hyrcanus (135–104 B.C.), Hyrcanus's son, made notable strides toward his goal of restoring the boundaries of the former kingdom of David. This ambition was more nearly realized by Simon's son, Alexander Jannaeus (103–76 B.C.), who was more ambitious than his father and more ruthless in his tactics. Using mercenary troops, he even attacked Jews who opposed his desire for expansion, and put to death many of the Jewish leaders. Under Alexander Jannaeus, the religious aims of the original Maccabean Revolt were all but obliterated, and most Jews looked upon him as disloyal to the cause of the original Maccabean heroes.

After Alexander Jannaeus's death, his widow Alexandra (76–67 B.C.) restored some degree of stability to the Jewish nation. Among those who supported her efforts was a group known as the Pharisees. Josephus, the Jewish historian who wrote at the end of the first and opening of the second century A.D., depicts them as "a body of Jews with the reputation of excelling the rest of their nation in the observances of religion, and as exact exponents of the law" (*Jewish Wars*, 1:109). They exercised great political power with the blessing of Alexandra, even to executing those who opposed them. By adopting new concepts and teachings, such as the doctrine of the resurrection of the dead, which could not be found in the Jewish scriptures, they could simultaneously affirm their ancient tradition and accommodate to the modern world. They could justify living under pagan domination, so long as Jews obeyed the Torah—as interpreted by their group.

On Alexandra's death, a dispute sprang up between her two sons over the succession. Each had his following among the Jews, and each sent an embassy to Pompey, in Syria, to seek Roman support. A third embassy, representing the Jewish people, requested that Pompey reject the monarchy altogether and restore the Jewish nation to its pre-Maccabean nonpolitical status.

Under Roman Rule: The Herodians

In 63 B.C., with Pompey's arrival in Jerusalem, the political independence of the Jews was ended once again. The territory now passed under Roman rule and was made subject to Rome's representative in the territory of Syria. Hyrcanus II, a son of Alexandra who was appointed High Priest by Pompey, faithfully carried out Rome's policy with the help of his minister, Antipater, an Idumean who was clearly motivated by personal ambition. During the long period of disturbances in Rome at the close of the Republican period, Antipater and his son Herod, through political astuteness and cunning, managed to stay in favor with a succession of Roman leaders. In 40 B.C., Rome named Herod ruler of both Judea and Samaria, with the title of king, although disturbances in Jerusalem made it impossible for him to ascend the throne until 37 B.C. Herod's rule (37–4 B.C.) was confirmed by Augustus Caesar in 30 B.C. Before Herod died, his kingdom had come to include not only Idumea, Judea, and Samaria, but also Perea in Transjordan, Galilee, and a territory north and east of the Sea of Galilee. It was this Herod who was ruler at the time of Jesus's birth.

Herod proved one of the most successful of Rome's puppet rulers, and he came to be known as Herod the Great. He restored some degree of law and order to troubled Palestine and set it up as a buffer state between Rome's territories and the marauding Arab peoples who constantly threatened the peace and Rome's lines of communication. Furthermore, in the fashion of a true Hellenistic monarch, he tried to foster in his kingdom Augustus's hopes for a common Greco-Roman culture throughout the Roman empire. Herod gave support to the imperial cult and built temples honoring Augustus in cities of Palestine and Asia Minor. He rebuilt many old cities according to the Hellenistic pattern, and throughout the land he constructed gymnasia, theaters, and stadia to encourage the Hellenistic way of life.

But most Jews despised Herod for his Idumean ancestry and for his tire-

A modern, large-scale model of the Temple and adjacent structures, based on careful analysis of ancient historical sources. The massive retaining wall is still intact. The building to the upper left is the Temple proper; the colonnade is the so-called Porch of Solomon. Tunnels led upward through the wall to give access to the Temple courts from the old city. The steps and arched entrances are visible here, center, left, and right.   (*Gordon N. Converse*)

less efforts to Hellenize the kingdom. Furthermore, his ambitious building programs cost money that had to be raised by excessive taxation. Desperately jealous of his power and fearful lest he lose it, Herod filled the land with secret police and severely punished any Jew who aroused the least suspicion of disloyalty. He went so far as to have his mother-in-law, two of his sons, and his favorite wife (he had nine others) murdered because he suspected their loyalty.

Herod did try, though in vain, to conciliate the Jews by easing their taxes in hard times and providing food during famines. In 20 B.C. he began the construction of a beautiful new temple in Jerusalem, though it was not completed until after his death. But all these efforts were to no avail. The land was seething with dissatisfaction, and there is evidence that Herod shrewdly played one group off against another to heighten the internal unrest.

It is not surprising, then, that when Herod died in 4 B.C. the Jews sent an embassy to Augustus asking that Rome refuse to execute Herod's will, in which he had appointed his sons as successors. When riots broke out in Judea, Varus, the Roman governor of Syria, was sent to quell them, and Augustus shortly approved Herod's will dividing the kingdom among his three sons. Archelaus was appointed ethnarch in Judea (4 B.C.–A.D. 6), Herod Antipas tetrarch of Galilee and Perea (4 B.C.–A.D. 39), and Philip tetrarch of Iturea, Trachonitis, Batanea, Auranitis, Gaulinitis, and Panias. Philip, most of whose subjects were Gentile, enjoyed a very successful rule. Herod Antipas was relatively successful in the eyes of Rome but distasteful to the Jews: It was under his rule that John the Baptist and Jesus carried on their ministries. Archelaus, who tried to conceal his incompetence by ruthless repression and by slaughter of his opponents, was deposed after offending both Jews and Romans. Following Archelaus's deposition, Jerusalem and Judea passed under direct Roman rule administered by a succession of procurators. There was just one short break in the administration (from A.D. 41 to 44), when Herod Agrippa I, Herod the Great's grandson, was granted the rule of his grandfather's entire territory. Since the welfare of the Jewish nation during the years of Roman rule depended directly on the relations between the people and the procurators, we must consider more carefully the events of this period.

The Procurators (A.D. 6–66)

No less than fourteen procurators were sent to Judea during the sixty-year period from A.D. 6 to 66. As the years passed, tension between Rome and the Jewish people increased steadily, partly because of the character of the procurators themselves. With few exceptions, these men failed to measure up to the highest standards of Roman administrative personnel, and their caliber seemed to decline with each successive appointment. Repeatedly, they made foolish judgments in administration, and often they were guilty of inordinate cruelty in carrying out official policies.

But the lot of the procurators was not easy, for they were appointed to govern one of the most troublesome territories under Roman rule—a territory that had grown increasingly resentful under years of alien control. Furthermore, they could not understand the Jews' stubborn resistance to Greco-Roman religion and culture, and their persistent loyalty to their own religious faith—a faith the procurators looked upon as superstitious and barbarous. In the name of that faith, minor figures arose time and time again promising release from Roman rule. To the Romans, such promises carried with them the threat of political treason. A good example of the procurators' failure to understand the Jews occurred under Pontius Pilate (A.D. 26–36), before whom Jesus stood trial. On one occasion, in order to build a new aqueduct, Pilate appropriated funds from the Temple treasury in Jerusalem that were specifically designated for maintaining sacrifices. Then, when the people protested this outrage against their religion, he turned them away by force of arms. On another occasion, he offended the religious sensitivity of the Jews by bringing military insignia bearing the emperor's image into the city of Jerusalem. Pilate finally had to be removed from office when he commanded his soldiers to attack a crowd of defenseless Samaritans who had gathered to watch a self-styled prophet perform a miracle on Mt. Gerizim.

As time went by, an increasing number of Jews were drawn into groups (Zealots) that openly or secretly favored armed rebellion. Open hostility often flared up. Under Felix (A.D. 51–60), before whom the Apostle Paul was brought for a hearing, the Jewish reactionary groups became even more fanatical, and assassinations on both sides were common. Felix's ruthless reaction to his opponents drove still more Jews to adopt radical ways of showing their hatred. Albinus (A.D. 62–64), who was recalled by Rome because of his graft and his maltreatment of innocent people, emptied the jails of prisoners before he left Judea, flooding the country with brigands. By the time of Florus (A.D. 64–66), the last of the procurators, open fighting had become common. To add to the fury, Florus plundered the Temple treasury, and when the people demonstrated against his action he ordered many of them crucified. By A.D. 66, the situation had become so critical and the promise of improvement so remote that organized revolt against Rome finally broke out. The impact of this event on early Christianity is apparent in the New Testament, especially in the Gospel of Luke, which reports "Jerusalem surrounded by armies" (Luke 21:20) as a sign of God's judgment.

But the rebellion of the Jews against the Romans was lost before it began, for the trained and powerful forces of the empire could not be overcome. Under the Roman generals Vespasian and Titus, the war was successfully concluded by Rome in A.D. 70, though the last remnants of resistance were not wiped out until A.D. 73. The city of Jerusalem suffered heavy damage during the fighting, and the Temple itself was destroyed. For the third time in their history, the Jews had suffered what appeared to be annihilating defeat. Yet once again they managed to survive.

Although political, social, and economic factors contributed to the outbreak of the Jewish War, the desperate venture sprang primarily from religious motives. Most of the leaders of the revolt saw themselves as the true successors of the Maccabean heroes, and they fought the enemy for the sake of their faith. Like the revolt itself, the Jews' survival as a community can be understood only in terms of faith. And, since it was the religious development within the community that determined to a large degree the community's capacity for survival, we must turn now to the faith of the Jewish community in order to see the various ways in which groups within Judaism responded to these pressures and crises.

THE FAITH OF THE JEWISH COMMUNITY

After the calamity wrought by the Babylonians in 587 B.C., a resurgence of commitment to covenant existence had brought about the reconstitution of the Jewish community. The Jewish prophets and leaders during the Exile boldly declared that the victory of the Babylonians was not a sign of the weakness of their God Yahweh, but rather the means whereby he had revealed his judgment on his people for their sins. Looking back to the words of the great prophets—Amos, Hosea, Isaiah, and Jeremiah—the Jews saw that through them God had repeatedly warned his people that continual refusal to obey his commands would lead to destruction. In the Exile, destruction had indeed come as testimony to the truth of all that the prophets had said, but the promise of the new covenant (Jer. 31:31) would surely be fulfilled.

The prophet whose words are found in the last chapters of the Book of Isaiah (40–66) saw in Cyrus's permission to the Jews to return to their homeland a sign of God's continuing concern for his people. By granting them an opportunity to renew their loyalty to him, God had provided the Jews with further evidence that he was not only their God, but the only true God in all the universe. It was Israel's privilege and obligation to become "a light to the nations" (Isa. 49:6), which meant that its knowledge of God was not merely to be treasured as a private revelation, but proclaimed to "the ends of the earth." Non-Israelites were to share in the blessings and benefits of the relationship with Yahweh.

The conviction that the God of Israel was the sole sovereign of the universe was vividly expressed by this prophet of the Babylonian exile:

> "Before me no god was formed,
>   nor shall there be any after me.
> I, I am Yahweh,
>   and besides me there is no savior.
> I declared and saved and proclaimed,
>   when there was no strange god among you.
> And you are my witnesses," says Yahweh.
> "I am God, and also henceforth I am He;
>   there is none who can deliver from my hand;
> I work and who can hinder it?"
>   —ISA. 43:10a–13

This disdain of other gods shows that in exile, the Jews were purged of polytheism. They no longer had the option of choosing whether they would serve Yahweh or some other god, as their ancestors reportedly had to decide on entering the Promised Land (Josh. 24:14–15). There is no God but Yahweh.

There are several possible implications of this conviction, however, and all of them raise problems. For a better understanding of the diversity of Judaism after the Exile, it is essential to examine some of the issues raised by the affirmation that there is only one God.

There Is No God But Yahweh: Monotheism

EXCLUSIVISM.   The first question is this: Why does the one sovereign God who has chosen Israel as his covenant people allow misfortune to befall them? A simple answer was that the disasters experienced by Israel were God's measures to bring his people back into obedient relationship with himself. The argument ran like this: First, the Jews had succumbed to idolatry and had turned to foreign gods rather than to Yahweh alone. Second, they had not worshipped Yahweh in purity, but had permitted their worship to become corrupted by all manner of foreign practices. Third, they had not obeyed the moral and ritual commandments he had given them. Therefore, God sent them into exile to purge them.

But under the impact of the Persian religion, with its theory of cosmic conflict between the beneficent powers of light and the hostile powers of darkness, Jewish thought began to speak of God's adversary—Satan (the Semitic term for the divine antagonist). Accordingly the pre-exilic account of an act of disobedience like David's prideful taking a census of Israel in order to inflate his own ego and to intensify his control over his subjects is attributed to the anger of Yahweh (2 Sam. 24:1). The same incident in a post-exilic account (1 Chron. 21:1) is described as instigated by Satan. The late sixth-century prophet Zechariah pictures Satan as a functionary of the heavenly court—a kind of prosecuting attorney leveling charges against God's servants. But by the fourth century, and perhaps even earlier, Satan was seen to be the cosmic opponent of God and his purpose. The seeming miscarriages of justice and the consequent miseries that befall God's people are blamed on Satan.

The human instruments through which Satan's evil designs are accomplished are described in the literature of the Hellenistic period in elaborate symbolic forms, as in the series of "beasts" who represent the successive pagan world empires depicted in the dream vision of Daniel 7: the lion stands for the Babylonians; the bear for the Medes; the leopard for the Persians; the dragon with the many horns for the succession of Hellenistic rulers. All these are defeated by a human being ("one like a son of man," Dan. 7:13), who is God's instrument to reassert his authority over his creation. That instrument is the faithful minority within Israel: "the saints of the Most High" (Dan. 7:22).

For a group sharing this conviction, as well as for those who saw in the catastrophe of the exile a divine punishment, the appropriate response was to maintain purity as the people of God. These convictions led to what has been called Jewish "particularism" or "exclusivism." It was not merely their belief that they were God's Chosen People that set the Jews apart from all other people. Given their firm conviction that belief, conduct, and worship were all of one piece, it was inevitable that they would seek to separate themselves from any mode of life that threatened the purity of any of the three. The books of Ezra and Nehemiah show the lengths to which this particularism was carried, for in them the Jews returning to Judea after the captivity are forbidden to marry foreigners, and those who have married non-Jews are asked to put them aside. Such exclusivism can be understood only in the light of the religious zeal that prompted it—the earnest desire to avoid at all costs the disloyalty which had resulted in judgment and in jeopardy of Israel's survival as a distinct entity. And since loyalty to Yahweh involved every aspect of life, it was dangerous to enter into any close relations with those who lived in accordance with other ways. This exclusivism at its worst could become a cloak for the derision and hatred of other peoples. But at its best it was the Jews' testimony to the reality of the God they worshipped and the way of life into which faithfulness to him inescapably led them.

In the Hellenistic Age, when polytheism and idolatry were commonplace, and when religion and morality were not so clearly related as they were in Judaism, the exclusivism of the Jews stood out sharply against the pagan world. Concerted efforts to Hellenize the Jews drove loyal Jews to defiance, since they felt that their way of life had been given by God himself, in the form of the Jewish law. More than anything else, it was the law that provided the bond between Jews and that distinguished them as a community from all other people.

SYNCRETISM. Very different responses to the belief in God's universal sovereignty also appeared in the post-exilic period, however. The first of these was the assumption that since there was one God over all humanity, truth was one in spite of its outwardly dissimilar forms. Those who adopted this position could set out to identify the correspondences between the best of human wisdom and the divine self-disclosure in the Torah given to Moses. Hellenistic philosophers were employing the allegorical method to show the philosophical truths behind the seemingly crude myths of classical Greece. The narratives of the gods were treated as poetic expressions of the interplay of cosmic principles and of the working of the laws of nature in human experience. Jewish interpreters influenced by Platonic and Stoic thought undertook allegorical interpretation of the Torah with analogous objectives in view. Thus, the instruction to Moses to build the tabernacle and its equipment "according to the pattern which was shown [to him] on the mountain" (Exod. 25:40) was interpreted as claiming that Moses was enabled to see the eternal heavenly archetypes or ideals of which earthly phenomena are impermanent copies. Thus Platonic ontology is discerned within the Mosaic Torah. In a more general way, when Greek-speaking Jews translated the Torah as *nomos* (law), they assumed that the all-pervasive laws of the Mosaic code were simply alternative ways of setting forth the laws of nature, which the Stoics taught gave structure and order to the universe. Hesiod, the Greek poet of the eighth century B.C. whose works included a myth of successive ages of human history culminating in a Golden Age, was thought to be expressing the same aspirations as Jewish prophecy with its teaching of a renewal of the creation, as in Isaiah 65:17–25, where new heavens, new earth, new Jerusalem, new conditions of human and animal existence are predicted. Daniel's ages of history climaxing in the Rule of God seem to parallel Hesiod.[2]

Yet in a more general way, the very notion that human wisdom is as much a divine gift as is Mosaic law manifests an important development in Jewish thought of the period. Wisdom in Proverbs, and especially in Ecclesiasticus is not merely proverbial lore, but is personified as a female consort of God who invites human beings to enjoy her company (Prov. 9). In Proverbs 8, she is God's companion and co-worker in the process of creating the world. Similar views are expressed in Sirach 1, 24, and especially 43, where the ordering of creation may be perceived and understood by those whom God has granted wisdom. The same gift of wisdom enables the faithful to discern God's providence at work in the history of Israel (Sirach 44–50). The whole of the Wisdom of Solomon (written originally in Greek, not Hebrew) extols wisdom and her role in the creation of the world, using the technical terminology of Hellenistic philosophy (Wisd. of Sol. 7:25–26). According to this point of view, there is no basic conflict between human and divine wisdom, but God's self-revelation to his people enables the wise to perceive more clearly his purpose and the order of creation. It was Philo of Alexandria, whose work we noted briefly above, who developed most fully this approach to philosophy as the handmaid of revelation.

A second approach to the question of human knowledge and divine revelation was to assume that all human striving to understand God was in vain unless one were a member of the favored few to whom God chose to disclose his truth. That was the basic attitude operative in apocalyptic circles, which produced Daniel and that section of Zechariah (9–11) that was also written in the Hellenistic period. Other apocalypses include writings attributed to Enoch.[3] This outlook is prevalent in the Dead Sea documents.

GNOSTICISM.   By the middle of the second century A.D., however, there were Christian groups who regarded the creation as presently dominated by the powers of evil but soon to be liberated. They denied the essential goodness of the created order and sought deliverance from what they regarded as human imprisonment in the physical world. The material universe was fundamentally evil, the product of a power hostile to the true God. The latter granted to his faithful elect knowledge of his purpose, brought to human beings by his agent. This movement, known as Gnosticism, may have had antecedents in Jewish wisdom speculation. But in its developed form, which depicts a heavenly messenger who comes from the realm of light, reveals the truth, and makes possible liberation from the material realm of darkness, it can be documented only from Christian or quasi-Christian sources.

Until the middle of the present century, our knowledge of the Gnostics was largely limited to attacks on them in the writings of the Church Fathers in

[2] Noted by Martin Hengel in *Judaism and Hellenism,* vol. I (Philadelphia: Fortress Press, 1974), pp. 233–34.

[3] These writings were claimed to be from Enoch, who according to Genesis 5:24 did not die but was taken up to God. Fragments of several of the Enoch writings were found among the Dead Sea scrolls.

the second and subsequent centuries. But in the 1940s a library of Gnostic writings was discovered in Egypt; most of the documents have been published, although all are still in the process of analysis and study. It is possible that some of these esoteric Gnostic writings incorporate fragments of earlier Jewish speculative works, especially myths about Seth and other ancestors of the Hebrew people in Genesis 1–11. But the redeemer figure and the matter-spirit dualism seem to have had no demonstrable Jewish antecedents. Gnosticism, as we know it from actual documents, is apparently a phenomenon of developing Christianity, and will be dealt with accordingly at the appropriate point in our historical survey (see Chapter 13).

The Centrality of the Torah

The one factor shared by all Jews of whatever persuasion, and vital to their sense of identity as God's covenant people, was their scriptures, even though they were not in agreement about what constituted scripture apart from the universally authoritative Torah given by God to his people. The Jews fervently believed that this law, given by divine revelation through Moses, was recorded in the Pentateuch (the first five books of the Old Testament). It is now common knowledge that these books contain materials that were gradually brought together over many centuries and that it was not until the end of the fifth century B.C. that they reached their present state.

By the end of the third century B.C., the prophetic books (Amos, Hosea, Isaiah, and so forth) had also assumed the form in which they now appear and had been accepted as part of God's divine revelation. In the New Testament, the phrase "the Law and the Prophets" is a reference to God's revelation to his people as it was contained in these holy scriptures. By the end of the first century B.C., all the books in the Old Testament, except for a very few, were regarded as divine revelation.

The English term *law* is not an adequate translation of the Hebrew word *Torah*, a fact that is obvious to anyone who reads the Pentateuch carefully. For the Pentateuch contains a great deal of legend, history, and myth, as well as specific rules and regulations. To the Jews, *Torah* was a very inclusive term that referred to all that God had revealed about himself, their history, and the conduct that was required of them. In time, the entire written revelation came to be referred to as *Torah*, though in the more narrow sense *Torah* always meant the Pentateuch, and often specifically God's commandments.

It is this centrality of the Torah in Judaism that accounts for the rise of a body of Jewish scholars known as the Scribes (*Sopherim*). Since knowledge of the Torah was so essential, there had to be authorities who were competent to interpret the meaning of Torah to the people. In the early post-Exile period, the priests had been the learned men who were looked to as authorities. By the end of the third century B.C., some laymen had become Scribes, charged with the responsibility of preserving the writings and giving the official interpretation of them. The conviction was widespread by that time that God was no longer revealing his will through prophets, but that the authority for understanding and interpreting God's will now resided largely with the Scribes, who accordingly thought of themselves as the successors to the prophets.

The Torah, then, provided the basis for the common belief and conduct that characterized Jewish life and bound Jews together wherever they might be. But no institution in Judaism was more important in transmitting knowledge of the Torah and in nurturing deep reverence for it than the synagogue (transliterated from a Greek word meaning "assembly"). It is impossible to speak with certainty of the precise origins of the synagogue. It may have had its inception during the exile in Babylonia, when the Temple no longer stood and the Jews, far from their home, came together for worship, deliberation, and mutual support. Long before the end of the first century B.C., the synagogue had become a well-established institution, though its significance had evolved gradually. Wherever Jews lived throughout the Greco-Roman world, the synagogue served as the center of Jewish life and thought. Weekly they heard the scriptures expanded, whether in Hebrew, in Aramaic[4] paraphrase, or in Greek. The gathering to listen to the scriptures was a central factor in Jewish identity. Indeed, the term *synagogue* referred not so much to a place of meeting as to the coming together of Jews in any locality. It was an assembly for worship for Jews who had no temple. God was as much present among them in the Torah shrine, which was the central feature of the synagogue, as he was in the temple of Jerusalem. From excavated remains of synagogues in Palestine and elsewhere we know that Hellenistic influence was at work there also. By the year A.D. 200, the characteristic decoration of the synagogue was the mosaic pavement, which featured a representation of the Torah shrine and of the menorah (the seven-branched lampstand); around the edge of the central room were the twelve signs of the zodiac, and in the center the sun chariot, representing Yahweh himself as sovereign of his people, of time, and of history. And it was in the synagogue that the "elders," the respected advisers of the local Jewish community, sought ways in which the Jews could adjust to an alien environment without being unfaithful to the Torah. When the Romans destroyed the temple in A.D. 70, the synagogue continued as the vital center of Jewish faith and life.

The Temple and the Priesthood

When the Jews returned to Jerusalem from the exile after 538 B.C., one of the first things they did was to rebuild the Temple.

The Old Testament books of Ezra and Nehemiah are supplements to the official post-exilic history of the Jews that we know as 1 and 2 Chronicles, which were written from the priestly point of view and simply assume that restoration of the worship of Yahweh in his "house" is essential for the well-being of his people. Ezra details events in the fifth century, when the Persian King Cyrus encouraged the Jews to return and restore their sanctuary. The returnees were carefully organized in spite of their huge numbers—more than 600,000 according to Ezra 2:67. Nehemiah's first task was to repair the wall of

[4] A Semitic dialect widely used throughout the Middle East, especially from the Persian period on.

The Holy Place in the Temple. The Temple proper consisted of a series of enclo-
sures, surrounded by the public Court of the Gentiles. Jewish women could enter
only the first courtyard enclosure behind the barrier visible in this picture. Male Israelites could go into the next court. The priests alone had access to the sanctuary
proper, but only the High Priest could enter the innermost section, where the Ark of
the Covenant was kept and where Yahweh dwelt in the form of a radiant
cloud.   (*Gordon N. Converse*)

Jerusalem (Neh. 1–7). The law was read to the male heads of households by
Ezra, who combined the roles of scribe (scholarly interpreter of Torah) and
priest (Neh. 8:13ff). The people were stricken with guilt, which they confessed
(Neh. 9:26–36), vowing to keep the law (Neh. 10:28–39) and especially to rebuild the Temple and to restore the worship there. Special emphasis was laid
on abstinence from all work on the Sabbath and on the avoidance of marriage
with non-Israelites (Neh. 13:15–27).

The result of these reforms was that Israel resumed its existence as a cli-
ent state with qualified local autonomy, led by priests concerned to preserve
the separateness of Jews. The priests who did the final editing of the Law of
Moses (Torah) were careful to include specific instructions on the temple
structure and the form of temple worship. The Temple itself consisted of a
series of courts; the innermost court was the Holy of Holies, which only
the High Priest was permitted to enter. This secret chamber was the place
where God dwelled, and it symbolized his presence with his people. Naturally
enough, the Holy of Holies provoked endless curiosity among non-Jews, who

circulated scandalous rumors about the contents of the room and what went on inside.

The heart of worship consisted of sacrificial offerings, including daily sacrifices morning and evening, and special sacrifices and more elaborate rituals on festival occasions. Then there were daily private offerings by individuals to cover the multitude of sacrifices required by the Torah. The temple area was constantly crowded with priests and Jews making offerings and with the sacrificial animals and the men who sold them. In addition, moneychangers were always on hand, since the Torah required that financial transactions in the Temple could be carried on only with a particular kind of coin.

It is impossible to discover what personal religious meaning the sacrifices had for the average Jew in the Hellenistic-Roman period. Apparently it was sufficient reason for performing them that the sacrifices and ceremonies were required in the Torah. Obedience to Yahweh was achieved, therefore, no matter what the significance of the act to the worshipper may have been. The stress on conformity to the Torah, combined with the decentralization of Judaism (which inevitably resulted from the spread of the synagogue movement), led to the aspiration of Jews to participate in the worship requirements directly, and to do so where they lived. The Torah had described Israel as "a kingdom of priests and a holy nation" (Exod. 19:6). In living up to that description, Jews must obey the laws of purity and worship in their own homes and not merely in the Temple. This emphasis contributed fundamentally to the ability of Judaism to survive the destruction of the Temple and of independent political existence.

Yet the Temple and the priests did provide a visible and psychological rallying point for a people recently escaped from exile. To officiate at the numerous sacrificial rites there were multitudes of priests from a long line of families whose genealogies were recorded in the Torah. Admission to the priesthood was carefully controlled, since the Jews were determined that worship be conducted only by properly qualified men. Only descendants from the sons of Aaron could be priests, although descendants from the line of Levi could perform restricted functions alongside the priests. The Torah's regulations to ensure the purity of the priests were meticulously observed, as was the Torah's requirement that the priests and the Levites be supported from offerings made by the people.

At the head of the priesthood was the High Priest, an office that seems to have emerged during the Persian period. As the titular head of the Jewish people, the High Priest carried on negotiations with the various governments to which the Jews were subject. From the beginning, this meant that the High Priest, together with the other priests whom he represented, exercised unusual authority in the community. By the second century B.C., and perhaps earlier, he served as head of the Sanhedrin, a court that handled cases involving infractions of the Torah. Since the Jews made no distinction between civil and religious law, the Sanhedrin could control every aspect of the daily life of the Jewish people. In practice, however, the Sanhedrin concerned itself with only the most obvious infractions of the Torah. Since the Romans recognized the Sanhedrin as the ruling body over the Jews, except in matters of treason, the Sanhedrin with the High Priest at its head wielded a great deal of authority.

In the Temple itself, the High Priest's importance was most dramatically symbolized on the Day of Atonement (Yom Kippur), when he entered into the Holy of Holies, into the very presence of God, as the representative of all the Jews. There he offered sacrifices for all the unwitting sins committed by the people during the year, and in response God assured the Jews of his continuing presence and love.

Although the High Priest and the priesthood continued to occupy a place of great importance up to the time of the destruction of the Temple in A.D. 70, their influence had begun to wane. Since the families from which the High Priests came were typically wealthy and aristocratic, they were separated in sympathy and understanding from the masses of the people. Probably the most important factor in the decline of the priesthood was the rising influence of the Pharisees, who were in dispute with the priests on many points of interpreting the Torah and who usually represented a position more sympathetic to the people.

Nevertheless, as long as the Temple stood it provided a unifying bond. Whether in Palestine or the Diaspora, the Jew looked to the Temple as a symbol of his status as one of God's people. Every year, Jews throughout the world sent their contribution to the Temple, and most Jews longed to make a pilgrimage to the Temple in Jerusalem at least once in their lives. When the Temple was destroyed, however, the growing importance attached to personal and household obedience to the law, combined with the institution of the synagogue, made it possible for Judaism to survive the catastrophe of the obliteration of the temple worship. But it was only a remarkable resurgence of religious faith and the renewed affirmation of the Torah that enabled the community to survive.

THE FUTURE OF THE COVENANT PEOPLE

The hope for the restoration of Israel was expressed vividly by Ezekiel the prophet, sharing and reporting his visions with his fellow exiles in Babylon, speaking in a situation of despair and helplessness. The Lord showed him a valley strewn with "very dry" bones, and then told him to prophesy to the bones, promising them life. Ezekiel complied: "Lo, I prophesied as I was commanded; and . . . there was a noise, and behold a rattling; and the bones came together." Then the prophet is told to command breath (or spirit) to breathe on the bones, "and breath came into them, and they lived." The revivified bones are "the whole house of Israel" (Ezek. 39:1–11). Similar themes using different imagery appear in other prophets: the new creation (Isa. 66:22), the liberation of prisoners (Isa. 42:7); the changing of the desert into a fertile land (Isa. 44:3–4); the river of life flowing from the temple and transforming the Dead Sea to a fresh water lake (Ezek. 47); the new covenant (Jer. 31); the defeat of the hostile pagan powers (Dan. 7; Hag. 2:20–23). The expectation of renewal was widespread; but how it would come about and the role of the nation in the process of transformation was variously perceived.

With the uprising of the Maccabees in recent history there was an answer attractive to many: Military force to achieve political autonomy seemed the only sure means of national renewal. That solution was suppressed for the most part until the middle of the first century A.D.; and in spite of severe defeat, it rose again in the 130s. As we learn from Josephus's *Wars*, however, the military-political movement appealed to prophecy and miracle as a way of guaranteeing that it was divinely sanctioned (II, 258–63).

The Sadducees

During the Maccabean period, especially as the secularization of the ruling princely-priestly Hasmonean family became more evident, groups offering options other than the purely nationalistic aspiration concerning Israel's future were formed in Palestine. One of these was the *Sadducees*. Described by Josephus as a philosophical school (not a sect in the modern sociological sense), the Sadducees seem to have been linked with the temple administration. Even the meaning and derivation of the name are uncertain. They are first mentioned by Josephus in describing events from the time of John Hyrcanus (135–104 B.C.). According to one hypothesis which has received considerable support, the term *Sadducee* was derived from *Zadok* (*Zadokite*). In the Old Testament the legitimate priestly office of Aaron is said to have been given to Zadok and his descendants. According to this hypothesis, since the principal claim and concern of the Sadducees was the legitimate succession of the priestly office, this derivation of the name and the movement seems justified.

Since no literature of the Sadducees is extant, and our knowledge about them is derived from the writings of rival movements, it is difficult to reconstruct a full and accurate account of their beliefs and practices. In comparison with the *Pharisees* and the *Essenes*, their religious outlook was probably conservative. Their exclusive guide in religious matters was the Law of Moses, the first five books of the Old Testament. In these books are contained the basic rules and regulations governing the Temple, the priesthood, and the sacrificial rites. How the scribes of the Sadducees interpreted the meaning of the sacrifices is not known, but this much seems clear: they believed that faithful and literal fulfillment of God's provision for sacrificial worship in the Temple was the crucial requirement in maintaining Israel's covenant relationship with God.

The influence and prerogatives of the Sadducees appear to have reached beyond the confines and activities of the Temple and its priesthood. They enjoyed a dominant position in the Sanhedrin, the local council whose presiding officer was the High Priest. Considering the authority of the Sanhedrin, the potential for wielding influence over the life of the Jews is quite obvious. Only the Pharisees, who gradually increased in strength, were powerful enough to challenge the Sadducees' influence and their interpretation of the Torah. Through their dominant role in the Temple and the Sanhedrin, the Sadducean priesthood and its supporters were the official spokesmen for the Jews in their dealings with Rome. Drawn largely from the wealthy, aristocratic, priestly families, they were concerned and in close touch with both the economic and political problems of the harassed nation. When possible, they followed the road of peaceful coexistence with the civil authorities. Nevertheless, on occasion they were capable of resistance when a political authority ventured to control and manipulate the office of High Priest, or plundered the treasury of the Temple.

Placing supreme value upon the Law of Moses, the Sadducees relegated the prophetic and other writings of the Old Testament to a place of secondary importance. They were particularly opposed to apocalyptic and eschatological thought, on the grounds that such speculation was not compatible with the Torah. For the same reason, they disavowed the popular belief in angels, demons, evil spirits, and the resurrection of the dead. They saw the life blood of Judaism pulsing in the Temple cult and looked with particular fear and horror on eschatological speculation and apocalyptic hopes, especially when these fanned the flames of anti-Roman nationalism.

While the Sadducees' political sagacity undoubtedly was an important factor in keeping a potentially hot war cold, the succeeding years were to show that the Sadducees had cut themselves off from those vital movements in Jewish religious life and thought that were to play such a decisive role in the resurgence of Judaism after the tragedy of A.D. 70. From that date, when the Romans sacked Jerusalem and destroyed the Temple, the Sadducees quickly disappeared from the Jewish scene. Their understanding of the Torah was so literal and unimaginatively limited, and their religious piety was so narrowly centered in the Temple, that once the Temple was destroyed their reason for existence ceased. The disappearance of the Sadducees marked the triumph of their chief rivals, the Pharisees.

The Pharisees

The origin of the Pharisees was in some way related to the revolt of the Hasidim in the Maccabean period. The Hasidim in the second century B.C. sources and the Pharisees as depicted in later sources were both rigorous supporters of the Torah. According to their own traditions, they looked back to the time of Ezra as the formative period for their group's ideals and aspirations. But even if the Pharisees claimed such early antecedents for their movement, it was not until after the Maccabean Revolt that there emerged the patterns of thinking that led to their subsequent development. It was also in this period that they became a coherent force in Jewish life.

Concerning the derivation of the name Pharisee, there is even less agreement among scholars than in the case of the Sadducees. One plausible hypothesis derives the name from a Hebrew word meaning "separatists." Whether this was a self-designation or a derogatory label of their opponents is uncertain. The problem of determining specifically what it was from which they were separated is likewise difficult to decide. One possibility would be the group's withdrawal of support from the Hasmonean monarchy, when in the second century B.C. it pursued a more decidedly political course and tended to veer from a distinctly religious orientation.

One certain feature of the history of the Pharisees, however, is that they were politically involved in the dynastic struggles at the end of the second century B.C., as Josephus attests. But their strategy seems to have been to acquiesce in whatever foreign power dominated their land so long as they—the Pharisees—could shape the lives of the Jewish people. This goal was to be achieved by political involvement that could coerce Jews to obey the Torah, as Jacob Neusner has shown,[5] and could give them the power to execute with royal support those who opposed them and their tactics. Josephus reports that when Alexandra became queen (76–67 B.C.), she turned over to the Pharisees the administration of the Jewish state: "If she ruled the nation, the Pharisees ruled her" (*Wars,* 1:112). He describes the Pharisees as having a reputation for "excelling the rest of their nation in the observance of religion and as exact exponents of their laws." They were able to manipulate the queen to preserve the façade of her royal authority while actually controlling the lives of her subjects by forcing conformity to their interpretation of Torah.

Like the Sadducees, the Pharisees looked upon the Torah of Moses as the definitive revelation of God's will. Unlike the Sadducees, they also venerated the prophetic writings and another group called "holy writings" (*hagiographa*) that were eventually to be accepted as authoritative. Indeed, it was the Pharisees who finally (about A.D. 90) determined the contents of the Hebrew Bible. But the Pharisees went a step further, for they also stressed the existence and validity of an oral Torah (oral tradition). According to rabbinic tradition, it had its inception with Moses himself. In this point they were in radical conflict with the Sadducees, who rejected the oral Torah and all doctrine not found in the written law.

By the time of the formation of the early rabbinic traditions into what is known as the Mishnah (between A.D. 180 and 200), the theory had emerged that what the rabbis taught went back in an unbroken line of orally transmitted teaching to the time of Moses. The homogeneity of the Mishnah, however, and the impossibility of tracing with certainty any older sources contained within it, make that claim unlikely and place it beyond proof. What we learn of the Pharisees through the Mishnah, therefore, is an indistinguishable mixture of second-century rabbinic idealization and some possible traces of authentic earlier tradition. The aim attributed to the oral law is, in retrospect, admirable: By their hypothesis of the oral Torah, the rabbis seem to have exercised a liberalizing influence on Judaism; through the oral Torah it was possible for Judaism to keep the written Torah relevant to changing conditions. If the Mishnah portrays faithfully what the Pharisees were like—even with minimal accuracy—then we can see that, although God had fully revealed his will in the written Torah, new rules of conduct had to be worked out if the written Torah were to be understood and obeyed in the face of ever-changing external circumstances. It would have been their firm conviction that every decision in life must be governed by the Torah that led them to develop elaborate principles of interpretation whereby they could derive specific rules to govern conduct in every conceivable situation. A rule or instruction so derived to set forth the relevant meaning of the written Torah was called a *halakah*. In the development of these *halakoth* (plural) the Pharisees

[5] Jacob Neusner, *From Politics to Piety: The Emergence of Pharisaic Judaism* (Englewood Cliffs, N.J.: Prentice-Hall, 1973), pp. 64–66.

employed an important principle called the "hedge." According to their tradition an important early Pharisaic teacher had said, among other things, "Build a hedge around the Torah." In practice this meant the formulation of additional *halakoth* to assist in faithfully obeying the requirement of some injunction of written Torah or previously formulated *halakah*.

But the oral Torah consisted of more than these succinct instructions. It also contained *haggadah*. *Haggadah* could take a variety of forms, such as a parable, simile, legend, myth, historical reminiscence. Its purpose might be to illustrate and elicit response to the moral injunctions of written or oral Torah. But its range of concern was much broader. In it such subjects as the relation of God to Israel and the world, the meaning of Israel's past, present, and future, the problems of life, death, sin, and temptation were dealt with in an imaginative way. If the *halakah* served as an arrow pointing to God and his will, the *haggadah* was intended not only to emphasize the urgency of following the arrow, but to evoke the faith, understanding, and motivation that brought active response.

Through the oral tradition the Pharisees found an outlet for their religious imagination, always of necessity oriented toward the written Torah. Among other things, it enabled the Pharisees to incorporate into their thinking the apocalyptic and eschatological insights which became increasingly important during the second century B.C. and later. Such expectations as the victorious coming of God's kingdom, the coming of the Messiah, and the resurrection of the dead, assumed an important place in Pharisaic thought. They were accustomed to thinking of the history of Israel and all humanity in terms of the "two ages": "this age" and the "age to come." By "this age" they referred to the then present world situation, wherein evil powers and lawless men sought to frustrate God's purposes and God's will. Within "this age" the one certain path was that of obedience to the Torah, through which the powers of temptation and sin could be overthrown and overcome. In God's own time he would bring the "age to come," in which his final victory over sin and evil would be disclosed to mankind, and a new order of existence would characterize human life. But as we will see, compared with such a sect as the Essenes, most Pharisees were restrained in their attitude toward eschatological[6] speculation.

By the beginning of the Christian era, however, major political changes had taken place in Palestine that directly contributed to the transformation of the Pharisees and of the subsequent history of Judaism as a whole. The coming of Pompey in 63 B.C. and the installation of the Herodian family as puppet kings of the Jews resulted in political impotence for Jews in general and the Pharisees in particular. Presumably under the leadership of Hillel (ca. 30 B.C.–A.D.10) the Pharisaic movement abandoned its political tactics and concentrated instead on the purity of its members. Although historical certainty is unattainable in this matter, it appears that Hillel transformed the Pharisees from a political cabal to a table fellowship. The Gospels, hostile though they are toward the Pharisees, picture them as primarily concerned about purity

---

[6] *Eschatological,* from a Greek word meaning "last," is a scholarly term for religious views concerning an expected end of the world, or of the present age.

issues: personal purity, food laws, sacrificial offerings, Sabbath observance. That emphasis is discernible in the oldest layers of the rabbinic tradition, which—though they were written down in their present form centuries later—probably reflect the concerns that dominated the Pharisaic movement in the period before A.D. 70.

Their overwhelming ambition—at least as it is later represented—was to create a covenant people obedient to Yahweh by the norms of their interpretation of his will in the oral and written law. The essence of Judaism, according to this strand, traced back in the Mishnah to the time of Hillel, was the relevance of the Torah for individual and social existence. For these Pharisees, even hope for the "age to come" was understood basically from the standpoint of obedience to the law. There were some Pharisees who claimed that if Israel should obey the Torah for one day, then the kingdom of God would come. So their zeal for the Torah was conditioned not only by their desire for Israel not to be faithless as in the past, but also by their belief that obedience would determine the future. It is in this context that their rigorous emphasis on obedience to the law must be understood.

To the Pharisees, as the Mishnah portrays them, the Torah was God's great gift to Israel, and through Israel, to all people. They taught that it was sin that stood between people and God. Residing in each person's heart is an evil and a good desire, the former leading to sin, the latter to obedience and good deeds. God gave the Torah in order that his good desire might overcome the evil. When the Pharisee spoke of the "joy of the law" he meant not only its ability to show what God requires, but also its power to lead humans to overcome evil desire. And if he failed, God in his mercy had also offered the gift of repentance. The power of the law and the power of repentance were two great themes of Pharisaic teaching.

The Pharisees seem to have set a rigid standard of adherence to the Torah that few could follow, but there is no doubt that many respected them. Their influence was dominant in the synagogue, whose existence and style or mode of worship was validated by oral tradition, and in the home, where they encouraged study and obedience to the Torah. On the other hand, it was inevitable that their rigorous attitude would tend to cut them off from many Jews, and bring with it the danger of self-righteousness, a problem they recognized and combated in their teachings.

The fact that the attainment of purity and the offering of fitting sacrifice could take place in the home or in their table fellowship as a group meant that for them the Temple was not essential to true piety. They presumably participated fully in the Temple worship, but in the Pharisaic view its inaccessibility to millions of Jews in the dispersion or even its disappearance did not hinder their being a holy people.

Not surprisingly, therefore, it was the Pharisees who led the Jewish community to recovery after the fall of Jerusalem and the destruction of the Temple. The Pharisees had no love for Rome or its puppet rulers in Palestine, but the majority of leaders seem to have cautioned against open revolt. They were not motivated by political or economic ambitions, but by their understanding of the Torah and their belief that the destiny of the Jews was religious rather than political. Even during the terrible siege of Jerusalem, they managed to smuggle out Yochanan ben-Zakkai, the famous teacher who was later to play a major role in religious recovery. Strengthened by a religious faith and piety deeply grounded in the Torah, the Pharisees were able to withstand the shock of the destruction of the Temple, and to create an even greater unity of life in the Jewish community—a unity that has persisted to the present day.

Driven from their capital city, Jerusalem, following the failure of their revolt against the Romans in A.D. 70, Jews would have been leaderless and devoid of direction had not the Pharisees (with Roman approval) launched a process at Yavneh (or Jamnia) on the coast that sought to formulate a consensus about Judaism and Jewish destiny. Learned debates were carried on concerning issues of legal interpretation. Decisions were reached as to which writings were to be considered authoritative scripture. Probably it was at Yavneh that Jews began differentiating Christians from themselves; at the same time Christians were making polemical statements about Jews (see Chapter 5). Above all, the basic patterns of scriptural interpretation and legal obligation that were to characterize rabbinic Judaism down to the present day were laid down at Yavneh.

The Essenes

The Essenes were the third distinctive group to develop in the Jewish community during the last two centuries B.C. Although they are not mentioned in the New Testament, they have long been known from the writings of both Philo and Flavius Josephus, the Jewish historian of the first century A.D.

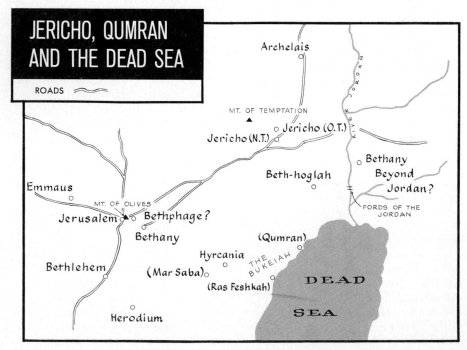

Until recently, many questions regarding the Essenes and their origins had never been answered. However, new light has been thrown on the Essene movement with the discovery (beginning in 1947) of the Dead Sea Scrolls, more recently called the Qumran Scrolls after the name of the site (Khirbet Qumran) of the community's dwelling. From the beginning, scholars recognized certain differences and omissions in the accounts of Philo and Josephus, as compared with the scrolls themselves. There is now general agreement that these discrepancies can be explained, and there is little doubt that the community which composed and treasured these scrolls belonged to the Essene movement. Since the day when a shepherd accidentally stumbled upon the first cave in the rugged hills on the western shore of the Dead Sea, numerous caves (eleven are of major importance for the sect) have been found, and their valuable manuscripts and fragments of manuscripts recovered. The task of publication and research is not yet complete. Nevertheless, study of the literature has proceeded sufficiently to provide a tentative reconstruction of the beliefs, practices, and history of the sect. The information derived from the documents has been enhanced by the knowledge gained from archeological excavation and study of the ruins at Khirbet Qumran.[7] Because the Essenes are less well known to the general reader and because the discovery of the Dead Sea Scrolls has led to extravagant claims about connections between the Essenes and the Jesus movement, we shall offer a more detailed description of this group than of the Sadducees or Pharisees.

The Essenes, like the Pharisees, were spiritual descendants of the movement of religious protest generated by the Hasidim. In the case of the Essenes this protest, culminating in the establishment of the community at Qumran, entailed a radical withdrawal from normal social and religious associations. Scholars continue to debate the date of the sect's origins; suggestions range from the beginning of the Maccabean Revolt (167–165 B.C.) to the reign of Alexander Jannaeus (103–76 B.C.). Archeological evidence points decisively to settlement within the reign of John Hyrcanus (135–104 B.C.). On the basis of the primary literary evidence, mainly Josephus's works and the historical allusions in the scrolls, the events that motivated the withdrawal to Qumran can be satisfactorily harmonized with what is known of Jewish history at that time. There are good grounds, however, for believing that the Essene movement antedated the withdrawal to Qumran. According to one interpretation of an important Essene writing, the *Damascus Document,* the sect existed for "twenty years" before the crisis that sparked the withdrawal to Qumran. It is quite possible, however, that "twenty" has a symbolical meaning. On one fact there is general agreement: the establishment of the community at Qumran, and the circumstances accompanying that event, were decisive in the formation of Essene religious life and thought as they are described in the scrolls.

---

[7] There is an immense bibliography for Qumran studies. Among the many excellent works, the following are notable for their conciseness as well as their dependability: Frank M. Cross, *The Ancient Library at Qumran and Modern Biblical Studies* (Garden City, N.Y.: Doubleday, 1958); and G. Vermes, *The Dead Sea Scrolls in English* (Middlesex, Eng.: Penguin Books, 1962). Many of the important documents are included in A. Dupont Sommer, *The Essene Writings from Qumran* (Cleveland: World, 1962; reprinted by Peter Smith, Gloucester, Mass., 1973).

Site of the Dead Sea community; the excavated ruins, with the Dead Sea in the background. The cave in the cliff in the right center foreground is one of many in the area that contained manuscript fragments of the Dead Sea Scrolls.   (*Israel Department of Antiquities and Museums*)

The withdrawal of the sect to Qumran represented a drastic reaction to the increased Hellenizing and secularizing tendencies of the Hasmonean rulers, and a repudiation of their illegitimate claims to the high priesthood. The specific event that provoked the departure was the persecution of the Righteous Teacher, whom the sect venerated as its founder, by a "wicked priest." Efforts to identify these persons with known historical figures has produced a flood of hypotheses. This much seems certain: the wicked priest was one of the Hasmonean rulers. Concerning the Righteous Teacher, there has been less success. His significance for the development of the Essene movement is acknowledged by all, but most interpreters are inclined to limit our knowledge about him to the information contained in the sectarian writings. Specific references are scarce, and in certain cases downright controversial. Fortunately, the writings are clear on two essential facts about the teacher. In the first place, his followers believed that he was the true representative of the legitimate line of priesthood, the Zadokite. This, in part, accounts for the priestly character of the sect and its violent opposition to the established priesthood in Jerusalem. In the second place, they believed that God had revealed to the teacher a new interpretation which was the true interpretation of the law and the prophets. According to their *Habakkuk Commentary*, God had

Pools at Qumran. Because of the steps that lead down into these pools it is likely that they were not used merely for storage of water, but served as places of ceremonial washing for the members of the Dead Sea community.   *(Israel Department of Antiquities and Museums)*

revealed to the Righteous Teacher "all the secrets of the words of his servants the prophets." Through their inspired teacher the Essenes were constituted as the community that alone possessed and exercised the legitimate priestly offices, and alone had received the authoritative interpretation of the Torah.

INTERPRETATION OF AND OBEDIENCE TO SCRIPTURE. Like the Hasidim, who rallied in Maccabean times to the defense of the Torah, the Essenes shared with the Pharisees the firm commitment to understand and obey the holy scriptures. However, their peculiar mode of interpretation disclosed the distinctive features of their life and thought. Fortunately, among the scrolls are several commentaries on biblical books, the earliest extant literature of this type. From these, the Essenes' peculiar way of interpreting the sacred writings can be discerned. While it is questionable if any of these writings can be attributed to the teacher, the method of interpretation, which the sect called the *pesher,* very likely derives from him. Simply stated, the members read the sacred writings, especially the prophetic books, in the belief that the words and events contained in them were written with specific reference to the events occurring in their own time. For example, their understanding of a passage from Isaiah (40:3) was of crucial importance: "Prepare in the wilderness a way . . . make straight in the desert a highway for our God." It is clear

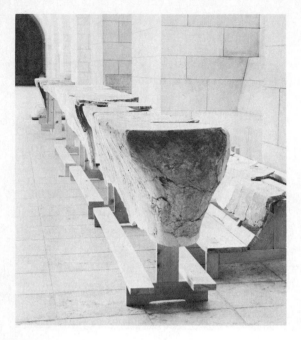

Tables or benches on which scribes of the Qumran sect copied manuscripts. Inkwells found nearby contain traces of dried ink. At the far end is a ceremonial basin in which the scribes washed their hands before copying the sacred writings. (*Israel Department of Antiquities and Museums*)

that they read these words as if they were spoken to them, and their retreat to Qumran was seen as the obedient response to prepare in the wilderness for the coming of God's kingdom.

It was not only their belief that the prophets were to be understood in terms of the sect's contemporary history that was important. Equally significant was the conviction that the prophets' words referred to the last days before the final victory of God's kingdom. The Essenes believed they were living in those last days. Their religious outlook was eschatological—i.e., concerned with the final things of the transition from this age to the next. This way of viewing history exercised a decisive influence over all they thought and did. The Essenes were an eschatological community; more than any other Jewish group they were nourished on the eschatological hopes that touched the lives of so many Jews during the troubled times of Hasmonean, Herodian, and Roman domination. The strength of these hopes was evident in their rigorously disciplined life, which they believed was God's true way for his people during the short interval before his long-expected deliverance.

The community was organized on the pattern of the early days of Israel's history when the people paused on the edge of the wilderness, preparing to enter into the inheritance of the Promised Land as the consummation of God's covenant with them. The Essenes clearly thought that the end of Israel's earthly pilgrimage would be a recapitulation of the beginnings under Moses and Aaron and Joshua. But they were forced to recognize the actual situation in their day as they saw it. The Promised Land was in the hands of the wicked Jewish leaders, who were unfaithful to the covenant and ignorant of the truth of the law and the prophets. But now God was about to bring to fulfillment the new covenant he had promised. It was an eternal covenant. If its fulfill-ment involved the defeat of the enemies within and without Israel, its culmi-nation was eternal life. The Essenes believed God had called them into the wilderness in order to lead them out by way of the new covenant; indeed, they called themselves the Community of the New Covenant. They alone were the true Israel, the faithful remnant.

THE DISCIPLINE AND ROUTINE OF THE COMMUNITY.   The Essenes residing at Qumran lived, as we have said, a life of strict discipline. The char-acter of this discipline is reflected throughout their writings, but particularly in the Rule of the Community (or Manual of Discipline), a document that sets forth their principal doctrines, rites, and rules and regulations, with pre-cise penalties for infractions. The community was tightly organized into groups of Priests, Levites, and Laymen, each enjoying a special status deter-mined by specific privileges and responsibilities. A central council consisting of twelve Laymen and three Priests served as a judiciary body to deal with certain well-defined areas. The superior status of the Priests clearly indicates the character of the community's organization. This division into orders was set within the context of a strong sense of unity. Indeed, the characteristic Hebrew word used by the Qumran sect to designate themselves can be trans-lated as "unity" as well as "community."

Daily life included work, assemblies for prayer and worship, study of the law, and meals of a distinctly religious significance. Members engaged in trades necessary to furnish a modest subsistence for the group, each in return drawing on the communal goods for his needs. In the ruins of Qumran were found the remains of a smith shop, pottery kilns and shop, bakery, grain mills, and storage silos. The sect also appears to have occupied an additional site at 'Ain Feshka, about two miles south of Qumran, where they engaged in small-scale irrigation farming and maintained their herds. Those who entered the community pooled their possessions voluntarily. A vow of poverty was a fea-ture of their discipline—they also called themselves the Congregation of the Poor. As their commentary on Psalm 37 shows, they were the "meek [who] shall inherit the earth"—of course, in the eschatological sense in which they understood "inheritance."

Early in the morning, before going about their work, and again in the evening, the sect assembled for prayers, probably in the large assembly hall located in the central building at Qumran. The many original psalms found in the scrolls, especially the Thanksgiving Scroll, and remains of liturgical texts, suggest the form of their worship. It is probable that reading and expo-sition of the Torah were important parts of their worship. Study of the Torah absorbed much more of their time. The discovery of a large *scriptorium* at the Qumran site, as well as the many remains of biblical texts, bear witness to the energy they devoted to studying, copying, preserving, and commenting upon the scriptures. According to the Rule of the Community, the Torah was to be read throughout the night for one-third of the nights of the year, in the pres-ence of the whole community.

Two daily meals, at noontime and evening, were central to their life of religious devotion. The Rule of the Community designates participation as one of the privileges of full membership. The Rule stipulates that these meals were to take place in the presence of an officiating priest, whose prayer of blessing was of primary importance. It is generally maintained that these meals should be understood within an eschatological framework. They were eaten in anticipation of the great Messianic feast in which the Essenes expected to participate when God's final victory had been achieved.

Throughout the year the Essenes celebrated the great religious festivals of the Jews, such as Sabbath, Passover, Pentecost, and the Day of Atonement. However, they followed a religious calendar at variance with the authoritative calendar of the Jerusalem Temple—undoubtedly an important source of contention in their continuing conflict with the established priesthood. To understand the significance of this feud it is necessary to recognize the Essenes' strong conviction that the times for the great religious festivals were ordained by God and fixed according to the movements of the heavenly bodies. Since a solar calendar was employed at Qumran and a lunar calendar in Jerusalem, discrepancies were inevitable. To the Essenes, irregularities at Jerusalem were a violation of God's will.

In view of the freedom and ingenuity that marked their scriptural interpretation and their absence from the Temple, the Essenes' rites probably varied from those of the Jerusalem Temple. One important problem concerns their attitude toward sacrifices. There is no clear evidence that they performed sacrifices at Qumran, and good reason to believe that they tended to "spiritualize" the concept of sacrifice. How far they went in this direction remains a question. Did they abstain from sacrifices at Jerusalem merely because of their opposition to the priesthood? Or did their abstention reflect a radical reinterpretation of sacrifice, consequently reflected in their theology and rites?

INITIATION, RITES, AND DOCTRINE.   Entrance into the community was preceded by a two-year-long novitiate of instruction and of testing the candidate's "knowledge," culminating in full membership. The Rule of the Community describes the ceremonial rite of initiation in which each of the orders—Priests, Levites, and Laymen—had its special part to play. The new members were placed under the solemn oath of secrecy and confronted with an impressive recitation of curses and blessings, a testimony to the consequences of disobedience or obedience to their vows. Apparently the admission of new members was an annual event, at which time the old members submitted to an examination of their obedience and renewed their vows. The initiation was climaxed by a purificatory rite of baptism, in which the baptized was purified by the Holy Spirit. The Essene writings, as well as the discovery of cisterns and water channels fed by aqueduct from Wadi Qumran, testify to the importance of ritual ablutions and probably of baptisms. From the time of his initial baptism the Essene was admitted to the privilege of, and obligation for, such ritual ablutions.

The zeal with which the Essenes embraced their discipline is to be understood in the context of their dualistic interpretation of the world and their hopes. Beyond the visible world there existed a host of wicked angels or spirits under the dominion of their ruler, Belial, also called the Spirit of Wickedness and the Prince of Darkness. Arrayed against them were the heavenly hosts of God, led by the Spirit of Truth, also named the Prince of Lights and the Angel of Truth. God, they believed, had permitted Belial and his forces to pursue their wicked course, but only for an allotted time. Why God had permitted this was one of the deep mysteries known only to God. But there is no suggestion that Belial existed outside the realm of God's ultimate sovereignty. There is no hint of an absolute or metaphysical dualism. This has led scholars to coin the phrase *eschatological dualism* to describe it. The wicked course of Belial was manifested principally through men of Belial's lot, Sons of Darkness, who rejected God and his will. These men were identified not only with the enemies of the Jews, such as the Roman oppressors, but also with Jews who were not a part of the true remnant. Against these angelic and human forces were arrayed the angels of God's lot, and the men of God's lot, the Sons of Light, the Community of the New Covenant.

According to the Essenes, God had predestined the lot of every human being. Entrance into the community was evidence of being in God's lot, and assured anyone of the support of the Spirit of Truth. Destiny for the Essene would be fulfilled when Belial's allotted time came to an end, and he and those of his lot were destroyed. For the Essene, life was already a battle against the Spirit of Wickedness; the struggle served as a discipline and preparation for the final conflict. For the end of Belial's lot was to come in a mighty battle. In one of their writings, the *War of the Children of Light against the Children of Darkness,* the details of the progressive states in that holy war, and the military organization of the community, are meticulously described. The Essenes with the hosts of God would prevail in the battle that marked the end of the hosts of wickedness, both angelic and human. Their conviction was that the leadership of Israel was corrupt and that therefore most Jews were disobedient to God's law and ignorant of his purpose. The Essene community had been granted privileged insight into God's plan—a mode of self-understanding that marks them as a true sect in the sociological sense of the term. A frequent characteristic of sects is the conviction that God has granted them a distinctive role in the divine purpose and special insight into the process of its fulfillment. At Qumran this belief was central.

THE ESCHATOLOGICAL HOPE OF THE COMMUNITY. Messianic speculation played an important role in the group's eschatological expectations. Their preoccupation with messianism is especially evident in their Testimonia Document, a collection of scriptural verses which they interpreted as messianic prophecies. Like many other Jews, the Essenes looked forward to the coming of a prophet as the forerunner of the messianic age. They were distinctive in their expectation of *two* messiahs, the messiah of Aaron and the messiah of Israel, the former from the priestly line, the latter from the royal line. The messiah of Israel was to be instrumental in leading the community in its victorious war; the messiah of Aaron was to be instrumental in the establishment of the New Jerusalem and the New Temple. It is significant that the messiah of Aaron takes precedence over the messiah of Israel. This precedence undoubtedly harks back to the centrality of the priesthood in Israel's early history. No doubt it was further strengthened as a result of the disillusion over the secularistic tendencies of the Hasmoneans, and the later despair of the victory over the Romans. This messianic speculation regarding Israel in the new age was consistent with the Essenes' belief concerning God's purpose for Israel throughout history. The community was to be a priestly people whose only king was God, and a holy people whose only law was Torah. On the basis of this conviction, the sect withdrew to achieve the life such a purpose demanded.

A very important question concerns the extent to which the Righteous Teacher was the subject of the Essenes' messianic speculation. Since the discovery of the scrolls many theories regarding the teacher have been promulgated—such as the theory that he had been crucified and had risen from the dead. Further study has decisively shown that this particular theory was founded on a mistaken reading of the texts. On somewhat firmer grounds other scholars have assigned a messianic role to the teacher, identifying him with the expected prophet (as in Deut. 18:18, Mal. 3:1) or even one of the messiahs. His role as the herald of the last days, of the messianic age and its figures, must be described as eschatological.

Nurtured on their eschatological hopes, the Essenes viewed the present world order pessimistically. We have already noted that, staunch in their biblical doctrine of God the creator and sovereign over his creation, they avoided anything approaching a metaphysical dualism. But in their writings, especially their psalms, there is an emphasis on the lowliness of humanity which goes beyond the biblical writings in intensity. It is not so much the problem of the weakness of the body or human sensuality that troubles them; it is the perverseness of the heart, mind, and will—the inadequacy of all human righteousness, the hopelessness of humanity apart from the righteousness of God. Such thinking stands in an unresolved tension with their predestinarian tendencies, but it also mitigates clear-cut legalistic tendencies. It is also in harmony with their confession that only through the guidance of the Holy Spirit do they achieve purity, obedience, and salvation. However much their pessimism must have been accentuated by the repeated political and religious frustrations of the Jewish people during 200 troubled years, it was basically rooted in their conviction of human moral weakness and the necessity of God's action.

The monastic life of the Essenes at Qumran must have had a peculiar appeal for many Jews who were world-weary, and looked to God for a new understanding of his ways with his people, Israel. The fact that there were Essene communities in places other than Qumran has long been known from Josephus's account. One of their writings, the Damascus Document, describes the organization of these camps, which were founded on a nucleus of ten persons, provided one was a priest. Obviously, changes in religious practices were necessary for the communities that did not enjoy the seclusion of Qumran. But the monastic life and thought at Qumran surely exercised a continuous influence upon them. Numerically the movement was small (Josephus says 4000). However, the Essenes must have played an important role in spreading and nurturing the eschatological hopes and apocalyptic visions that pervaded Jewish religious thought. This is one of the most important aspects of the discovery of the Dead Sea Scrolls. Now, in a way that was not possible before, we can better understand this atmosphere. It is significant that the sect's library included a number of writings which are either identical with, or bear a literary relationship to, extracanonical writings called by modern scholars the Apocrypha and Pseudepigrapha.[8] Essenes undoubtedly were the authors of many such writings. It is particularly important for the student of the New Testament to have some understanding of the mingled despair and hope represented by the Essenes. For it was this same eschatological mode that was a major characteristic of the thought of Jesus and the New Testament writers.

THE END OF THE COMMUNITY. The conclusions of the archeologists point to the grim fact that sometime during the siege of Jerusalem (probably in A.D. 68) Roman legions attacked and devastated the settlement at Qumran. The disappearance of the sect after A.D. 70 affords persuasive evidence that the community pinned its hopes on the expectation that this was the Holy War for which they had waited. It appears that those who did not suffer death in the war with Rome came to the shocking conclusion that their way of understanding Torah had been wrong. Their precious library, which they managed to conceal in their caves before the Roman onslaught, bears testimony to their incredible zeal for God and his Torah, and their consuming desire to be the faithful community established by his covenant.

Jewish Mysticism

Although there is no indication of a separate sect or group in Judaism before A.D. 70 that was predominantly mystical in its outlook, at Qumran and in other documents from this period there is evidence of a special type of mysticism that centered on the chariot throne of Yahweh as the locus of personal revelatory experience. Combining the vision of Isaiah 6 and that of Ezekiel 1, where the prophets were enabled to see Yahweh on his chariot throne, these mystical writings described the experience of faithful persons who, having endured suffering obediently, are granted a vision of God and a promise of ultimate vindication. In an apocryphal document, the Testament of Job, for example, Job explains that he was able to endure all his trials because early in his life he had seen the divine chariot throne.

In the experience his face and garments became radiant, as did the face of Moses according to Exodus 34:29 and as did Daniel's appearance (Dan. 10:8). Similar visions of God's throne are mentioned in liturgical fragments from Qumran, as they are in the document known as 3 Enoch (which has survived in a late reworked form). This tradition became important in Judaism, and seems to have influenced both Jesus and Paul, as we will note later. These mystical visions were not understood as an escape from earthly difficulty, but as a way of understanding it and overcoming it.[9]

---

[8] The so-called Apocrypha of the Old Testament are easily available in many editions of the Bible. The most complete edition of the Pseudepigrapha is that edited by J. H. Charlesworth (Garden City, N.Y.: Doubleday (Anchor Books), Vol. I, 1983; Vol. II, 1984.)

[9] Known as Merkabah mysticism, this aspect of Jewish piety has been studied by Gershom Scholem, *Major Trends in Jewish Mysticism* (New York: Schocken, 1941) and more recently by Michael Stone in *Scriptures, Sects, and Visions* (Philadelphia: Fortress Press, 1980).

The existence of these mystical movements in the period of the second Temple shows a degree of diversity in Judaism that is often overlooked. Yet, divergent as they were in the solutions each offered, these groups were united on the central issues at stake in their continued existence as those called to be God's covenant people. There was at this period no normative Judaism, and efforts to posit such an orthodox system in the period before the destruction of the Temple must rely on later rabbinic developments from the second to the sixth centuries. When the Pharisees came into the ascendancy in Palestine under Roman auspices after A.D. 70 and began the process of solidifying Jewish thought and practice in the absence of Temple and priesthood, it was the Pharisaic viewpoint which became the norm. In the pre-70 period, diversity reigned. Yet even though each group in Judaism interpreted the Torah and Jewish tradition in a different way, and sought to preserve the distinctiveness of covenant existence by different standards, two factors gave the Jews an overarching sense of unity: their devotion to the Torah and their claim to descent from Abraham, from Jacob, and his twelve sons.

This unity of life and thought must have attracted many non-Jews by its religious and ethical fervor; yet others were repelled by its exclusiveness. Part of the difficulty lay in the fact that while men and women of the time sought eagerly for membership in a religious community, the Jews claimed to have been *born into* such a community. The Jews had made efforts to share their religious life with Gentiles, but with little success. Now, however, there arose out of Judaism a new movement—one that succeeded in the matter of inclusiveness. We turn next to a consideration of this new community: the Christian Church, which, like the Dead Sea sect, considered itself to be the true heir of the new covenant.

ANNOTATED BIBLIOGRAPHY

CHARLESWORTH, J. H., ed.   *The Pseudepigrapha.* Garden City, N.Y.: Doubleday (Anchor Books), Vol. I, 1983; Vol. II, 1984.   A comprehensive collection of introductions, translations, and notes for the Jewish writings, produced for the most part under the names of Jewish worthies from the past, which demonstrates in detail the rich diversity of Judaism during the period of the rise of Christianity.

NEUSNER, JACOB.   *Method and Meaning in Ancient Judaism.* Third Series. Brown University Judaic Studies. Chico, Calif.: Scholars Press, 1981.   A superb set of essays which traces the rise of rabbinic Judaism, the development of the Pharisaic movement, and the antecedents of the Talmud and Mishnah.

NICKELSBURG, GEORGE W. E.   *Jewish Literature Between the Bible and the Mishna.* Philadelphia: Fortress Press, 1981.   A careful and comprehensive analysis of Jewish writings during the centuries before and after the birth of Jesus. Includes material never recognized by official Judaism as well as interpretations of scripture that prepared for the rise of rabbinic Judaism.

PETERS, F. E.   *The Harvest of Hellenism.* New York: Touchstone (Simon and Schuster), 1970.   Presents a fascinating, detailed overview of the Mediterranean world under the social and cultural influence of the Greek and Roman rulers.

RUSSELL, D. S. *The Jews from Alexander to Herod.* Oxford: Oxford University Press, 1967. An excellent survey of the historical and religious developments within Judaism under the impact of Greek and Roman culture.

VERMES, GEZA. *The Dead Sea Scrolls in English.* London and Baltimore: Penguin, 1974. A handy and comprehensive collection of the writings found in the caves and ruins near the site of the Essene community by the Dead Sea.

PART II

THE COMMUNITY
OF THE
NEW COVENANT

Introduction:

The Rise
of the
New Covenant Community

No one would question that Jesus is the central figure of the New Testament. Without him, the New Testament writings would never have been produced. Yet there is nearly as much space in the New Testament devoted to the career of Paul and to writings by him or attributed to him as there is to the Four Gospels that tell the story of Jesus. It was Paul's encounter with the risen Christ that called him to his apostolic mission, and there is scarcely a paragraph in his letters which does not spell out for his readers what the meaning of Jesus Christ is to those who seek to follow him. But the fact remains that there are important differences between the writings that concentrate on the portrait of Jesus—the Gospels—and the Epistles of Paul. The difference is not that the letters merely expand on the Gospels; rather, the differences are more basic.

The Gospels concentrate on the career of Jesus, especially his teachings and activities during the brief period between the launching of his mission in Galilee and his death in Jerusalem. We read in the Gospels of his conflicts with religious and civil authorities, culminating in his execution as a threat to

71

the Roman order. In all the Gospels there are hints or even promises that God will raise him from the dead in order to fulfill his work of preparing God's people for the coming of God's rule, the kingdom of God or the new age. Only Mark fails to describe the post-Crucifixion appearances of Jesus to his followers, but even Mark anticipates that the Resurrection is soon to occur. In all the Gospels the disciples are commissioned by Jesus to carry forward the work he had launched, and that commission is confirmed in the post-Resurrection scenes depicted in Matthew, Luke, and John. In addition, Matthew and Luke describe the circumstances of his birth and provide a genealogy, even though they differ between themselves in details.

Neither in the Epistles of Paul, however, nor in the sermons attributed to him in Acts, do we learn anything more about Jesus's career than that he lived in full obedience of God, who vindicated him by raising him from the dead. Except for the repetition of the words spoken by Jesus at the Last Supper, there are no more than traces of Jesus's teaching in the Epistles. Ironically, the one direct quotation outside the Gospels about the blessedness of those who give (Acts 20:35) does not appear in the Gospel tradition. In the non-Gospel material, both Pauline and later, stress falls on the role of Jesus as deliverer, as sacrifice for sins, as the one who in victory establishes God's rule. Aspects of those roles are present in the Gospel tradition as well, but there they are always linked with some aspect of Jesus's public activity: his exorcizing the demons, his welcoming the poor and the outcasts. None of these details is present in Paul's picture of Jesus as savior and lord: attention is given rather to the power of God through Jesus and to the redemptive results. Rather than recalling the past of Jesus—apart from the general references to his obedience and death—Paul's emphasis is on the future when through Jesus God will triumph over all opposition and establish his rule on the earth.

The Gospels and Epistles are in agreement on certain broad themes, however: Jesus was God's agent to renew the creation; his death was central to that purpose, and God vindicated him by raising him from the dead; those who see in him God's instrument of redemption share in the life of his people. But in matters of ethics and group organization there are fundamental differences. The Gospels base ethical demands on Jesus's teaching, and especially on his reinterpretation of the law of Moses. Paul's ethic is also based in large measure on scripture, but it is set in a framework for which there is no scriptural equivalent, with a stress on the human conscience and an appeal to moral qualities deriving from Stoic thought, such as endurance, integrity, and self-control (Gal. 5:22–23). The leadership of the movement in the Gospels consists of itinerant preachers who move from village to village; urgency rather than organization is their primary concern (Mark 6:6–13). Although Paul is also a traveling preacher, he takes care to organize communities, to work out distribution of responsibilities, to arrange for handling finances, and he worries about what outsiders will think of the enterprise. The disciples claimed to have been commissioned for their work by the earthly Jesus, although his post-Resurrection appearance confirmed that call. But Paul had never seen Jesus, except in an inner or at least a private vision (Gal. 1:16), although he considered that to be as valid for his apostolic role as the experience of those who had journeyed with Jesus during his career in Palestine (1 Cor. 9:1).

How are we to account for these differences? Do they involve more than personal idiosyncrasies? They reflect the basic differences between the cultural and social background of Paul on the one hand, and of the writers of the Gospels on the other. In spite of superficial similarities, the difference in cultural context, and therefore in response to Jesus, is perhaps as great among the evangelists as it is between all of them and Paul. Paul's background in Jewish speculation, his apparent training in Hellenistic philosophy, and the necessity to reach people who lacked any background in Judaism in the course of his mission meant that Paul laid stress on the cosmic significance of Jesus and on mystical communion with him. The writers of Matthew, Mark, and Luke, on the other hand, were influenced by the Jewish prophetic tradition, especially in its eschatological aspects. That is, the expectation prevails in the first three Gospels that through a divinely endowed agent the prophetic hope of the defeat of the evil powers, the establishment of God's rule, and the renewal of his covenant people (Chapter 3) will be fulfilled. Like the ancient prophets of Israel—Amos, Isaiah, Jeremiah—their own personal experiences are intermeshed with their message about what God is soon to do in behalf of his people.

Although it is that outlook which dominates the material included in the Gospels as we know them, each writer has modified the tradition to a greater or lesser degree, in keeping with his own cultural context, perceptions, and values. Mark, the oldest of the Gospels, stands closest to the Jewish apocalyptic tradition, with its stress on the suffering that lies immediately ahead and must be endured before the day of divine vindication arrives. Jesus is the prototype of the witness who is faithful to death. There are no hints of community organization; the expectation of suffering and deliverance is the focus (Chapter 4).

Matthew, however, was apparently written at a time late in the first century when the break between Christianity and Judaism was becoming formal, as the Jews gathered in consultation to draw the limits of thought and action for participation in the Jewish community. The Christians of the Gospel of Matthew seem to be reacting to the Jewish process of self-definition. The emphasis therefore falls on Jesus as the true interpreter of the law and on how disputes are to be settled within the Christian community (Chapter 5).

Luke, however, is deeply concerned about the relationship of the Church to the wider Roman world. His portrait of Jesus stresses his reaching out to outsiders. He takes care to show that from the beginning the Christian movement was involved in the decisions of pagan rulers, but that God's purpose worked through them, so that neither Jesus nor his followers was ever politically subversive. In the second volume of his work, which we know as Acts, he makes references to pagan writers and employs literary styles and patterns in use among pagan writers of the time. His aim was not to secularize Christianity, but to enable the new movement to gain some measure of respect among thoughtful pagans of the period by demonstrating that the case for the new faith could be made in intellectually respectable ways. There is also in Luke a dimension of compassion and tenderness that was and is universally appealing. Ernest Renan, a French skeptic of the early nineteenth century, called Luke "the most beautiful book ever written," largely because of these qualities.

John has adapted the outward form of a Gospel to his own purposes, rearranging some material from the other Gospels and adding much that is his own. Although he includes many vivid narratives, as well as accounts of exchanges between Jesus and his opponents, the major thrust in John is on Jesus's declaration of who he is and of his significance for the community of faith. Like Luke, John seeks to achieve this by employing the language and literary forms of the contemporary world in an effort to show to his readers the deeper meaning of Jesus as God's redemptive agent (Chapter 6).

Luke was not content to picture the reaching out of Jesus during his lifetime, but appended to his Gospel the story of the launching of the Gentile mission from Jerusalem. The coming of the Spirit, as well as the details of the spread of the worldwide mission, are presented by Luke in Acts as not only the working out of a divine plan, but also as in fulfillment of scripture. Yet the entire strategy of the Apostles as Luke describes them is to meet their contemporaries on common ground, speaking their language, recognizing the validity of their aspirations and the powerful hold of their religious traditions. Luke takes these factors into account not to compromise the Christian message, but to enable it to be spread more effectively (Chapter 7).

WHICH HAS PRIORITY,
GOSPELS OR EPISTLES?

One might suppose that the historical development of Christianity would have begun with the Gospels, and then simply have moved to Paul and his more abstract theological image of Jesus. But in fact, the Epistles of Paul are probably anywhere from twenty to fifty years older than the Gospels. And there is no evidence of an evolutionary development from the Gospels to the Pauline Epistles. Rather, these two bodies of literature reflect independent but parallel lines of development within the first-century Christian movement and into the early second century. In spite of scholarly claims, there is no evidence of a conceptual link between Mark's Gospel and Paul.[1] As we noted above, there are some broad common elements between the Gospels and Paul, but none of the characteristic Pauline emphases is to be found in Mark, or vice versa.

Matthew shows no signs of direct links with Paul, and the outlook of the first Gospel in the New Testament sequence is very different from Paul's teaching of justification by faith. Matthew asserts the claims of the Jewish legal tradition on the followers of Jesus (Matt. 5:18–20) in a manner that is simply unthinkable for Paul. Luke, on the other hand, has Paul as the central figure in his second volume, Acts. Yet the words he puts in Paul's mouth are

[1] An oft-repeated dictum is that Mark is a setting forth of the Pauline Gospel of Jesus's atoning death, with an extended introduction. But this misrepresents both Paul and Mark.

significantly different from what we read in Paul's own letters. And Luke reports Paul as compromising on the question of dietary and ritual obligations for Christians (Acts 15:20) in a way that seems in direct conflict with Paul's unequivocal position on the subject of Christians' relationship to the Jewish law (Gal. 2:14–16). Although Matthew and Luke were written three or four decades after Paul had been martyred, they show that there was not yet a single Christian point of view on the Jewish law. John, as we have noted, is primarily concerned with mystical communion. He reduced ethical obligation to the law of love (John 13:34–35). In his Gospel, the Jews are present chiefly as "the bad guys," without discussion of specific ritual or ethical issues (John 7:1). Once more, there is no evidence of a single evolutionary line with the Gospels at certain points along it and Paul on the same continuum.

It seems appropriate, therefore, to explore separately the two main lines within the New Testament: (1) the Gospels (Part II), and (2) the Epistles of Paul (Part III). In Part IV we turn our attention to the later and more miscellaneous New Testament and subsequent writings. There is a certain arbitrariness in this arrangement, since two or perhaps three of the Gospels seem to be contemporaneous with the so-called later books of the New Testament. A further complication lies in the fact that this strategy requires us to look at a book that treats of Paul—Acts—before we have looked at his own surviving works. But the rationale here is that it is preferable to look first at the documents that focus on the figure of Jesus, his career and teaching and death, since this cluster of events provided the starting point for the entire Christian movement. Then in Part III we turn to the parallel development which is, so far as we know, inaugurated by Paul and carried forward in the Pauline tradition. When we come to a consideration of Paul's career, we will examine in detail the significance of Acts as an historical source for our knowledge of his life and thought. But we begin by trying to look behind the Gospels to the oral stage of the Jesus tradition, and by exploring the possibility that written records of Jesus antedate the Gospels.

3

Jesus, Prophet of the New Age

Jesus of Nazareth is the historical base for the Christian claim to be the community of the new covenant. Yet, as we have observed, our documentary evidence about him was written long after his death, probably in the last half of the first century. Our records are a series of responses to Jesus by those who saw in him the agent of God, not the reports of detached observers. In the process of analyzing these documents of faith we learn about Jesus, but we also learn about the communities in which the tradition about him was treasured and transmitted.

THE SYNOPTIC GOSPELS AND JOHN

The first three Gospels, in spite of important differences, share a basic structural core. Beginning with Jesus's baptism by John and continuing to the report of the women at the tomb, the narrative sequence in Matthew, Mark, and Luke is essentially the same. There are minor variants and rearrangements, but the common pattern is evident. John, on the other hand, diverges from the other three in sequence and in content. In John, Jesus is never actually baptized; his ministry is carried on extensively in Jerusalem, rather than in Galilee and vicinity. In John, Jesus cleanses the temple early in his ministry; in the other three, his doing so is the final offense that turns the Jerusalem authorities against him. The exorcism of demons, which is so important in the first three Gospels, is missing from John. The only miracle story found in all four is the feeding of the five thousand, but in John alone it is the occasion for a discourse on the Bread of Life. Jesus's style of teaching is different in John, with long speeches apparently intended for his followers only, in contrast to public statements consisting mostly of clusters of short sayings in the other accounts.

Scholars commonly designate the first three Gospels as *synoptic,* since they share a common perspective. Yet once that is said, there are important qualifications, as we will see in detail in this and the next four chapters. Although the three share a common sequence of events from the time of Jesus's baptism to his entombment, they differ in the ways they begin and end. Both Luke and Matthew have birth and infancy stories, but the details are wholly diverse, except that both report the birth as occurring in Bethlehem. Similarly, the post-Resurrection appearances of Jesus differ in Matthew's and Luke's accounts. At the same time, Mark has nothing about Jesus's birth, genealogy, or childhood, and no account (in the oldest manuscript copies of Mark) about Jesus's appearing to his disciples after his death. In addition,

The Jordan River begins near the mountains of Syria and Lebanon, travels to the Sea of Galilee, and finally empties into the northern part of the Dead Sea. Although the exact spot of Jesus's baptism in the Jordan is not known, the traditional site is believed to be at the lower portion of the river just outside of Jericho, where the waters are shallow and calm.   (*Gordon N. Converse*)

there are extended sections of Mark that are missing from one or two of the others, and very long segments of Matthew and Luke which they share but which are not in Mark, or which one or the other of them alone includes. Our procedure will be to look first at the tradition shared by the synoptists (Chapter 3), and then in the succeeding four chapters, focus on the distinctive features of each of the Gospels, including John.

THE GOSPEL TRADITION
BEFORE THE WRITTEN GOSPELS

The differences among the Gospels are there: They can be ignored, or they can be approached carefully, analytically, and with due sensitivity to the aims of the writers and to the cultural milieu out of which they were written. Obviously, the latter method is the only way to responsible study of the Gospels and to reliable results.

Before looking at the written sources, however, we must investigate the

Nazareth, in Galilee. An insignificant village in Jesus's day, it was expanded by the Crusaders and given the appearance of a provincial town of northern Italy. *(Gordon N. Converse)*

oral stage of the tradition concerning Jesus. Although there were public scribes in the cities and towns of the Roman world to whom one could dictate letters, there is no indication that such a role was assigned to one or more of Jesus's followers. The attempt by some scholars to show that Jesus required his disciples to memorize his teachings rests on no sure evidence, and has persuaded few others.[1] In spite of scholarly claims, it is untenable to regard the Gospels as the elaboration of the Pauline preaching about Jesus as Lord,[2] since Paul shows no interest in the earthly career or teaching of Jesus. Much more plausible are the studies of the Gospels that compare them with what is known of the transmission of oral tradition in non- or semi-literate societies.[3] These analyses have shown that there is a wide gulf between oral and written tradition. So before we analyze the Gospels as a literary form, we must look at the oral tradition which, by any theory, preceded the appearance of the earliest written version.

[1] Harald Riesenfeld, *The Gospel Tradition* (Philadelphia: Fortress Press, 1970).

[2] For example, Rudolf Bultmann, in *The History of the Synoptic Tradition,* trans. John Marsh from the third German edition (New York: Harper & Row, 1963).

[3] Albert Lord, "The Gospel as Oral Tradition," in *The Relationships among the Gospels,* ed. Wm. O. Walker, Jr. (San Antonio, Tex.: Trinity University Press, 1978), pp. 34–90. Walter J. Ong, S.J., *The Presence of the Word: Some Prolegomena for Cultural and Religious History* (New Haven, Conn.: Yale University Press, 1967). Erhardt Güttgemanns, *Candid Questions concerning Gospel Form-Criticism,* trans. W. G. Doty (Pittsburgh: Pickwick Press, 1979).

The Oral Stage of the Gospel Tradition

Several factors contributed to the fact that the oldest tradition about Jesus was preserved orally rather than in writing. The most obvious of these is that the disciples were apparently illiterate (Acts 4:13). They did not write about Jesus because they could not write. Even if there were literate persons among the earliest followers, the sense of urgency arising from the limited time to complete the work would have diverted their energies from preparing an official report. Of what use would a permanent, documentary record have been for a community that expected the end of the age within a matter of months? Of equal importance is the evidence that, even in later generations, the oral tradition about Jesus was more highly regarded than any written account could ever have been, so that in the early second century there still were those who treasured the oral word above that of the written.[4]

Apart from the diverse features of the Jesus tradition in its written form, what evidence is there, or what likelihood is there, that the oral tradition would have preserved verbatim accounts of his life and teaching? Studies of the transmission of oral tradition in other cultures—ancient as well as modern primitive societies—show that, while poetry assumed a fixed form, oratory and narrative did not.[5] In a detailed study of oral transmission among peoples all over the world, it was determined that there is not a single verifiable case of verbatim memory for extensive oral utterance.[6] Similar studies of folk traditions in Central Europe by Albert Lord, using modern recording techniques, reached the same conclusion. Each presentation has in it the element of a fresh performance, adapted to the needs and responses of the audience at each moment, so that the basic themes survive relatively intact, but there is no such thing as exact repetition.

The themes, and much of the illustrative material, used by the orators was standard, but each presentation had to be adapted to the special situation of the hearers. Although some of the elements of such a speech would follow familiar patterns—such as references to a person's family, homeland, occupation—the public presentation was a creative response to the moment of its delivery. In fact if it came across to the hearers as a recitation of something composed previously, it would be regarded as insincere.[7]

The implications of these observations for study of the teaching activity of Jesus are clear. We cannot expect verbatim reports. We should expect to find variations on themes, rather than simple repetition. But even if we had available copies of oral statements by or about Jesus, two other factors must be taken into account when analyzing the Gospel tradition. The first of these is the fundamental shift that occurs when a culture moves from an oral to a

---

[4] Helmut Koester, *Synoptische Tradition bei den apostolischen Vätern* (Berlin: Akademie Verlag, 1957).

[5] Ong, *Presence*, pp. 26–27.

[6] Ong, *Presence*, p. 32, quotes these words from the conclusion reached by H. M. and N. K. Chadwick in their three-volume study, *The Growth of Literature* (Cambridge, Eng.: Cambridge University Press, 1932–40); he adds that twenty-two years later Mrs. Chadwick confirmed that her research in the interim had found no verifiable instance of exact oral reproduction in the "communal recital of entire texts."

[7] Ong, *Presence*, p. 57.

literary stage. At the oral stage, however powerful the expectation of the listener that there will be set units of tradition arranged in familiar patterns and sequence, a major source of interest is to see how the speaker will rework and adapt the traditional material. Imaginative variations on the otherwise commonplace delight the hearer and testify to the skill of the speaker. Once the tradition is written down, however, patterns and content are fixed. In a culture using script, the copyist can still expand or rework the material. But in a culture that employs printing, there is an impression of order and a fixed quality about the text that conveys a sense of control and constitutes the organization of reality.[8]

These differences between an oral and a written text were seriously underestimated by scholars around the turn of the twentieth century. Until recently, many New Testament scholars assumed that the Gospels were a kind of folk literature so close to the oral tradition that it did little more than reproduce it. There was some question about whether it was even appropriate to speak of those who produced the Gospels as writers.[9] Since the 1920s, however, there has been growing awareness that the Gospels include material which was worked over by the writers or even produced by them. In Mark, as we will see, the extended narrative sequence of the story of Jesus's last days in Jerusalem shows the writer's hand throughout, however much the smaller units of what he incorporates may have derived from oral tradition. Specifically, parts of Jesus's last speech to his followers (Mark 13) and the series of interchanges with his antagonists (Mark 11–12) are found in other contexts in the other Gospels and therefore may come from oral tradition. But in their present form and arrangement, they give evidence of the work of the writer.

From Oral to Written Gospels

Earlier critics assumed that in the first century a simple shift occurred from the oral tradition to the inclusion of that material in the written Gospels. But the Gospels are far more than and substantially different from a mere accumulation of sayings and oral narrative tradition.[10] A unified outlook pervades the component parts of each Gospel and is apparent in the connective tissue by which each writer has linked the various parts; it provides the dramatic movement from the beginning of Jesus's ministry in Galilee to the end in Jerusalem. The result is of a different order from any of the parts out of which the whole has been shaped. We will consider the aims of the Gospels as a literary form in Chapter 4, when we analyze the oldest, that of Mark. But does this conclusion about the gulf between oral forms and the first Gospel mean it is useless to explore the oral stage?

There is an important, positive value in such a study of formal patterns within the tradition. By comparing the different ways in which the tradition has been preserved, we can recognize the typical forms and variations from those forms. In the early decades of this century, biblical scholars began to

---

[8] Ibid., pp. 135–36.
[9] Martin Dibelius, *From Tradition to Gospel* (New York: Scribner's, 1935).
[10] Güttgemanns, *Candid Questions,* pp. 80–81.

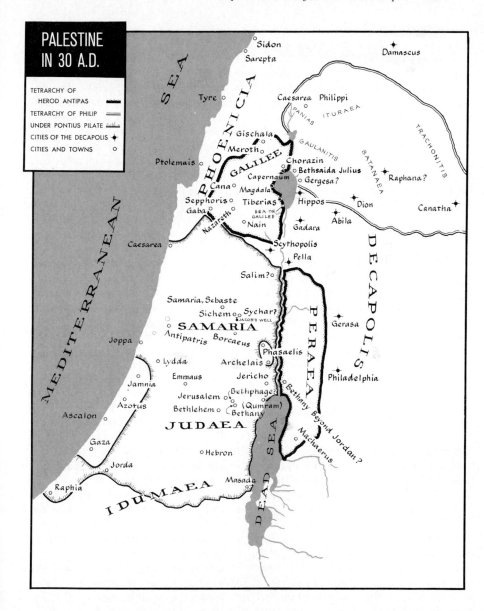

PALESTINE
IN 30 A.D.

TETRARCHY OF
HEROD ANTIPAS
TETRARCHY OF PHILIP
UNDER PONTIUS PILATE
CITIES OF THE DECAPOLIS ✦
CITIES AND TOWNS ○

Sidon
Sarepta
Damascus
SEA
Tyre
Caesarea Philippi
PANIAS ITURAEA
PHOENICIA
Gischala
Meroth
GALILEE
Ptolemais
Chorazin
Bethsaida Julius
Gergesa?
Raphana?
Capernaum
TRACHONITIS
GAULANITIS
BATANAEA
Cana
Magdala
Sepphoris
Tiberias
Hippos
Dion
Canatha
Gaba
SEA OF
GALILEE
Nazareth
Nain
Gadara
Abila
MEDITERRANEAN
Caesarea
Scythopolis
Pella
DECAPOLIS
Salim?
Samaria, Sebaste
Sichem
Sychar?
JACOB'S WELL
SAMARIA
Gerasa
Antipatris
Borcaeus
PERAEA
Joppa
Phasaelis
Lydda
Archelais
Philadelphia
Jamnia
Emmaus
Jericho
Azotus
Jerusalem
Bethphage?
Ascalon
Bethlehem
(Qumram)
Bethany
Bethany Beyond Jordan?
JUDAEA
Gaza
Hebron
Machaerus
Jorda
Raphia
Masada
IDUMAEA
DEAD SEA

perceive that in and behind our present gospels were formal patterns of narrative and speech which had apparently been taken over from an earlier stage in which the tradition circulated orally. This analytical method, known as *form-criticism*,[11] classified the material that underlies our Gospels. These forms ranged in size and complexity from extended narratives, such as the detailed accounts of the cure of the Gerasene demoniac (Mark 5:1–29) or elaborate parables (such as the prodigal son, Luke 15:11–32), to oft-repeated brief sayings, such as "Let whoever has ears to hear, hear." The formal unit of tradition itself can often be distinguished from the literary setting in which the Gospel writer has placed it, as when Mark writes in 1:21, "And they went into Capernaum; and immediately on the Sabbath. . . ," from which he launches into the story proper. Similar stylized conclusions are added at the end of the narratives: "And they were all amazed" (Mark 1:27).

If formal analysis of this kind is carried out, one can see how the individual writer has modified the material to suit his own purposes, by editorial touches or by substantive changes. It may be possible in some instances to distinguish earlier from later forms of the tradition, although that is often a subjective undertaking. But in other instances, the results are clear and persuasive. For example, when we compare Luke's version of the Parable of the Great Supper (Luke 14:16–24) with Matthew's (Matt. 22:1–14), there is a decided shift in the use of the parable. In Luke's version, there is a rather general comparison between (1) a festal meal at which outcasts replace the originally invited guests and (2) Jesus's opening up participation in the kingdom of God to the religiously and socially disapproved. In Matthew's version, on the other hand, there is an allegorical reworking of the parable, according to which God (the king) prepares a marriage feast (symbol of the new age) for his son (Jesus), which ends with the punishment of the unrighteous (the judgment of the wicked at the end of the age). A formal analysis shows that Luke's is the earlier stage of this parable. Similarly, the Markan saying about becoming as a child in order to enter the kingdom (Mark 10:15; Matt. 18:3) is transformed in the Gospel of Thomas, so that "becoming as a child" is elaborated and interpreted to mean that the Christian must be divested of sexuality, becoming androgynous ("when you make the male and the female into a single one," Thos. 22). The latter is clearly a later development of the Markan version.

More is at work here than formal distinctions, however. The deeper question is this: What is the world view or *life-world*[12] in which the tradition is being appropriated and in which it now functions? In the older tradition there is a positive view of the created world, although it has gone astray from God, its creator; he is seen to be at work through Jesus and his followers to bring the creation and his own people back into obedient relationship with himself. In the Gospel of Thomas, however, the created order is inherently evil, and the goal of the good God is to enable the favored few to escape from involvement in the natural structures of human existence in order to find true life in the

---

[11] The classic form-critical studies are R. Bultmann, *The History of the Synoptic Tradition,* trans. John Marsh (New York: Harper & Row, 1963), and Martin Dibelius, *From Tradition to Gospel* (New York: Scribner's, 1935).

[12] See Appendix I for the significance of *life-world.*

realm of the spirit. There is no interest in the Gospel of Thomas in what we would call nature or history. In the canonical Gospels, the goodness of creation and the fulfillment of God's purpose in history are both affirmed. The formal similarities between units of tradition must not, therefore, lead to the assumption that there is a single, uniform way in which the tradition is being understood. Rather, one must ask not only about form, but about function and about the world view of the writer utilizing the tradition.

Written Sources of the Gospels

Although no copies have survived, it is likely that collections of similar materials—parables, wonder stories—were utilized by Mark in writing his Gospel. It is virtually certain, however, that in addition to their use of Mark, one source used by Matthew and Luke was a collection of sayings, known by scholars as Q (probably from the German word *Quelle* meaning "source"). In the early nineteenth century the attempt was made to prove that Matthew was the oldest of the Gospels, and used as a source by Mark and Luke. But at many points Luke is closer to Mark than to Matthew, and in spite of their occasional divergences from Mark's order, Matthew and Luke follow Mark with astonishing consistency from the precise point where Mark's narrative begins to the dangling sentence (Mark 16:8) where it ends.

Up to and subsequent to those points in the narrative, Matthew and Luke are completely independent of each other. Where Matthew or Luke differs from Mark in detail—such as in the erroneous attribution of a prophecy to Isaiah in Mark 1:2, which the other two evangelists set straight—each makes the correction in his own way. It is easier to understand that Mark's acknowledgments of Jesus's limitations were eliminated by Matthew and Luke in their own ways (cf. Mark 6:1–6 and Matt. 13:57–58 and Luke 4:16–30) than that Mark came up with this confession of Jesus's incapacity to perform miracles on the basis of having read Matthew or Luke. These and hundreds of other comparative details emerge when one studies the Gospel tradition with the aid of *Gospel Parallels*,[13] or any similar publication that prints the synoptic Gospels in parallel columns where they offer common material.

Recent efforts to discredit the theory that Mark is the earliest Gospel and the basic source for the other two have succeeded only in showing that analysis of the Gospels cannot rest on a process that deals exclusively with supposed literary sources. To do so is to ignore the creative contribution of each of the evangelists.[14] But to the extent that literary analysis is useful, the hypothesis of two sources—Mark and Q—can best explain both similarities and differences among the synoptic Gospels.

[13] *Gospel Parallels*, ed. Burton Throckmorton (Camden, N.J.: Thomas Nelson & Sons, 1957).

[14] The classic statement of the literary sources for the gospels is B. H. Streeter, *The Four Gospels* (New York: Macmillan, 1925), which traces not only Mark and Q, but M (material unique to Matthew) and L (material unique to Luke). Streeter's analysis, however, as well as more recent ones that rely almost entirely on the reconstruction of literary sources, are of limited value in understanding the distinctive features of each writer.

THE Q SOURCE

When one works through the synoptic parallels, noting the material that is not in Mark but that is shared by Matthew and Luke, the result might seem formless and random. But in fact that is not the case. Detailed comparison of the Q material with Matthew's and Luke's versions of it suggests that Luke has done less adapting than Matthew has. Matthew has not only changed details to suit his purposes, but he has positioned material in keeping with his rather elaborate structure, which we will consider in Chapter 5.

Once this tradition has been separated out from its present setting in Matthew and Luke,[15] it becomes clear that a central interest pervades the whole: the preparation for the coming of the new age. That eschatological expectation characterizes the call to discipleship, the prophetic role of Jesus and his followers, the message of repentance and judgment they preach, and the depiction of Jesus as God's agent to reveal his purpose and to establish the new age. The Q material may therefore appropriately be grouped on the following thematic basis (with the references to Luke):

1. Discipleship: Privileges and Trials

6:20–49	The blessedness and obligations of discipleship
9:57–62	Break with home and family for the sake of the kingdom
10:2–20	Participation in proclaiming the kingdom in word and act
10:21–23	God's special revelation of his purpose
11:2–13	God will sustain his people and give them the kingdom
12:51–53	Jesus the divider of households
14:16–24	Those included and those excluded from the messianic banquet
14:26–27	Discipleship shatters ordinary human relationships
16:13	The demands of discipleship
17:3–6	Forgiveness and faith: essentials for community life

2. The Prophet as God's Messenger

3:7–9, 16–17	John the Baptist as forerunner of Jesus and prophet of doom

[15] See Appendix III for a reconstruction of the Q source, reprinted by permission from my *Jesus in History,* 2d ed. (New York: Harcourt Brace Jovanovich, 1977).

11:49–51	The fate of the prophet and of his emissaries
12:2–3	The promise of revelation of God's purpose
12:4–10, 11–12, 42–46	God's care for and vindication of his messengers
13:34–35	Jerusalem's rejection and martyrdom of the prophets
16:16–17	John as boundary of the old age; God's word is sure

3. Repentance or Judgment

11:33–36	Warning about darkness and light
11:39–48, 52	Woes against the religious leaders of Judaism
12:54–59 13:14–29	Prepare for the impending judgment
17:23–30, 35, 37	Judgment will be inescapable when it falls
19:12–13, 15–26	Reward for the faithful, but punishment for those lacking ambition, perseverance

4. Jesus as Revealer and Agent of God's Rule

4:2b–12	Jesus's successful struggle with the Devil
7:18–35	Jesus as agent of liberation: greater than John
10:24	Jesus as son, agent of revelation
11:14–22	Jesus as agent of God's kingdom
13:20–21	Leaven at work now
15:4–7	God's joy at reconciliation of a sinner
22:28–30	God grants the share in the kingdom to those for whom it has been covenanted and who have endured the trials

Let us turn now to an analysis of this material in order to see how, before there was a written Gospel, the message and meaning of Jesus were understood by that segment of the early Church that preserved the Q tradition.

Who Is To Be Included in the Covenant People?

In the sole narrative passage considered to be part of Q there is the story of a centurion (an officer in the Roman army) who asked Jesus to heal his slave (Luke 7:1–10; Matt. 8:5–13). One would expect pious Jews who observed ritual purity laws to want to have nothing to do with a Gentile, and politically sensitive Jews would scarcely want to help a member of an occupying military force. Yet this man had built a synagogue for the Jews, and was therefore presumably sympathetic toward the faith of Israel. The man's respect for Jewish standards of purity was evident in his reluctance to enter the house where Jesus was, but his confidence in Jesus's power to heal, which he communicated by the messengers whom he sent, was so great that Jesus did heal the slave. What is important is Jesus's observation that he had not found such faith "even in Israel" (Luke 7:9). The man shares in the benefits of God's grace even though he is not a member of the traditional covenant community.

The same theme is evident in two other Q passages: the words of John the Baptist (Luke 3:8; Matt. 3:9), and the Parable of the Supper (Luke 14:16–23). In the Q version of the preaching of the Baptist, John not only announces that "the mightier one" is coming, but redefines the covenant people. It is not enough, he declares, to claim descent from Abraham; God is able from the stones—that is, from a wholly unlikely source—to raise up a people for himself. The fact that these words were uttered in response to the self-styled religious elite, the Pharisees and Sadducees, makes the point all the sharper. Indeed, the religious types are denounced as offspring of snakes who falsely claim membership in the covenant people.

Similarly, in the Parable of the Supper (leaving out the modifications by Luke and Matthew), there is a contrast between those who ought to participate and those who in fact do. The former are the insiders, "those who had been invited"; the latter are those in the back alleys of the city and those living outside the city walls. Yet it is these unlikely guests who actually share in the banquet. When we take into account the fact that a feast is a favorite designation in Jewish tradition for the joyous time to come when God has achieved his purpose in the world and gathered his own to his company, it becomes clear that the parable indicates a radical redefinition of the covenant people from an eschatological point of view.

Discipleship: An Extraordinary Life Style

In both ancient Israel and in the culture of Rome, personal identity was intimately bound with the family. In Jewish families, the male son regularly carried the father's name. Much of the ritual commanded in the Torah was observed within the family context. Similarly, the worship of the household gods was considered by Romans to be essential for the stability and security of the family and of the state as a whole. When the emperor became the *pontifex maximus* for the nation, the assumption was that he was now the father-priest for the whole Roman family. The emperor felt it appropriate to adopt his chosen successor as his son in order to provide familial continuity for the Roman state. Paul, as we will see, takes pride in being able to trace his lineage to the tribe of Benjamin, and thereby to assert his impeccable credentials (Phil. 3:5).

Jesus overturns this pattern utterly, according to the Q tradition. He has no home, and accepts that fact as a badge of identity, even of authority (Luke

9:58). In the Markan tradition, his family thinks he is mad (Mark 3:21, 31), and he is forced to leave his hometown (Mark 6:1–6). But in the Q tradition the case is even stronger against the family as the locus of identity and security. Routine family obligations—burying one's father, even bidding the family farewell—are to be ignored in light of the urgency of announcing God's kingdom as disciples of Jesus (Luke 9:59–62). The issue is put even more strongly in Luke 14:26, where Jesus tells his disciples that they must "hate . . . father and mother and wife and children and brothers and sisters." The break with the family and the associated network of ordinary obligations is radical and total.

The values to be adopted and embodied by his followers are the exact reverse of ordinary hopes and the usual goals of human life: It is the poor, the hungry, the sorrowful, the hated and the rejected, who are said by Jesus to be blessed of God (Luke 6:20–23).[16] The disciples are not called to be masochists, but to look to the new age rather than to present possessions or social acceptance for fulfillment. All that they seek from God is bread sufficient for each day and forgiveness for unfulfilled obligations. Their continual prayer is for the coming of God's kingdom, whereby his name will be honored throughout creation (Luke 11:2–4).

The actual mode of life demanded of his disciples by Jesus is sketched in Mark (6:6–13) and in Q (Luke 10:1–16). Having abandoned house and family, the disciples live an itinerant existence, spending the night in whatever village offers them hospitality. They set out with neither food nor money, dependent on whatever is offered them. Their task is threefold: to expel demons from those possessed by them; to heal disease; to announce the coming of God's rule (Luke 9:1–5). These factors are closely related in terms of Jewish prophetic tradition, since in that literature the defeat of the demons is essential to overcoming the grip of Satan on the world, and thus preparing for God's rightful reign. The healing of diseases was promised in Isaiah 29:18–19, 35:5–6, and 61:1 as part of the reversal of human fortune that would come with God's new age. The disciples' life and work is to prepare for and to share in that experience.

This tradition is not likely to have been preserved by an early Christian group for whom it had no personal meaning. Rather, it seems to have been kept in corporate memory because it depicted the mode of life the leaders of the community had indeed adopted as their own. From non-Christian sources we know that there were other itinerant preacher-teachers in this same period, although their message and life-world were significantly different from those of the disciples. These pagan itinerants combined a scorn of society with certain aspects of Stoic teaching ("live according to nature"), and wandered from town to town haranguing listeners in the marketplace, and scoffing at wealth and respectability.[17] Operating under no visible authority, they were

---

[16] Matthew has tempered the force of the Beatitudes. For example, he changed "poor" to "poor in spirit," "hunger" to "hunger and thirst after righteousness." See also Chapter 5.

[17] A sketch of the early Christian itinerant movement is offered by Gerd Theissen in *The Sociology of Early Palestinian Christianity* (Philadelphia: Fortress Press, 1978).

what sociologists of religion call *charismatics:*[18] to others unpredictable and irresponsible, but to themselves guided by the divine spirit. The historian Ramsay MacMullen has given us a vivid picture of these wandering teachers:

> Identified by their long hair, beards, bare feet and grimy rags, their wallets, staffs and knapsacks: by their supercilious bearing, paraded morals, scowling abuse . . . shameless they seemed, and half-educated, vulgar, jesting; beggars for money, beggars for attention . . . clustered at temples or street corners, in cities and army camps; loud-mouthed shouters of moral saws driven to a life of sham by poverty.[19]

By their being prohibited from using a beggar's bag or a knapsack or staff, the Christian itinerants were even more completely devoid of resources or defenses against a hostile world than were their pagan counterparts. Yet this was the style of life the Q tradition sets forth as mandatory for true followers of Jesus.

The disciples' resources are intangible, but from their viewpoint they are powerful and of paramount value. First, Jesus's followers go out in confidence that they are his deputies. The response they encounter—whether acceptance or rejection—is equivalent to the world's response to Jesus (Luke 10:16). In their work of proclamation, the kingdom itself has drawn near to their hearers (Luke 10:9). They are in the fullest sense the authorized representatives of Jesus. Second, they may be confident that their needs and requests are heard by God. Whatever they request will be granted, whether it be something to eat, access to some opportunity, recovery of what is lost or sought, or the Holy Spirit to enable them to carry out their work (Luke 11:9–13). But the third and most important resource is the insight God has granted them to perceive his purpose, a perception that those who consider themselves wise will never gain, but that God has given to these "little children" (Luke 10:21–22).

What we may see in the community that kept the Q material is what sociologists call a *sect,* by which they mean a religious group in which participation is not by reason of cultural heritage or family tradition, but by conscious decision to depart from the established religious system. Sects arise in any age or culture when "something in the environment or social system has broken through a taken-for-granted system of meaning, and has thereby rendered it inadequate. Groups arise to create new islands of meaning or a new identity. . . ." Feeling helpless and threatened by a breakdown in the social order, one turns to a message or a messenger that offers "a relevant way of interpreting present disorder in the light of a future event."[20] In the Jesus movement as it is reflected in the Q source, it is the promise of deliverance from the sense of powerlessness that motivates the disciples and rallies support for their enterprise.

[18] Max Weber, *On Charisma and Institution Building,* ed. S. N. Eisenstadt (Chicago: University of Chicago Press, 1969).

[19] Ramsay MacMullen, *Enemies of the Roman Order* (Cambridge, Mass.: Harvard University Press, 1966), p. 59.

[20] Hans J. Mol, *Identity and the Sacred* (New York: Free Press, 1977), pp. 181, 182.

The Prophet of the New Age

Although it is John the Baptist who sets the stage for the role of Jesus in Mark, the Q material (in which John is represented) gives greater sharpness to the image of what God has destined Jesus to do and be. That destiny includes the offer and the achievement of doom or deliverance to those who hear his message, from him or from his followers. As we noted, the new covenant people in Q include religious and ethnic outsiders (Luke 3:7–9). But there is the warning that those who fail to respond properly will be cut down and burned like worthless fruit trees. The imagery is changed when John, after announcing Jesus's coming and his endowment with the Spirit of God, warns that the useless "chaff" will be consumed by the fires of judgment (Luke 3:17).

One evident characteristic of the career of Jesus and his followers in the Q tradition is struggle. Like the prophets of ancient Israel, Jesus's preparation for public ministry includes a period of testing and wrestling with temptation to do other than God's will. Jacob, Moses, Elijah, and Jeremiah are reported in the Old Testament as undergoing periods of solitary conflict and reflection before they were ready for their divine mission. The period mentioned in Mark 1:13, forty days, matches precisely the testing time of Elijah (1 Kings 19:8). And the coming of Elijah at the end of the age, which is given by the prophets (Mal. 3:1; 4:5), is recalled by Mark in connection with the advent of Jesus (Mark 1:2). Thus the synoptic tradition as a whole links Jesus with the widespread Jewish hope of the coming of the eschatological prophet; Q builds on that tradition in the story of Jesus's testing.

The Devil does not try to entice Jesus into committing grossly sensual acts or flagrant violations of the commandments. Indeed, he quotes scripture to try to lure Jesus into disobeying the will of God (Luke 4:10; Ps. 91:11–12). The diabolical proposals are for Jesus to attain kingly power by exploiting his extraordinary powers in order to attract a following and by subjecting himself to a will other than that of God. The conflict in which Jesus is here seen as engaged is not merely with earthly authorities, but with his own inner commitments and with the unseen powers that lie behind and are at work through visible instruments of authority; that is, "the kingdoms of this world."

But in the poignant scene from Q (Luke 7:24–35) where the doomed, disillusioned John the Baptist sends from prison to ask about Jesus's mission, it is made clear that the coming of God's kingdom is not to be attained by political-military triumph or by some kind of supernatural annihilation. Instead, Jesus draws attention to the works of mercy, to the extension of benefits of divine grace to the unlikely, the deprived, the outsider. These redefinitions of the covenant participation are couched in phrases taken from the later prophets of Israel: the blind receive sight, the lame walk, the lepers are cleansed, the deaf hear, the dead are raised up—and above all, the poor have good news preached to them (Luke 7:22). The ill, the helpless, the handicapped, the deprived are the ones who share in God's new age, which he is inaugurating through Jesus. Important as his role was, John the Baptist has brought to a close the old era; with the coming of Jesus and the launching of his mission through the disciples, a new era has dawned (Luke 16:16). Their special relationship to God and the unique blessing under which they live and work is that God has revealed to them the secret of his purpose for the creation, a vision concealed from all earthly rulers (Luke 10:24).

The essence of that divine disclosure is that through Jesus the powers of evil are already being defeated in preparation for the coming of God's rule. The Q tradition has a brief but important supplement to the Markan account of the controversy between Jesus and his opponents as to the source of his power to expel the demons from possessed persons (Mark 3:22–27). The Q version acknowledges that others can cast out demons, but insists on the distinctive significance of Jesus's exorcisms: they are signs of the coming of God's rule (Luke 11:19–20). In describing his activity, Jesus uses a term, "the finger of God," which occurs in the story of the plagues that Moses brought on Egypt through God's power in order to effect the release of the Israelites from slavery (Exod. 8:19). The God who was at work through Moses to liberate his people is now at work through Jesus to free and vindicate his new covenant people.

The performance of healings and exorcisms is not to be carried out in order to persuade potential followers to join the Jesus movement. The contemporaries of Jesus, the Q material declares, want miracles to be performed as proof of Jesus's divine authority—that is, they seek a "sign" (Luke 11:29)—but their demands will not be met. Rather, Jesus has come as Jonah did to the ancient pagan city of Nineveh, with a call to repentance (Luke 11:32). "Repentance" does not connote, as in modern popular usage, feeling sorry for misdeeds or failure; rather, it implies a change of mind, a shift in goals and life direction. Non-Israelites had their outlook on life transformed by responding to God's messengers. The implication is that Gentiles will respond to Jesus's message, since "someone" (Jesus) who is greater than Solomon or Jonah has come forward with wisdom and preaching.

The theme of the expected rejection of Jesus and his followers by ethnic Israel is a pervasive one in the Q material. In pronouncing divine woes on the Pharisees, who thought of themselves as the guarantors of purity, Jesus portrays them as identifying themselves with those who built the prophets' tombs, and therefore as having a share in the hostility that culminated in the killing of the prophets. From Jewish sources contemporary with the New Testament period, such as the Martyrdom of Isaiah, we know that there was a cult of the martyred prophets. Jesus declares that those who appear to honor the prophets by building tombs in their memory and by pilgrimages to the burial sites actually incriminate themselves in responsibility for the death of God's messengers (Luke 12:47–51). Indeed, the history of Israel as recorded in the Jewish scriptures can be read as a series of murders of God's agents, beginning with Abel in the first book of the Bible (Gen. 4:8) and ending with Zechariah in the last book of the Jewish canon (2 Chron. 24:20–21). All this is a precedent for the treatment Jesus and his followers may expect from the religious establishment of their day: the martyrdom of the prophets and apostles (Luke 11:49).

The attitude toward the Jews and Jerusalem is one not of vindictiveness but of sorrow at the failure to respond to the good news about the new covenant. Jesus pictures God as a mother hen, seeking to gather her own around her. But the people of Jerusalem refuse to heed the maternal call. Instead, they kill the prophets and stone God's messengers. They will not be able to discern who Jesus is until they come to the point of saying of him, "Blessed is the one who comes in the name of the Lord" (Luke 13:34–35). These words are quoted from Psalm 118, the last of six psalms recited by Jews in celebration of the deliverance from Egypt and in anticipation of God's ultimate vindication of his people in the age to come. The Q tradition sees Jesus as applying to himself this promise of future hope; it is through him that Israel's aspirations and longings are to be fulfilled.

Guidelines for Life in the Community

As in the Parable of the Supper (Luke 14:15–24), participation in the new community is open to religious, moral, and social outsiders. The parable often called "The Lost Sheep" is actually a picture of God as The Joyous Shepherd, since there is "joy in heaven" (Luke 15:3–7) when the alienated individual is restored and reconciled. Neither religious condition, moral performance, ritual purity, respectability of occupation, or any other human criterion is a prerequisite for admission to the people of God. The only requirements are to be "lost"—that is, alienated, estranged, alone—to acknowledge it, and to accept the invitation to be "found"—that is, to accept reconciliation with the shepherd and the flock.

Religion is not concerned with ritual purity or ceremonial performance, but with the moral integrity of the person. True cleanliness is not a matter of washing hands or dishes, nor is righteousness a question of giving alms. Rather, purity is of the heart, of the will, of concern for other human beings and of love for God (Luke 11:37–41). Otherwise public piety becomes an empty show, mere religious ostentation. There can be no presumption that a decent life of orderly respectability makes anyone right with God. What was calamitous for contemporaries of Noah who were abandoned and excluded from the ark was not their wanton or sensual mode of life, but their preoccupation with the ordinary routine: eating, drinking, marrying, burying, selling, making a living. Their fatal failure was their indifference to the message of judgment through God's spokesman (Luke 17:22–37). The person who strives merely to preserve life will awake on the Day of Judgment to find all that he or she lived for has vanished. The one who is willing to abandon security and ephemeral values of ordinary life in exchange for a life devoted to the Gospel may experience a martyr's death, but in the end will find authentic fulfillment.

What is called for, therefore, is watchfulness. In a pair of vivid images, Jesus warns his hearers of the importance of readiness (Luke 12:35–46). The first is the master of a house who, on returning from the extended festivities of a marriage feast, finds some of his servants faithful in their duties, while others are lazy and careless; the second is a homeowner who does not even notice when a thief breaks into his house. There will be rewards for those who faithfully discharged their responsibilities, and judgment on those who failed to do so. In a vivid parable, Jesus compares the farsighted disciple who understands the urgency of his situation with an accused person who pays off the judge in advance rather than face the consequences of a trial. The line of argument seems to be this: In coming to terms with the eschatological crisis that confronts you and the whole human race (Luke 12:57–59), be at least as shrewd as this scoundrel.

Yet the life of the follower of Jesus is not at all to be characterized by anxiety about one's fate. Instead, his disciples are called to live lives free of concern about food, shelter, clothing, since they live in confidence that the same God who cares for wild creatures and clothes the earth with beauty can care for his own people (Luke 12:22–34). Their single objective is to be his kingdom and its coming. Once that solitary goal is the focus of their lives, all routine needs will be met.

The kingdom, however, is not something to be achieved by their striving, nor is it granted as a reward for fidelity. Rather, it is the gift of divine grace. It is God's pleasure to *give* to his own flock a share in his kingdom (Luke 12:32). Those who participate in the new age are contrasted with the indifferent who failed to respond to his message. Like householders who refuse to open the door to those who knock for admittance, claiming that they know the master from watching him work among them, Jesus dismisses those who belatedly acknowledge him. They will be excluded from the kingdom by reason of their indifference to his message, while others from all over the world will share in the eschatological feast, together with the patriarchs of the old covenant community (Luke 13:23–29). The people who participate in God's rule are not the decent religious types, but those who respond in faith to the message of good news for the poor, of acceptance for the outsider, of liberation for those possessed by the powers of evil. It is they who "sit at table in the kingdom of God" with the founders of the covenant people.

There is one aspect of this new relationship with God that depends on human action: integrity and courage in identifying oneself with Jesus as God's agent of human redemption. Whoever publicly identifies himself or herself with the Son of Man (Jesus) now will be vindicated by the Son of Man in the future. Conversely, everyone who refuses to acknowledge Jesus now will be doomed on the Day of Judgment in the presence of God (Luke 12:8–9). Therefore one's stance toward Jesus in the present age determines one's standing before God in the age to come.

Jesus as Son of Man

The term Son of Man derives from a Semitic idiom used in the psalms and by some of the prophets that calls attention to the limitations which characterize the human race. For example, in Psalm 8 the writer asks and then answers the question of why God has placed human beings in charge of the created order (described in Genesis 1). By contrast with the vast splendor and shining glory of the stars and the universe, why is God interested in puny "man" and why does he care for "the son of man" (which in the poetic speech of the Hebrew language refers to human beings)? The psalmist does not really answer his own question, but proceeds to restate the glory and honor and responsibility that God has placed upon human beings, the apex of his creation.

In the prophetic tradition of Israel, Ezekiel uses the phrase "son of man" to call attention to his own frailty and fallibility. When the prophet prostrated himself before God following a vision of the divine throne, he was told to get up: "Son of man, stand on your feet" (Ezek. 2:1). By this phrase he is continually reminded of his shortcomings. In Daniel 7, however, the phrase is used to contrast the fantastic beasts (which symbolize the wicked, pagan empires that have dominated this world) with those whom God has chosen to exercise sovereignty in his behalf over his kingdom:

> I saw in the night visions,
> and behold, with the clouds of heaven
> there came one like a son of man [i.e., like a human being],
> ... And to him was given dominion and glory and kingdom
> that all peoples, nations, and languages should serve him;
> his dominion is an everlasting dominion,
> which shall not pass away. . . .
>
> —DAN. 7:13–14

The prophet soon explains that the "one like a son of man" is the body of God's faithful people, or as he calls them, "the saints of the Most High" (Dan. 7:18, 22, 27). In still later Jewish literature the term became a title, so that the Son of Man was a designation of God's agent in establishing his rule.[21] It is presumably this later use of the term that lies behind the title given to Jesus in the Q tradition, as well as in Mark's gospel.

The hostility and exclusion experienced by Jesus's followers is not to be viewed as an indication that God has abandoned them; rather, it is to be seen as a sign of their special blessedness. The basis of the opposition lies not in them but in the Son of Man; although he has been rejected as the prophets of old were, he has already laid up in heaven a reward for them, to be given for their fidelity to him on the Day of Judgment (Luke 6:22–23). The same idea is present in Luke 12:8, where Jesus promises to vindicate before God those who stand firm in behalf of the Son of Man. Elsewhere the Q material stresses the future role of the Son of Man in rewarding his own and in judging those who have opposed him (Luke 17:24, 26, 30).

The later Jewish prophetic literature, which reports visions of things to come, often with elaborate, even fantastic, imagery, and which insists that this promise of future deliverance from oppressive evil powers has been granted by God solely to a small elect group, is called by scholars *apocalyptic,* from the Greek word *apokalypsis,* meaning "revelation" or "disclosure." In the one Jewish apocalyptic writing where the Son of Man appears as a title, the Parables of Enoch, it is used of a heavenly figure whose redemptive role lies wholly in the future. In Q, however, the Son of Man is already visible in the earthly life

[21] The simile, "like a son of man," became a title, "Son of Man," in the Similitudes of Enoch, which were probably written by a Jewish apocalypticist in the first century. The Enoch tradition goes back to the third century B.C.; the later material—the Similitudes—has been carefully analyzed by David Suter in *Tradition and Composition in the Parables of Enoch* (Missoula, Mont.: Scholars Press, 1979).

of Jesus. It is he, the Son of Man, who "has nowhere to lay his Head" (Luke 9:58). It is in his capacity as the friend of such political outcasts as tax collectors and such religious reprobates as "sinners" that Jesus is designated Son of Man. It is the fully human behavior of eating and drinking that leads opponents to denounce this Son of Man as "a glutton and a drunkard" (Luke 7:34).

The composite picture of Jesus that emerges from the Q material is one of compassion and judgment, of inclusiveness and denunciation. His promise to his followers is that they must suffer, but that he and they will be vindicated by God when his purpose is fulfilled.

The Historical Implications

What does this Q tradition have to contribute to our historical inquiry? There are at least two outcomes. The first is that we have the main outlines of a community which sees itself as in direct continuity with Jesus's ministry, which has renounced ordinary human security, which is prepared to accept suffering and even martyrdom, but which lives by faith in God's sustaining power and his future vindication of his people. There would be little point in preserving the tradition about the abandonment of home, family, and worldly security unless the members of the community had adopted that life style as their own. It is the itinerant, charismatic model of Jesus they have chosen for their own life style.

But is that historically the way Jesus lived? Are these features of the life of obedience as outlined in Q what Jesus really taught and embodied? There can be no absolute answer to these questions, but in view of the fact that the other New Testament writings move away from this picture of unstructured existence, characterized by movement and urgency, one can scarcely imagine early Christians inventing such a portrait of Jesus that would have been irrelevant for them. The strong likelihood, therefore, is that in the Q tradition we come closest to what Jesus taught and how he lived, as well as to what he expected of his followers. As that tradition shifted from oral to written form it was modified and in many cases toned down as the writers adapted it to their own situation and sense of what was needed for their segment of early Christianity. For an analysis of the range of ways in which the Jesus tradition was appropriated and modified in changing circumstances and in a range of cultural settings, we turn now to a study of the individual Gospels.

4

The Beginning
of the Gospel:
Mark

literary - having to do with literature

"Beginning" is the opening word of the Gospel of Mark. The writing of that document marked the beginning of a new stage in the history of the Jesus tradition. Until then, no sequential account of Jesus had been prepared. All the subsequent gospel writers were indebted to Mark. Gospel, or "good news," was not only a shorthand term for the message God had sent through Jesus; it was now also an important and enduring literary form in which the story of Jesus and the significance of his life and teaching were preserved.

The oldest Gospel is anonymous, never once mentioning the person whose name it now bears. Almost certainly, the fact that it gave special attention to Peter (mentioned seventeen times) and yet made no claim to have been written by him led to the assumption that its author was a companion of his. Acts reports that Peter, following his conversion (Acts 12), lived in the household of Mark. In I Peter 5:13 the author, who calls himself Peter, refers to Mark as "my son." Actually Matthew mentions Peter more frequently than Mark does and gives him a more exalted position, but ancient tradition attributed the earliest Gospel to Mark of Jerusalem. We use his name for convenience, but assume unknown authorship.

WHEN AND WHY WAS MARK WRITTEN?

The best clue we have to the time of the writing of Mark is the great importance attached by the writer to the attack on Jerusalem and the desecration of its temple in Mark 13. We know that the siege of the city and its subsequent fall occurred in the years A.D. 66–70. Since the description of the attack is vaguer in Mark than in Luke (who mentions excavating a deep trench around the city to prevent the inhabitants from escaping, a military tactic indeed performed by the Roman army), it is possible that Mark was writing in anticipation of the fall rather than after it. In any case, we have a firm date near which Mark was produced. The writing could not have appeared long after 70, on the other hand, since the writer pictures Jesus as telling his followers that some of them will live to see the end of the age (Mark 13:30). Followers of Jesus who were young adults about A.D. 30 could not be expected to live much beyond 70.

It would be inadequate and inappropriate, however, to assume that Mark was written as a historical archive when the eyewitness generation of Jesus's followers was about to die off. The urgency and motivation implicit in Mark are far more intense than mere recordkeeping. There is a cluster of crises at hand—not only the desecration of the Temple and the fall of the Holy City,

98

and not only the dwindling of the first generation of disciples. Some members of the community have become lethargic (Mark 13:36). Others have been swept off their feet by persons claiming to be special messengers from Jesus (13:6). Faithful Christians are undergoing trials and persecution, so they wonder whether God has abandoned them (13:9–11, 19). Members have betrayed other members to the authorities (13:12). The community feels profoundly threatened and helpless. This collective state of mind is precisely what gives rise to apocalyptic sectarian movements, as we have noted.[1] Given the fact that the Jesus tradition was apocalyptic from the outset, it is fully comprehensible that the Markan community in such circumstances would have produced what we know as the Gospel of Mark.[2]

Mark is the foundation document of an apocalyptic group within early Christianity. Its story of Jesus is not in any sense a biography, since it tells us nothing of his birth or upbringing; it describes only his brief period of public activity, culminating in his death. Like Daniel, it promises vindication. But its promise of future deliverance does not even go so far as to describe the resurrected Jesus—an omission made up for in the other three Gospels. Jesus is the paradigm of divine power, of compassion for the penitent and needy, and of fidelity unto death.

Of equal importance is the series of specific instructions on moral and ritual issues that occupy several chapters in Mark, and that are touched on in relation to Jesus's healings and exorcisms. Those scholars who regard Mark as "a passion story with an extended introduction"[3] or as a biography of a Hellenistic miracle worker[4] are at a loss to account for the lengthy sections on such subjects as divorce and paying taxes. When Mark is seen as a foundation document, however, these regulations are precisely what we should expect to find. Instruction is offered concerning the power and authority available to the group through Jesus, concerning the nature of the enemy (the powers of evil) and the certainty of suffering that the community must undergo, just as Jesus did. Concrete rules are presented for dealing with Jewish authorities, with the interpretation of scripture, and with the Roman imperial power. Beyond all

[1] See Chapter 3. A fuller description of the social situation implicit in Mark is offered in my *Community of the New Age: Studies in Mark's Gospel* (Philadelphia: Westminster Press, 1977), pp. 77–105. Reprint, Macon, GA, Mercer University Press, 1983.

[2] The various theories about the literary antecedents of Mark are summarized and criticized in my *Community of the New Age,* pp. 14–49. There is no real precedent for Mark in ancient literature. Perhaps the closest we can come to prototypes for Mark are the Dead Sea Scrolls and some of the apocalyptic literature. Two foundation documents for the Dead Sea community were found at Qumran: the Damascus Document and the Scroll of the Rule. In the former there is a brief account of the trials the founder underwent until God called him to found the sect. In the Scroll of the Rule instructions and encouragement are offered for the sect to live by until the time of their vindication by God, when they will be established as the true leaders of Israel's devotion to God. Similarly, in the book of Daniel, the first part concerns the difficulties and threats of martyrdom endured by Daniel and his faithful followers; the latter part depicts the deliverance that is to come. Scattered throughout are the guidelines for the life of the faithful in the interim.

[3] The place of the passion story within the whole of Mark's gospel is discussed in some detail in my *Community,* pp. 30–32.

[4] The attempts to trace Mark's aim in writing his Gospel to mostly later popular accounts of miracle workers are discussed in *Community,* pp. 17–18, 22–30.

these interim problems, there is the assurance of divine vindication when the Son of Man appears in triumph and the kingdom of God comes in power (Mark 8:38–9:1). Meanwhile, God will preserve those who endure faithfully to the end (Mark 13:13b).

Mark is written in a peculiar style, awkward in syntax and construction, yet remarkably vivid in detail. That it was written by someone who knew Greek reasonably well is evident from the fact that the quotations from scripture are taken from the Septuagint rather than directly from the Semitic original. Yet there are traces of Semitic terms and syntax behind the Greek, and in some places Aramaic phrases are quoted and then translated (Mark 5:41; 7:34). Possibly the writer lived in a community that spoke Greek, but whose heritage was Semitic.[5] The frequent mention of place names on the border between what we call Palestine and Syria, together with the preservation of such cultural details as mud-roofed houses (Mark 2:4), omitted or altered by the other Gospels, suggests that Mark was written in southern Syria. Supporting this suggestion is the information from Josephus that this is where Jewish nationalists turned against co-religionists who refused to side with them in the fight for political independence—precisely what the Markan community is urged to refuse to do (Mark 12:13–17).

These are the circumstances that seem to have produced the earliest Gospel. But detailed analysis is required to discern how the Markan community perceived in Jesus and the tradition linked with him its origins, its present responsibility, and its divine destiny. The roots of all those elements are found by Mark in the Jewish scriptures. His first words, after announcing the Gospel as the theme of his book are: "Just as it has been written . . ." (Mark 1:2).

AS IT IS WRITTEN IN THE PROPHETS

Accordingly, Mark first turns to the scripture, which he believes was fulfilled with the coming of John the Baptist. *Gospel* could be intended here to refer to the good news about Jesus, or to the good news Jesus proclaims, but the net result is much the same: God has begun something for human redemption, Mark is declaring, yet it is a reappropriation of the old promise made through the prophets. And for those who see in this message good news, it provides the basis for a new covenant community.

The scripture reference is said to be from Isaiah; actually it is a combination of a verse from Malachi 3 and one from Isaiah 40 (what scholars call Second Isaiah, since it was written after the exile of the Jews, rather than prior to it, as was most of Isaiah 1–37). Mark, or the source he is quoting, has modified the pronouns of Malachi 3:1 slightly so that they can better serve his purpose. The Hebrew text says that Yahweh is sending a messenger before him; Mark says the messenger is to prepare "thy" way. Instead of referring to Yahweh, as in the Hebrew original, the texts are used by Mark to point to Jesus, whom the Church acclaims as Lord, and for whose coming John the Baptist is seen

---

[5] A careful, detailed analysis of the extent to which Semitic linguistic features underlie the Greek of the Gospel of Mark has been carried out by Elliott C. Maloney in *Semitic Interference in Markan Syntax* (Chico, Calif.: Scholars Press, 1981).

The wilderness of Judea; the eastern slopes of the mountain ridge running the length of Palestine on the crest of which Jerusalem sits. The rain clouds coming from the west drop nearly all their moisture on the western slopes, while the eastern slopes remain utterly barren, reaching down to the Jordan Valley and the Dead Sea. (*Gordon N. Converse*)

to be the preparer of the way. Other changes have been made in the text as well: Isaiah 40 speaks of someone crying, "In the wilderness prepare the way...," but Mark, recalling that John's preaching was carried on in the wilderness, describes him as "crying in the wilderness." These subtle shifts in wording might seem to us tricky or even deceitful, but we know from the Dead Sea Scrolls that similar alterations of scriptural texts were performed at Qumran in order to bring prophecy and fulfillment closer together. And the fact that the sacred texts had such possibilities testified to their divine origin rather than exegetical chicanery. The scriptures were regarded as containing divine wisdom for the redemptive history of the world; it was essential to show that each detail of what the Christian claimed for Jesus could be found in scripture.

JOHN THE BAPTIZER APPEARED

From Mark we learn much less of Jesus's relationship with John the Baptizer (literally, the John who baptizes, to distinguish him from others of that name) than we do from Q documents and the Gospel of John. But we are told of

John's calling men to accept baptism as an expression of their penitence, and we have the crude garb and diet of John vividly described to us (1:6). The mightier one who is coming may have meant in John's mind some undefined agent of judgment who would appear at the end of the age, but Mark wants his readers to understand it as a reference to Jesus, whose "mightier" acts are to be depicted in the miracle stories that characterize Jesus's ministry in Mark's account. Curiously, no mention is made in Mark of the baptism with fire; all that appears is the contrast between the preparatory role of baptism with water at the hand of John and the baptism with the Spirit by which individuals will be incorporated into the new covenant people. And among those who came seeking baptism was Jesus of Nazareth (1:9).

A VOICE FROM HEAVEN

Missing from Mark's account of Jesus's baptism are a number of features from the other Gospels which readers of the New Testament have come to regard as essential. But it is important to note what Mark does not report: There is no hint of recognition of or special treatment of Jesus by John. The implication is that Jesus is just one among the crowds streaming to John to receive baptism. The vision of the Spirit descending and the sound of the divine voice seem to be private experiences of Jesus, since the words are addressed to him alone rather than to John or to the crowds. The voice from heaven is heard in a dual allusion to scripture: "Thou art my son," recalls Psalm 2, where the king is hailed as God's agent ruling on the earth, and therefore as God's son; "with thee I am well-pleased," echoes Isaiah 42:1, where Yahweh is addressing his servant, who in his gentle way is establishing justice on earth. He is enabled to do so by the power, or spirit, which God has granted him: "I have put my spirit upon him . . ." (Isa. 42:1b).

Some interpreters have suggested a link between the voice and the rabbinic notion that God would attest the right interpretation of the Law of Moses by a celestial echo, *bath qol* (meaning "daughter of the voice"), since Jewish piety assumed that the voice of God itself could not be directly heard by humans. But a more fitting analogy is to the Old Testament tradition of theophanies and divine auditions by which chosen persons received their commission from God, as in the case of Moses at Sinai (Exod. 3:4ff), Elijah on Horeb (1 Kings 19:12ff), or Daniel on the bank of the Tigris (Dan. 10:2ff). In Jewish usage of the time, the term Son of God designated a man who had been chosen and empowered by God to do his will, and especially to exercise authority in God's stead. Hence, it was a familiar way of referring to the king, both the historical kings of Israel (Pss. 2, 45, and especially 72), and the idealized ruler whose coming was to usher in the new age (Isa. 9:6, 7). Although it is often asserted to be the case, there is no evidence that the term Son of God was used even in Hellenistic circles to refer to a divinized man. From the time of Augustus on, however, the Roman emperors were on occasion described as "son of the divine Caesar." The voice acclaiming Jesus as "Son" is therefore to be understood as the agent of his commissioning for the task of establishing God's rule on earth. What that role involves is clarified in the remainder of the text.

THE KINGDOM HAS DRAWN NEAR
[MARK 1:14]

Mark quickly sketches the conflict into which Jesus entered as he launches his career in behalf of the kingdom, tested by Satan and ministered to by the angels. A succinct summary of the message of Jesus follows: The present age, dominated by Satan and his agents, is coming to a close; and the new age, for which people may now prepare themselves by believing Jesus's announcement of its advent, is about to dawn. The rest of the Gospel is occupied with showing the nearness of the kingdom and the urgent necessity of heeding the summons to prepare for it.

The work of preparing people for the kingdom is not restricted to Jesus alone; as with any rabbi or eschatological leader, there is a group of disciples who gather around him to assist in his work and carry forward his program. Choosing initially from a handful of Galilean fishermen, Jesus is said to have designated them at the outset as "fishers of men" (Mark 1:17). Later on, Mark describes Jesus's sending them out on an extended tour (Mark 6:7–13). In view of the urgency of their message and the shortness of time before the end of the age, they are to make no preparations for their daily needs. Like the itinerant charismatics of the Q tradition, they are to rely on whatever hospitality is offered them from village to village. Their actual work is specifically stated to be an extension of Jesus's ministry in overcoming disease and demonic possession, which is for Mark the chief sign of the nearness of the kingdom.

HAVE YOU COME TO DESTROY US?
[MARK 1:24]

Significantly, the first act Mark depicts Jesus as performing is an exorcism carried out in the synagogue at Capernaum, the lakeside village in Galilee to which Jesus seems to have moved (Mark 2:1) from Nazareth, following his rejection there (Mark 6:1). By "teaching" Mark means far more than merely the message of Jesus: it encompasses the whole of his public activity. And its chief characteristic is that it is authoritative. It does not carry the sanctions of the appropriate religious officials, since that is the exact opposite of the case, but brings its own conviction. Its warnings are urgent and lead people to repent; its promises of deliverance are effective, as the results show.

In the story of the demoniac in the Capernaum synagogue, even the demons are aware of this power. Before Jesus addresses himself to the demo-

Synagogue at Capernaum as reconstructed by an artist from the second century A.D. ruins. In Jesus' time, "synagogue" probably referred to the assembly itself, rather than to a special meeting house.

niac's problem, the demons sense that in Jesus they have met one who is not only their conqueror, but is also to be the victor in the cosmic conflict. Jesus's commanding word, with the effective results, shows conclusively that the demons' question implies, "You have come to destroy us, haven't you?"

In keeping with his overall literary approach, Mark does not simply tell his reader what he wants him to know or merely get out the truth about Jesus. Instead, he proceeds by a series of questions which invite the response Mark believes is the only proper one. He wants his readers to respond affirmatively to the demons' question: "Yes, Jesus will defeat the demons." And he wants them to ask themselves what sort of man could possibly possess the insight and authority Mark attributes to Jesus. The novelty of his teaching lies not only in its specific content, but also in the effectiveness of his whole ministry. The doom of the demons is not merely announced—there would have been nothing novel in that—but effected: "He commands even the unclean spirits and they obey him."

All that follows in the remainder of Mark 1 is an elaboration of this theme: Jesus's authority is portrayed as extending to overcoming fevers and conquering diseases, even leprosy. The tradition here (1:43) links the healing of leprosy with one of the technical terms for the commanding word of Jesus by which the evil powers are overcome and the way prepared for the coming of God's rule. Up to this point, Mark has used the traditional language of Jewish apocalyptic literature to depict the coming of God's kingdom. From this point on, however, he has introduced his own special views and terms for portraying Jesus as the fulfillment of those hopes.

THE SON OF MAN HAS AUTHORITY
ON EARTH
[MARK 2:10]

Unlike the apocalyptic writers who developed the term Son of Man as a way of depicting God's agent (based on Dan. 7), Mark wants to show that even before the kingdom has been consummated, Jesus, during his earthly activity, is the authoritative agent of God and as such spoke of himself as Son of Man. In Jewish eschatology, God would pronounce the forgiveness of sins on the Day of Judgment that would bring to an end the present age and bring in the new. By shifting the focus from the paralyzed condition of the man lowered through the roof by his friends to the question of moral responsibility for his ailment, Mark has transformed the tradition from a straightforward healing story into a claim that Jesus already possesses power to pronounce the forgiveness of sins.

Some interpreters have pointed out that the Aramaic phrase, *bar nasha* (or in Hebrew, *ben adam*), can mean simply "a human being," as it does in Ezekiel 2:1. Others have conjectured that Son of Man was used as a circumlocution for "I," though this remains highly unlikely. But as Mark uses the term (Mark 2), the force is not simply that humans in general can forgive sins (2:10) or can set aside the ancient Sabbath law (2:27, 28), but that during his ministry Jesus has the authority to act in these ways, so that for Mark he is the eschatological Son of Man even before the new age has fully come.

Closely grouped with these two stories into which Mark has apparently introduced the Son of Man idea—in both 2:10 and 2:28 the narrative would read more smoothly without this factor—are three other pericopes in which Jesus is represented as setting aside established patterns of Jewish piety and separatism. The first has to do with Jesus's enjoying the hospitality of the religiously unacceptable (2:15–17); the second offers a justification for the failure of the disciples to fast (2:18–22); the third is another report of a healing performed on the Sabbath day (3:1–5). The second of these stories is particularly revealing about Mark, since in addition to explaining the more libertarian attitudes of Jesus and his followers during his lifetime, it also shows why the Church after his time did adopt the practice of fasting: because the bridegroom had been taken from them (2:20), an interpretation which is probably added by Mark. The string of sayings (2:21–22) has only a general link with what goes before, although this section as a whole makes the point that the new thing happening through Jesus cannot be forced into the structures of the old covenant.

More important for Mark's overall aims in this passage is the pair of references to the death of Jesus. The first of these alludes to the taking away of the bridegroom (2:20), the second to the coalition of religious and civil powers that destroy Jesus (3:6). Mark wants his readers to know from an early stage of the narrative that the death of Jesus was in view, although it is an exaggeration to say with Martin Kähler that the Gospels are Passion stories with extended introductions.[6] The reader has been forewarned about Jesus's death, however, before the predictions of the Passion begin at 8:31.

BINDING THE STRONG MAN
[MARK 2:27]

The paradox of increasing success and opposition is simultaneously portrayed in 3:7–35. In a summarizing statement, Mark describes the crowds flocking to Jesus to be healed as coming not only from his native Galilee, but also from the more distant Jewish territory around Jerusalem and even from the non-Jewish regions of Tyre, Sidon, Idumea, and the region east of the Jordan. They are reported as acclaiming him Son of God, although the significance of the title has not yet been clarified. The command to be silent about his activity (3:12) comes from Mark, and is in keeping with his conviction that there is no direct path to deliverance and triumph that does not pass through suffering.

After another brief mention of the circle of followers Jesus summoned to assist in his work of announcing and evidencing the kingdom of God (3:13–19), Mark goes on to indicate the various sources of opposition Jesus encountered. Typical of his literary method, Mark has divided a story in the middle and inserted another incident between the halves. The result of the determination by Jesus's family to remove him from the public scene reads smoothly if one passes directly from 3:21 (reading "his family" instead of the unwarranted translation "his friends" as in RSV) to 3:31, where his mother and brothers are directly mentioned. The link between the two stories lies in the supposition in each case that Jesus is the victim of some kind of aberration: his family assumes he is out of his mind (3:21), while his official opponents infer from his success in performing exorcisms that he is in league with demonic forces (3:23). Employing one of his favorite editorial devices, by which he appends to a saying of Jesus an explanation of his somewhat less than self-evident teaching, Mark has Jesus explain "in parables" (by analogy and metaphor) why the prince of demons would not assist Jesus in establishing God's rule by diminishing the control demons hold over human beings. The first figure is that of a dynasty, and the argument runs that Satan is not likely to work toward the destruction of his own "house." But then the figure changes to that of a household which cannot be stripped of its possessions (i.e., Satan's hold over the present age) until the householder (Satan) is deprived of his power. This is what Jesus is accomplishing by the exorcisms.

But then the argument moves on to deal with issues that are not as appropriate to the life of Jesus as to the life of the community: What sins are forgivable? How does the community regard someone who attributes to Satan what is in fact the work of the Holy Spirit? (3:28–30). This subject is not unrelated to that of the source of power behind Jesus's exorcisms—but the situation has altered significantly, since Mark is more interested in addressing the needs of the community in his own time than in accurately reconstructing

[6] See p. 99, note 3.

the circumstances during the lifetime of Jesus. Or more precisely, he believes that the power of Jesus once known among his disciples is still evident through the Holy Spirit in the life of the community. For him, therefore, the transition is obvious and inevitable.

THE SECRET OF THE KINGDOM
[MARK 4:11]

The Parable of the Sower, which was probably intended by Jesus to encourage his followers as they proclaimed the coming kingdom, becomes in the hands of Mark a kind of riddle (the Semitic word for parable, *mashal*, can mean riddle, enigma, puzzle), the meaning of which can be discerned only by the inner circle of the followers (4:11–12). The allegorical explanation of the parable that follows is clearly addressed to the congregation in Mark's day rather than to the disciples of Jesus.

The seed is identified as *the Word*, which is not a general message or a random theme, but the specifically Christian proclamation. The hearers are the various kinds of soil in which the Word is sown, at least in 4:15, where Satan (the birds) snatches away the seed soon after it has been sown. By 4:16 the allegory becomes inconsistent, and the hearers are now equated with the seed that has been sown on rocky ground—although by the end of that verse, the seed has once more become the Word and the hearers are the unreceptive soil. But in spite of the awkwardness of the allegory, the fault with the members of the community is painfully obvious. When tribulation or persecution on account of the Christian message becomes a real possibility, they fall away from the faith. Others are turned aside by preoccupation with worldly obligations (4:19). The very fact that riches could be an obstacle to faith indicates that the community for which Mark is writing is not a handful of impoverished itinerant preachers, but an organization of the kind that can attract the wealthy and that is faced with the problems of holding on to those whom it has converted.

The final note in the allegorical interpretation is an encouraging one, however, pointing as it does to the enormous effectiveness of the proclamation of the Gospel among those who are prepared to hear and respond faithfully. It is followed by a string of sayings, originally independent of each other, which Mark develops to stress the importance of spreading the light of the Gospel (4:21, 22) and to declare that refusal to heed the message will deprive people of even the opportunity to hear it (4:25). The section ends with two more parables concerning seed growing unnoticed (4:26–29) and the mustard shrub (4:30–32), both of which point to the contrast between the small beginnings of the Gospel and the great results of its proclamation that will become visible only on the Day of Judgment (harvest). Thus the parables have been adapted by Mark to serve the dual purposes of warning the careless and encouraging the faithful. But only those chosen by God are able to discern what is taking place; that is, Jesus has announced the elect status (13:20, 27) of those to whom the mystery of the kingdom has been disclosed.

WHO IS THIS?

[MARK 4:41]

The older miracle stories of the Gospel tradition point to the significance of Jesus's ministry: The demonic hold on the present age is being broken by Jesus's healings and exorcisms. In the later stories, the focus shifts to the direct question of who Jesus is that he is able to perform these wonders. The issue is not the personal question of how Jesus can deliver people from the present age but the theological question as to what it means to call Jesus "the Christ."

The first of the stories in this series depicts Jesus as stilling a storm on the Lake of Galilee (4:35–41). The language includes the technical term for commanding the demons (wrongly translated "rebuke," 4:39), which is here addressed to the wind (in Greek, *pneuma*) rather than to an "unclean spirit" (which would also be *pneuma*). Mark wants his readers to infer from this story that Jesus is the agent of God's rule over the whole cosmos, not merely over human needs. But his question, "Have you no faith?" is addressed as much to the community of his time as it is to the disciples in the boat. In the time of impending stress, it was essential that the members of the Markan community be reminded that the God who delivered the disciples from a storm through the Word of Jesus is able to save them from whatever fate might threaten.

The miracle stories of Mark 5 are among the most elaborate and detailed in the Gospel tradition. The details of the demoniac's plight and the stages of his release have parallels in Hellenistic exorcism stories of the time, and at the same time the technical terms of the older exorcism accounts are missing.[7] That Mark is more concerned about his own contemporaries than those of Jesus is apparent in the wording of 5:19, "Go home to your friends and tell them how much the Lord has done for you. . . ," where Mark uses the Church's confessional designation for Jesus—Lord—rather than a title such as "rabbi" or "teacher," by which his own disciples might have addressed him.

Mark interrupts the story of the healing of Jairus's daughter (5:22–24, 35–43) by inserting the account of the woman with the hemorrhage (5:25–34). By doing so, the drama of the first story is heightened, especially since the reader is given the impression that the delay may have resulted in the girl's having died (5:39). But perhaps the contrast between death and sleeping is Mark's way of contrasting Christians' attitude toward death, which was in fact referred to as "sleeping" (1 Thess. 4:13, 15), and the views held by some Jews and many pagans that death was final. Giving her food is a way of proving that her return to life is a physical reality and not merely an illusion, just as the developing Gospel tradition will describe Jesus as eating food following his resurrection from the dead (Luke 24:39–42).

The section ends (6:1–3) with a series of questions addressed by Mark to readers requiring them to come to some conclusion as to who this person is

[7] The older Gospel traditions employ a special term, *epitimān*, which translates a Semitic term used in the Hebrew Bible for God's exercising control over the powers that oppose him, and in the Dead Sea Scrolls for a commanding word that brings the demoniac under control.

who is able to exercise such extraordinary powers. Mark places the questions on the lips of Jesus's detractors, and thereby effects a transition from the description of what Jesus has done where he is responded to in faith to the limitations imposed where there is no faith.

A PROPHET WITHOUT HONOR
[MARK 6:4]

In contrast to the estimate of Jesus offered by those who have benefited from his abilities to heal and to release from demonic power is the reaction by his fellow villagers from Nazareth. They can see in Jesus only a carpenter, whose rather large family is well-known to them. His words and actions seem to them no more than vain pretensions. In having Jesus refer to himself as a prophet, Mark may well be preserving an authentic tradition, since as we have noted, prophet is a likely role for Jesus to have adopted for himself. Now, Mark tells us, the rejection of his prophetic role is complete: Both family and friends deny that he is sent by God. Their unbelief deprives them of the benefits of his God-given powers; it is not merely that he *will* not, but he *cannot* do his mighty works among them, Mark declares (6:5).

Even as he reports Jesus sending out the disciples on their missionary tour (6:7–13), Mark provides his reader with a none-too-subtle warning about what the fate of any messenger of repentance is likely to be, especially one whose mission is identified in the public mind with that of a prophet (6:15). In vivid detail Mark describes the fate of John the Baptist at the hand of Herod Antipas, son of Herod the Great and tetrarch of Galilee and Perea, the two territories where Jesus and John, respectively, carried on their major activity. Once again Mark has sounded an ominous note to prepare his readers for the predictions of death that are soon to appear in the narrative.

IT IS I
[MARK 6:30–56]

Mark has bracketed together two stories that attribute cosmic powers to Jesus: feeding the multitude and walking on water. These accounts have stimulated the imagination of rationalistic interpreters of Jesus to come up with ingenious explanations (Jesus shamed the crowd into bringing out and sharing the lunches they had concealed in their sleeves; the water was shallow and Jesus was merely wading). But the stories were preserved because they had become vehicles for describing the community's belief in the continuing spiritual presence of Jesus in their midst. The technical language of the communion sacrament has found its way into the narrative: "he blessed . . . he broke . . . he gave. . . ." The Greek phrase that translates "It is I" can also be rendered "I am," and is the way the Septuagint translated the name of God, Yahweh, that was disclosed to Moses at Sinai (Exod. 3:14). Since the Septuagint was the Bible of the Greek-speaking church for which Mark was writing, readers would have been familiar with the terminology of the theophany at Sinai, just as they would have associated this story with Yahweh's promise of safe deliverance of his people from the threatening waters (Isa. 43:2, and especially 43:25, where the Greek phrase is identical with Mark 6:50). The incident concludes with Mark's account of the mounting popular response to Jesus, which contrasts sharply with the coalescing official opposition.

WHAT DEFILES A PERSON
[MARK 7:20]

One of the major features of both Pharisaic and Essene Judaism in the time of Jesus was the maintenance of ceremonial purity. The Essenes were so obsessed with the question that many of them[8] withdrew from society—even Jewish society—so that they could pursue the pure life in their desert monastic community. It was for them essential to maintain their purity so as to be ready to enter with the rest of God's elect into the age to come, which they believed he was about to establish. Mark depicts Jesus as sharing a concern comparable to that of the Essenes for preparing the elect for the new age, but he is portrayed as in total disagreement with them about the importance of ceremonial purity. Whether Jesus himself went as far as Mark suggests—that is, to the point of setting aside all regulations about cleanliness (7:19)—is doubtful. But for Mark's community the regulations have no positive value at all; rather, what is essential is integrity and inner moral purity. The human being is corrupted by an evil heart (7:21), not by externals with which he or she comes in contact. It would appear that whatever may have been the original links between Mark's community and Jewish Christianity, the Jewish traditions of separateness have been abandoned.

CHILDREN'S BREAD FOR DOGS

Although the geographical indications are somewhat confusing, it appears that Mark wants his reader to see the next series of events in the life of Jesus as occurring in a Gentile setting: Tyre, Sidon, Decapolis, Caesarea Philippi. And the point of the stories is that where there is faith among Gentiles, they have as ready access to the elect community as do Jews. The sarcastic words of Jesus questioning the appropriateness of taking what was originally intended for Jews ("children") and giving it to Gentiles ("dogs") is replied to in kind by the quick-witted, determined Syrophoenician woman with the ailing child. And the result is that her daughter is healed. Similar results are reported with the deaf-mute in the Decapolis and the blind man at Bethsaida. The crowd is fed in Gentile territory (8:1–10), just as another crowd had been fed in a Jewish district (6:35ff). The numbers of baskets of remaining fragments—twelve and seven (8:19–20)—correspond exactly to the number of leaders said to

---

[8] According to Josephus (*Jewish War,* II. 114–125), some of the Essenes lived in the towns and cities, unlike those at Qumran.

Gerasa has been remarkably well preserved. The theaters, temples, and extensive baths of this city of the Decapolis are evident among the ruins. Most manuscripts of Mark report that it was outside the city of Gerasa that Jesus healed the demoniac.   (*Howard C. Kee*)

have been chosen by the Jerusalem Church for its Jewish and Gentile missionary enterprises, respectively (Acts 6:1–6). Mark wants to be certain his readers recognize that the Church's mission to the wider Gentile world was not an afterthought or an expedient once the mission to the Jews had failed, but was a part of the divine plan from the outset, sanctioned by the example of Jesus himself.

WHO DO YOU SAY I AM?

[MARK 8:29]

Up to this point, Mark has been content to raise questions about who Jesus is only editorially or by implication. Now he represents Jesus as addressing the question of his identity directly to his disciples. The suggestions as to who Jesus is offered by those other than the disciples are inadequate, but not wide of the mark. His message does resemble that of John; it does match well the eschatological function of Elijah; he can be compared with the eschatological prophet whose coming was announced in Deuteronomy 18 and who was awaited at Qumran. At first Peter seems to have given the correct answer: "You are the Christ." But the moment Jesus declares that his messianic role involves suffering and death Peter rejects the notion, showing that he has not understood Jesus's intention. Although some scholars see in this passage the effort of the historical Jesus to redefine the traditional messianic conceptions of Judaism—which had no concept of a suffering Messiah—it is far more likely that this is one of the main aspects of Mark's own interpretation of Jesus, in keeping with the overall apocalyptic framework in which he has placed his portrait. Mark simply asserts *that* Jesus must suffer, without indicating how that suffering will contribute to the coming of the Kingdom of God or to the redemption of people.

Mark 8:31 is the first of three increasingly detailed predictions of the suffering and death and resurrection of Jesus (the others are at 9:31 and 10:33–34), all of them tied in with the term Son of Man. Although the one "like a son of man" in Daniel 7 comes in triumph rather than as a sufferer, the elect community to whom the kingdom is to be given (Dan. 7:22) is promised that God will deliver them from whatever punishment the worldly authorities may require them to undergo, whether a starvation diet (Dan. 1:8ff), exposure to wild animals (Dan. 6:16ff), or being burned alive (Dan. 3:19ff). One of the frequently recurring images in apocalyptic writings is that of birthpangs, which must be endured if the new age is to be born. There is no direct logical significance assigned by Mark to suffering, as there might be in a doctrine of vicarious sacrifice, where the victim suffers so much to produce equivalent benefits. Suffering is simply declared to be inevitable if the redemptive outcome is to occur.

By refusing to accept these painful dimensions of Jesus's messianic role, Peter is portrayed as not only denying what is essential to Jesus's function as Son of Man, but as also rejecting the role of suffering and persecution that is a major feature of discipleship. Mark tells us this by appending to the prediction of the Passion the words about the cost of discipleship (8:34–38). The clue to Mark's choice of Son of Man as messianic designation for Jesus becomes clear in 8:38, where those who endure suffering on Jesus's behalf are promised vindication by Jesus when he appears in triumph at the end of the age. Taking as his starting point the authentic Son of Man words that speak of his future coming, Mark uses the term Son of Man to depict both the authority of Jesus and the necessity of suffering for him and his followers. That vindication, Mark quotes Jesus as affirming, will come during the lifetime of the first generation of followers—which confirms the other evidence that Mark was writing about A.D. 70, when the original disciples would be starting to reach the limits of their life expectancy. Indeed, the problem may well have been made the more urgent by the death of some of the earliest followers.[9]

In addition to the verbal assurance of vindication in the end (9:1), Mark describes an apocalyptic vision granted to the inner circle of disciples, Peter, James, and John (9:2–8). Like the theophanies of the Old Testament, the setting for this experience is a remote mountain where Jesus takes his followers and where they are addressed by a heavenly voice. The presence of the two

[9] No historically reliable accounts of the death of the apostles have been preserved, but some of the traditions and legends surrounding the death of Paul are sketched on pp. 291–98. Other legendary stories of the martyrdom of the apostles appear in the apocryphal Acts. See *New Testament Apocrypha II* (Philadelphia: Westminster Press, 1963 [1976]).

additional eschatological figures, Moses and Elijah (both of whom were expected by Jews of the period to return to earth before the end of the age), gives the experience added significance. The glowing of the garments of Jesus is reminiscent of what happened to Moses, whose face shone after seeing God (Exod. 34:29 ff), and even more precisely of Daniel's vision (Dan. 10:2–14), even to the point that Daniel's disciples could not grasp what was happening and were in any case enjoined to silence about what they had seen (cf. Mark 9:9). The conversation that Mark places following the vision (9:9–13) confirms the link between the eschatological messenger and suffering. Whatever this tradition may originally have meant, it now refers to John the Baptist, who is Jesus's forerunner in both his message and his death.

YOU DO NOT KNOW WHAT YOU ARE ASKING

[MARK 10:38]

The entire section of Mark from 9:14 to 10:45 is occupied with a series of accounts of misunderstandings or misconceptions on the part of the disciples. The inability of the disciples to cure the demon-possessed mute (10:14–29) is seen as evidence of their lack of faith, and contrasts with the availing faith of the father of the demoniac (9:24). The second announcement of the Passion is greeted with fear and incomprehension (9:32). The two appeals by the disciples for places of special privilege (9:33–37; 10:35–45) are met, respectively, by lessons on the need to be childlike and on the necessity of accepting suffering and death for the sake of the coming kingdom. Warnings are issued against rejecting anyone who performs good deeds in the name of Jesus, even though he is not a member of the community (9:38–41), and against leading astray any "little children" in the faith by one's insensitive or irresponsible actions (9:42–50). A similar theme is repeated in 10:13–16.

PREPARING FOR LIFE OF THE AGE TO COME

[MARK 10:17]

Two questions which must have been considered important by the community which Mark is addressing, but which are presented as wrongheaded in Mark's form of the Jesus tradition, are these: (1) Under what conditions are divorce and remarriage permissible? (2) How good does a person have to be in order to be sure of entering the life of the age to come? To the first, Mark has Jesus reply that God intended man and woman to be inseparably united, so that divorce is a concession to human weakness, not a divine provision. Mark adds further, using his characteristic literary device of a private explanation following a public pronouncement (10:10), the arguments against man or woman taking the initiative in divorce. Since women lacked this right in Jewish law, Mark has clearly adapted the tradition to the Gentile situation in which the Romans had provided for the rights of women.

The second question becomes the occasion for a denunciation of riches, apparently on the ground that people cannot differentiate between what they have acquired and their own self-esteem. It is not how a person ranks on the achievement scale of the divine commandments or in the acquisition of wealth that is the essential question, but the intensity of commitment to the work of preparing for the kingdom of God (10:17–31). It is possible that Mark has modified the more stringent original declaration of Jesus against possession of wealth by suggesting a three-stage development: (1) initial renunciation of wealth; (2) an intermediate stage of mingled reward and persecution; (3) the ultimate reward of eternal life, or life of the age to come.

The third prediction of the Passion (10:32–34) arouses fear and astonishment rather than comprehension. Even the detailed attempt to clarify the difference between the route of power by which the nations exercise authority and the route of service and acceptance of suffering that Jesus and his followers must follow does not penetrate to the disciples. How the roles of Son of Man and Son of God (King) fit together eludes them. Ironically, there is one man who can discern who Jesus is: the blind Bar-Timaeus, who calls out to Jesus for help as he is passing through Jericho (10:46–52). Addressing Jesus as Son of David, Bar-Timaeus not only affirms Jesus's role as king, but, by associating Messiah and Son of David with restoration of sight, implicitly recalls that in the eschatological kingdom the eyes of the blind will be opened (Isa. 35:5; 42:7; 42:16; 43:8), that this promise is given to the city of David (Isa. 29:1, 18), and specifically that the power to open blind eyes is assigned to the Anointed (in Septuagint, *christos*) of Yahweh (Isa. 61:1). In sharp contrast to the imperceptive disciples, the blind beggar is able to see clearly who Jesus is.

HE WHO COMES
IN THE NAME OF THE LORD
[MARK 11:9]

Mark describes Jesus as entering Jerusalem, apparently for the first time, by way of the Mount of Olives, with its spectacular view of the Temple and city spread out below. The old Roman road that came up from Jericho (800 feet below sea level) through the arid wilderness of Judea twelve miles or so to the crest of the ridge (2800 feet above sea level) led steeply down the western slope of the Mount of Olives, across the dry bed of the Kidron, and up the slope of Zion. As Mark depicts the journey, it is in apparently conscious fulfillment of the prediction of Zechariah 9 that Jerusalem's king would come to her in humility, not on a white horse, but on a lowly donkey. Unlike the later Gospels in which Jesus is addressed as king (Matt. 21:9), the crowds acclaim Jesus as one who comes in the Lord's name, referring to Psalm 118:26, which was quoted in Jesus's day as an eschatological hope of the establishment of God's kingdom, as Mark 11:10 affirms. There is no hint in Mark of any immediate consequences to this act performed by Jesus. Some scholars think that if Jesus had actually entered the city in this way and permitted his acclaim by the crowd, he would have been seized instantly by the authorities as a messianic claimant and therefore as a threat to political stability. It was as such that he was finally arrested and condemned, though we cannot be certain historically that he provided the occasion for his seizure by this overt act. For Mark, however, it is the appropriate way for the true Son of David to enter the city which is about to reject him.

The hostility of the leaders of the city toward him is symbolized by the strange account of the cursing and the withering of the unproductive fig tree (11:12–14; 20–22), just as the unsuitability of the Temple as a place of approach to God is asserted in Jesus's act of purging the courts (11:15–18). The place where the Gentiles should have been able to worship the God of Israel (11:17, "for all nations") had become a place of greed and commerce. Pressed by the officials for the source of his authority in performing these arrogant actions in the carefully regulated Temple enclosure, Jesus only throws the question back at his interrogators (11:27–33). In an allegory which is itself based on Isaiah's allegory of the faithless nation, Israel (Isa. 5:1–7), Mark reports Jesus to have represented his impending rejection and death as the climax of a long series of events in which Israel had rejected the messengers sent by God.

The result is that the nation has forfeited its special place as the people of God; Jesus is now to be seen as the founder of the new covenant people (12:10–11). As such, this people is to be characterized by faithfulness in prayer (11:22–24), by neither arrogance toward nor dependence upon the civil authorities (12:13–17), by assurance that God will create new conditions of life for his own people in the age to come (12:18–27), by obedience to the twin commandments of love of God and neighbor (12:28–34), by acceptance of a worldly position of humility and poverty (12:38–44). Characteristic of this people will be their conviction that Jesus, the true Son of David, is the one acclaimed in the Church as Lord (12:35–37).

END OF THE TEMPLE AND END OF THE AGE
[MARK 13:1–4]

The editorial hand of Mark is once more evident in the shift from the public pronouncement of the Temple's impending destruction (13:1–2) to the private explanation offered to the disciples. Mark has here assembled the longest consecutive string of sayings to be found in his entire Gospel. The sayings are not arranged in a strictly logical order, and some scholars even think Mark has copied all or part of this material from a written source, as the reference to "the reader" in 13:14 implies. The discourse as it stands attempts to balance two viewpoints: (1) The new covenant people is facing persecution which, if endured faithfully, will not last longer than they can bear; (2) but this people should not be deceived into assuming too quickly that the end of the age has come or that every messiah claimant is to be credited. The disturbances that will mark the coming of the end are political (13:7, 8), interreligious (13:9), intercommunal (13:12), and cosmic (13:24–25).

The unambiguous clue to the approaching end will be the desecration of the Temple (13:14), but in the interim the task of evangelism among the Gen-

Fallen stones from the Jerusalem Temple, dating from the time of Herod, lie on the stepped street where they fell during the destruction of the Temple in A.D. 70. The largest stone measures about 8 by 10 by 6 feet; the slab still in position along the left is nearly 30 feet long.   (*Howard C. Kee*)

tiles must be carried out universally (13:10). Although there is no way to determine the precise time of the end, since that is a secret known to God alone (13:32), the new covenant people can be sure it will occur within the life of the first generation of its members (13:30). It is the responsibility of the community to be ever faithful and ever watchful (13:35–37).

The language and point of view of the discourse in Mark 13 are dependent on the book of Daniel.[10] The other synoptic writers have expanded this part of Mark considerably, drawing in large measure on Q material. But the basic structure and the place of the discourse within the overall picture of Jesus's career are the contribution of Mark, who wants readers to see a parallel between the desecration of the Temple in Daniel's (actually, Maccabean) times and the destruction of the Temple predicted by Jesus. What was expected by Daniel but did not occur—the establishment of the kingdom of God—is affirmed by Mark as now about to take place. With this assurance in mind, the reader is prepared to see beyond the sad story of rejection and death to the promised deliverance.

The prediction of the Temple's destruction provides us with our best clue to the historical circumstances for the writing of Mark. In the decade of

---

[10] See Lars Hartmann, *Prophecy Reinterpreted: The Formation of Some Jewish Apocalyptic Texts and of the Eschatological Discourse, Mark 13 and par.* (Lund: Gleerup, 1966).

the sixties occurred a series of events that profoundly affected the early Church. The leading apostles were put to death: Peter and Paul in Rome, and James in Jerusalem; Jerusalem and its temple fell into Roman hands; the Jerusalem Christians fled from the city. The community for which Mark wrote was gravely concerned over these developments. Its members needed assurance that the new age would arrive within the lifetime of at least some of the apostles (Mark 9:1). The flight of the Jerusalem Christians and the destruction of the city—whether Mark wrote shortly before or just after these events took place we cannot ascertain—had to be explained to the community in terms which affirmed the power of God to fulfill his promises and to judge those who rejected his messenger, Jesus. Just as the Maccabean crisis in the days of Antiochus IV had led to the writing of Daniel (about 168 B.C.), so the Roman invasion of Palestine and the disruption of the life of the Christians in Jerusalem seem to have been the occasion for the writing of Mark. So significant were these events for the future of the Church that we review them here in broad outline.

In the years A.D. 66–70, the position of the community in Jerusalem had become increasingly difficult as a result of the Jewish revolt against Roman occupation. The cruelty and corruption of the Roman procurators had been increasing. Nero had made important concessions to the Gentiles in Palestine, and they had begun to interfere with Jewish worship in the synagogues. In the year 66, as a reaction against maltreatment at the hands of the Roman administrators, the Jews refused to permit the sacrifices to the emperor to continue, although these sacrifices were required by Roman law. Riots broke out in every city; Gentile towns were burned; the Roman garrisons were attacked in cities where they were weak; and Jews were slaughtered in reprisal in cities where the garrisons were strong. At first, the Jews succeeded in liberating parts of the land from Roman control; the independence of the Jewish nation was declared, and Jewish coinage was issued. But the poorly armed bands of revolutionaries could not withstand the 60,000 seasoned troops Rome sent in to quell the revolt. By the year 69 all of Palestine, except for Jerusalem and some outlying fortresses near the Dead Sea, was once again under Roman control.

Vespasian, who commanded the Roman troops, could have destroyed all resistance, but his mind was occupied with other matters. The emperor, Nero, had died under mysterious circumstances in 68, and Vespasian's

A shekel of Israel as minted by the Jews during the Jewish revolt of A.D. 66–70. The reverse side is inscribed "Jerusalem the Holy." (*James T. Stewart*)

Vespasian invaded Palestine in A.D. 67. He left his son Titus to capture Jerusalem while he returned to Rome to be acclaimed emperor in 69. *(Alinari/Editorial Photocolor Archives)*

chances of succeeding him were excellent. Accordingly, Vespasian held back from the fighting for a time to see what the outcome of the contest for the imperial throne would be. When it became clear that the army in the East would declare for him, he returned to Rome. His rivals faded from the scene, and he became emperor in 69. His son Titus, who had been left in charge of the troops in Palestine, pressed the siege of Jerusalem.

The Fall of Jerusalem

The city's resistance might have been greater if the people had not been torn by internal dissension. At the start of the revolt there had been two main parties: the peace party, whose members believed God would free the nation from Rome in his own time and by his own methods; and the resistance party, whose adherents were convinced that the time had come for them to take the initiative in driving the Romans out. With the advent of the Roman troops, the peace party was overwhelmed by the rebels. But any prospect of success for the revolt was ended when the rebels began to fight among themselves under rival leaders. The civil strife continued within the city even during the siege. Although the revolutionaries had killed Annas, who had caused James's death, the Christians appear to have been in sympathy with the peace party.

They believed that the hope of the nation lay in the return of their Messiah to establish the reign of God, not in military victory. The siege, which began in April of the year 70, lasted five months, and during this time thousands died of starvation. Then, when the city fell, the Romans laid it waste and demolished the Temple. A generation later, during the reign of Hadrian, the Jews attempted a second revolt (A.D. 132–135), but at the order of Hadrian the city of Jerusalem was leveled and a pagan city called Aelia Capitolina was built on the site.

The Flight of the Christians

Eusebius, the fourth century Church historian, reports that just before the siege began the Christians decided to flee to a place of safety. At first glance, it seems clear that the reason they would have fled was to escape destruction at the hands of the Romans. But Eusebius tells us they went to the Gentile city of Pella, east of the Jordan in the region of the Decapolis, in response to a divine oracle. If we were to take his report as historically reliable, certain questions would immediately arise: What was the nature of the oracle? Why did it tell them to go to a despised Gentile city like Pella, which had been among those attacked by Jewish nationalists only a few years earlier? Why were the Jewish Christians—traditionally so fastidious about maintaining separateness from Gentiles—willing to seek refuge in a Gentile stronghold? Conjectural answers to these questions (in reverse order) might suggest that the Jerusalem Christians would have been willing to compromise their religious scruples for the sake of saving their own necks. The only place of safety in the whole area for Jews who had opposed the revolt would be a place like Pella, which was Gentile and hence free of Jewish nationalist feeling. There they would be safe from the Romans, who might have taken them for rebels in Jerusalem, and safe from the rebels, who might have killed them as traitors. Recent analysis of this tradition suggests, however, that it rests on a claim by the Christians of Pella to possess continuity with the apostles through the migration of the Jerusalem Christians to their city.[11] There is no way to verify their claim, and it tells us nothing about the nature of Jewish Christianity in Pella or elsewhere, even if it were authentic.

Eusebius gives another theory to explain the flight of the Christians from Jerusalem. He suggests that the Roman emperors, from Vespasian on, sought out all descendants of David in an effort to exterminate the Jewish hope of a revival of the Davidic dynasty. Since Jesus was from "the seed of David" (Rom. 1:3), he and his relatives would have been in the royal line, and his brothers and other surviving relatives would have been the victims of Vespasian if they had remained within his reach at Jerusalem. On this theory, the flight to Pella would have been a communal effort to protect Jesus's family, to whom had passed the leadership of the Jerusalem community. This story of

---

[11] For a detailed critical analysis of the Pella tradition, see Gerd Lüdemann, "The Successors of Pre-70 Jerusalem Christianity: A Critical Evaluation of the Pella Tradition," in *Jewish and Christian Self-Definition,* ed. E. P. Sanders (Philadelphia: Fortress Press, 1980), pp. 161–73.

JERUSALEM IN THE TIME OF JESUS

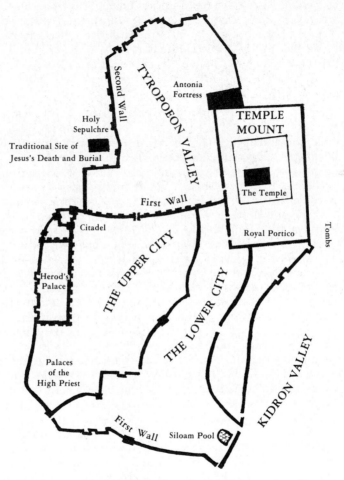

Eusebius bears the marks of legendary embroidering, and really conveys little more than the general impression that (1) the Romans did not understand the nature of Christian messianic beliefs, and mistakenly identified them with the nationalistic hopes of Judaism, and (2) the Jerusalem wing of Christianity had already lapsed into such complete obscurity by the end of the second century that there were no precise recollections of what had happened to it after the city fell to the Romans.

Although we do not know what happened to the Christians after they fled from Jerusalem, we do know that the destruction of Jerusalem by the Romans was interpreted by Christians generally as a divine judgment on Judaism for its rejection of Jesus as the Christ. This conviction is plainly and repeatedly stated in Eusebius, and it is easy to read it between the lines of the Gospels. As noted in the opening part of this chapter, the very fact that the apocalyptic section mentioned above was incorporated into Mark shows that the fall of Jerusalem was considered by its author to be a major event in the unfolding of the purpose God had begun with the coming of Jesus. The destruction was understood to be the final proof that the old dispensation had come to an end; the new age was already beginning to dawn.

LAST SUPPER AND NEW COVENANT
[MARK 14:24–25]

Although we have noted that Jesus's last meal with his disciples was probably an eschatological celebration, as Mark 14:25 clearly implies, it was recalled in the Church's tradition in light of two other factors: (1) an analogy between the Jewish Passover and the death of Jesus, and (2) the concept of Jesus's death as the sacrifice that sealed the new covenant promised by Jeremiah (Jer. 31:31). The Passover in Jewish tradition recalled the act of deliverance by which God freed his people from slavery in Egypt and led them into the new land. The death of Christ was itself identified with the Passover in the Pauline churches (1 Cor. 5:7); and in Johannine circles, Jesus was regarded as the Lamb of God (John 1:29; Rev. 5). The annual celebration of the Passover as a ceremony of recommitment probably provided a rough parallel for the Christian's periodic celebration of the Eucharist, which was considered in Pauline circles as a covenant renewal ceremony (1 Cor. 11:25), where the term "new covenant" is actually used (as it is in some manuscript copies of Mark at 14:24). Mark's version of the tradition has not fully developed a theological interpretation of the death of Jesus; it declares only that the life he offered up ("blood" was equivalent to life in Hebrew) was linked with the (new) covenant, and was to the benefit of "many" (14:24). The later Church expanded this seminal notion, developing from it doctrines of the atonement as substitution, as propitiatory, as expiatory. But just as Mark was content to affirm only that the death of Jesus was necessary, without explaining why or how, so he simply states that Jesus's death is in behalf of others. This is what the community of Mark celebrates in the communion, while looking forward to the completion of the number of the elect in the new age.

DENIAL AND BETRAYAL
[MARK 14:26–72]

In a series of vivid narrative passages, Mark depicts the instability of the disciples even as Jesus is seen struggling to carry out his destiny. There is no hint of what Judas betrayed, although imaginations, pious and otherwise, have long speculated on the subject. Probably he did no more than to lead the guards outside the city walls to the place of Jesus's rendezvous with his followers, and identify him positively for arrest. Mark suggests vaguely that Judas was offered money to betray Jesus, but Matthew fills out the detail to make the incident conform to scriptural prophecy (Matt. 26:14–15; Zech. 11:12).

Scholars have suggested that Judas was disappointed because Jesus failed to side with the revolutionaries, but there is no evidence that Judas was himself a zealot. Theories about plots are unfounded guesswork. All we can be sure of is that Jesus was put in the hands of the authorities by one of his own followers. Even Peter, when pressed, professed to have had no acquaintance with Jesus.

CONDEMNATION AND DEATH

The stories of the charges brought against Jesus by the authorities and the various hearings where he was called to account are confused in Mark's account, and hence in the other Gospel narratives that are dependent on his. In general, however, the issues raised in the presence of the High Priest and the Jewish leaders gathered as the Sanhedrin are all religious and Jewish. Chief among the accusations is his threat to the Temple (14:58), although instead of having predicted its destruction he is quoted by his opponents as having vowed to destroy it. The second issue has to do with Jesus's claim to be the Son of God ("Blessed," since Jewish piety avoided pronouncing the name God). According to Mark 14:62, Jesus for the first time states unequivocally that he is the Son of God, but goes on to define that title by a combination of scriptural quotations, one of which is a reference to the Davidic king seated at God's right hand, the place of power (Ps. 110:1), and the other a paraphrase of Daniel 7:13, where (one like) the Son of Man comes on the clouds of heaven to assume authority in God's kingdom. Here we have the central point in Mark's understanding of Jesus as Messiah: He combines the kingly role of the Son of David, with its title Son of God, and the eschatological role of representative of the "saints of the Most High" in Daniel to whom the kingdom of God is assigned. Although the High Priest is represented as horrified by this claim, no action is taken by the Sanhedrin, which turns over responsibility for Jesus to the civil powers represented by Pontius Pilate, the Roman procurator, who was resident in Jerusalem at the time of the festival rather than at his official seat in Caesarea.

Pilate's questions concern the political matter over which he would have jurisdiction: the possibility that Jesus was a claimant to the Jewish kingship and therefore a potential leader of a revolt (15:2). Jesus's response is equivocal, and he refuses to offer any word in his own defense. Although the story of the release of a political prisoner Barabbas is not documented outside the Gospels as having been Roman policy in Palestine or the Eastern provinces (and is likely to have been created by the Christians), it keeps its focus on what was probably the historical point at issue in the hearing before Pilate: Was Jesus an insurrectionist? The terms used of Barabbas, "rebel . . . who had committed murder in the insurrection" (15:7), fit well with such a situation, as does the form of execution that was finally decided upon, however reluctantly, by Pilate: crucifixion. If Jesus had been executed by the religious authorities, a legal possibility at this time, he would have been stoned to death. But the unanimous evidence that he was crucified points to his having been condemned on a political charge: that he claimed to be the king of the Jews.

He was treated as an insurrectionist by the soldiers who tormented him and by those who were crucified with him. The sign placed on the cross (15:26) makes the charge explicit. Even though many of the details of the Crucifixion scene may be legendary elaboration (15:33, 38), based in part on a Christian reading of the scriptures (15:34 is a quotation from Ps. 22, which also lies behind other details of the account such as Jesus's thirst), the general outline of the story is credible, including the faithful watch of the women (15:40–41) at the cross and the hasty burial of the body in a stone-cut tomb (15:45–46) in order to avoid polluting the Sabbath by allowing a dead body to be exposed.

YOU WILL SEE HIM AS HE TOLD YOU
[MARK 16:7]

The women take the first opportunity to prepare the body properly with spices—that is, at daybreak on Sunday morning (16:1–2). Their chief concern is how they will manage to roll back the stone. This wheel-like slab of stone

The steps and entrance to this rock-hewn tomb are of the type referred to in the story of Jesus's burial and Resurrection. The circular slab of rock that served to block access to the tomb can be seen at the right; when the block holding it back was removed, it would roll down the groove and cover the entrance. In the Gospel story, it is found rolled back. *(Gordon N. Converse)*

was made to roll down a hewn track by gravity and close over the opening of the tomb, which was a chamber cut out of the rock. To their astonishment, the stone has been rolled back and the body of Jesus is gone. A young man— the later Gospels will have angels—is there to reassure them. He asserts that Jesus has risen, that he will fulfill his promise (14:28) of going before the disciples to Galilee, where he will be seen by them (16:7). Instead of the rapturous joy one might expect at such news, Mark declares that the women were filled with trembling, astonishment, and fear. The three terms used here by Mark are all to be found in the Septuagint version of Daniel 10:12, where Daniel is responding to an apocalyptical vision of the eschatological king.

The open-ended way in which Mark brought his Gospel to a close was part of the apocalyptic tradition that shaped his outlook and his literary contribution. But it was not satisfying to the other writers, who added endings of their own, or to later copyists, who provided Mark with a more nearly standard conclusion. These are often reproduced in study editions of the New Testament, and were actually included as part of the text in the King James Version. But a formal literary conclusion is unnecessary for Mark. He has informed his reader repeatedly that Jesus's suffering and death are essential stages on the path to glory. For those who await him, he will appear in triumph when God's purpose for his creation is complete. The specific timing is known only to God (Mark 13:32). The obligation of the community is to fulfill its mission, to stand firm, and—above all—to "watch" (Mark 13:37). The Gospel of Mark is the fundamental document that enables and encourages the community to fulfill the injunction to preach and heal, to wait and watch.

5

The True Community
of Israel:
Matthew

From the second century down to the present, the Gospel of Matthew has been considered the first Gospel not only in the list of the New Testament books, but in importance as well. Its place at the beginning of the canon means, of course, that it is probably the most frequently read of all the New Testament writings. But more significant than its location is the fact that the words of Matthew's Gospel are among the most familiar of all New Testament themes. The coming of the Wise Men, the Sermon on the Mount, the familiar form of the Lord's Prayer, the coin in the fish's mouth, the parable of the sheep and the goats are found only in Matthew. Only in this Gospel does Jesus address Peter as the Rock on which the Church will be built. There can be no question why Matthew has taken and held the prime place among the Gospels in the esteem of the Church.

The prime place assigned to Matthew within the New Testament and the relative familiarity of its contents may obscure for the reader what is distinctive about this Gospel with regard to the circumstances of its origin and certain features of its contents. A careful reading of the book will disclose a paradox: Matthew is at the same time the most Jewish and the most hostile of all the Gospels—or indeed, of all the books of the New Testament—toward what was to emerge in the second and subsequent centuries as normative Judaism. The basic issue Matthew shares with all the Jews, as well as with other New Testament writers, is this: How does one qualify for inclusion in the covenant people? The distinctive quality of his response is influenced not only by his and his community's point of view, but by historical circumstances within the Jewish community at the time he was writing.

In Chapter 2 we considered briefly the reshaping of Judaism that is associated with Yavneh on the Mediterranean coast and that took place in the closing decade of the first century. The discussion about which books were to be considered authoritative, as well as which regulations of Jewish law according to what interpretation were to be binding on Jews, set the basic pattern for Jewish identity down to the present day. An important aspect of that definition process, from our standpoint, is the way in which Jews felt obligated to draw the lines of identity against the burgeoning Christian movement. Some of the polemical results of that undertaking are apparent in the later Jewish traditions, which claim that Jesus was the illegitimate offspring of a Roman soldier.[1] In these traditions, Christians are dismissed as heretics.

---

[1] For a discussion of this allegation, see my *Jesus in History,* 2nd ed., New York: Harcourt Brace Jovanovich, 1977), pp. 48–54.

The other side of this mounting hostility toward Christians is apparent in the Gospel of Matthew, which, as we shall see, contains some of the harshest statements in all of early Christian literature against what was to become mainstream Judaism. At the same time, in claiming to be the true heirs of the promises to Israel, the community for and to which Matthew wrote is emphatic and persistent that what God intended through his self-disclosure in the law and the prophets has now come to fulfillment in Jesus and his people. The result of this paradoxical attitude is that Matthew appears to be at the same time the most Jewish and the most anti-Jewish of the Gospels. That link with the Hebrew heritage is by no means a strictly modern interest; its origins go back to shortly after Matthew was written.

Papias, bishop of the Hierapolis in Asia Minor in the early second century, stated that Matthew was the compiler of the sayings (in Greek, *logia*) of the Lord in Hebrew, and that every man interpreted or translated them as he was able. This testimony of Papias (written presumably about A.D. 140) has usually been understood to refer to the Gospel of Matthew, and therefore to affirm that that Gospel was originally written in Hebrew.

There are many difficulties with Papias's testimony. First of all, we cannot be at all sure that he was talking about the Gospel of Matthew when he spoke of the "logia" of Jesus. If *logia* means "sayings," as it sometimes does, then we note immediately that Matthew's Gospel contains far more than merely sayings; it is a careful blend of narrative and discourse material. In any case, Papias could not be referring to Matthew as we know it.

It has been suggested that *logia* was a term used in the early Church for collections of Old Testament texts used by the Church to prove that Jesus was the fulfillment of the Hebrew prophecies. Among the manuscripts found at Qumran was a sheet of Old Testament passages that may have served to provide a ready list of messianic proof texts among the Essenes of the Dead Sea community. But Matthew, while attaching great importance to the fulfillment of the Old Testament, has far wider interests and includes much more than quotations.

Papias has further been charged with error in his claim that the *logia* were in Hebrew, since the language in common use in Palestine in the first century was Aramaic, a Semitic dialect closely related to Hebrew. But the discovery of the Dead Sea Scrolls, most of which are in Hebrew rather than Aramaic, has weakened the force of this argument, since it is now evident that Jews in first-century Palestine were using Hebrew as the official tongue of their religious communities. But whether Papias meant Hebrew or Aramaic, he can scarcely have been referring to the original of the Gospel of Matthew, since it was clearly written first in Greek, and dependent on Greek sources.

At an early period in the Church's life, however, there were those who claimed to have found the Hebrew original of the First Gospel. In the fifth century, Jerome (famous for his translation of the Bible into Latin, known as the Vulgate, the official Roman Catholic version) announced that he had discovered and translated the "original Hebrew" form of the Gospel of Matthew. What he actually found was a paraphrase in Aramaic of the Greek Gospel of

Matthew.[2] The paraphrase was known as the Gospel of the Nazarenes, a Jewish-Christian group that flourished in that part of Syria through which the Euphrates flows. Other fathers of the Church mistook other books—some of them heretical—to be the Hebrew original of Matthew. The fact is, however, that the Gospel of Matthew is based on the Greek Gospel of Mark, although of course the oral tradition drawn upon by Mark, as well as the tradition embodied in Matthew's other written sources, go back ultimately to the Semitic speech spoken by Jesus and his contemporaries in Palestine.[3]

There is no need to repeat here the evidence that Matthew had Mark before him, as well as a document (now known as Q) consisting mostly of sayings of Jesus. What should be noted here, however, is the great skill with which Matthew has reworked and edited his material, supplementing it here, abridging it there.[4] Throughout, he has handled his materials in such a masterful way that both the overall structure and the development of details contribute effectively to his major theological and polemical aims. Before turning to an analysis of Matthew's aims, however, we direct our attention to the question of the probable time and place of writing of this influential document.

WHEN AND WHERE
WAS MATTHEW WRITTEN?

Allusions to the Gospel of Matthew in the writings of Ignatius of Antioch (ca. 115) provide us the latest date to which the writing can be assigned. That Ignatius quotes it as authoritative suggests that it had been in circulation for some time, perhaps since at least A.D. 100. On the other hand, Matthew's dependence on Mark as one of his sources proves that the Gospel could not have appeared earlier than A.D. 70. This supposition of a post-70 date is confirmed by the direct mention in Matthew 22:7 of the fall of Jerusalem and the burning of the city, which took place in the year 70. A likely date for the writing of Matthew would be, therefore, about 90 to 95.

To settle on so late a date as this virtually excludes the disciple Matthew from consideration as the author. We shall see that on other grounds it is not likely that this book was written by a disciple, since a person so closely connected with Jesus would not have had to depend on Mark, who at best was reporting at secondhand the recollections of an apostle. Indeed, the Gospel of

[2] B. W. Bacon has denounced Jerome's claims of discovery as fraudulent; see his *Studies in Matthew* (New York: Holt, 1930), pp. 478–81. This Gospel is also discussed in Hennecke-Schneemelcher, *New Testament Apocrypha*, I (Philadelphia: Westminster Press, 1963), pp. 139–46.

[3] An older standard assessment of the Semitic element in the language of the Gospels is presented by M. Black, *An Aramaic Approach to the Gospels and Acts* (Oxford: Clarendon Press, 1967). For a more complete and reliable analysis, see Joseph Fitzmyer, S.J., *A Wandering Aramaean* (Missoula, Mont.: Scholars Press, 1979), especially the opening chapter on the Aramaic background of the New Testament.

[4] For a concise summary of the modification Matthew has made in the Markan material, see my *Jesus in History,* 2nd ed. (New York: Harcourt Brace Jovanovich, 1977), pp. 166–85.

Matthew itself makes no claim to have been written by an eyewitness, much less by one named Matthew. It is true that only in Matthew is the tax collector who became a follower of Jesus (Mark 2:13–14) called Matthew (Matt. 9:9; 10:3), but there is no hint of a connection between this man and the writer of the Gospel. The divergences among the lists of disciples found in the three synoptic Gospels are such as to warn us against basing historical judgments on variations in the name. We must confess that, as with the other three Gospels, we do not know who the author of Matthew was. For the sake of convenience, however, we shall continue to refer to him as "Matthew."

The author's use of a Greek source makes it obvious that Matthew was originally written in Greek, as we have noted. This conclusion is strengthened by the fact that a number of the quotations from the Old Testament are taken not from the Hebrew text, but from the Septuagint, the widely used Greek translation of the Old Testament that had been prepared in the third and second centuries B.C. for the use of Jews throughout the Hellenistic world who no longer understood Hebrew. We look, then, for a city or region where there

Seleucia, port city for Antioch-on-the-Orontes in Syria, where Paul resided during an early stage of his missionary career, and where he had the confrontation with Peter that he describes in Galatians 2:11. According to Acts 13, it was from this port that Paul and Barnabas set sail for Cyprus as their mission to the Aegean area began. (*Gordon N. Converse*)

were Greek-speaking Christians of Jewish origin as the likely place where Matthew was written. Alexandria has been proposed, but there is no evidence to connect Matthew with that city. Caesarea has been suggested, but largely on the basis that Peter, who is given a place of special importance in Matthew (especially 16:16–19), was the one through whom the Church was established in Caesarea, according to Acts 10. But the story of Peter at Caesarea serves the author of Acts as a stylized account of the transition from Jewish to Gentile evangelism rather than as a straightforward historical report. Antioch is the city where the first echoes of Matthew are heard in the form of quotations and allusions in the writings of Ignatius. The dominant view among biblical scholars has been that Antioch is in fact where Matthew was written,[5] although it is more probable that it originated in a community in the area to the east of Antioch near the Euphrates Valley. We know of the existence of strong Jewish communities in Aleppo, Edessa, and Apamea[6] in this period, and that Christian communities flourished there in the second century. The interest in the Magi and the miraculous star are fitting in such an environment, although astrological speculation had pervaded the whole of the empire by this time.

At best we can only conjecture, on the basis of hints from within the work itself, about the specific type of community in which the Gospel of Matthew might have arisen. It was, as we have seen, a Greek-speaking group, but one strongly influenced by Jewish perspectives and aspirations. We have already observed that there is on the part of the author of this Gospel a paradoxical attitude toward Judaism. On the one hand he is deeply sympathetic with Judaism, especially its law and the moral demands contained therein. On the other hand, he is profoundly, at times bitterly, critical of Judaism, especially of its leaders, whom he regards as hypocrites (Matt. 23:1–36, especially vv. 13, 15, 16, 23, 25, 27, 29). The reader senses that Matthew has the mind and attitude of a convert from Judaism who loves its institutions and shares many of its convictions, but who is profoundly troubled by what he considers to be its inability to grasp the fuller truth God has now revealed in Jesus Christ.

This truth is not antithetical to the faith of Judaism, but it is more than a mere supplement. Christianity is for Matthew the divinely disclosed fulfillment of the law and of Jewish hopes; he cannot comprehend that those who stand in the tradition of the law could fail to discern the truth as it is in Jesus. In presenting his Gospel, therefore, Matthew meets his Jewish opponents on their own ground, arguing from scripture and employing typically Jewish methods of debate.

But although the Gospel of Matthew contains polemics against Judaism, it is not written primarily as a polemical document; rather, it is a book of instruction for those living in a situation of tension with Jews. The author does

---

[5] The classic statement of this position is given by B. H. Streeter, in *The Four Gospels* (London: Macmillan, 1924). Streeter connects each of the Gospels with one of the four great centers of Christianity.

[6] See the discussion of the possibility of this area as the place of origin of Matthew by B. W. Bacon, *Studies in Matthew* (New York: Holt, 1930), pp. 24–36.

not refute the claims of the Jewish scriptures; he claims instead that the Church is the true Israel,[7] while the people that calls itself "Israel" has actually forfeited that claim by its failure to recognize Jesus as God's Messiah.

The theory has been advanced that the primary aim of Matthew was "to supply, from the treasure of the past, material for the homiletical and liturgical use of the Gospel in the future."[8] But apart from the traces of liturgical phraseology that have been introduced into the material included by Matthew in the Sermon on the Mount,[9] there seems to be no greater interest in worship here than in any of the other Gospels. A more fitting characterization of the book is a manual of Church instruction and administration, roughly comparable to the Dead Sea community's so-called Manual of Discipline.[10] In our examination of the themes and motifs that characterize the Gospel of Matthew, we shall see how devoted the author is to the matter of maintaining order in the Church.

STRUCTURE IN MATTHEW'S GOSPEL

Many interpreters of Matthew have drawn attention to the fondness for structure which is evident throughout the book. In the genealogy that opens the book, the author has arranged the generations in sets of 14, even though this process obviously requires the omission of several links in the genealogical sequence (Matt. 1:2–17). But the most striking instance of Matthew's having structured his material is in the main body of the Gospel, which he has divided into five sections, each of which concludes with some such phrase as "When Jesus had finished these sayings . . ." (cf. Matt. 7:28; 11:1; 13:53; 19:1; 26:1). Each of the sections begins with a series of narratives concerning the activities of Jesus, and each concludes with an extended discourse. Preceding the first such section is the story of the birth and infancy of Jesus; following the fifth discourse is the account of the Passion and Resurrection. The opening and closing parts of the Gospel are, however, far more than mere prologue and epilogue; they are essential elements of the story as a whole. The structure of the Gospel of Matthew can be viewed schematically as shown on the following page.

[7] This understanding of the Church by Matthew has been convincingly developed by W. Trilling, *Das Wahre Israel* (Leipzig: St. Benno-Verlag, 1959).

[8] Thus G. D. Kilpatrick, *The Origins of the Gospel According to St. Matthew* (Oxford: Clarendon Press, 1946), p. 99.

[9] For example, the Beatitudes and the Lord's Prayer are both given by Luke in simpler form than by Matthew. Luke has Jesus pray simply, "Father"; Matthew has the more elaborate form suited for liturgical use: "Our Father who art in heaven." Luke presents the Beatitudes as direct address ("Blessed are *you* poor . . ."), while Matthew reproduces them as general statements ("Blessed are *the* poor in spirit").

[10] This theory was developed by K. Stendahl in his *The School of St. Matthew* (Uppsala: C. W. K. Gleerup, 1954; rev. ed., Philadelphia: Fortress Press, 1968).

I. The Coming of Jesus as God's Messiah—Chapters 1 and 2

II. The Ministry of the Messiah—Chapters 3 through 25

   1. Preparation and Program of the Ministry—Chapters 3–7
      Narrative: Baptism, Temptation, and Call of Disciples—
         3:1–4:25
      Discourse: Sermon on the Mount—Chapters 5–7

   2. The Authority of Jesus—Chapters 8 through 10
      Narrative: Healing and Forgiveness of Sins—8:1–9:38
      Discourse: Sending of the Twelve Disciples—10:1–42

   3. The Kingdom and Its Coming—Chapters 11–13
      Narrative: Controversy Resulting from Men's Inability to Dis-
         cern the Kingdom's In-breaking—11:1–12:50
      Discourse: The Parables of the Kingdom—13:1–58

   4. Life of the New Community—Chapters 14–18
      Narrative: Anticipations of Hostility toward and Common Life
         within the New Community—14:1–17:27
      Discourse: Regulations for the Common Life—18:1–35
   5. The Consummation of the Age—Chapters 19–25
      Narrative: Intensified Conflict between Jesus and Judaism—
         19:1–24:2
      Discourse: The End of the Age (Synoptic Apocalypse)—
         24:3–25:46

III. The Humiliation and Exaltation of the Messiah—Chapters 26–28
    The Passion and the Resurrection Stories; The Final Commission-
    ing of the Disciples for the World Mission

A careful reading of the Gospel following this outline will disclose that Matthew has not followed through his scheme with complete consistency. In Section II (4), for example, it is difficult to differentiate between narrative and discourse. In Sections II (1) and II (2), however, there is no mistaking the division, since the narrative portion in each case closes with a summarizing account of Jesus's public ministry. Thus Matthew 4:23 reads:

> And he went about all Galilee, teaching in their synagogues and preaching the gospel of the kingdom and healing every disease and every infirmity among the people.

And Matthew 9:35 reads similarly:

> And Jesus went about all the cities and villages, teaching in their synagogues and preaching the gospel of the kingdom, and healing every disease and every infirmity.

The other subsections of Section II are *not* thus marked off by summarizing statements.[11]

Some interpreters have suggested that the structure of Matthew's central section is a conscious imitation of the Torah. Thus Jesus would be giving the new law on the mountain in Galilee as Moses had given the original law on the mountain in Sinai. But this proposal has several weaknesses. First, there is no real development in Matthew of the image of Jesus as a second Moses,[12] although Moses is depicted as appearing to him on the Mount of the Transfiguration (Matt. 17:3ff), as is the case in the other synoptic accounts. More significantly, one of the main arguments of Matthew is that it is precisely the law (of Moses) and the prophets that have their fulfillment in Jesus (Matt. 5:17). In addition to this explicit reference to the fulfillment of the law, the book is marked from beginning to end by the claim that what God has done in Jesus Christ has been to effect the fulfillment of the scriptures. This leads us to an examination of the main themes developed by Matthew.

GOD'S MIGHTY WORKS

Although all the Gospel writers present a picture of Jesus marked by marvelous powers on his part and by miraculous events that accompany his ministry, Matthew lays greater stress on this than do the other evangelists. The birth story consists almost entirely of divine disclosures through dreams and miraculous occurrences, chief among which is the supernatural conception of Jesus in the virgin's womb. Only slightly less wonderful is the guiding star that led the Magi to the birthplace. All these miracles are told in distinctive passages.

Matthew reproduced nearly all the miracle stories found in his sources, Mark and Q. At times he has abridged them; at other times he has expanded them. On occasion his modification has had the effect of heightening the miraculous element, such as when the ruler's daughter is not merely at the point of death, but dead (cf. Mark 5:23 with Matt. 9:18), and when the blind man at Jericho in Mark 10:46 becomes two men (Matt. 20:30). But for the most part, Matthew's changes in the miracle stories serve his theological objectives by concentrating on the faith of the persons healed, or on the authority of Jesus, or on the demands of discipleship.[13]

The sheer joy in the miraculous, however, comes out most clearly in

[11] This and other inconsistencies in the structural arrangement of Matthew have been noted by F. V. Filson in his article, "Broken Patterns in the Gospel of Matthew," *Journal of Biblical Literature*, LXXV (1956), 17ff. For another view, see Jack Dean Kingsbury, *Matthew: Structure, Christology, Kingdom* (Philadelphia: Fortress Press, 1975), pp. 1–37.

[12] See the treatment of the theme, "New Exodus and New Moses," in W. D. Davies, *The Setting of the Sermon on the Mount* (Cambridge, Eng.: Cambridge University Press, 1964), especially pp. 92, 93.

[13] The way in which Matthew has brought out these motifs in the miracle stories, partly by expansion of his sources and partly by condensing them, is set forth in detail by H. J. Held in his long essay, "Matthew as Interpreter of the Miracle Stories," in *Tradition and Interpretation in Matthew*, by G. Bornkamm, G. Barth, and H. J. Held (Philadelphia: Westminster Press, 1963), pp. 164–299.

Matthew's account of the empty tomb. Mark soberly describes the stone as already rolled back, and a young man present who announces that Jesus has been raised from the dead. Matthew reports a great earthquake, an angel descending from heaven, the terror that strikes down the guards. At the death of Jesus, according to Matthew alone, there had been an earthquake, and the bodies of many saints were raised even before the Resurrection of Jesus took place (27:52). The intention of all this is not simply to impress the reader with miraculous detail, but to demonstrate that God was at work throughout the whole of the earthly life of Jesus, and that his (God's) action had culminated in the greatest of all miracles, the Resurrection.

THE SCRIPTURES ARE FULFILLED

God's action in Jesus's behalf was not to be thought of as arbitrary or random; rather, it was the unfolding of a divine plan which the eye of faith could see as having been given beforehand in the Hebrew scriptures.

The Fulfillment of "Prophecy"

The foretelling of Jesus's ministry was not limited to the obviously prophetic sections of the Old Testament, but included passages that did not appear to be predictive at all, or that to an outsider might not even seem to apply. At least one scripture quoted by Matthew cannot be found in the text of the Hebrew Bible as we know it; there is nothing in the Old Testament that corresponds to the words that purport to be a quotation from the prophets: "He shall be called a Nazarene" (Matt. 2:23). Possibly the Old Testament reference the writer had in mind was Judges 13:5, or Isaiah 11:1, or a combination of the two. In the first of these passages, a person who in a special way is dedicated wholly to God is called a Nazirite; in the second, the coming Messiah of the Davidic line is called (in Hebrew) *nezer* (meaning "a shoot which springs from a cut-down stump"). The meaning is that, although the royal line that began with David is apparently dead, there will yet come one from that family who will be the ideal king. Since the Jews believed that the consonants (which alone were written in the original text of the Hebrew Bible) were sacred, and that they were capable of several meanings, depending on what vowels were supplied to fill out the words, perhaps Matthew recognized that a different set of vowels used with *nezer* would provide scriptural confirmation for Jesus's association with Nazareth.

A distinctive feature of Matthew's quotations from scripture is an introductory formula he uses eleven times: 1:22; 2:5; 2:15; 2:17; 2:23; 4:14; 8:17; 12:17; 13:35; 21:4; 27:9–10. With variations, the formula runs: "This was done to fulfill what was spoken by the Lord through the prophet. . . ." It must be acknowledged that, by current standards of biblical interpretation, none of these prophecies means in its original context what Matthew has made it mean in his setting. For example, "Out of Egypt have I called my son" is in Hosea a reference to the exodus of the nation Israel from its bondage in Egypt; here it is a prediction of God's calling Jesus back from his temporary residence in Egypt after the death of Herod, who had threatened his life. In at least one instance, Matthew seems to have created a story (27:3–10) to fit his combination of two or three prophecies (Zech. 11:12–13; Jer. 32:6–15; 18:2–3). The actions of the prophets in none of these passages has reference to the betrayal of the Messiah or to money received as a bribe. None of the other Gospels reports this incident at all, so it would appear to be a product of Matthew's concern to demonstrate how God's purpose revealed in scripture was fulfilled even in Jesus's betrayal by one of his own followers.

Although the prophecy of the king coming on an ass seems to lie behind the Markan version of Jesus's entry into Jerusalem, Matthew makes the allusion to Zechariah 9 explicit. In doing so, however, he shows that he does not understand the nature of Hebrew poetic form in which the prophecy is set forth. Hebrew poetry is characterized by parallelism, in which the meaning of the first line is echoed or amplified in the second:

> The earth is the Lord's, and the fulness thereof,
> The world and those who dwell therein.
>
> —PSALM 24:1

When Zechariah wrote of Israel's king coming "on an ass, and on a colt the foal of an ass" (Zech. 9:9, as rendered literally from the Hebrew in the King James Version), he had in mind only one animal, as the other evangelists have recognized. Matthew, on the other hand, finding mention of two animals in the text, reports Jesus as giving orders to procure for his entry "an ass . . . and a colt."

Although it may not be warranted to speak of a school of interpretation standing behind these formula quotations,[14] there is a parallel between the method of applying the scriptures freely to the present situation, as was done at Qumran, and Matthew's procedure. In both instances, it was assumed that the group interpreting the scripture was an eschatological community awaiting the last days and the consummation of God's purpose. To them had been granted special insight into the future by means of the unlocking of scriptural mysteries. Therefore, even though—or perhaps more precisely *because*—the surface meaning of a passage of scripture did not seem to apply to the present, the inspired interpreter could see in these writings a clue to the divine purpose at work in the present historical circumstances.

The Fulfillment of the Law

The scriptures were also understood by Matthew to be fulfilled in another than the prophetic sense: that is, in fulfillment of the ethical demand contained in the law and the prophets. This claim is set forth in the opening section of the Sermon on the Mount (Matt. 5–7). Although Luke has also re-

[14] This is the view of K. Stendahl, *The School of St. Matthew* (Uppsala: C. W. K. Gleerup, 1954), especially pp. 20–35. For a study of school tradition in the Greco-Roman world and its bearing on biblical interpretation, see R. Alan Culpepper, *The Johannine School* (Missoula, Mont.: Scholars Press, 1975).

Mount of the Beatitudes, a traditional site identified as the hill referred to in Matthew 5, where Jesus is depicted as having assembled his disciples for instruction, just as Moses had gathered his people at Mt. Sinai in the days of the Exodus from Egypt. Nearby is Capernaum, which was probably the home base for Jesus's mission activity.   (*Gordon N. Converse*)

produced a "sermon" (Luke 6:20–49) that shares some features in common with Matthew's better-known sermon—both evangelists apparently drawing on Q—Matthew has given distinctive qualities to his version, and has included far more than Luke. The Beatitudes which open the Sermon show that Matthew does not regard ethics as a matter of mere conformity to legal standards; membership in the people of God cannot be attained by meeting legalistic requirements. Rather, God's people are those who have received as a gift of his grace all that they have. By this world's standards they are the poor, the bereaved, the despised, the persecuted; but in the age to come, it will be evident that they are the special beneficiaries of divine favor: theirs is the kingdom, they shall inherit the earth, they shall see God (Matt. 5:3–8). They are the salt of the earth, the light of the world: let them perform now their proper functions in doing good works, that men may glorify their heavenly Father (Matt. 5:13–16).

The heart of Matthew's attitude toward the law, however, is disclosed in two passages: the general statements about the law (Matt. 5:17–20) and the series of antitheses ("You have heard that it was said to the men of old . . . but

I say to you . . ." Matt. 5:21–48). Since these statements are found only in Matthew in this form, it is likely that they originated with him, or at least that they have been shaped by him to suit his purposes. Let us examine this passage in three parts:

> (1) Think not that I have come to abolish the law and the prophets;
> I have come not to abolish them but to fulfill them.
>
> —MATTHEW 5:17

The first part of the verse implies that the charge has been leveled against Jesus (or against the Church which honors him) that Christianity seeks the destruction of the Jewish law. This accusation is denied, countered by the claim that Jesus intends to *fulfill* the law and the prophets. "Fulfill" cannot mean in this context what it meant in the formula quotations discussed above; instead, it means that Jesus has come to accomplish what the law promised, to actualize in human existence the will of God which the law summons humans to obey. That the weight falls on the ethical demand is obvious from the third general statement in verses 19 and 20.

> (2) For truly, I say to you, till heaven and earth pass away, not an iota,
> not a dot, will pass from the law until all is accomplished.
>
> —MATTHEW 5:18

A parallel to this statement appears in Luke 16:17, where it is apparently ironical; that is, Jesus mocks the Pharisees who would rather have the whole creation pass away than for a single stroke or dot of the written law to be changed. As Matthew reproduces the saying, however, it is not ironical but affirms the unchangeability of the law with an absoluteness that even some of the rabbinic interpreters did not enjoin. Matthew is convinced that what has been wrong with the nation that called itself Israel is that it has not expected the law to be fulfilled in the proper and complete way; now the new community for which he is the spokesman looks forward to the true and total accomplishment of everything promised and commanded in the law. Although this principle is not carried out with complete consistency in the interpretation of the law that Matthew gives in the antitheses, the point of view expressed there is a full, radical affirmation of the law. There is no hint of reducing the law to a single principle, such as the law of love, nor is the law presented as an instrument that will drive people to despair of their own moral abilities and thereby throw them back in repentance upon the grace of God. Interpreters of Jesus have read these passages in this way, but without warrant from the texts themselves.

> (3) Whoever then relaxes one of the least of these commandments and
> teaches men so, shall be called least in the kingdom of heaven; but
> he who does them and teaches them shall be called great in the
> kingdom of heaven. For I tell you, unless your righteousness exceeds that of the scribes and Pharisees, you will never enter the
> kingdom of heaven.
>
> —MATTHEW 5:19–20

Several features of this astonishing passage must be noted. First, the role of the member of the community is twofold: doing and teaching. Unlike the Pharisees, whose teaching may conform to the law but whose way of life does not (see Matt. 23:3), the true child of the kingdom teaches rightly and lives rightly. The person who aspires to leadership by assuming a teaching role in the community takes upon himself a serious and solemn responsibility.

The second part of this passage, rather than denouncing the Pharisees as immoral persons, calls for the member of the true Israel to go beyond them in obedience to the law. The popular caricature of the Pharisee is that of a pedant, a prude, a prig—and a hypocrite. While denouncing the hypocrisy of the Pharisees (especially in chapter 23), Matthew has no quarrel with the moral demands they make; his complaint is that they do not live up to their own standards. The new people of God should not only live up to Pharisaic standards, but should go beyond them in the stringency of their interpretation of and conformity to the law. The law, therefore, is understood to be binding in a most radical way.[15]

JESUS'S ATTITUDE TOWARD THE LAW.   In the synoptic tradition as a whole, Jesus is represented as at times setting aside what is explicitly permitted or prohibited in the law, and at other times as going beyond the statement of the law to a more profound demand. Of the first type is the teaching about divorce, a practice explicitly permitted in Deuteronomy 24:1. The rabbis of the first century disagreed as to the conditions implied in the specification of adequate grounds for divorce ("because he has found some indecency in her"), some interpreting the phrase strictly to apply only to adultery, others interpreting "indecency" more broadly. According to the version of Jesus's word on divorce in Mark 10:11–12, there were to be *no* conditions under which divorce and remarriage were to be permitted. In Matthew's versions of this saying (he reproduces the word twice: 5:31–32 and 19:9), there is provision for divorce in case of "unchastity." In this passage, Matthew therefore depicts Jesus as less radical than he actually seems to have been, according to the older form of the tradition preserved in Mark.

On the other hand, the radical nature of obedience is powerfully set forth in the words of Jesus on murder (5:21–26), on adultery (5:27–30), on retaliation (5:38–42), and especially on love of enemies (5:43–48). In each instance the moral issue is moved out of the realm where one can calculate what is legally permissible and what is not. Not the overt act of murder, but hatred of one's brother is forbidden. Not extramarital intercourse, but lusting after a woman who is not one's wife is condemned. Not acquiescence in performing a burdensome duty, but willing cooperation in demands and obligations is enjoined. One is not to have love only for those who are friendly and close at hand, but for one's enemies as well.

These commandments are radical not merely in the sense that they are

---

[15] See in this connection the essay of G. Barth, "Matthew's Understanding of the Law," in G. Bornkamm, G. Barth, and H. J. Held, *Tradition and Interpretation in Matthew* (Philadelphia: Westminster Press, 1963), pp. 85–105; also H. C. Kee, "Introduction and Commentary on Matthew," in *Interpreter's Commentary* (New York and Nashville: Abingdon Press, 1970).

stringent and demanding, but because they get at the root of human relationships rather than dealing with the externals of human interchanges. It is too
simple to say that Jesus is here pictured as concerned with the spirit rather
than the letter; he is concerned about the letter of the law as well, as we see
from his appeal, in defense of his position on divorce, to the prior principle of
God's intention in instituting marriage: "[So] God created man ... male and
female ... and they became one flesh." "What therefore God has joined together, let not man put asunder" (Mark 10:6–9; Matt. 19:4–6—cf. Gen. 1:27;
2:24).

The basic appeal of the ethics of Jesus as shown in Matthew is to the
nature and purpose of God himself:

> But I say to you, love your enemies and pray for those who persecute
> you, *so that you may be sons of your Father who is in heaven;* for he makes his
> sun rise on the evil and on the good, and sends rain on the just and on
> the unjust. . . . You, therefore, must be perfect, as your heavenly Father
> is perfect.
>
> —MATTHEW 5:44, 45, 48

The term "perfect" here does not mean simply absence of moral imperfection,
but the wholeness and singlemindedness by which God goes about fulfilling
his purposes and by which standard humankind is called to obey him.[16] Luke
has toned down the force of this demand in his parallel form of this saying by
substituting the word "merciful" (Luke 6:36), but Matthew is closer to what
was likely the original intent of Jesus's word.

Obedience to the law, as Matthew describes it, was not confined to *ethical* performance, however: it included participation in such typical Jewish acts
of piety as prayer (6:5–8), giving of alms (6:1–4), fasting (6:16–18), and apparently offering the appropriate sacrifices as prescribed by the Temple regulations in the law. These may have been empty requirements by Matthew's
time, since the Temple was no longer standing,[17] but they show that in principle Matthew did not make our modern distinction between the ceremonial
law (as not binding on Christians) and the moral law (as valid).

having to do c̄ right & wrong

THE WAY OF RIGHTEOUSNESS

A characteristic term of Matthew's is "righteousness." He has introduced incidents into this account where the term is used, and inserted it in accounts
where he is paralleling Luke. (An example of the latter is Matt. 6:33: while
Luke 12:31 reads "seek first his kingdom," Matthew adds "and his righteousness.")

[16] See the discussion of this term by Barth, "Matthew's Understanding," pp. 97–103.

[17] K. W. Clark has sought to show that, even after the destruction of the Temple in
A.D. 70, the sacrificial worship was continued, presumably in the ruins. This would account
for mention of bringing sacrifices to the altar (in Matt. 5:23), as well as the reference to the
Temple cult as continuing, in Heb. 8:4, 5. See "Worship in the Jerusalem Temple after A.D.
70," *New Testament Studies*, VI (July 1960), 269ff.

The theme of righteousness is laid down at the very beginning of Jesus's ministry in Matthew's account (3:15). At this point in the narrative of the baptism of Jesus, John protests that he is inferior to Jesus and needs to be baptized by him. Jesus, however, insists that "it is fitting for us to *fulfill all righteousness.*" Each of these italicized words is important. The demands of God's will are to be *fully* met. Even Jesus—nay, Jesus most of all—is under obligation to meet these demands. Righteousness is to be complied with in its *totality;* partial obedience will not suffice. Although the context in Matthew 3 does not tell us precisely what "righteousness" implies, we can see from the evangelist's use of the term throughout the Gospel what it involves, and how Jesus is presented as the embodiment of righteousness. But that the term does not mean only ethical performance according to the will of God is made clear from Matthew 21:32, which speaks of John the Baptist as having come "in the way of righteousness."

There is an eschatological dimension to righteousness which is important for Matthew. This aspect is implied in Matthew 6:33, where "kingdom" and "righteousness" are linked. That is, the will of God is not fully achieved by the obedience of individuals; the whole sweep of human history is involved in the unfolding of God's purpose. Only when his goals are fulfilled in history—when his kingdom has come in its fullness—will the "way of righteousness" reach its divinely determined end. One aspect of that goal is set forth graphically by Matthew 25:31–46, in the Parable of the Last Judgment. Strictly speaking, this is not a parable, but a highly stylized picture of the end of history, when all people—Jew and Gentile—are brought to account before God. In it we can sense Matthew's blending of eschatology and ethics: Human behavior is the prime criterion in God's action to effect the consummation of history.

The specifics of the ethical demand are spelled out in the Sermon on the Mount as a whole, though especially in the antitheses, in which Jesus reportedly contrasts his interpretation of what the law requires with the way it was understood by his Jewish contemporaries. Apart from one instance in which "righteousness" is used as a term for the alms given by the pious (Matt. 6:1), the word itself occurs in the Sermon in more general statements. That it has been introduced into the tradition by Matthew is evident from the comparison with the Lukan version of the same passages. Luke reads: "Blessed are you that hunger now" (Luke 6:21); Matthew reads, "Blessed are those who hunger and thirst *for righteousness*" (Matt. 5:6). In contrast to Luke, who simply reports the blessedness of those whose names will be reviled on account of the Son of Man (Luke 6:22), Matthew has a unique passage in which he declares blessed those who are persecuted "for righteousness' sake." It is not only for confession of the name of Christ ("on my account," Matt. 5:11), but for following the way of life called forth by Jesus's interpretation of the will of God.

Matthew does not stop with the general appeal to do "good works" (Matt. 5:16); in the Parable of the Last Judgment he gives concrete examples: feeding the hungry, clothing the naked, visiting the imprisoned, welcoming strangers into one's home. Conversely, to fail to perform these acts of mercy is to invite condemnation on the Day of Judgment. Yet the parable does not imply that works of kindness are to be done *in order to* achieve a reward. On the contrary, those who (according to the parable) performed them did so solely on the grounds that they had encountered another human being who was in need. They are represented as wholly astonished that they have done anything worthy of reward: "Lord, when did we see thee hungry . . . ?"

The way of righteousness, therefore, is not a path of legalism, by which the commandments are obeyed in order to "keep the rules." It is a way of life according to which the commandment to love is put into concrete action. It is not the one who says "Lord, Lord," but the one who does the Father's will who enters the kingdom (Matt. 7:21); it is not the one who *hears* Jesus's words, but the one who *does* them whose work endures (Matt. 7:26). It is to such, Matthew tells us (25:34), that the king will say at the judgment: "Come, O blessed of my Father, inherit the kingdom prepared for you from the foundation of the world." It is they who are in truth "the righteous" (25:37).

Righteousness: A Community Responsibility

The way of righteousness is more than a matter of individual behavior; for Matthew it involves the life of the individual in the corporate experience of the community as well. In Matthew 18, the writer has reworked synoptic material in such a way as to lay stress on community responsibility within the Church. Mark's account of the dispute of the disciples among themselves, as to which was greatest, is modified by Matthew (18:1–5) to a general statement that becoming humble like a little child is the way to greatness in the kingdom. Further, every true disciple is to be ever concerned for the welfare of the weaker members of the community. He is to exercise great care lest he offend one of the "little ones" (18:6–9). The Parable of the Lost Sheep, which in Luke (15:3–7) depicts the joy of God at the recovery of one of his lost creatures, has become in Matthew a warning to the Church to guard with care even the lowliest of its members from harm. In a unique verse (18:14), the point is made that God will hold the Church responsible for the loss of even "one of these little ones."

In 18:15–35, Matthew has brought together material from several sources to stress the obligation the Christian has for trying to restore an erring brother and to forgive one who has offended. Not seven times, but seventy times seven, the true follower of Jesus must be willing to forgive. A parable which must originally have carried the point that one dare not take advantage of God's forgiveness, lest it be withheld in the Judgment,[18] has been attached by Matthew to the appeal that the Christian be willing to forgive a brother or sister repeatedly. While the parable does not intend to depict God as in every way like the king—complete with his own official torturers (18:34, where "jailers" should be translated "torturers"), he does want to impress his reader with the seriousness of the command of Jesus for Christian brothers and sisters to forgive one another.

---

[18] J. Jeremias, *Parables of Jesus,* rev. ed. (New York: Scribner's, 1963), pp. 210–14. The Kingdom of God in its present form is discussed by Kingsbury, *Matthew: Structure, Christology, Kingdom,* pp. 137–49.

GOOD AND BAD IN THE CHURCH

While Matthew, as we have seen, sets before the Church the goal of perfection, he is fully aware that the Church, like any other human institution, will have obedient members and disobedient ones, and that the leadership must be prepared to deal with disobedience. The mixed nature of the Christian community is clearly pictured in Matthew's versions of the Parables of the Kingdom, together with the interpretation of these parables which he offers. In addition to the general terms "kingdom" and "kingdom of heaven" (kingdom of God), Matthew speaks of the "kingdom of the Son of Man" and the "kingdom of the Father." The former refers to the Church in the present age in its mixed form, including good and bad. The kingdom of the Father is the age beyond the consummation, when only the faithful are present among the people of God.

In the Parable of the Weeds, which is found only in Matthew (13:24–30), and in the interpretation of it that is given (13:36–40), we have two different points. In the original form of the parable, the point was that the messenger of the Gospel should go about his work without stopping to evaluate the outcome or to remedy unwanted results. The focus of the parable is on the eschatological Judgment, portrayed under the figure of the harvest. God will evaluate on that day; the human task is to sow, leaving the results to God. Matthew, in the interpretation attributed to Jesus, has transformed this story into an allegory, warning members of the Church that some of them are worthy and some are not. The latter will be cast into the furnace of fire, where they weep and gnash their teeth (13:42). The task of sorting out on the Day of Judgment will be handled by the Son of Man, whose angels will gather "out of *his* kingdom" (the kingdom of the Son of Man) the causes of sin and the evildoers. But the righteous "will shine like the sun in the *kingdom of the Father.*"

The Parable of the Net (Matt. 13:47–50), which originally was addressed to the messengers of the good news, encouraging them to leave to God the estimation of the results, is likewise made into an allegory warning those in the community that they should not be "bad fish" whose destiny is to be thrown into the furnace. What we see at work in Matthew's modification of this tradition is concern about the mixed state of affairs in the Church. He is here warning the members to examine themselves, to see whether they will find their lot with the good or the bad on the Day of Judgment.[19]

Although there is no contrast between the kingdom of the Son of Man and the kingdom of the Father in Matthew's addition to the Parable of the Feast (Matt. 22:1–14; compare Luke 14:16–24), the lesson is once more that the people of God are a mixed group. Luke's version of the parable stresses that the religious outcasts have responded to the Gospel invitation and are now certain of a place in the eschatological community. Matthew reshaped the parable so that those who have finally come to the feast are "both good and bad" (Matt. 22:10). Among them is one man who lacks the appropriate

---

[19] A detailed analysis of these parables is given by J. Jeremias in *The Parables of Jesus,* rev. ed. (New York: Scribner's, 1963), pp. 81–85, 224–27. Jeremias shows that on the grounds of vocabulary alone, the interpretations of these parables cannot be regarded as coming from the tradition; they originate with Matthew.

garb. He is cast out into outer darkness. Presumably the garment is the cloak of righteousness, which conforms to what we have already seen to be a dominant theme in Matthew.

The Church cannot wait, however, until the Judgment to settle matters of good and evil within its own group. There must be some system of adjudicating disputes and some structure of authority. Matthew alone makes provision for this need. The story of Peter's confession of Jesus as the Christ is expanded by Matthew (16:17–19) to include the designation by Jesus of Peter as the rock on which the Church will be built. This passage cannot be original, since Mark, whose interest in Peter is great and obvious, would scarcely have omitted it from his account. Although "Church" would not here mean institution but eschatological community,[20] it is probably anachronistic to attribute such a statement to Jesus.[21] For Matthew, however, Peter's central role is not that of broad ecclesiastical administration but the exercise of authority in regulating the inner life of the community. The binding and loosing mentioned here are repeated in Matthew 18:18, and echoed in John 20:22–23. One of the functions of the rabbis, referred to in Jewish tradition as "binding and loosing," was the formulation of interpretations of the legal parts of the Old Testament in order to determine the situations in which a given law was or was not applicable. Matthew has obvious interest in and respect for rabbinic practices. In Matthew 13:52, Jesus is quoted as comparing a "scribe who has been trained for the kingdom of heaven" with "a householder who brings out of his treasure what is new and what is old." The leadership role in the Church, therefore, includes the task of interpreting the law—whether old or new—in relation to the daily needs of the Church's life.

The strange and difficult Parable of the Laborers in the Vineyard, found only in Matthew (20:1–16) was originally a vindication of Jesus against his critics.[22] God's nature is to be merciful toward all; he does not match his grace to human performance. By adding the free-floating saying, "So the last will be first, and the first last," Matthew has shifted the meaning, so that the parable is in his setting a defense of the fact that the late-arriving Gentiles gain priority over God's people, the Jews, who were there from the beginning. As was the case with Paul in his struggle over the place of Israel in the purpose of God, Matthew here suggests that they have lost their place of special favor in God's sight. Whether this implication was intended by Matthew in 20:1–16 or not, it is clearly his meaning in his addition to the Parable of the Wicked Tenants in 21:33–46. Verse 43 reads:

> Therefore I tell you, the kingdom of God will be taken away from you and given to a nation producing the fruits of it.

[20] For a defense of the authenticity of these words, see K. L. Schmidt, "The Church," in *Bible Key Words*, ed. J. R. Coates (New York: Harper & Row, 1951), pp. 35–50; also translated by G. W. Bromiley, in *Theological Dictionary of the New Testament*, vol. 3 (Grand Rapids: Eerdman, 1965), pp. 501–36.

[21] O. Cullmann in the revised edition of his *Peter: Disciple, Apostle, Martyr* (Philadelphia: Westminster Press, 1962), argues that the words were spoken in a post-Resurrection appearance, rather than at Caesarea Philippi (pp. 161–217).

[22] See Jeremias, *The Parables of Jesus*, pp. 33–40.

Lest the reader be in any doubt as to the force of these words, he continues:

> When the chief priests and the Pharisees heard his parables, they perceived that he was speaking about them.

The most interesting feature of this prediction that the kingdom of God will be given to others is the use of the term "nation" to refer to the Church. The true nation, Israel, is no longer the Jewish people, Matthew declares: it is the Church.

What of the fate of Old Israel? In one of the bitterest passages in all the New Testament, Matthew describes the Jewish leaders as inviting upon themselves full responsibility for the death of Jesus: "His blood be on us and our children!" (Matt. 27:25). Regrettably, this bit of polemic has been seized upon by anti-Semites ever since. But Matthew did not stop there: in 23:32–36 he went on to bring down on the heads of the Jewish leadership the guilt for the murder of all God's messengers, from the days of Cain and Abel to the present. Israel has, as Matthew sees it, forfeited its right to be called the people of God; that privilege has been granted the Church.

EXPECTATION OF THE END

The theme of the nearness of the kingdom of God (literally, of the heavens) is sounded by John the Baptist, according to Matthew. The other Gospels speak only of its preaching of repentance. Drawing on Markan and Q material, Matthew builds up a vivid picture of John as announcing the coming of the kingdom, and as the instrument by which Jesus inaugurates the way of righteousness (Matt. 3:14). Only in Matthew, among the synoptic writers, is John aware of Jesus's sonship at the moment of his baptism (Matt. 3:16). Jesus is represented as taking up John's message when, in Matthew 4:17, he begins his public ministry. The eschatological nature of the kingdom is emphatically stressed in Matthew's account of Jesus and John.

The summarizing statements in Matthew 4:23 and 9:35 concerning Jesus's ministry both use the peculiar phrase "the gospel of the kingdom," thereby pointing to the eschatological nature of his message. The signs that point to the coming of the kingdom are evident in the works of healing and the exorcisms Jesus performs. Similarly, the discourse on the sending of the Twelve (Matt. 10) instructs the messengers that they are to preach the nearness of the kingdom (10:7) and to manifest the signs of its coming. The eschatological dimension of their work is heightened by the inclusion in the mission discourse of Markan material that is found in the synoptic Apocalypse (cf. Matt. 10:17–25 with Mark 13:9–13), and which is obviously tied in with the judgment that Matthew believes fell when Jerusalem was destroyed; the Markan passage (Mark 13:9–13), which Matthew has lifted out of its context and inserted in his mission discourse, leads directly into the prediction of the destruction of Jerusalem (Mark 13:14ff; Matt. 24:15ff). From various parts of Mark and Q, Matthew has brought together a series of sayings he has modified in order to point up one of his major concerns, the coming (*parousia*) of the Son of Man: Matthew 24:3 (where mention of the consummation is also added to the Markan form of the word); 24:27, where a Q word mentioning the Son of Man "in his day" is converted into an explicit prediction of the *parousia;* 24:29–31, where the Markan prediction of the coming of the Son of Man is expanded; 24:37, 39, where the Q expression "days of the Son of Man" becomes a direct reference to the *parousia;* 24:42, where Matthew introduces a distinctive word about watching, lest the Lord come on a day when he is not expected.

In three parables included by Matthew in his version of the apocalyptic discourse, the point is in each case the need for watchfulness in view of the delayed *parousia.* The Parable of the Faithful and Wise Servant (Matt. 24:45–51) furnishes both encouragement for those who remain faithful and ready in spite of the delay ("My Lord delays his coming," Matt. 24:48), and a solemn warning of the judgment that will fall on those who are not watching at the time of his coming. It reinforces the point we noted earlier, that the Church of Matthew is composed of worthy and unworthy, watchful and indifferent. In the Parable of the Ten Maidens (Matt. 25:1–13) the point is once more that when the *parousia* occurs, some will be ready and some will not. "No one knows the day nor the hour—watch, therefore." The Parable of the Talents, which like that of the Wise Servant comes from Q, calls for faithful stewardship of one's gifts during the interval before the coming of the master. That the interval is protracted in Matthew's view is evident from his adding the phrase (25:19): "after a long period of time" the Lord came again. Twice Matthew underscores the catastrophic consequences of failure to be ready, by appending his gloomy warning: there will be weeping and gnashing of teeth (24:51; 25:30).

There are hints in Matthew, however, that the interval between the first coming of Christ and his *parousia* in glory is not to be viewed as an insignificant period of waiting. Rather, a new responsibility and a new reality have come into being as a consequence of the Resurrection. The new responsibility is the obligation of the followers of Jesus to preach the Gospel and to instruct all the people of the world. In contrast to the universal outreach commanded in the post-Resurrection words of Jesus in Matthew 28:19, 20, the mission discourse specifically instructs the disciples to limit their evangelism to the "lost sheep of the house of Israel" (Matt. 10:5, 6), by which is meant not that all Israel is lost, but that the abandoned ones—the outcasts—from within Israel are to hear the good news. We see in the next chapter that this theme is developed by Luke. Nevertheless, the mission is to the Jews. The mission to the Gentiles has been anticipated, however, in the opening words of Matthew describing Jesus's public ministry (4:12ff, especially v. 15), where Galilee is mentioned as "Galilee of the Gentiles [or nations]." The fact that there will—indeed must—be a mission to the whole world before the consummation can occur is explicitly affirmed in Matthew's apocalyptic discourse, 24:14:

This gospel ... will be preached throughout the whole world [Greek, *oikoumene*], as a testimony to all nations, and then the end will come.

It is a fitting climax to this development, therefore, when the risen Christ commissions his followers to launch this world mission in 28:19, 20.

The new reality referred to above is the Church itself, composed not only of good and bad, but of Jew and Gentile. We have noted that the Church is represented by Matthew as a new nation, which will produce the fruits of righteousness that the people Israel have failed to do (Matt. 21:43). Upon Israel within the then-present generation will fall the doom appropriate to its guilt (Matt. 23:32ff):

> Fill up, then, the measure of your fathers. You serpents, you brood of vipers, how are you to escape being sentenced to hell? Therefore I send you prophets and wise men and scribes, some of whom you will kill and crucify, and some you will scourge in your synagogues and persecute from town to town, that upon you may come all the righteous blood shed on earth from the blood of innocent Abel to the blood of Zechariah the son of Barachiah,[23] whom you murdered between the sanctuary and the altar. Truly I say to you, all this will come upon this generation.

This fearful and vindictive indictment is surely written out of a situation of direct conflict between the growing church of Matthew and the Jewish community, torn as it was with conflict with Rome and with the Church. Although the prediction of doom is addressed against the Pharisees (Matt. 23:13ff), it reads as a denunciation of the whole Jewish nation. These passages tell us a great deal about Matthew and his attitudes; they tell us nothing about Jesus. It is simply not possible to square this cruel invocation of wrath with the command of Jesus—ironically, also reproduced by Matthew (5:44)—to love one's enemies. The supreme irony in Matthew's viewpoint, however, is not that he denounces the Jews, but that he expects the Church to take over so much of Jewish institutions and practices: scribal interpretations, ceremonial requirements, alms, fasting, and so on. He is able to view the Church in this way because, as we have already noted, the Church is for him the true Israel, which takes the place of the nation that did not see in Jesus God's Messiah.

In the interval before the return of the triumphant Son of Man, the new community is to continue to confess him before men: if they fail to do so, they will not be vindicated by him at his *parousia* (Matt. 10:33). This Markan word (Mark 8:38) has been placed by Matthew in the midst of instructions to the messengers of the Gospel. In fulfilling their work as witnesses, they function under the authority of this risen Christ: "All authority in heaven and on earth has been given to me" (Matt. 28:18). It is by this power that they are to carry on their ministry, the specific tasks of which correspond precisely to the ministry Jesus himself performed: healing, exorcisms, preaching the Gospel (Matt. 10:7, 8). In addition, they are now to perform baptisms, and to do so in the trinitarian name of God. This is one of the few instances in the entire New

---

[23] Abel is the first one murdered in the first book of the Bible; Zechariah is the last one to be murdered in the last historical book, 2 Chronicles. Matthew has, however, confused his Zechariahs, since the son of Barachiah was not a priest, but a prophet (Zech. 1:1) and was not murdered, so far as is known.

Dividing the Mount of Olives (in the background) from the Jerusalem Temple Mount, the Kidron Valley has been lined from Hellenistic times with tombs and cemeteries, as well as with monuments honoring worthies of Israel's past.   (*Gordon N. Converse*)

Testament canon of an explicitly trinitarian formula; elsewhere, there are usually only implications of the Trinity (e.g., 2 Cor. 13:14). Their lives are to be characterized by complete obedience to the commandments he has given them during the period of his ministry among them; they are not only to teach these commandments, but to see that they are observed. They may rest assured that, though their Lord is not visibly present, he is nonetheless among them: "Lo, I am with you always, to the close of the age" (Matt. 28:20).

In this way, Matthew alleviates the problem created by the nonfulfillment of the *parousia* expectation. On the one hand, the passage of time must not permit the members of the community to grow lax or to lose their zeal, since the return of the Son of Man is certain; on the other hand, to consider him as absent is to misunderstand the facts, since he has promised his continuing presence in their midst until God's purpose through him is consummated and the old age has given way to the kingdom of the Father.

6

The Mystical Community:
The Gospel of John

WHAT DIFFERENTIATES JOHN
FROM THE OTHER GOSPELS

The narrative scope of the Gospel of John resembles that of the other Gospels—at least in a general way. But the differences are very great, both in content and style.

Unlike Matthew and Luke, John has no stories of Jesus's birth or childhood, and insists that he was born in Nazareth rather than in Bethlehem (John 7:41–42) and that Joseph was his father (John 1:45). Although John is filled with miracle stories about Jesus, none of them reports exorcisms, which play such a prominent role in Mark and the Q tradition. Although Jesus comes to John to seek baptism, there is no report of John actually baptizing Jesus. Yet Jesus and his disciples are described in John 3:22–4:2 as carrying on baptismal activity on their own—something they are never pictured as doing in the synoptics, which do report John's baptizing Jesus. The narratives of John are on several occasions left incomplete—or rather the accounts of an interchange between Jesus and a potential follower (such as with the Samaritan woman at the well in John 4) never really conclude, but instead drift off into lengthy discourses from which the original interrogator is missing.

Still more striking is the difference between Jesus's teaching in the synoptics and his discourses in John. The former consists of loosely grouped series of sayings. Many of them can stand independently of the context in which they are placed by the writers, and indeed they are often inserted at different points from one Gospel to another. In John, Jesus speaks in a lengthy, sometimes repetitive manner, discoursing on a single theme, such as the light of the world or the bread of life. Instead of referring to himself indirectly by a title such as the Son of Man, in John Jesus declares straightforwardly: "I am the light of the world, the vine, the good shepherd." The significance of the feeding of the five thousand is left implicit in the synoptics, although the use of eucharistic language ("he took, he blessed, he broke, he gave") gives strong clues. But in John the discourse on the Bread of Life makes explicit that Jesus is the true, spiritual food of the new covenant people: ". . . whoever eats me will live because of me. This is the bread which came down from heaven, not such as the fathers ate and died; whoever eats this bread will live forever" (John 6:57–58).

Another important stylistic feature characteristic of John is the use of words with double meaning. The author does not want his reader to choose one meaning rather than the other, but to discern that both are appropriate. For example, Jesus's response to Nicodemus is to tell him that, although he is a respected teacher of Israel, he must be born "again" in order to enter God's kingdom. The Greek word, *anōthen,* can mean "from above" or "again." Both meanings are important for John's Jesus: The child of faith (John 3:14–16) enters into a life so completely new it can only be depicted as a new birth, but it is not merely an extension or a repetition of the old life; it is made possible by the spirit that comes from above. Another instance of double meaning may be found in John's references to the lifting up of Jesus (John 3:14; 8:28), apparently pointing to his being raised up on a cross to die. But from John 12:32–34 it is clear that his Crucifixion is at the same time his exaltation, so that the paradox of shameful death and divine glorification are linked (in Greek) in this single ambiguous word, "lift up" the Son of Man.

Similar duality of expression and meaning is evident in John's representation of Jesus's message of hope for the future. Unlike the synoptics, where finding or gaining life is seen as a future expectation (Mark 8:35–38), in John Jesus speaks of life as what the Christian already possesses, and of the new age as having already come: "Whoever hears my words and believes . . . has eternal life; he does not come into judgment but has passed from death to life. . . . The hour is coming and now is, when the dead will hear the voice of the Son of God" (John 5:24–25). The future hope is not abandoned, but it is transformed by the claim that in Jesus the faithful have already begun to experience the life of the age to come. What kind of person in what set of circumstances would have produced such a document?

WHO WROTE THE GOSPEL OF JOHN?

None of the Gospels makes a direct reference to its author, but in John there are indirect indications of a special witness of Jesus's career, and particularly of his death. Thus, in John 19:35 the description of blood and water flowing from the side of the crucified Jesus is given special attestation by someone who claims to have been an eyewitness. At several crucial points in the narrative of the last days in Jerusalem mention is made of a "disciple whom Jesus loved" (John 13:23; 19:26; 21:7, 20), who is given special responsibility to care for Jesus's mother. Do these references mean that the Gospel of John was written by an eyewitness?

That seems scarcely likely, since the Gospel tradition as we have it in John seems to have undergone an even more extended and thorough process of reflection and theological interpretation than is the case with the other three. Further, there is mention of specific practices described in technical terms that apparently did not develop until late in the first century. Specifically, the term used for exclusion from the synagogue, with which the parents of the man born blind are threatened in John 9:22, seems not to have come into use until after the Council of Jamnia (Yavneh) in A.D. 90. Or again, direct mention of the destruction of the Temple seems to have been written down after that event had actually occurred, which would be after A.D. 70. While it is conceivable that an aged disciple would have transmuted the Jesus tradition as extensively as seems to have occurred in the Gospel of John, it scarcely seems likely. Rather, what we have in this book is the end product of two or more generations of treasuring the Jesus tradition and at the same time of interpreting it in altered circumstances.

Early Theories

Second-century Christians, however, who linked the synoptic Gospels with companions of the apostles, were by about 180 asserting that the Gospel of John was written by John, the son of Zebedee. It identified this "John" as Jesus's most intimate disciple—that is, "the disciple whom Jesus loved." In an era when apostolicity was being appealed to as a guarantee of authority and accuracy, the direct association of John's Gospel with "the disciple who leaned on Jesus's breast" (John 13:23) added greatly to the value of this document ecclesiastically, theologically, and in terms of personal piety. To read the Gospel of John was to become an intimate associate of Jesus, the theory implied. Careful examination of the ancient evidence shows, however, that there is no substance behind the theory. It was first clearly formulated by Irenaeus about A.D. 180. He declared that, following the writing of the first three Gospels, "John, the Lord's disciple, who had leaned on Jesus's breast, published the Gospel himself, as he was staying in Ephesus." This claim, which is quoted in Eusebius's *Ecclesiastical History* (V.8.4), matches other views that have come down from the late second century, but they all rest on a series of assumptions: (1) that a certain John the Elder who was in residence in Ephesus in Asia Minor in the first quarter of the second century is identical with John the son of Zebedee; (2) that John the disciple is the same as the beloved disciple mentioned in the last third of John; (3) that that disciple wrote the Gospel we now call by the name of John. All these assumptions are unlikely, and none can be proved. Within the Gospel itself, there is a clear hint that the beloved disciple did not long survive the death of Jesus, and even if he did, he appears as an observer rather than as the author. In short, the late second-century claims about the Gospel of John tell us more about the value attached to apostolicity than about the authorship of the Fourth Gospel.[1]

The Johannine Life-World

What might have been the life-world* in which this Johannine interpretation took place? Since the end of World War II two collections of ancient documents have been discovered in the Middle East, each of which has been declared by certain scholars to provide the key to the origins of Christianity in general and of Johannine Christianity in particular. One group of documents is the Dead Sea Scrolls. The other is the Gnostic library from Nag Hammadi in Upper Egypt. Both were found in the 1940s; neither has yet been fully published. But the availability of the major writings in both cases makes pos-

---

[1] Speculation about the authorship of the Gospel of John and the probable time of its composition is conveniently summarized in W. G. Kümmel, *Introduction to the New Testament*, trans. H. C. Kee (Nashville: Abingdon Press, 1975), pp. 234–47.

* For a more detailed discussion of the technical term life-world, see Appendix I.

sible an informed judgment about the bearing of these materials on Christian origins.

THE EVIDENCE OF THE DEAD SEA SCROLLS. The contrast between light and darkness in the opening lines of John (1:4, 8, 9) and throughout the Gospel correspond with a book from the Dead Sea caves known as The War of the Children of Light and the Children of Darkness. The importance attached to Jesus as the Light of the World (8:12) and the link with his followers who walk in the light, who are later in the same chapter portrayed as the true children of Abraham, show that covenant relationship with God is being represented as the privilege of those who are children of light (12:36). It would be a mistake, however, to assume an identical meaning for the phrase "children of light" at Qumran and in John.

The Dead Sea community believed its members were the only ones who obeyed the law with sufficient strictness to qualify to carry on the true worship of God in the Jerusalem Temple. They were biding their time in their desert settlement until God would intervene, drive out the unworthy priesthood that had usurped the leadership of Israel, and vindicate the faithful children of light by establishing them in the Holy City. That event was expected to take place in the near future. The Johannine community, on the other hand, foresaw the destruction of the Temple and its replacement by a new locus of worship, "the temple of his body" (John 2:19–21). In John, Jesus has nothing to do with the Temple during his final visit to Jerusalem, and does not even bother to denounce it, as he does in Mark 13 and parallels. Furthermore, covenant participation is not restricted to certain Jews, as among the Qumranians, but is open to seeking Gentiles, as symbolized by the Greeks who come to "see Jesus" (John 12:20–23). There is in John no hint of cosmic warfare and no promise of an immediate, dramatic delivery from the hands of the enemy, both of which appear in the Dead Sea writings. The apocalyptic language and expectation of the Qumran people are missing from John. Thus we cannot conclude that the Johannine community is a Christianized version of the Dead Sea sect.

THE EVIDENCE OF GNOSTIC WRITINGS. The Gnostic writings from Nag Hammadi also use the imagery of light and darkness, and they depict a divine redeemer figure who descends from the heavenly realms in order to liberate the faithful from their imprisonment in the material world. At first glance, this sounds like John's portrayal of Jesus as the Son of Man who descended from heaven (John 3:13; 6:62). In what is universally recognized as one of the oldest of the Gnostic writings, the Gospel of Thomas, the world is represented as fundamentally evil: "Whoever has known the world (*kosmos*) has found a corpse" (Gospel of Thomas 56). The goal of salvation is to overcome the sexual differentiation that has characterized humanity from the beginning ("Male and female created he them," Gen. 1:27), but which according to the Gospel of Thomas is to be replaced by androgynous existence (Gospel of Thomas 4, 22, 37, 114). In John, however, the created order is the work of God through the Word made flesh (John 1:3, 10, 14). Neither the

God who made the world nor the world he made is evil, as in Gnostic thought. And the goal of redemption is, through love, to bring life to the world (John 3:16–17). What hinders redemption is not the material nature of the world, but the willful refusal of human beings to live in obedience to God (3:19). The Gospel of Thomas depicts the redeemer figure as "not born of woman" (Thomas 15), but John asserts the full fleshly humanity of Jesus (1:14). Both the affirmation of the creation as the work of God and the hope of redemption through the Word made flesh place John literally in a world removed from the Gospel of Thomas, to say nothing of the more advanced dualistic speculations of later Gnostic writings from Nag Hammadi.

THE EVIDENCE OF JEWISH WISDOM.   Although scholars have tried to link John with Greek philosophy (because of the use of the technical term *logos* in the prologue) and with later speculative religious writings—such as the Hermetic literature of Egypt[2] or the Mandaean[3] material from Iraq—the clearest ties are between John and Jewish wisdom literature. As Judaism in the period during and following the Babylonian exile came to place more stress on the transcendence of God, there was an apparent need to posit the existence of an intermediary through whom God might be thought to have created the world and by which knowledge of him would be transmitted to humans. That instrument was wisdom, conceived of in almost personal terms. In Proverbs 8, for example, wisdom is a female companion of God who shares with him in the pleasurable work of creating the world. Her role is elaborated in Sirach 24, where she appears as a mother figure, calling God's people to compassion and obedience.

Elsewhere in the wisdom tradition, wisdom is an emanation of divine glory; she illumines the path of human beings; she descended from heaven to dwell among men and women, to lead them to life, truth, and knowledge of God's purpose. She addresses her hearers in the first-person singular (Prov. 8; Sir. 24), and she gathers around her those who seek to obey the divine will. Her role as the communicator of God's purpose is epitomized in the prayer attributed to Solomon in a document of Hellenistic Judaism known as The Wisdom of Solomon:

> Wisdom was with you; she who knows your works and was present when you made the world; she who knew what was pleasing in your sight, what was in accord with your commandments. O send her out from your holy heavens and from the throne of your glory, so that, through her being present with me, I may know what is pleasing to you.
>
> —WISD. OF SOL. 9:9–10

Scholars analyzing the Jewish wisdom tradition against the background of the literature of the ancient Near East have long recognized the links be-

---

[2] See the brief sketch of the Hermetic literature, with excerpts and references to possible conceptual links with John, in H. C. Kee, *The New Testament in Context: Sources and Documents* (Englewood Cliffs, N.J.: Prentice-Hall, 1983).

[3] On the sect of the Mandaeans, see E. L. Drower, *The Mandaeans of Iraq and Iran* (Leiden: Brill, 1962); for a discussion of the Baptist background of the hymns, see C. H. Kraeling, *John the Baptist* (New York: Scribner's, 1951), pp. 166–71.

tween the developing concept of wisdom within Judaism and the changing role of Isis in Egyptian religion of the same period. By the fifth century B.C. Isis had taken over from Ma'at, the more ancient goddess of wisdom, three primary roles: the functions of (1) creating and (2) sustaining the world, as well as (3) becoming a figure of mercy and compassion toward all who sought to do the will of the gods. Those are precisely what wisdom does within Judaism. But unlike Jewish wisdom, Isis's benefactions came to be understood in the Hellenistic period in wholly tangible ways; she was the healing goddess who enabled the blind to regain sight or the ill to be restored to health. Hundreds of inscriptions and literary texts attest to her role as benefactress of the faithful. By the early second century A.D. she had also become the central figure in a widespread cult, so that devotees gathered to honor her in cities and towns throughout the empire, as we have noted (Chapter 1). Isis combines three roles by which she ministers to basic human longings: (1) as the agent of creation; (2) as the central figure around whom the faithful rally; and (3) as the proclaimer of divine wisdom, addressing her hearers in the first person singular, "I am Isis." The analogies with wisdom and with the figure of Jesus in John are obvious. Instead of the feminine word *sophia* to identify the agent of wisdom, John offers a masculine equivalent to match the sexual identity of Jesus: *logos.*[4] Unlike both Jewish and pagan speculation about wisdom, however, John insists that in Jesus divine wisdom assumed fully human form, and was self-revealed in a fully human life, culminating in death and a resurrection from the dead. Like Isis, however, Jesus is the instrument of miraculous ministration to human need, as the miracle stories of the Fourth Gospel attest. What we find in John, therefore, is a life-world strongly influenced by wisdom speculation with respect to benefactions, revelations, and mystical participation. But in its doctrine of incarnation—the *logos*-become-flesh—it stands in unique contrast to any pagan cult or Jewish personification of wisdom.

The Sources of John's Gospel

Although it is clear that John did not depend directly on Mark for his major source and structure, as did Matthew and Luke, the general pattern of a Gospel and even the broad sweep of Mark's narrative seem to have had an important influence on John. But since with very few exceptions, John's content is wholly independent of Mark, on what sources is it likely that John drew?

SIGNS SOURCE.   The fact that John starts to enumerate the "signs" of Jesus (2:11; 4:54) suggests that he had a sign source, although 20:30–31 implies that he did not use all the sign material available to him. Scholars have long sought to reconstruct the signs source used by John, but have not been able to agree about details, extent, or even what subject matter might origi-

---

[4] An analysis of the relationships between the *logos,* Jewish wisdom, and the redeeming goddess, Isis, is set out in H. C. Kee, "Myth and Miracle: Isis, Wisdom and the Logos," in *Myth, Symbol and Reality,* ed. Alan M. Olson (Notre Dame, Ind.: University of Notre Dame Press, 1981), pp. 145–64.

nally have been included. Some would limit the signs source strictly to miracle stories, while others would include the Passion narrative as well.[5] But should "signs" include other narrative material, such as the prediction of the destruction of the Temple (2:13–22), the encounter with Nicodemus (3:1–21) and with the Samaritan woman (4:1–45)? If so, then the designation of the healing of the official's son as "the second sign" is in error, at least so far as the present narrative sequence is concerned. The signs might include changing water into wine (2:1–11), cleansing the Temple (2:13–22), the dialogues with Nicodemus (3:1–15) and the Samaritan woman (4:1–42), the healing of the official's son (4:46–53), the healing of the lame man at the pool (5:1–18), feeding the five thousand (6:1–14), walking on the water (6:16–21), healing the man born blind (9:1–41), raising Lazarus from the dead (11). If we were to omit the dialogues and controversy stories, we should be left with seven signs. But there seems to be no reason to include the Passion narrative, since it contains no account of a miracle other than the concluding Resurrection story. The assumed signs source is by no means a unit, or even a uniform cycle of material.

DISCOURSE SOURCE.   The same problem is apparent in the attempt to reconstruct a discourse source. Many of the addresses attributed to Jesus include the first-person singular form of self-declaration, "I am," but by no means all. There is no unifying pattern which suggests that the speech material derives from a single source. We will examine below the claims made in behalf of Jesus in the Johannine sayings material, but it is important to note now how diverse in form this material is. At the same time, however, all the components of John—the sayings material, the signs accounts, the Passion story and the prologue—exhibit a remarkable unity of style and vocabulary. One can only conclude that, if John worked from existing sources, he has so thoroughly worked them over and adapted them to his own style and aims that they can no longer be distinguished as sources.[6]

It is a wholly subjective undertaking, therefore, to try to distinguish between the alleged sources of John and the finished product as we have it. There are some apparent editorial awkwardnesses, as in the end of the speech section in John 14:31 ("Arise, let us go hence," which is then followed by three more chapters of speeches), and the inelegant epilogue (21), which is tacked onto a natural ending (20:30–31). Since we cannot determine what John's sources were, if any, we cannot discover how he reworked them. Our only alternative is to analyze the Gospel as we now have it. Our procedure will be to ask first, "What historical information does John include in his Gospel?" Then we turn to the significance of Jesus's miracles, or "signs" as John prefers to call them. Next, the fundamental question "Who is Jesus?" is answered by his statements in the form of "I am" declarations. And finally we analyze how life within the community of faith was understood to involve mystical union with Christ, and through him, with God.

[5] For example, Robert T. Fortna, *The Gospel of Signs: A Reconstruction of the Narrative Source Underlying the Fourth Gospel* (Cambridge, Eng.: Cambridge University Press, 1970).

[6] D. Moody Smith in *The Composition and Order of the Fourth Gospel* (New Haven, Conn.: Yale University Press, 1965), pp. 114, 241.

THE HISTORICAL INFORMATION IN JOHN

Even though John regularly uses narrative as a launching platform for theological claims concerning Jesus, his Gospel does include valuable pieces of information that are probably reliable and that supplement what is available through the synoptic tradition. The first set of information concerns John the Baptist and Jesus's relationship to him. From the synoptics one can infer only that Jesus and John met when Jesus came seeking baptism. No further connections are hinted at, until John sends his poignant inquiry from prison as to who Jesus is. In John's Gospel, on the other hand, there are indications that the men who became Jesus's disciples were originally followers of John (John 1:35–37). Beyond that, the fragmentary and partly self-contradictory narrative that runs from John 3:22–4:3 indicates that Jesus and his disciples carried

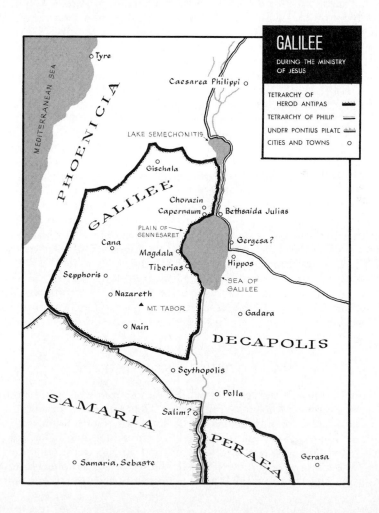

on baptismal activity in the land of Judea with a degree of success that was regarded by the Baptist's followers as in direct competition with John (3:22, 26). The results were obviously impressive (4:1), even though the text in its present form denies that Jesus himself actually performed any baptisms (4:2). The reason Jesus stopped this enterprise and returned to his native Galilee is not clear—the text of 4:1 seems garbled—but there is a hint in 3:24 that the reason for Jesus's launching an independent ministry is the same in all the Gospels: John the Baptist was imprisoned. Out of deference for John the Baptist, then, Jesus refrained from starting his own mission until John was off the scene.

Another area in which John's Gospel may offer tradition which does not merely supplement what we have in the synoptics, but which actually corrects it, is the chronology of the final days in Jerusalem. The synoptics assume that Jesus's final meal with his disciples was a celebration of Passover. Since that feast was fixed by the phases of the moon, it could come on any day of the week, including the Sabbath. If it fell on Thursday night through Friday up to sundown (in accord with Jewish computation of a day as beginning with sunset), it would be nearly unthinkable for pious Jewish leaders to take part in nocturnal conclaves, especially in association with pagan leaders, on the night of the solemn feast of Passover. If, however, John's chronology is correct (13:1), then Jesus's final meal was eaten on the night before the Passover, which would have begun coincidentally with the beginning of the Sabbath, at sundown on Friday. That would account for the eagerness of the Jews to have the body of Jesus removed before the Sabbath began (19:31), and would fit with the description by John of that Friday as "the day of Preparation." It would also explain the otherwise puzzling statement of Jesus in Luke's version of the Last Supper (Luke 22:15), according to which Jesus states that he had wanted to eat the Passover with his disciples but would not be able to do so. Almost certainly, John has preserved the historical tradition on this matter. The fact that the death of Jesus came to be interpreted by Christians as their equivalent for the Passover sacrifice led to the blending of the Last Supper and the Passover traditions, as Mark and Matthew report it.

John, therefore, is keenly interested in preserving historical records of Jesus. His theological interests do not eclipse his historical concerns. Rather, his conviction that in Jesus the Word became flesh (appeared in genuinely human form) led him to include historical evidence.

WHAT DO THE SIGNS SIGNIFY?

In the synoptic miracle stories, two related factors point beyond healings or exorcisms to a larger framework of meaning. The exorcisms, for example, are said in Luke 11:20 to be indications of the coming of God's reign: "If it is by the finger of God that I cast out demons, then the Kingdom of God has come upon you." Similarly, the response to John the Baptist's question about Jesus points to Jesus's acts of healing and recalls the scriptural prophecies in which the blind receiving sight and the lame walking were declared to be characteristics of the new age, when God's purpose for his creation would be accomplished (Luke 7:18–23; cf. Isa. 29:18–19; 35:5–6). In both cases, the miracles are set in an eschatological framework, as signs of the advent of the age to come.

The First Sign: Water into Wine

In the Johannine equivalent of the miracle stories—the signs—the meaning is very different. The first of the signs, changing water into wine (2:1–11), has at least two levels of significance. The fact that the miracle takes place at a wedding feast implies, through the Jewish imagery of the period, that joyous fulfillment is taking place. Jewish allegorical interpretation of the love poem known as the Song of Solomon pointed to the consummation of God's purpose for and through his people, Israel. Similarly, the synoptic tradition anticipated the new age with the image of the coming bridegroom (Mark 2:19; Matt. 25:1; cf. Isa. 61:10). But for John, the best wine is available now (2:10), not in an age to come. That is, *the joys of the new age are already available for the faithful.* The second level of meaning is purely symbolic, and centers on the linked factors of water and wine. Although one cannot be certain, the explicit contrast with the Jewish rites of purification (John 2:6) implies that Christian purification—that is, baptism—is being symbolized. And the climax of the story, the new wine, could be seen as pointing to the other Christian sacrament, the Eucharist. There can be no doubt, however, that the feeding story (John 6) has eucharistic meaning for John.

The Healing Signs

Of all the Johannine narratives, the story of the healing of the official's son (4:46–54) most closely resembles the miracle stories of the synoptic tradition. Even the implicit point of the story—that the official was linked with the half-Jewish monarchy that remained in power by collaborating with the Romans— is similar to the synoptic picture of Jesus as one who welcomed into the circle of his followers persons who were religiously, socially, or politically objectionable by current Jewish standards. The story of the lame man at the pool in Jerusalem, on the other hand, makes explicit through the long discourse that follows it that what is at issue is not Jesus's ability to heal, but the authority by which he carries on all his work. Jesus's capacity to heal is an indicator of the authorization he has received from God to judge, to forgive, to give life, to raise the dead. The works Jesus performs are testimony to his claim to have been sent and empowered by God. Only those who trust him, who respond to him in love, and who can see the outlines of his work anticipated in the Jewish scriptures are the true children of God. The rest will stand condemned by God and by the law of Moses, which they failed to understand properly.

The Sea of Galilee. This lake lies well below the level of the Mediterranean Sea. Beyond the lake were predominantly Gentile cities, including the Decapolis. Fishing in the clear, fresh water of the lake was an important feature of the local economy.   (*Gordon N. Converse*)

The Miracle Signs

The linked stories of the feeding of the crowd in the desert and of Jesus walking on the water are reminiscent of the miracles of divine care and deliverance told in the Old Testament about the exodus of Israel from Egypt. The passage through the Red Sea and the provision of food for the starving tribes in the desert are told in various forms in the books of Moses (Exod. 14:21; 15:1–18), in the Psalms (Ps. 66:5–6; 78:9–16) and in the prophets (Isa. 50:2; 51:9–11). God's mastery of the waters is a theme that goes back to the story of creation (Gen. 1:9), where the gathering of the waters is a sign and symbol of God's sovereignty over the created world. The report of the provision of miraculous food (*manna*) is also told repeatedly (Exod. 16:4, 15; Num. 11:8; Ps. 78:24; 105:40). When Jesus identifies himself in John 6:20 as "it is I," the link with Yahweh, the God of the Old Testament, is clear, since the emphatic Greek phrase, *ego eimi,* can mean simply "it is I," but it is also the way that the Septuagint translated God's special name, Yahweh (Exod. 3:14). Moses has been summoned to lead Israel out of Egypt, and when he asked whom he should tell Israel had called him to this role, God answered him, "Say this to the people of Israel, 'I am (*ego eimi*) has sent me to you.'" Similarly, in the prophetic poems of 2 Isaiah, God discloses himself and his redemptive purpose for his covenant people through direct address: "I am Yahweh; there is no other" (Isa. 45:6); "I, I am the Yahweh, and beside me there is no savior" (Isa. 43:11); "I am Yahweh your God, the Holy One of Israel, your Savior" (Isa. 43:3). The imagery and the terminology of these combined traditions of historic deliverance from slavery and of future deliverance into the new age are blended in the Johannine accounts depicting Jesus as provider of bread from heaven and as master of the waters.

Unlike the synoptic version of these stories, however, John does not leave the significance of these miracles at the level of the implicit. The discourse by Jesus which follows in John 6:25–65 explicitly recalls the miraculous feeding through Moses of the covenant people Israel. But it makes two emphatic contrasts as well: (1) The breadlike substance that floated down from the sky as food for Israel was subject to decay; and (2) it could do no more than sustain life within the normal limits of human existence. Jesus, however, does not merely provide bread: He *is* the true Bread from Heaven. And the life which is provided through this bread is eternal (6:51).

But how are we to understand the command to "eat his flesh and drink his blood"? In a literal sense, of course, this would be cannibalism, and would be strictly forbidden by Jewish law and abhorrent to most other human cultures. Is it intended in a purely figurative way? That is, is Jesus by this image inviting his hearers to full participation in the fellowship of the new covenant people, who have taken the place of Israel of old? Or is there here, as in the synoptic version, a reference to the sacrament of the eucharist, in which bread and wine symbolize the body and sacrificial blood of Jesus? To mix the metaphors, is Jesus here pointing to himself as "the Lamb of God that takes away the sin of the world" (John 1:29)? Although some interpreters of John think that he has dismissed the sacraments of baptism and the eucharist, it seems more likely that, in keeping with the highly symbolic nature of his book, he intends the discerning reader to perceive in the covenant ceremony of miraculous feeding the Christian rite of communion through partaking of the Bread from Heaven.

The Test Signs

The man born blind (John 9) is perceived by the religious leaders as a test case for Jesus on two counts: Jesus is asked to decide whose sin is the cause of the man's handicap; and the healing Jesus performs is regarded as a violation of the Sabbath law of the Jews. Once again, the miracle of restoring sight to the blind has an importance beyond the benefaction itself, although it is linked with the prophetic promise of restoration of sight to the blind at the end of the age (John 9:17; Isa. 29:18; 42:7). The central issue is Jesus's status before God: whether he as a violator of the fundamental law of Sabbath observance can be God's instrument of healing, God's agent of the new age. The estimate of Jesus that turns on this issue has become for John's community the criterion for acceptance into or rejection by those who call themselves the children of God. As we have noted, Jewish authorities by the end of the first century decreed that all who acknowledged Jesus as the Messiah were to be excommunicated from the synagogues of Israel (9:22). The supreme irony in this story is that the only one who can see clearly who Jesus is is the man born blind.

The final miracle story in John reports the raising of Lazarus from the dead. The bereaved sisters articulate confidence in Jesus's ability to help the sick ("If you had been here, my brother would not have died," John 11:21), as well as orthodox Pharisaic belief in the resurrection of the just at the end of the age (11:24). Lazarus's being raised from the dead becomes, therefore, a symbolic statement that Jesus embodies life as God intended it to be, and that that life is available now and forever (11:25–26). But another issue is raised in relation to faith in Jesus as the agent of life: For Jews to trust in him would bring about the end of the sanctuary and of Israel as a holy nation. John sees Jesus's significance as essential and constructive, since his death is in behalf of his people, and the "nation" he rallies in faith will be universal in its extent (11:51–52). But the issue of who the covenant people are involves the question of who Jesus is.

WHO IS THE SON OF MAN?

When Jesus asks the man born blind if he trusts in him, the man replies that he does not know who he is. The identity of Jesus is both affirmed and constantly refined from the opening of John's Gospel. He is the *logos*, the true light, the Word made flesh, the Lamb of God in John 1. But more traditional messianic titles are also applied to him from the outset: He is the Christ or Messiah (1:41), the one of whom Moses and the prophets wrote (1:45), the Son of God and the King of Israel (1:49). He enables his followers to experience the same vision that confirmed Jacob as the progenitor of the covenant people: the ascending and descending angels (John 1:51; Gen. 28:12).

The New Corporate Relationship

Yet even more important than traditional titles in John's portrait of Jesus are the cosmic functions he fulfills in behalf of God and his people. These are for the most part set forth in terms of the "I am" declarations of Jesus to which we made reference earlier, and which are a distinctive feature of John. It is essential to look at the "I am" sayings in association with the range of Jesus's roles as John presents them for his readers. Two features of these self-declarations of Jesus then become apparent, in addition to the obvious aim of describing Jesus as revealer of God. The first of these associated features is the repeated assertion that the revelation through Jesus requires a human response. It has no automatic efficacy, but demands a reaction of faith in order to become effective. The other feature is that the response always results in a new corporate relationship: men and women of faith are incorporated into the new community. That pair of themes is set forth in the promise to the disciples concerning the angels attendant upon the Son of Man, referred to above, but the combination is expanded in a series of subsequent images.

In John 3, the dialogue between Jesus and Nicodemus stresses newness of life under the image of the new birth or the birth from above. But that experience of launching into a new life of which Jesus speaks to the inquiring, puzzled rabbi is not an automatic process or a magical rite—it can occur only where the divine provision is accepted in faith: "Whoever trusts in Him has eternal life" (3:16). The reference to the experience of Israel in the desert of Sinai described in Numbers 21 makes the point: Only those who regard with faith God's remedy for the human condition benefit from that provision. Only the serpent elevated on the pole could ward off the baleful effects of the plague that beset disobedient, petulant Israel. The Son of Man, soon to be lifted up on a Roman cross, will be regarded with scorn or with malignant satisfaction by many who are glad to be rid of this troublemaker. But to those who look in faith, the tragedy will become the instrument of divine love to the world (3:14–15). The potential beneficiaries of the sacrificial victim are all of humanity, John declares (3:17).

The New Locus of Worship

John's report of Jesus predicting the destruction of the Temple may include historical allusions, such as how long the Temple was under construction (2:20), but clearly the significance of the prophecy is linked with Jesus's Resurrection ("in three days") and with the reconstitution of his followers in light of the post-Resurrection appearances (2:21–22). The term for his people, "body," is the same as Paul's preferred term for the Christian community as a whole (Rom. 12:4–5), where he notes that for all their differences, individuals are collectively united in "the body of Christ." Similarly, as John contrasts the soon-to-be-destroyed sanctuary in Jerusalem with Jesus's body, so Paul speaks of the "body" as "the temple of the Holy Spirit" (1 Cor. 6:19). The place of worship where God and his people meet is not a sacred building that can be geographically located, but the context of the community itself.

The question of the locus of divine worship is raised again in John 4, in the course of Jesus's interchange with the woman of Samaria. The Samaritans, descended from the northern tribes of Israel which broke away from what had been the central government and central shrine of Israel under David and Solomon, revived the worship of God at the sanctuary in Shechem, about thirty miles north of Jerusalem. That was where the twelve tribes had covenanted with Yahweh when Israel began the conquest of Canaan (Josh. 24). The well adjacent to the sanctuary was thought to be on land bought by Jacob when he moved to Shechem. Joseph, whose body had been carried up

From the massive stone ruins of Shechem one can look across the valley to the top of Mount Gerizim, where the Samaritan shrine stood. The structure overlooked the city of the Samaritans (called Neapolis, now known as Nablus), and was connected with the city in the early second century by a gigantic staircase.   (*Gordon N. Converse*)

from Egypt, was buried nearby (Josh. 24:32). Shechem was rich in tradition and memories of the founding of the covenant people and of its patriarchs. On nearby Mt. Gerizim the Samaritans had their proud match for the Judean temple on the eastern hill of Jerusalem.

Once Jesus began to press the Samaritan woman about certain embarrassing details of her personal life, especially her many spouses and male companions, she shifted the subject to the theoretical question about which of the two mountain shrines, Jerusalem or Gerizim, was superior (4:20). To her astonishment, Jesus denounced them both, rejecting all geographically localized worship of God. God is to be worshipped "in spirit and in truth" (4:24). The believing response of the woman is matched by faith on the part of other Samaritan inquirers, who recognize Jesus as "the savior of the world." The first stage of inclusiveness of the new community is to be discerned in this successful mission to the Samaritans, a factor we will see is important for the spread of the Gospel as described in Acts as well: "Beginning in Jerusalem and in Judea, *in Samaria*, and to the end of the earth" (Acts 1:8). The crucial step in the woman's recognition of Jesus comes when she asks him about the coming

Cut from the rock, this deep well is linked by tradition with Jacob, who bought land and settled in Shechem, erecting there an altar to the God of Israel (Gen. 33:19–20). A Christian church now has been built over the ancient site. *(Gordon N. Converse)*

Messiah, and he replies, *ego eimi*, "I am [he]." Her response makes her the nucleus of a new stage of the new community.

The Bread of Life

Jesus's defense of his having healed the lame man at the pool on the Sabbath requires him to meet directly the accusation that Jesus has made himself equal with God (John 5:18). In defining his relationship to God, however, Jesus does not lay claim to a simple identity, as though Jesus and God were interchangeable terms. Rather, Jesus points to the identity of what he is doing with what God is doing. The unity between Father and Son is functional: Jesus is carrying forward God's work in the world, and that is the explanation for the wonders he is able to perform. That divine activity will continue into the future, when Jesus as Son of Man is judge of the living and the dead (5:26–28). Here, incidentally, John comes closest to the apocalyptic role of the Son of Man as it appears in Daniel and Mark. Jesus's link with God is seen in the love he manifests, in the light he reveals, in the works he performs. Right reading of scripture will provide additional confirmation to the faithful that Jesus is indeed commissioned and empowered by God (5:39), since its testimony is to him.

That theme is resumed and expanded on in the discourse following the feeding of the five thousand. Unlike the bread from heaven provided by Moses, which merely extended human life, the bread Jesus provides—and which he *is*—transforms human life into the eternal sphere. It is not merely longer life; it is an entirely new kind of life (6:49–51). At this point, John reports Jesus as affirming his own preexistence: he was with the Father, he has now come down to earth, and he will return to be with the Father. That pattern of movement of the revealer figure is to be found in Jewish tradition about wisdom, as we have noted. The difficulty his contemporaries have with Jesus's claim is not inability to conceive of a descending-ascending revelatory figure, but with the fact that they know the human parents of the one who makes this stupendous assertion about himself. For John, of course, this is the heart of his concept of Jesus as the human incarnation of the *logos* of God. To eat the bread from heaven is not meant literally, but is a vivid figure for hearing in faith and heeding what Jesus says about God and his purpose: "The words I have spoken to you are spirit and life" (6:63). His disciples confirm their understanding of Jesus when they declare that he has the words of eternal life (6:68). Once more, recognition of who Jesus is—"the Bread of Life"— enables one to share in the life of the community that never hungers or thirsts (6:35).

The Messiah

The disparity between what Jesus claims for himself and his known humble origins serves as the basis for further clarification in John 7 of who Jesus really is. From the standpoint of Jewish messianic expectations, there were severe difficulties with the Christian assertion that Jesus was the Messiah. The most common form of messianic hope—renewal of Jewish political autonomy under a king from the Davidic line—figures importantly in Matthew's and Luke's infancy stories and is attested in part even by Paul in Romans 1:3, which attests that Jesus was descended from David. The prophecy of Micah 5:2 promises a ruler of Israel born in Bethlehem. Isaiah 7:13–14 predicts the rule of a member of David's house, whose reign will be one of such unprecedented peace and prosperity that his subjects will call him "God-with-us," or Emmanuel. In John, however, Jesus is linked with Galilee as the place of his birth (1:45–46) and as the seat from which his prophetic ministry was launched (7:40–44, 52). For the faithful, he will be the instrument through which God's spirit will be poured out, in fulfillment of prophetic expectation (John 7:38; Joel 2:28–29), an event which is reported as taking place following the Resurrection (John 20:22). But for the rest of his hearers, Jesus's statements about his relationship to God are offensive, contradictory to scripture, and deserving of punishment.

In John 8 a series of questions is addressed to Jesus: "Where is your father?" (8:19); "Who are you?" (8:25); "You are not yet fifty years old, and have you seen Abraham?" (8:57). Jesus's response is to claim continuity between God's work and his. But he goes on to deny that his antagonists are, as they claim, children of Abraham. They are instead children of the Devil, since they are rejecting God's messenger to them (8:44). His claim to be both superior to and chronologically prior to Abraham is audacious—indeed, from the perspective of Jewish tradition, it could only be regarded as a mixture of madness and blasphemy. But what is at stake is not Jesus's estimate of himself, but rather his role in the purpose of God and their response to him. The climax of his defense involves a distinction in technical terms that scarcely comes through in English. Greek differentiates "becoming" from "being." That is, human and other forms of physical existence are regarded as in a constant process of transition: "becoming." They assume their present form only to have it fade or decay, whether they are trees, rocks, or human beings. By contrast, the ideal or unchanging form—of which all transitory phenomena are impermanent copies—participate in true being. They eternally *are*. Using these two terms, John reports Jesus as saying, "Before Abraham became, or came to be, I am." In this phrase, "I am" (*ego eimi*), which we have considered in other connections, Jesus asserts his share in eternal being and at the same time identifies himself with Yahweh, who called Abraham into covenant relationship. The critical decision is up to his hearers: "I told you that you would die in your sins, unless you believe that *ego eimi*" (8:24).

The New Flock

There are two "I am" pronouncements in John 10, both of which focus at once on the identity of Jesus and on the nature of the community he is calling together: "I am the door of the sheep" (10:7); "I am the good shepherd" (10:11, 14). Yahweh's relationship with his people is commonly represented in the Old Testament as that of a shepherd and his flock. The most familiar is Psalm 23, "Yahweh is my shepherd." That role is projected into the future in Isaiah 40:11, where Yahweh's restoration of his people to their land is described with the image of Yahweh as feeding his flock, carrying the young, protecting the pregnant ewes. But the other side of this metaphor of tender care is the expectation that the covenant people will be dominated by wicked shepherds who will exploit and maltreat the flock. The leaders of Israel have betrayed their trust, have scattered the flock, says Jeremiah (23:1-4), and they will be replaced by faithful shepherds. Ezekiel paints an even more critical picture of Israel's "shepherds," describing them as fleecing the sheep, slaughtering the helpless, ignoring the plight of the weak and hungry, scattering God's people rather than gathering them for nurture and protection. God will expel the evil leaders and replace them by the single faithful shepherd who will make with them a covenant of peace and blessing (Ezek. 34). Although Jesus lacks the qualification for this role of Davidic descent (Ezek. 34:23), he proves that he is the good shepherd by laying down his life in behalf of the flock (John 10:18).

An important feature of John's portrayal of flock and shepherd stands in sharp contrast to Ezekiel's: for John, this is an inclusive community. The "other sheep, that are not of this fold" are the non-Israelites who join with believing Jews to constitute God's new flock (10:16). Participation in this new

Inscription from the balustrade of the Temple in Jerusalem built by Herod the Great, marking the point beyond which Gentiles were not permitted to pass. *(Quarterly of the Dept. of Antiquities of Palestine 6/1938)*

covenant people is not the result of divine decree but of human response: the true sheep recognize and heed the voice of the true shepherd, and thereby enter into eternal life in the new fellowship of God's people (10:27–28). Once they have become partners in that community, they are preserved by the care of the faithful shepherd and by the power of his Father. This interconnection of Jesus's work and God's continues to be for John the ground of Jesus's claim in his own behalf to be "one with the Father" and the basis of his rejection by the religious leadership, whose criteria for covenant participation are simply incompatible with those set forth here.

That the covenant people is open to Gentiles as well as to Jews is given succinct but dramatic expression in John 12. The story concerns seeking Gentiles who have come to worship the God of Israel at the sanctuary in Jerusalem. While there, they approached two disciples, both of whom had Greek names, Philip and Andrew. Their request was simple: they wanted to see Jesus. Taking into account John's fondness for words with multiple meanings, it seems that their search is not motivated by curiosity; they are not merely tourists who want to catch a glimpse of the controversial Galilean who has come to Jerusalem for the feast, and has audaciously ridden into the city as though to fulfill the prophecy of Zechariah concerning the eschatological king (Zech. 9:9). Rather, these earnest seekers want to know who Jesus is. When the report of their request reaches Jesus, it serves to inform him that his "hour has come"—that is, the hour of his Crucifixion and thereby of the launching of the inclusive community. His rejection by the religious leadership is seen as the fulfillment of the prophetic warning about Israel's disbelief (John 12:37–41; Isa. 6:9–10), but also as the opening of the invitation to all the world to share in the light God has provided through Jesus (12:32, 44–48). To reject Jesus is to reject God; to trust him and his word is to trust God. That is the ground for participation in the new community.

LIFE WITHIN THE NEW COMMUNITY

The images that John uses both for Christ and for his people describe not merely a formal relationship between the redeemer and the redeemed, but also involve participation by the faithful in a new reality. That reality is eternal life, and the participation in it is depicted by John in the language of mysticism: sharing in the divine life. This is evident in the bread which must be eaten, the shepherd whose flock must be tended and fed, the vine whose branches share in the new life.

As the opening lines of John 13 make clear, once his rejection and death are certain, the focus of Jesus's concern shifts to the interior life of the community. The symbolic act of washing the feet of the disciples serves a dual purpose of picturing Jesus in the role of a menial servant, who willingly takes on the necessary but ignoble task for the benefit of others, and of requiring the disciples to adopt similar roles in relation to one another for the welfare of the whole community. The love for one another which Jesus enjoins is not an attitude but a way of acting (13:14, 34–35). Yet within this inner circle of followers is the traitor, who foolishly assumes that because his own expectations of Jesus have been betrayed, he can destroy Jesus by turning him over to the authorities. But in the purpose of God, the moment of Jesus's betrayal by human agency is actually the moment of his glorification (13:31–32). Peter's protestations of fidelity are likewise seen to be the prelude to denial. Love will bind the community; pride will dissolve it. That theme is resumed in John 15:12–15, where the command to love is matched by the promise of God's preservation of his own. Jesus is both proclaimer and paradigm of love.

The resources of the community are embodied in Jesus: He is the way to God, the truth about God, and the life that God calls his people to live. Trust in him will enable his followers to perform works similar to his. Understanding of God and his purposes will be conveyed through the Spirit Jesus provides for his own. The Spirit will be their teacher, and will enable them to recall the tradition about Jesus. The power that binds the community together and to God is love. The appropriate response to God's love is obedience. God's response to human obedience is his mystical presence: "If anyone loves me, he will keep my word, and my Father will love that person, and we will come and make our home within that person" (John 14:23). That living presence will strengthen the faithful during the period when Jesus is visibly absent and the power of evil is at work in the world. They can "be of good cheer" because Jesus in his faithful obedience has overcome the world (16:33).

The most vivid of John's images for the community's organic unity in Christ is that of the vine. The image is not new, since it was used by Isaiah

(5:1–7) to depict the gap between Israel's potential as the people of God and actual performance. The theme of unfruitful Israel was developed by Jeremiah (2:21) and especially by Ezekiel (19:10–14), who describes the vine as stripped of its fruit, its stem withered, struggling for existence in a "dry and thirsty land." For John, on the other hand, the vine is a metaphor for the vitality, the productivity, the mutuality of support that characterizes the faithful community. The produce of the vine is not spectacular performances or vast enterprises but love and obedience, which bear testimony to all observers that those linked with the life of the vine are disciples of Jesus and members of God's family. There will be times of severe testing ahead (15:18–26), but the Spirit will counsel them, God's power will be at work through them, and his love will more than compensate for the hatred their stance will engender against them from the world that rejected Jesus and will reject them. Sociologically speaking, what John here depicts is a sect, a group which is humanly powerless and yet can live in confidence because of its conviction that it has knowledge of a divine purpose in which God's love enables it to share.[7] The central focus of the group's identity is Jesus, to whom the Spirit bears witness (15:26).

The kinds of hostility the sect can expect are named in John 16: expulsion from the synagogues and martyrdom. In Jesus's absence the Spirit has two roles: one toward the world and one toward the community. For the world, the Spirit's work is that of judgment, convincing humankind of its folly in rejecting Jesus. Within the community, the Spirit will be the guide to the truth that comes ultimately from God. One of the fundamental truths is that the suffering through which the community is soon to pass is not an indication of God's abandonment of his people, but rather a necessary stage through which it must pass. The familiar figure of the woman in childbirth is the analogy with the epoch of testing through which the disciples and their followers are about to pass (16:20–22). And all that will be forgotten when the joy of the new age arrives.

THAT THEY ALL MAY BE ONE

[JOHN 17:21]

In Jesus's own experience, as represented in John 17, his impending death is regarded as the accomplishment of his earthly work and as the prelude to his return to the Father. That expectation is made explicit in the words addressed to Mary Magdalene following his Resurrection. She had wanted to hold him, but he told her he must ascend to the Father (20:17). Jesus's prayer for his people is not for their removal from the world, but for their preservation in the world, so that through their testimony others might be brought into the community of faith (17:20). The ultimate achievement of God's purpose is the actualization of unity. In spite of differences of origin, they are to be seen as one, just as the differences in roles between Jesus and the Father lead to unity,

---

[7] See Wayne Meeks, "The Man from Heaven in Johannine Sectarianism," *Journal of Biblical Literature* 91 (1972), pp. 44–72.

rather than to division. The supreme testimony to God's word to the human race is to be expressed in the unity of his people (17:23). The effective bond of that unity is love, originating in the nature of God, manifested in the obedience of Jesus, and embodied in the new community.

The term Son of God was used in ancient Israel as a designation for the king. In the Psalm of Enthronement, as the king assumed royal power on Mt. Zion, he was addressed by God: "You are my son, today I have begotten you" (Ps. 2:7). This was not understood literally in ancient Israel as an act of divine begetting, but as a new relationship whereby the king became God's agent of rule over his people and their land. As the "anointed" (Messiah; in Greek, *christos;* Ps. 2:1), the king was chosen and empowered by God for the role, and hence was addressed as God's "son." The issue of Jesus's relationship to this religiopolitical tradition is raised understandably in the trial scene of John 18. If Jesus was laying claim to political sovereignty over Israel, that was a matter of deep concern both to the religious leaders of the Jews and to the Roman powers with their determination to put down any challenge to their authority. Pilate's question to Jesus, "Are you the king of the Jews?" would be quite proper historically for him to raise about someone who has been talking about the kingdom of God and allowing his followers to use messianic language concerning him. Jesus's reply is ambiguous: When he says his kingship is "not of this world," that could mean that it is an otherworldly enterprise, or it could imply that his rule will not be established by means and standards and expectation deriving from this world order. It is the latter meaning which is indicated by the disclaimer of the use of force to establish his rule. Yet Jesus does not deny that he is "a king" (18:37).

Just as Israel has been redefined, so Jesus here gives a radically new significance to the title king of Israel. It comes as no surprise, therefore, that the leaders of the nation refuse to accept Jesus as their king, preferring instead Barabbas, apparently a Jewish revolutionary. The final repudiation of Jesus is said to be the response to his claim to be Son of God. For reasons of political safety, they will say to the Roman overlord that the only political sovereign they acknowledge is Caesar. The title set above Jesus's cross bears the supremely ironic words: "Jesus of Nazareth, the King of the Jews." He should be from David's city, Bethlehem, not Nazareth. He is a king who refuses to exercise royal political or military power. He is a king spurned by the leaders of his own people.

WHY ARE YOU WEEPING?
[JOHN 20:15]

The angel's question to Mary Magdalene is a dramatic understatement addressed to the whole community. Instead of lamenting the absence of the Christ, they should rejoice in his Resurrection, his return to the Father, and the gifts for the Church he bestowed. They are commissioned by him to carry forward the work which he launched and which the coming of the Spirit now makes possible (20:21–22). An important feature of their new responsibility is to pronounce the forgiveness of sins. This was of paramount significance for the leadership of the church in the Matthean community as well. Thus control over who will be admitted or excluded from the community rests in the hands of its leadership, working with the power of the Spirit.

For an author like John, who has insisted on the reality of the incarnation, it is not surprising to have attention drawn to the corporeality of the risen Jesus. Twice in the narrative he displays his wounded hands and side as tangible evidence of the identity of their Galilean leader with the strange figure who now comes and goes among them (20:20, 25). The community is asserting that its faith rests in a resurrected person, not in a vision or an idea. That bodily presence evokes peace and faith for sustaining the life of the group.

Although the Gospel might well end, and probably once did end, at 20:31, the epilogue now makes even more concrete the resources and responsibilities that have been assigned to the community by its Risen Lord. The two vivid images of the disciples as fishermen and as shepherds serve to point up what their work is to be. First, they are to gather into the community all who will respond to the Gospel. The size of the haul is a token of the phenomenal success they may expect in their enterprise. The distribution of bread and fish serves another purpose as well: it is obviously a symbol of the Eucharist, by which the community celebrated the spiritual presence of the Lord in its midst. The shepherd-flock metaphor, on the other hand, points to the continual need of the leaders of the community to provide sustenance and nurture to new members. Profession of love is not enough: it must be demonstrated by loving care for the little ones who join the group.

Finally, the Risen Lord warns that there will be two kinds of problems besetting the community, neither of which is to be the occasion for doubt or discouragement: One is the inevitable experience of martyrdom that some will be called to undergo; the other is the gnawing doubt that some will experience as the years go by (14:1-3). As in the synoptic tradition, there is the expectation that some of the disciples will survive until the *parousia* (21:22-23), but John—apparently intentionally—leaves the result uncertain. To be a follower of Jesus may well lead to martyrdom (21:19), and certainly does not guarantee that one will live until his coming. As we will see, this problem troubled the Pauline community as well. For the Johannine community, it was sufficient to rely on what Jesus had promised and to celebrate his presence among them in the Eucharist and through the Spirit.

As the Christian communities became increasingly beleaguered—cut off from Judaism and persecuted by Roman authorities—the Gospel of John served an important function. It provided a framework of understanding for a group or groups within early Christianity that had to come to terms with persecution and with the delay in the expected *parousia*. The Fourth Gospel dealt with both issues directly. At the same time, it provided a theological framework for a community that was simultaneously inclusive and mystical. Its membership was open to all who would come in faith, and its members were mutually supported by love and by the strengthening, guiding, teaching power of the Spirit within. The Johannine life world contributed mightily to survival, to outreach, and to internal strength.

7

The Inclusive Community:
Luke-Acts

No one observing the itinerant fishermen and village craftsmen trying to launch an apocalyptic movement in Palestine in the name of an executed Galilean troublemaker would ever have supposed that by the end of the first century there would be flourishing communities of Gentile adherents in the major Mediterranean cities and in Rome itself. And surely no one observing that the original leadership of the movement included illiterates (Acts 4:13) could have imagined that its members would one day include skilled authors able to quote pagan poets, or to employ the literary styles of historians and popular writers of romances. Yet the story of the geographical shift of Christianity from Galilee to Rome and the production of a literarily skilled document worthy of the attention of thoughtful Greek and Roman readers is what we have in the two-volume work comprising the Gospel of Luke and the Acts of the Apostles. The author's detailed and accurate knowledge of the Roman world—including names, titles, and functions of the colonial administration of the empire—lend to his work an air of authority and learning. Who could have produced such a document?

WHO IS THE WRITER?

Ancient tradition, quoted by Eusebius of Caesarea in his *Ecclesiastical History,* affirmed that the Third Gospel was written by Luke, a physician and companion of Paul (Col. 4:14; 2 Tim. 4:11). Scholars were at one time inclined to think that this was a reliable account of the author, since he was supposed to have had a special knowledge of medical terms and to have shared the universalistic outlook of Paul. Closer study, however, has shown that his allegedly superior medical knowledge is no greater than might be expected of any well-educated Greek-speaking Gentile of his time, and his theological outlook turns out to be distinctively different from that of Paul. He acknowledges in the preface of his Gospel (Luke 1:2) that his information about Jesus derives from others who were eyewitnesses, and there is no reason to suppose that he had any more direct access to the career of Paul. Some scholars have inferred from the sections where the narrative is reported in the first-person plural (Acts 16:10ff) that the author was a companion of Paul for parts of his journeys; but the shift back and forth from first- to third-person narratives has parallels in the Hellenistic literature of the period. All that can be said is that the author of Acts may have utilized as one of his sources a travel account concerning Paul, although one must acknowledge that this document was more reliable in topographical and local detail than in its historical account of the career of Paul as a whole.

Even if we do not know the name of the author of this work, we can infer a great deal about his life-world. Luke, as it is convenient to call him, differs from both Paul, whose story he tells in his own way in Acts, and from the other Gospels. Formally he stands with the other two synoptics, since the basic outline he follows derives from Mark, with supplemental material from Q, in addition to his own distinctive traditions. He has smoothed out the awkwardnesses of Mark's syntax, although he has at many points effectively echoed the style of the Septuagint, which was obviously the version of the Bible he knew and used. His stories are framed by stylized statements (such as the opening lines of both Luke and Acts) and by chronological references, in keeping with the practice of secular historians of the period (Luke 3:1). We will comment on his qualities as a historian later on in this chapter, but it is important to recognize that he had the cultural background and the education to know how writers and historians went about their work. When he came to tell the story of Paul's missionary journeys around the Mediterranean world, he used precisely the style and technique that was being employed in his time (beginning of the second century) by writers of popular romances, such as Xenophon of Ephesus in his vivid, novellike account of the perilous travels of two devotees of Isis, whose wanderings take them to Athens and Ephesus, culminating in a storm at sea from which they are miraculously delivered. The similarities to the narrative of Acts are obvious.

It is not merely literary skill and cultural sophistication that differentiates the life-world of Luke from that of Paul or the other Gospel writers. Rather, Luke has a fundamentally different view of the place of the Church in history than the outlook of Q, or of Mark, or of Paul. These three believed that the present age was shortly coming to an end and regarded responsibilities for accommodation to the wider world and internal organization of their respective communities as a matter of expediency. A minimum of structure in order to achieve a maximum of evangelistic efficiency, one might say. What Luke has undertaken is to show that the ongoing life of the Church should not be regarded as an embarrassment (the delay of the *parousia*), but as prime evidence that God is working out his purpose in history through the Church and its leadership.

Luke presents this not in terms of a general theory, but in a concrete program manifested in a pattern of epochs that stretch from the creation of the world to the consummation of God's redemptive plan. The concreteness of this program is apparent in the changing geographical setting for the unfolding story, beginning in Galilee and culminating in Rome—although the consummation is apparently to take place in Jerusalem, where the two central saving events occurred: (1) the death and Resurrection of Jesus, and (2) the outpouring of the Spirit (Luke 23–24; Acts 1–2). One cannot be certain that Luke intended from the outset to write both volumes, but the two mesh smoothly. The Gospel obviously builds on synoptic tradition, and is written in a more nearly Semitic style, while Acts shows kinship with Greek historical and popular writing. But in spite of distinct characteristics, the work as a whole is skillfully unified in its outlook. And that overarching objective is not primarily to demonstrate intellectual or literary expertise. Why would he have wanted to write such an account?

WHY AND HOW A CHRISTIAN HISTORY SHOULD BE WRITTEN

There have, of course, been those in every century of the Church's existence who have looked on life in this age as merely transitional, and who claim to see no positive worth in anything this age has to offer. Everything they want will become theirs in the sweet by-and-by. Luke[1] was not content with this viewpoint, and instead set about describing the redemptive purpose of God in such a way as to show the essential role of the Church in the achievement of that purpose. In his view, the structuring of the Church was as much a part of the fulfillment of the divine plan as the act of Consummation itself. Indeed, the act of the drama in which the Church has the center of the stage is an indispensable antecedent of the end of the age. The Age of the Church is the midpoint in the whole drama, as Luke sees it.[2]

Luke's Historical Method

Luke's scheme can be discerned in detail not only from direct statements, but from the ways—at times subtle, at times more obvious—in which he modifies the tradition as he received it. The modifications are most clear, of course, where we have parallels from Mark and Matthew with which to compare Luke's handling of the material. But the special interests and even the distinctive vocabulary of Luke can be detected in material which he alone among the evangelists records. He was peculiarly well fitted for this task by his apparent knowledge of historical and literary methods of his own time, as well as by his thorough familiarity with the language of the Greek Old Testament. As a result of those two streams of literary influence, his work serves admirably as a bridge from the Jewish setting in which the Gospel arose to the Gentile world to which the message was to be interpreted. Luke is equally at home with the Semitic-sounding hymns of the infancy stories ("My soul magnifies the Lord," Luke 1:46) and the philosophical platitudes of the Hellenistic world ("In him we live and move and have our being," Acts 17:28).

Luke's knowledge of his world includes precise political and historical information as well. For example, in Acts 17:6 the city officials in Thessalonica are referred to as "politarchs." The term is used without explanation and occurs nowhere else in the New Testament. Inscriptions found in the region, however, confirm that the title was in use there and suggest that it was not

---

[1] On the question of the authorship of Acts and the use of sources, see the full and judicious discussion in W. G. Kümmel, *Introduction to the New Testament,* trans. H. C. Kee (Nashville: Abingdon Press, 1975), pp. 181–88.

[2] The basic work on Luke-Acts in which the redemptive periods are traced out is *The Theology of St. Luke,* by Hans Conzelmann (New York: Harper & Row, 1960). This study is translated from the original German, which is titled appropriately, *Die Mitte der Zeit*—that is, *The Mid-Point of Time.* A variant of this scheme is set out in H. C. Kee, *Jesus in History,* pp. 189–210. Luke, however, is more concerned with expanding spheres of evangelism (from Jerusalem Jews, to Samaritans, to Jews in pagan cities, to Gentiles throughout the Mediterranean, culminating in Rome) than with successive periods of time.

The Oracle at Delphi was the site where the priestess of Apollo, after ceremonial preparation, uttered statements, often enigmatic, which were understood to be answers to questions addressed to her concerning momentous personal and political problems.   (*Darryl Jones*)

used elsewhere. The accuracy of Luke's designation of the rulers of the city is thereby confirmed.

One of the few relatively fixed points of chronology in the whole of the New Testament is the stay of Paul in Corinth (Acts 18:12ff). Luke reports that the Roman governor in Corinth at the time of Paul's sojourn there was Gallio. From an inscription found across the Gulf of Corinth at Delphi it is possible to determine that Gallio began his term as governor in the first half of

Claudius as pictured on a coin of his reign (A.D. 41–54). He was the emperor who drove the Jews from Rome about the year 50. Some of the exiles found their way to Corinth and became Paul's aides.   (*James T. Stewart*)

A.D. 51. This confirmation of Luke's account receives further support from the mention in Acts 18:1ff that two Jews who had recently arrived in Corinth and who later helped Paul in his work there had fled from Rome following a decree of the emperor Claudius against the Jews in the imperial city. The date of that decree, as can be inferred from Suetonius's *Life of Claudius,* is approximately A.D. 49, which of course fits in precisely with Luke's account. In short, Luke has access to accurate information and uses it effectively in setting forth his story of the spread of the Gospel from Galilee to Jerusalem and on to Rome.

LUKE AS HISTORIAN. It would be unreasonable, however, to expect Luke to measure up to modern standards of historical reliability, much less objectivity. He compares favorably with his contemporary historians.[3] One sees this from the outset in the formal literary prefaces with which he has prefixed both volumes of his work:

> Inasmuch as many have undertaken to compile a narrative of the things which have been accomplished among us, just as they were delivered to us by those who from the beginning were eyewitnesses and ministers of the word, it seemed good to us also, having followed all things closely for some time past, to write you an orderly account, most excellent Theophilus, that you may know the truth concerning the things of which you have been informed.

> —LUKE 1:1–4

And the second recalls the first:

> In the first book, O Theophilus, I have dealt with all that Jesus began to do and teach. . . .

> —ACTS 1:1

The complexity of the sentences, the acknowledgment of predecessors in the field, the expression of purpose by the writer, and the address to the patron are all literary conventions of the time. Luke is making a bid to have his books regarded seriously by the sophisticated of his day.

It is easier to assess Luke's place among the historians of his time than it is to evaluate his work as a historian for the modern mind which seeks historical knowledge of the beginnings of Christianity. On the one hand, Luke uses his sources in much the same way as his contemporary historians, although the evangelistic purpose behind his work gives his books a special quality that the other historical writings lack. On the other hand, he raises problems for the modern scholar in search of "historicity" by adopting the first-century custom of inventing speeches or modifying the accounts of events. This was done even when the historian was an eyewitness, since his aim was not verbatim reporting but portraying what was characteristic or what he thought was

---

[3] For an appreciative study of Luke's literary and historical methods in comparison with those of other Hellenistic historians, see H. J. Cadbury, *The Making of Luke-Acts* (London: S.P.C.K., 1961), pp. 113–212.

significant in the incidents he was reporting. The late interpreter and historian of early Christianity, Martin Dibelius, has said:

> The ancient historian does not wish to present life with photographic accuracy, but rather to portray and illuminate what is typical, and his practice of aiming at what is typical and important allows the author of Acts partly to omit, change or generalize what really occurred. So it is that, where he sometimes appears to us today to be idealizing, and describing what was typical, he was really trying to discharge his obligations as an historian. Thus, through the literary methods of the historian, he was able to discharge his other obligation of being a preacher of faith in Christ.[4]

Basic for the work of a historian today is a chronological sequence of the events with which he is dealing; none was available to Luke, however. In all probability, Luke had only an itinerary of Paul to follow for the sequence of events he depicts in Acts. Even there, his other objectives lead him to halt the course of his account of Paul to introduce other interests or to insert speeches attributed to Paul. This is especially evident in the famous sermon on the Areopagus in Acts 17. In preparing the Gospel of Luke, there was no chronology or sequence of events available, except for Mark's. Luke follows Mark's sequence in a general way, but feels free to depart widely at the beginning and the end, and to make considerable modifications in the middle. His avowed purpose of setting forth "an orderly account" seems to refer not so much to chronological order but to logical or even theological order. As we shall see, it is to his purpose to have the story of Jesus's rejection at Nazareth come right at the outset of his public ministry (4), even though Mark locates it at the end of a period of successful activity in Galilee (Mark 6). It is important, therefore, to try to discover the pattern or "order" which guided Luke in the arrangement of his material.

A Christian Perspective on the Scope of History

Luke's undertaking is an ambitious one: He wants to place the ministry of Jesus and the work of the Church in the context of the universal purpose of God. Although the actual chronological scope of the events directly reported runs only from the birth of John the Baptist to the imprisonment of Paul in Rome, there are many factors in both volumes which point backward to the story of ancient Israel and forward to the consummation.

THE FIRST EPOCH: FROM ANCIENT ISRAEL TO JOHN THE BAPTIST.   The best clue to the way Luke regards history as divided into periods is Luke 16:16. In Matthew 11:12–13, the more original version of the saying reads:

> From the days of John the Baptist until now, the kingdom of heaven has been suffering violence, and men of violence are seizing it. For all the

[4] M. Dibelius, in "The First Christian Historian," from *Studies in the Acts of the Apostles* (London: SCM Press, 1956), pp. 136, 137.

> prophets and the law prophesied until John; and if you are willing to receive it, he is Elijah who is going to come.

Luke has greatly reduced this saying (or this cluster of sayings) and has omitted the reference to John the Baptist as Elijah. But more important than these changes is the attitude implied toward John the Baptist: For Matthew, John marks the beginning of the new era of violence that presages the coming of the kingdom. For Luke, John marks the *end* of the epoch of the law and the prophets:

> The law and the prophets were until John; since then the good news of the kingdom of God is preached, and every one enters it violently.
>
> —LUKE 16:16

In Luke's view, John the Baptist brings to a close the old era of the law and the prophets, during which the promises of redemption were given, but in which the promised deliverance did not occur. It is the period of the ministry of Jesus that brings about the fulfillment of the promise. Luke tells us this in a unique passage (4:16–30). He describes Jesus preaching in the synagogue at Nazareth. After reading the words of promised redemption ("good news to the poor, release to the captives, deliverance for the oppressed"), Jesus declares forthrightly:

> Today this scripture has been fulfilled in your hearing.
>
> —LUKE 4:21

Although he does not carry the theme of fulfillment to the extreme of Matthew, Luke is careful throughout his account of the ministry of Jesus to show how what Jesus did was the fulfillment of scripture. Before considering the subject of fulfillment in Luke in detail, we must identify the end of this period in Luke's scheme and the beginning of the next.

THE SECOND EPOCH: THE EARTHLY MINISTRY OF JESUS.   The period of Jesus's ministry is the second great epoch, and is itself divided into three phases. The first opens with the launching of the ministry with the programmatic sermon. By the time Luke reaches the point in his narrative that corresponds to Mark 9:38–41 (Luke 9:50), we should expect the ministry to be nearing its close, as is the case with Mark's report. Instead, the ministry is now ready to go into its next phase: the preaching of the Gospel outside the land of Galilee, as 9:52 shows. The significance of the first phase is the gathering of the witnesses in Galilee, as is shown by the special attention and miraculous circumstances surrounding their call into his service (Luke 5:1–11). The importance of these eyewitnesses has been anticipated in Luke's preface (1:2); it is confirmed by the special Lukan word to his followers on the eve of the Crucifixion, in which he addresses them as "you who have continued with me in my trials" (22:28), as well as by the choice of a replacement for the traitorous

Judas from among those "who have accompanied us during all the time that the Lord Jesus went in and out among us, beginning from the baptism of John until the day that he was taken up from us. . ." (Acts 1:21, 22).

According to Luke 4, the rejection of Jesus by his countrymen is expected from the outset. He must therefore turn to others in seeking a response of faith wherever it may be found. It is appropriate that Luke closes off the first phase of Jesus's ministry with the story of the strange exorcist, according to which Jesus rebukes the disciples for their exclusivism and encourages them to welcome support from whatever source (9:49–50): "Whoever is not against us is for us."

Although Jesus "must" now leave Galilee, he does not set out aimlessly: The clear goal that he has in view is Jerusalem, where his final rejection is to occur (9:51). Appropriately, this phase of his work is preceded by the sending of seventy evangelists to call men to repent and to announce the nearness of the kingdom of God (10:1–16, esp. v. 11). The number seventy seems to be here (as is often the case in Jewish tradition) symbolic of the seventy nations into which it was believed the human race was divided. Luke is here preparing for the mission to the Gentiles that is to be the theme of volume two of his work.

The event that signals the right time for the new phase is not simply the negative factor of the rejection in Galilee. Indeed, Luke reports widespread response to Jesus from Galilee, Judea, and Gentile regions beyond (6:17–19). The factor that brings about the change of locale and hence the change of procedure is the announcement by Jesus of his impending suffering and death (9:18–22). In Luke's version of the Transfiguration which follows the first prediction of the Passion, an incident occurs which he alone reports: the conversation of Jesus with Moses and Elijah ("the law and the prophets") concerning his "departure which he was about to fulfill in Jerusalem" (9:31). This theme is sounded again when Jesus's final departure from Galilee is recounted in 13:31–33. The immediate occasion for Jesus's statement is a report to him by Pharisees that Herod (Antipas, the tetrarch of Galilee) is seeking to destroy him:

> Go and tell that fox, "Behold, I cast out demons and perform cures today and tomorrow, and on the third day I finish my course. Nevertheless I must go on my way today and tomorrow and the day following; for it cannot be that a prophet should perish away from Jerusalem."

The first "journey" of Jesus and the seventy begins after the fact of his suffering has been disclosed, but before its significance is understood.[5] The final journey begins (13:33) when the suffering is about to be undergone. Luke moves up to this point his version of Jesus's lament over Jerusalem, in contrast to Mark (followed by Matthew), who assigns it to the last days of Jesus in Jerusalem. For Luke it serves as a symbolic indication that Jesus's rejection in Jerusalem and the subsequent judgment of God on the city are necessary elements in the working of the divine plan. The destruction of Jerusalem is men-

[5] See Conzelmann, *The Theology of St. Luke*, p. 65.

From Jerusalem down to Jericho. Traces of fortifications and hostels remain along the road which descends nearly 3000 feet from the crest of the Judean hills at Jerusalem to the depths of the Jordan Valley where Jericho lies. The barren, forbidding stretch seems never to have supported settlements.   (*Gordon N. Converse*)

tioned unambiguously by Luke (21:20), whereas in Mark (13:14) and even in Matthew (24:15) the desecration of the Temple and the fall of the city are alluded to or described only in veiled language. It is also in Jerusalem that the triumphant Christ is to be revealed as judge at the consummation of the age (Acts 1:8). Jerusalem, then, is central to the whole redemptive purpose of God in Luke's understanding, and it is to Jerusalem that Jesus *must* go.

The third phase of the activity of Jesus takes place in Jerusalem, beginning with the approach to the city by way of Jericho and reaching its climax in his rejection and crucifixion there. The nucleus of the new eschatological community is present at the Last Supper, according to a tradition found only in Luke (22:15–30).[6] The post-Resurrection appearances of Jesus occur in

[6] The account of the Supper is found, of course, in the other Gospels, but the emphasis on the eschatological nature of the meal (22:16) and the words addressed to the disciples as the beginnings of a new community (22:28ff) are distinctively Lukan. If one assumes that the so-called Western text of the Greek New Testament is the original, and omits 22:19b–20, the eschatological nature of the Supper is all the more striking.

Jerusalem or in that vicinity, in Luke's account. Matthew reports them as taking place in Galilee; and Mark, who does not describe any appearances, nevertheless expects them to occur in Galilee. According to Luke, it is from Jerusalem that the world mission of the Church is to begin (Luke 24:47), and it is there that the community will receive the gift of the Holy Spirit to empower it to fulfill its divinely appointed task (Acts 1:8).

THE THIRD EPOCH: FROM THE ASCENSION TO THE RETURN OF CHRIST.   The ascension of Jesus Christ—reported only in Luke—marks the transition to the third major epoch in Luke's scheme of the ages: the age of the Church's mission to the world. During this period, Christ is seated at God's right hand (Acts 2:33; 3:20, 21). Having poured out the Spirit upon the Church, his next great work will be that of judge of all at the end of the age (Acts 10:42; 17:31). God's work is, in the present epoch, being achieved by the power of the Spirit at work through the Church. It began with those who were eyewitnesses of Jesus's activity (Acts 1:21–22) and is continued by those who succeeded them in the community of faith. It does not matter, therefore, how long the Last Day may be delayed: The ground of the redemptive activity has been laid in the work of Jesus Christ in fulfillment of the law and the prophets. The power of God is at work in the Church as it was in the ministry of Jesus. All is leading to the promised day, whose coming is now made certain by God's provision of the Messiah, by his triumph over death, by the power of the Spirit, and by the activity of the Church in fulfilling its mission.

During the latest epoch, however, Christians who are not of Jewish background are to respect those who are. Thus, for example, Paul took a Nazirite vow on his final visit to Jerusalem (Num. 6:1–20), which involved special purification and shaving the head (Acts 21:23–26). He not only boasted of a "clear conscience toward God and toward men" (Acts 24:16), but denied that he had done anything contrary to the law of the Jews (24:14) or against the Temple (25:8). What he has proclaimed is "nothing but what the prophets and Moses said would come to pass" (26:22). There is no suggestion, therefore, that in the final epoch of the divine plan the Jewish concern to obey the law of Moses is out of place for Christians. Rather, as we shall see in Chapter 10, Paul agreed—according to Acts 15—that a minimum of the ritual requirements of the Jewish law should be observed by Gentile Christians.

ALL THINGS WRITTEN IN THE LAW
ARE NOW FULFILLED

Luke's conviction that the law and the prophets are fulfilled in Jesus Christ is far more pervasively present in both volumes of his work than the direct references to the fulfillment of scripture might indicate. We have already noted the explicit claim attributed to Jesus in his sermon at Nazareth that on that day the scripture was fulfilled in the hearing of those present (Luke 4:16–30). Luke's Gospel concludes on the same note; the doubting disciples are told:

These are my words which I spoke to you while I was yet with you, that everything written about me in the law of Moses and the prophets and the psalms must be fulfilled.

—LUKE 24:44

The sermons of Acts are full of allusions to the Old Testament and of the claim that the promises made to the Fathers (the Fathers in Israel) have been fulfilled now in Jesus Christ (Acts 2:16, 30; 3:18; 4:11, 4:25; 7:52; 8:35; 10:43; 13:32). But the direct claims and specific promises which are believed to have been fulfilled are only part of the work of Luke.

John the Baptist and the Old Testament

The stage is set for development of the theme of the Baptist's connection with the Old Testament in the opening verses of Luke, following the formal preface (1:1–4). The birth of John the Baptist is described in its priestly environment and in an atmosphere of pious obedience to the Jewish law. The miraculous circumstances surrounding John's conception and birth are reminiscent of the birth of Samuel (1 Sam. 1, 2). He comes in the spirit of Elijah, and his ministry will have its effect upon "the sons of Israel" (1:16, 17). The hymns of praise and gratitude uttered by the angels, by Mary, by Zechariah, and by the aged Simeon in the Temple (2:29–32) are written with the cadences, the vocabulary, the imagery of Old Testament poetry. So strong is the Semitic flavor of the language in these passages that some scholars think the hymns have been translated from Hebrew or Aramaic originals. The same could be said, indeed, of the narrative context in which Luke has placed them. It is possible that there were Semitic originals, but it is perhaps even more likely that Luke, with his great literary skill, has written the narrative in the style of the Semitic-flavored Septuagint with which he was familiar and from which he regularly quotes. It would have sounded to him like biblical language in much the same way that the language of the King James Version sounds "like the Bible" to us today.

The hymns may have originated in pre-Christian times and may have been adapted by Luke for his own purposes. It has been conjectured that they originally belonged to a sect that honored the Baptist as the eschatological prophet. Traces of such a sect may be discerned beneath the surface of John 3 and 4, as well as in Acts 18:24ff. A sect that honors John the Baptist as redeemer survives to the present day in Iraq.[7] Some ancient biblical manuscripts of Luke attribute the so-called Magnificat (1:46ff) to Elizabeth rather than to Mary, in which case the savior would be John and not Jesus. In any case, the continuity between the covenant people of Israel and the new is vigorously set forth in the opening chapters of Luke. The venerable worshippers, Simeon and Anna, both of whom are looking "for the consolation of Israel" (2:25, 38), with true prophetic insight recognize in the infant Jesus the realization of their hopes.

---

[7] The basic study is by Lady E. S. Drower, *The Mandaeans of Iraq and Iran* (Leiden: Brill, 1937, 1962).

Jesus's Ancestry as a Link to the Old Testament

The directness of the continuity between Jesus and Israel's hopes is affirmed in the genealogy of Jesus, which differs significantly from Matthew's (Luke 3:23–38; Matt. 1:1–17). Matthew traces Jesus's ancestry back to Abraham; Luke traces it back to Adam. When linked with the expansion of John's quotation from Isaiah 40 to include the words "all flesh shall see the salvation of our God" (Luke 3:6), it is obvious Luke wants his readers to know that Jesus Christ is the *world's* redeemer, not merely the deliverer of Israel. Although we can recognize the artificiality of the genealogy, and although it is impossible to harmonize it with Matthew's, Luke's "historical" purpose still stands clear: God's guiding hand is to be seen throughout the whole range of history, culminating in the history of Jesus and the redemption of the world that is made possible through him.

Israel's Misunderstanding of the Prophecies

Even while affirming the hand of God at work in the history of his people, Luke asserts that the nation Israel has come under judgment because it has failed to comprehend the will of God through the prophets. The speech of Stephen in Acts 7 is the fullest and most vivid evidence of this, with its climactic accusation:

> You stiff-necked people, uncircumcised in heart and ears, you always resist the Holy Spirit. As your fathers did, so do you. Which of the prophets did not your fathers persecute? And they killed those who announced beforehand the coming of the Righteous One, whom you have now betrayed and murdered, you who received the law as delivered by angels and did not keep it.
>
> —ACTS 7:51–53

The fault lies not with the law or the promises contained in it, but with the people who have failed to hear in it God's word for them. Yet even their rejection of his word has been turned by God to good purpose. The Crucifixion itself, though accomplished "by the hands of lawless men," was nonetheless "according to the definite plan and foreknowledge of God" (Acts 2:23). Or in the words that Luke attributes to the risen Christ, "Was it not necessary that the Christ should suffer these things and enter into his glory?" And Luke goes on to say:

> And beginning with Moses and all the prophets he [Jesus] interpreted to them in all the scriptures the things concerning himself.
>
> —LUKE 24:27

THE SPIRIT POURED OUT ON ALL FLESH

The effective agent in the accomplishment of God's purpose in the epoch of preparation through the prophets, the epoch of Jesus's ministry, and the epoch of the Church's mission, is the Holy Spirit. Thus David's prophecy about the Messiah and the demonic opposition he would encounter were uttered "by the Holy Spirit" (Acts 4:25). Israel's resistance to the word of God proclaimed by the prophets was, according to Stephen's speech, "resisting the Holy Spirit" (Acts 7:51).

The Spirit Commissions Jesus

Similarly, the Spirit is operative in the preparations for the coming of Jesus Christ in the infancy stories of Luke 1 and 2: John the Baptist will be filled with the Holy Spirit; the Spirit will come upon Mary so that she may conceive and bear a son; Elizabeth is filled with the Spirit when she greets Mary; Zechariah prophesies by the Holy Spirit, as does Simeon. Luke alone

Shepherds' Field and Bethlehem. Although it was known as the City of David, Israel's most renowned king, its population was limited by a lack of agricultural resources. Then and now, shepherds are a familiar part of the scene.   (*Gordon N. Converse*)

depicts the coming of the Spirit upon Jesus at baptism as being "in *bodily* form, as a dove" (Luke 3:22). The anointing by the Spirit characterizes Jesus's ministry from the outset, both in the initial return from the Jordan to the desert (4:1) and from the desert to Galilee (4:14), and in the sermon based on Isaiah 61, which Jesus claims to be now fulfilled in him.

Although Jesus's bodily presence among his followers is depicted by Luke as terminating with his ascension, his spiritual presence is vividly described as an ongoing process which obviously did not end with his being taken up and which is seen to have three facets. The first of these is Christ's presence in the reading of scripture. (1) Jesus is himself the interpreter who expounds all three parts of the Jewish scriptures for the disciples—the law, the prophets, and the psalms (Luke 24:44)—in order for them to see how these sacred writings have found their fulfillment in him. (2) The second mode of his presence is in the partaking of bread, the eucharistic ritual (24:30). In both cases, it is Jesus himself who is "made known" in the word and sacrament, not merely information about him. (3) Finally, the Spirit which they are about to receive, following Jesus's departure, is sent by him in the name of the Father (24:49), in order to enable them to be qualified, empowered witnesses (24:48). That is precisely the designation by which Jesus addresses his followers at the moment of his ascension (Acts 1:8), as they are commissioned for their worldwide task.

The Spirit Empowers the Church

The coming of the Spirit on the Day of Pentecost (Acts 2) is for Luke the sign that the promise made through Joel is being fulfilled: God's Spirit will be poured out on all flesh (on all humanity) and whoever (whether Jew or Gentile) will call on the Lord's name will be saved. The day of universal salvation, or universal opportunity for salvation, is here. The miracle of simultaneous translation described by Luke (Acts 2:5–11) is told in a manner that parallels the Jewish tradition about the marvelous manifestations of divine power that accompanied the giving of the law at Sinai. According to this Jewish legend, there were seventy tongues of fire on the mountain, representing the seventy languages of the seventy nations of the earth. The law, however, remained largely the private possession of Israel, its light rarely reaching to the Gentiles. Now at the end of the age, Luke is telling his reader, the goal is achieved: all people come under the power of the Spirit of God. Furthermore, the divine judgment at the Tower of Babel is reversed: Humankind, which was then divided by language barriers into many hostile peoples, is now brought into one by the power of the Spirit in order to prepare all to hear the one Gospel that can redeem the race.[8]

The Spirit is the effective power in enabling the ministry of the community to perform its work. The disciples, forbidden by the religious officials in Jerusalem to speak the message of God, are given courage through the Holy Spirit to defy the authorities and to speak (Acts 5:9). The criteria for selection

---

[8] See the discussion of this difficult passage in E. Haenchen, *Acts of the Apostles* (Philadelphia: Westminster Press, 1971), pp. 166–75.

of the "deacons" to assist in the ministry of the community include that they must be "full of the Spirit" (6:3). Stephen is given strength to go to a martyr's death by the power of the Holy Spirit (7:55). The validity of the evangelistic work done among Samaritans (8:19) and Gentiles (10:44) is confirmed by the fact that those who hear the Gospel in faith receive the Holy Spirit. It is the gift of bestowal of the Spirit that the mercenary Simon Magus tries to purchase (8:18). The seal of Saul's conversion is the reception of the Spirit (9:17). The Spirit leads the community and its ministry in selecting persons for special tasks (13:2), in shaping the itinerary of the traveling evangelists (13:4; 16:7; 19:21), and in the supervisory roles within the community itself (20:28). Angels at times lend assistance, according to Luke (Acts 8:26; 10:3; 12:7; 27:23), but it is the Spirit who is the chief agent of God's purpose in this age.

THE MISSION OF THE CHURCH
TO THE WHOLE WORLD

The first clear indication that Luke gives us of his concern for the universal benefits that are to come through Christ appears in the words of the aged holy man, Simeon, whose utterance now forms an important part of the liturgy of the Church:

> Lord, now lettest thy servant depart in peace,
>   according to thy word;
> for mine eyes have seen thy salvation
>   which thou hast prepared in the presence of all peoples,
> *a light for revelation to the Gentiles,*
>   and for glory to thy people Israel.

—LUKE 2:29, 30

The Light for the Gentiles

There is ample precedent in the Old Testament for the thesis that Israel's mission is to be a light to the Gentiles (Isa. 42:6; 49:6), but Simeon as he beholds the infant Jesus affirms that it is through this child that the promise is to be fulfilled. We have already noted that Luke quotes a more extended passage from Isaiah 40 in connection with the ministry of John the Baptist, with the result that the savior for whose coming John prepares the way is the savior of "all flesh" (Luke 3:4–6). Even before Jesus launches his public ministry, Luke is letting his reader know that the benefits Jesus brings are to be extended to all humanity, and are not to be the exclusive privilege of the Jewish nation. In this way Judaism is not excluded from the grace of God, but the scope in which the grace of God is at work is extended beyond ethnic bounds. In the words of the angels' song:

> Glory to God in the highest, and on earth peace among men with whom he is pleased.

—LUKE 2:14

Peace is for all who respond in faith, rather than the prerogative of a chosen few.

The occupations of the two groups of persons who are reported by Luke to have repented at John's preaching are such as to exclude them automatically from religious acceptability by Jewish standards. A tax collector was considered a traitor to Judaism because of his collaboration with the hated Roman overlords and the dishonest dealings that seem to have been characteristic of his trade. Soldiers, who were subject to duty on any day, could not possibly keep the Jewish laws against work on the Sabbath. Jews were excused from military service by Roman law; if a Jew chose a military career, he virtually forfeited his claim to participation in the life of the covenant people. Luke tells us, however, that it was persons of this sort—that is, religious outcasts, by Jewish standards—who heard John's message and repented. Even before Jesus appears, then, Luke is preparing us for the fuller story of the God who in Jesus Christ seeks the outcasts and accepts those who know their need and acknowledge it.

The Good News for the Outsiders

The converse of this concern for the outcasts is the constant attack on the rich. The theme is also sounded in the hymns of the infancy stories:

> He has scattered the proud in the imagination of their hearts,
>   he has put down the mighty from their thrones,
>   and exalted those of low degree;
>
> He has filled the hungry with good things,
>   and the rich he has sent empty away.
>
> —LUKE 1:51–53

The opening theme of the sermon at Nazareth is the claim that "The Spirit of the Lord . . . has anointed me to preach good news to the poor." The word "poor" resounds throughout the Gospel of Luke. Instead of the religious designation in the Beatitude recorded by Matthew, "Blessed are the poor in spirit," Luke has simply, "Blessed are you poor" (6:20). Only in Luke's version of the Parable of the Great Supper is it explicitly stated that those who are brought into the feast after the group originally invited has declined are the "poor and maimed and blind and lame" (Luke 14:21). The invitation is symbolic of the Gospel invitation to share in the joys of the age to come. The Jews to whom the invitation was originally extended have refused to come; the offer now goes out to the outcasts. Only in Luke do we hear of the rich fool whose wealth is his sole ground of security (12:13–21) and of the wretched Lazarus, who enters the realm of the blessed while the rich man lingers in torment (16:19–31).

Although Luke shares with Matthew the tradition about the questioners who come from John the Baptist, in which Jesus points to the works of healing and the proclamation of good news to the poor as evidence of his mission (Matt. 11:5; Luke 7:22), Luke alone develops the theme. At times this motif appears in the form of a modification of material used by the other evangelists. For example, Matthew and Mark report at the end of Jesus's public ministry the story of the woman who anointed him for burial. In Matthew 26:8 and Mark 14:4, the disciples complain about the waste of money, which might better have been given to the poor. Jesus's famous reply is that the poor are always on hand, but that he will not be on hand for long. In Luke's version, however, the story has become an account of the pronouncement of forgiveness to an outcast, a woman who is a "sinner." She comes to him in a spirit of devotion, seeking nothing. He offers her forgiveness and salvation (Luke 7:36–50, see esp. 48, 50). No mention is made of anointing for burial, and the whole point of the incident centers on the forgiveness of sin even to the one who most obviously violates the moral and ceremonial laws of Judaism. Luke underscores this by locating the incident immediately following the report of the contrast between Jesus and John the Baptist, in which Jesus quotes his critics as calling him "A glutton and a drunkard, a friend of tax-collectors and sinners" (7:34).

The same note is sounded in the story, reported only by Luke, concerning Zacchaeus, the tax collector (Luke 19:1–10). Once more, Jesus violates the Jewish laws of ceremonial purity by not merely having contact with a tax collector, but actually inviting himself to his house for a meal. As in the case of the woman who anointed him, Jesus announces that "salvation has this day come to this house." The story is rounded off by a saying in which Jesus epitomizes his redemptive program: "The Son of man has come to seek and to save that which is lost."

God Takes the Initiative Toward the Outcasts

In these narratives, Luke is telling us that not only is God willing to *accept* those who are estranged from him and to forgive those who are sinners, but that he is actively *seeking out* those who are far from him, whether Jews who were excluded from the life of the covenant people or Gentiles who never had a part in the covenant. Luke underscores this conviction in both narrative and discourse material. Nowhere has he set this forth more powerfully than in three parables he presents in sequence: the Lost Sheep, the Lost Coin, and the Lost Son (Luke 15:1–32). The last two of these are found only in Luke, and the first appears in an expanded version (cf. Matt. 18:12–14). In each case, the title of the parable might well be changed to stress the joy of the one who has recovered what has been lost, thereby making the point of the parable the nature of God rather than the condition of the one who is lost. Accordingly, the parables would become the Joyous Shepherd, the Joyous Housewife, and the Joyous Father. The story of the rejoicing father is actually in two parts, with the second focused on the disgruntled older brother who refuses to welcome back his wayward brother. He will not even acknowledge him as his brother, preferring to refer to him as "that son of yours." Luke (or Jesus?) is here striking out against the critics of his message of God's grace by comparing them with the self-centered, unforgiving, graceless brother, just as Jesus rebukes those who condemn him for his forgiving attitude toward the sinful woman. Luke views Jesus as the foe of prideful moralism and as the spokes-man for God, whose grace flows out to all who will acknowledge their need and receive that grace by faith.

The Outcasts Are Ready to Respond

The readiness of the Gentiles to accept the grace of God is indicated by the two illustrations that bring to a close Jesus's sermon in the synagogue at Nazareth. The only person who was miraculously fed during the famine in the time of Elijah was a Sidonian woman—that is, a Gentile. Similarly, only the Gentile leper, Naaman, was healed in the time of Elisha. The implication is that others do not benefit from the divine redemption available to them be-cause they are not ready to receive it. If God's grace can evoke no response of faith in Israel, it will turn to the Gentiles.

As we noted earlier in this chapter, Luke anticipates the Gentile mission when he depicts Jesus as sending out the seventy. This mission of the seventy is in addition to the sending of the twelve that Luke has taken over from his Markan source (9:1; cf. Mark 6:7ff), and which Matthew has greatly ex-panded in his account of the mission of the disciples (Matt. 9:35–10:16). Per-haps Luke intends the sending of the twelve to symbolize the initial mission of the Gospel to Israel, and the sending of the seventy to represent the subse-quent turning of the messengers of the Gospel to the nations of the world. The shift of attention from the mission to Israel to the world mission is specifically pronounced in Acts. In Antioch of Pisidia, where Paul and Barnabas have been evangelizing, the success of their efforts has aroused violent hostility from the Jewish community. The apostles' reaction to their attack is a turning point in Luke's description of the apostolic mission:

> And Paul and Barnabas spoke boldly and said: "It was necessary that the word of God should be spoken first to you. Since you thrust it from you, and judge yourselves unworthy of eternal life, behold, we turn to the Gentiles. For so the Lord has commended us saying, 'I have set you to be a light to the Gentiles, that you may bring salvation to the utter-most parts of the earth.' "
>
> —ACTS 13:46, 47

The belief that the Gospel was to be heard first by the Jews and then by Gen-tiles is not peculiar to Luke (cf. Rom. 1:16), but it is declared by him with unique clarity and persistence.

Going into All the World

Just as Luke's Gospel begins with a sermon outlining the ministry of Jesus, so the Book of Acts begins with a program laid down by the Risen Christ to be effected by the power of the Holy Spirit through the Church. The disciples—now to be styled *apostles,* or *sent ones*—are to bear witness to the Gos-pel of Jesus Christ; first in Jerusalem, then in all Judea, then in Samaria, and then to the end of the earth (Acts 1:8). It is appropriate that the witness

Agora at Samaria, the Roman Forum, and part of a temple at Sebaste, the Greek-style city of Samaria built by Herod the Great and named in honor of Augustus— "Sebaste" in Greek.   (*Howard C. Kee*)

begins in Jerusalem, since, as we have seen, Jerusalem is for Luke the place of revelation *par excellence*. The proclamation of the Gospel in Judea brings the message to the Jews, in keeping with the divinely ordained order ("the Jew first"). The shift to Samaria brings the opportunity to hear the good news of Jesus Christ to those who are alienated from Israel but who share a common heritage. As noted in Chapter 6, the Samaritans were a Semitic people who shared with Judaism the belief that the law of Moses was the word of God, although their version of it differed slightly from the accepted Jewish version. But their chief point of disagreement was on the place of worship (Mount Gerizim rather than Jerusalem), where they had their own priesthood distinct from the Jerusalem priesthood. Samaria was a kind of enclave within predominantly Jewish territory. Once the preaching of the Gospel moved beyond the borders of Palestine, it would know no bounds until it reached the ends of the earth.

Luke does not merely set out the program, however: He describes the progress of the Gospel as it moves on toward what is at least a symbolic achievement of its goal. The first seven chapters of Acts depict the efforts of the apostles to proclaim the good news in Jerusalem. Their work met with considerable success (". . . and there were added that day [of Pentecost] about three thousand souls," 2:41), as well as with violent opposition. As a result, the disciples were imprisoned, interrogated, warned (4:17–22), beaten, and forbidden to speak in the name of Jesus Christ (5:40). The threats and punishments were ineffective, however, and the work of evangelism in Jerusalem is described by Luke as continuing until, following the belligerent speech of Stephen, the Jewish leadership had little choice but to launch a counterattack. In that speech Stephen denounced the nation as having never been ready to hear God's messengers when they came (7:51–53), including Jesus, whom they have murdered. In response, the authorities turn on the infant community; as a result of the great persecution which follows, the friends and co-workers of Stephen flee (8:1b).

That this scattering is symbolic of the spread of the Gospel rather than a historical occurrence in which the Jerusalem community was dispersed is evident from Luke's own account, since he reports continuing activities of the apostles in Jerusalem down to the time of the arrest of Paul there (21:17ff). Jerusalem continues to be the base of operations for the evangelists even in this same chapter of Acts (8:14, 25). The victims of the persecution and the subsequent scattering seem to have been, not the original circle of twelve disciples, but men whom Luke refers to as "Hellenists" (6:1), all of whom bear Greek names. Their assigned role in the Church is that of "deacon," which means "servant" or "assistant" (6:2, 3). Although their original assignment is reported by Luke as caring for "tables" (that is, taking care of the menial and more secular aspects of the community's life), they very soon are engaged in preaching the word of God. This is most obvious in the case of Stephen (6, 7) and Philip (8).

It would appear that Luke has reworked some traditional material in such a way as to document several convictions: (1) that the division in the Church between Jewish Christians and Gentile Christians was by agreement and divine intention rather than a result of conflict; (2) that the proclamation of the Gospel to non-Jews carried the full sanction of the Jerusalem community; and (3) that the death of Stephen was the divinely planned occasion for drawing Saul (Paul) under the influence of the Gospel, thus preparing him for the distinctive role he was to play in the spread of the Gospel to the Gentiles. There is a splendid irony in the fact that it is Paul who leads the very persecution that results in launching the Gentile mission of the Church (8:3). Apart from a general description of himself as a persecutor of the Church (Gal. 1:13), we have no word of this from Paul, so that we cannot determine whether or not it may rest on historical fact. But it is used here by Luke in a fitting way to show how the work of God's Spirit proceeds not only in spite of, but by means of, human opposition (8:4).

The Progress of the Gospel

The spread of the Gospel to the end of the earth has been anticipated by Luke in his description of the Day of Pentecost. This is the case not only in the symbolic significance of the tongues of fire, but in the enumeration of the widely scattered lands from which the dispersion Jews have come (2:9, 10).

Luke goes so far as to say that they were present "from every nation under heaven" (2:5). Luke depicts them as including (1) Jews who had moved to these lands and were returning for the feast; (2) Gentiles who, by accepting baptism and circumcision, had become proselytes, members of the community; and (3) devout Gentiles who had come to participate in the Jewish festival. But here for Luke they represent the whole of humanity. All people will soon have opportunity to hear the Gospel, Luke is telling his reader; from the outset these representatives had opportunity to witness the power with which the Gospel goes forth. The miracle of simultaneous translation was itself enough to fill them with awe and to foreshadow the coming of the Gospel to every nation:

> "We hear them telling in our own tongues the mighty works of God." And all were amazed and perplexed, saying to one another, "What does this mean?"
>
> —ACTS 2:11, 12

Luke is not content, however, merely to anticipate the world mission of the Church: he depicts each stage of its development. The first is of course the preaching to the crowds in Jerusalem, and especially in the Temple itself, the religious center of Judaism (3:11–26), and before the Sanhedrin, Judaism's chief governing body (5:27–32). Following the first persecution (8:1ff), the next stage is launched when Philip preaches the Gospel in Samaria with impressive results, Luke reports (8:4–8). Soon thereafter the Gospel moves to a wider circle when Acts recounts the conversion of an Ethiopian eunuch (8:26–40). According to the Mosaic law, a eunuch could not have participated in the covenant worship (Deut. 23:2), but the term "eunuch" is often used of a powerful court figure, without any of the usual connotations of the word. The story is filled with miraculous movements and coincidences. That the Ethiopian official was prepared in advance to hear the Gospel is evidenced by his reading from the Jewish scriptures the suffering servant text from Isaiah 53, which Philip immediately interprets for him as a prophecy of Jesus Christ (8:33–35). This story must have originated in Hellenistic circles, perhaps connected with Philip the evangelist, whose daughters joined him in his work (21:9), but it has been worked over by Luke to serve the overall objectives of his work. Here it paves the way for the Gentile mission, which begins in full force with the conversion of Cornelius (10:1–48).

The importance of this story for Luke is emphasized by the fact that it is first told (Acts 10) and then retold (Acts 11). What is significant is not only that the Gospel was heard and received by a non-Jew, but that God had placed his stamp of approval on this by sending his Spirit on the new believers (10:44). The point is reaffirmed (10:45), and then put in question form by Luke (through Peter) to any potential critic of the practice of evangelizing Gentiles: "Can anyone forbid water for baptizing these people who have received the Holy Spirit just as we have?" (10:47). The apostolic circle in Jerusalem, Luke reports, approved the evangelism and gave its sanction to the results (11:18): "Then to the Gentiles also God has granted repentance unto life."

Opening the Door of Faith to the Gentiles

For a century and a half, critical study of the New Testament has debated the question as to why Acts depicts Peter as the one through whom the Gentile mission is launched, while the Letters of Paul give one the impression that he was the pioneer in this field. An ingenious solution that still exerts wide influence originated with the so-called Tübingen School of interpretation, which was dominated by Hegel's philosophy of history. According to Hegel's theory, all history moves by the emergence of an idea (*thesis*) which evokes its opposite (*antithesis*); the conflict between the two continues until there emerges a third possibility (*synthesis*). By this view of history, Peter's Jewish-legal understanding of Christianity is the thesis, and Paul's law-free Gospel is the antithesis: from it emerges the universal synthesis of catholic Christianity, of which Acts is a chief document.[9]

It is possible that at the basis of Luke's story is a historical tradition of an encounter of Peter with a Roman officer who became a Christian. It is difficult, however, to square the story as it is told, including all the divine sanctions for the conversion, with Peter's refusal to have table fellowship with Gentiles as reported in Galatians 2. Luke, however, lays heavy stress on the reluctance of Peter to go along with the Gentile mission and on the necessity of repeated divine intervention in order to convince Peter to visit Cornelius. Luke demonstrates to his reader that the decision to open the common life of the Church to all without forcing submission to the Jewish law was not Peter's idea, nor Paul's, but God's.[10]

In the chapter following Peter's report to the apostolic circle, Luke describes another period of persecution—this time by the civil authority, Herod Agrippa I—and after a brief term of imprisonment, from which he is miraculously delivered, Peter disappears from Jerusalem and from the narrative of Acts. A possible exception is the inclusion of "Symeon" (Peter?) in the Apostolic Council detailed in Acts 15. But Peter's main mission is fulfilled for Luke when he has broken down barriers and become the first agent of Gentile evangelism.

Meanwhile, the apostolic circle had commissioned a man named Barnabas to exercise authority in Antioch, which was becoming a center for a new Christian community (11:19–26). As his co-worker, he chose Saul of Tarsus, whose conversion had proved something of an embarrassment to the Jerusalem church according to Acts (9:1–30). After effective evangelism in Antioch, Paul and Barnabas went on a tour of Cyprus and southern and central Asia Minor (13 and 14). Their procedure in each town was to preach first among the Jews, and then, when opposition was encountered, to turn to the Gentiles (14:27).

But not everyone at Antioch was pleased with the results of Paul's work, Luke tells us. Certain persons from Jerusalem (whether official inspectors or

[9] For a summary of the view of the Tübingen School, see A. Schweitzer on F. C. Baur, in *Paul and His Interpreters* (London: A. and C. Black, 1912), pp. 12–21. For a critique of the view, see J. Munck, *Paul and the Salvation of Mankind* (Richmond, Va.: John Knox Press, 1960), pp. 69–86.

[10] See Dibelius, in *Studies in the Acts of the Apostles,* p. 122.

self-appointed busybodies is not stated) came to Antioch insisting that obedience to the precepts of Mosaic law was necessary for participation in the life of
the Christian community. Superficially, at least, this sounds like the situation
of which Paul writes in Galatians 1 and 2. According to Acts 15 and Galatians, it was decided to have Paul and Barnabas go to Jerusalem to work out a
settlement of a disagreement over the proper basis for admitting Gentiles.
Closer examination, however, shows that the consultation in Acts 15 and the
one described by Paul in Galatians can scarcely be the same. In Acts, the
meeting in Jerusalem is a kind of public hearing, at which the entire community (15:12) is present and listens to the verdicts handed down by the leaders
of the apostolic circle. Paul makes a point in Galatians 2:2 that the conversation was a private one, with "those who were of repute." Titus is present in
Paul's account; he is not mentioned in Acts. Even more striking is the difference between the agreement reached according to Acts and the one referred to
by Paul in Galatians 2:10. According to Paul, it was agreed that he and his
associates would carry on the evangelism of the Gentiles, while the Jerusalem
group would restrict itself to work among Jews. The only further requirement
was that Paul, and presumably the churches established by him, were to "remember the poor." This seems to be a reference to the practice attested to in
the two preserved Letters to the Corinthians by which the Gentile churches
collected and submitted an offering to the Jerusalem church.

THE APOSTOLIC DECREES.   In Acts, however, Paul agrees to commu-
nicate to the Gentile churches the so-called apostolic decrees. These were four:
(1) abstinence from idolatry; (2) abstinence from blood—that is, from food
containing blood and therefore unclean by Jewish dietary rules; (3) abstinence
from eating animals that had been killed by strangling, again in accord with
Jewish food laws; (4) abstinence from unchastity. In one group of New Testament manuscripts known as the Western text the words "and from things
strangled" are omitted while others add a form of the Golden Rule. This
allows for an interpretation of the three remaining requirements as strictly
moral rather than cultic or dietary. "Blood" would be interpreted as a decree
against committing murder. This would ease the problem somewhat by saving us from having to assume that Paul agreed to certain legalistic food laws
as a prerequisite to acceptance into the family of faith. But even with the three
rules, we are left with the sense that Paul must have compromised his teaching
of justification by faith if he agreed to these laws for admission. Although he
would not have condoned such practices as were here forbidden in the
churches under his care, it would have clouded the issue of faith to have held
these particular rules up as prerequisite to accepting the Gospel of grace.
Some scholars have conjectured that Paul agreed to these rules, but never
sought to enforce them among the Gentile Christians; others have proposed
that he made the simpler agreement reported in Galatians first and then accepted the more stringent rules later.

THE NOAHIC LAWS.   It would appear that Acts 15 and Galatians are
simply incompatible, so that Paul could not have accepted two such contradictory sets of regulations. The details of Paul's own position are explored in

Chapter 8. Perhaps the explanation for the non-Pauline viewpoint is to be found in the correspondence between the fourfold requirement of Acts (in the non-Western text) and the way in which Jerusalem understood the force of the decrees connected with the covenant of Noah in Genesis 9:1ff. These No-ahic laws were considered by first-century Judaism to be binding on all humanity, rather than as especially enjoined on Israel alone. The regulations of Acts 15 would be one version of the minimal requirements for Gentiles if they were to remain in God's favor. Some scholars think they find a further trace of these "decrees" in Revelation 2:20–23. But it appears that Luke has included them here because he thought they were appropriate, not because he found them in a document reporting the decision reached at any apostolic council. The actual decision between Paul and the Jerusalem church was the one reported by Paul in Galatians 2; the decisions described in Acts 15 were written at a time when the tensions between Jewish and Gentile Christians had subsided—and, one might conjecture, after the full force of Paul's doctrine of justification by faith had been eclipsed by a surge of moralistic Christianity, such as we see in James and other late New Testament books. For Luke, this council marks an important turning point in his story: The leadership of the Jerusalem church has passed from the apostles to the elders. Probably "Symeon" is Peter, but he is no longer the leader of the group; that role has been assumed by James, the brother of Jesus. Luke is showing that there was a common agreement and a unified set of ground rules by which the Church everywhere would from that time on operate. But already the center of attention for Luke has shifted from the historical and eschatological center in Jerusalem to the spread of the Gospel among the Gentile cities, culminating in Rome.[11]

THE CENTER OF ACTS. The story of the conversion of Cornelius marks the center of the book, both in the aim of the author and in amount of material.[12] From that point on, Luke is interested in showing how the Gospel evoked faith among the Gentiles, first in the cities of Asia Minor, then on the mainland of Europe (Acts 16). Each step along the way is taken by divine hindrance (16:7) or divine call (16:9). None of the many civil authorities before whom Paul and his associates are brought can find anything worthy of punishment. The movement, Luke is telling his readers, is the work of God and is not in conflict with the human laws. Whether it be in a jail (16:24ff), before the venerable Athenian court of manners and morals known as the Areopagus,[13] or at a public hearing before a Roman proconsul (18:12ff), Paul has an appropriate word from God. There are none, of whatever origin or station in life, who are to be denied an opportunity to hear the Gospel. And from every stratum there is a faithful response, whether from a jailer (16:34) or an Areopagite (17:34). Paul's preaching is varied in approach, ranging from capi-

[11] A full statement on the details of Acts 15, on the history of its interpretation and critical judgments concerning the historical elements in Luke's account, are to be found in E. Haenchen's *The Acts of the Apostles* (Philadelphia: Westminster Press, 1971), pp. 440–72.

[12] Ibid., pp. 305–8.

[13] Meaning "Hill of Mars." Originally the court met on this hill, overlooking the *agora* or marketplace. Later it met in its own building, though we cannot tell where Luke understood it to have met on the occasion he describes.

The Acropolis at Athens, with the hill of Areopagus in the foreground. According to Acts 17, Paul defended himself and his message before the court that traditionally met on the Areopagus. *(Darryl Jones)*

talizing on the jailer's terror to quoting Greek poets before the members of the Areopagus. Paul's faithfulness in his mission provides him with opportunities to preach the word before the rulers of the Greek cities, the territories of Palestine, the Jewish authorities, and finally in the city of Rome itself. In capsule form, the whole sweep of the world mission of the Church is discernible in the work of Paul and his aides. Its symbolic consummation is represented in his stay in Rome, where he is able to proclaim the Gospel of the kingdom, preaching about Jesus Christ without restraint (Acts 28:31). It is on this joyous note that the work of Luke-Acts ends, even though Luke has given us full notice of the impending death of Paul (Acts 20:17–38).

EARLY CHRISTIAN PREACHING
ACCORDING TO ACTS

The Jesus tradition is of basic importance for Luke; otherwise he would not have written volume one of his work, in which the story of Jesus and the excerpts from his teaching are set forth with such dramatic and poetic power.

Strangely, however, the sermons attributed to the apostles in volume two touch only lightly on the career of Jesus, and not at all on his teachings as preserved in the Gospel. Although Acts 20:35 reports Paul as asking his hearers from Ephesus to "remember the words of the Lord Jesus," the saying itself—"It is more blessed to give than to receive"—does not appear in Luke or elsewhere in the Gospel tradition (Chapter 2). Furthermore, there is no real difference between the sermons of Peter and the sermons of Paul in Acts, in spite of Paul's acknowledgment in Galatians 1 and 2 of the great tensions and disagreements between them. Two questions confront us: What is the unity that links these sermons? And to what source should this unity be traced? The following themes appear in the sermon summaries of Acts:

1. Jesus is from the posterity of David.
2. Jesus's ministry was approved by God, as may be inferred from the mighty acts which Jesus performed through the Holy Spirit.
3. The Jews put Jesus to death and, without realizing it, thus fulfilled the scriptures which point to his suffering.
4. Gentiles ought to recognize God's concern for them in that his divine provisions for their needs are everywhere apparent.
5. God has placed his stamp of approval on Jesus by raising him from the dead on the third day after his burial. Now God has exalted him and through him has sent the Holy Spirit.
6. All people are called to repent and to receive salvation through the name of Jesus, who is destined to be the judge of humankind.

These themes and the terms for interpreting the significance of Jesus—even in the sermons attributed to Paul (Acts 13:16–41; 14:15–18; 17:22–31)—are decidedly non-Pauline. The preexistence of Jesus, his self-humiliation, the value of his death, his exaltation following his death, and the creation of the Church as his body are central for Paul. All are missing from Acts. *Sōma* (body) occurs scores of times in Paul's letters, for example, mostly as a figure for the corporate Christian community. Its single appearance in Acts (9:40) is a reference to a corpse.

Another significant omission from this list is the interpretation of the death of Christ as somehow related to the forgiveness of sins. Nowhere does Peter or Paul say in Acts: Christ died *for our sins*. Yet this is paramount in Pauline theology. Attempts have been made by New Testament scholars to find a substratum of common affirmation behind the Acts sermons on the one hand and Paul on the other.[14] Except for the importance of the Resurrection as God's demonstration of his approval of the humiliated and crucified Jesus, there is no real identity. And even the Resurrection receives a different inter-

[14] The classic statement of the position that finds in Paul and the Acts sermons evidence for a pre-Pauline common message is given by C. H. Dodd in *The Apostolic Preaching and Its Development in the New Testament* (New York: Harper & Row, 1951). A vigorous critique of this theory is given by C. F. Evans in "The Kerygma," *Journal of Theological Studies*, N.S., VII (1956), 25–41.

pretation in Paul from the one given it in these sermons. For Paul it is the ground of human justification as well as the basis of hope of participation in the age to come (Rom. 4:25; 1 Cor. 15:20–22), whereas in Acts the Resurrection is the exaltation of the rejected Christ, by which he remains at God's right hand until the time has come for his work as judge of all humanity.

The appearance in these sermons of certain unusual terms, such as the reference to Jesus in Acts 4:30 as "thy Holy Child," has led some interpreters to assume that we have archaic theological language, antedating the more sophisticated terminology, for example, of Paul. Luke's use of rather awkward turns of expression in his otherwise smooth Greek narrative, especially in these early chapters of Acts, led others to the conclusion that Luke was utilizing an Aramaic source, which he had rendered into Greek.[15] But as we have already remarked, the language of Luke-Acts is influenced by that of the Septuagint, which was of course the Bible of the Greek-speaking early Church for which Luke was writing and in which he was likely reared. As for the archaic theological terms, H. J. Cadbury has warned us:

> There is danger of arguing in a circle, since our ideas of early Christianity, with which the speeches in Acts are said to conform so exactly, are derived in large part from those very speeches.[16]

The sermons in Acts, it would appear, are not to be considered evidence for the earliest Christian preaching, though one cannot exclude the possibility that there are some reflections of older tradition included in them. Rather, they are to be regarded as having been composed in the same manner used by historians roughly contemporary with Luke, who attributed speeches to various figures in their historical narrative. Whether the historian wrote about his own contemporaries or whether he wrote of a distant past to which he no longer had direct access, much less reliable documents, he saw his task as composing the speeches in such a way as to serve the overall purpose of his book. There was an obligation to write the speeches so as to convey what the author deemed appropriate to the occasion he was describing.[17]

The fact that the speeches attributed to Paul do not correspond with the vocabulary and theological perspectives we find in Paul's own Letters would not in itself mean that Luke was not the companion of Paul and did not have access to Pauline material. It would signify rather that Luke's purpose in setting forth his grand design of the divine plan of salvation, working out in history under the guidance of the Spirit, was better served by what Luke wrote for Paul than it would have been by direct quotations from Paul himself. The

---

[15] This theory was propounded by C. C. Torrey in *The Composition and Date of Acts* (Cambridge, Mass.: Harvard University Press, 1916). A more cautious assessment of the evidence is to be found in M. Black, *An Aramaic Approach to the Gospels and Acts* (Oxford, Eng.: Clarendon Press, 1963).

[16] H. J. Cadbury, *The Beginnings of Christianity*, V, ed. F. J. Foakes-Jackson and K. Lake (London: Macmillan, 1933), p. 416.

[17] See the discussion of the style of speechwriting among Hellenistic and Roman historians in H. J. Cadbury, *The Making of Luke-Acts* (London: S.P.C.K., 1961), pp. 184ff. Also see the chapter on "The Speeches in Acts and Ancient Historiography" in Dibelius, *Studies in the Acts of the Apostles*, pp. 138–85.

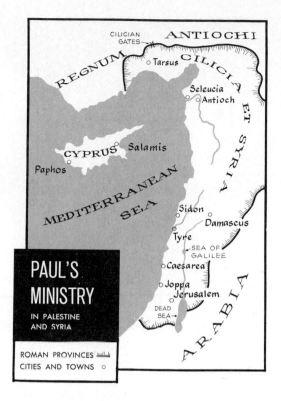

content and the unity of the speeches is to be derived from Luke's consistent point of view set forth in both volumes of his work, and not from his faithful reproduction of a peculiar way of proclaiming the message that was shared by all the apostles. Even if there were such uniformity among the apostles, we should not be warranted in inferring it from the reports of the sermons in Acts. Luke's skillful literary method would have smoothed over the differences in serving his wider objective. The Acts sermons show us, therefore, not necessarily what the apostles preached, but what Luke thought they ought to have preached. The question remains, however: If Luke was so free in creating speeches for Paul and the other apostles, how much credence can we place in his account of Paul's travels and ministry?

ACTS AS A SOURCE FOR THE LIFE OF PAUL

Both in regard to his speeches and to the apostolic council in Jerusalem, Luke has created material that serves his purpose rather than limiting himself to repeating whatever authentic information was available to him. Does this mean that Acts is worthless as a historical source? It does mean that for many of the historical questions to which we should like answers, Acts pro-

The harbor at Troas. A huge system of breakwaters make Troas a fine harbor, from which Paul is reported by Acts 16:8–11 to have set sail for the mainland of Europe, in response to an appeal in a vision of a man from Macedonia. *(Gordon N. Converse)*

vides no information. But, in keeping with the conventions of the time, Luke does provide us with references to contemporary incidents or persons by which we can ascertain the relative time of the events he is describing. This is notably the case in the famous synchronism of 3:1, 2, where Luke ties in the beginning of the ministry of John the Baptist with the reigns of various rulers in the eastern end of the empire. There are some historical difficulties involved in it,[18] but it does provide us a useful basis for establishing a relative chronology of the life of Jesus. That is, according to this chronology, Jesus would have begun his ministry in the year A.D. 26–27 or 27–28. Similarly, the references to pagan rulers in Acts have given us a fixed point: the accession to the governorship of Gallio, the Roman proconsul of Corinth in A.D. 52.

It would appear further that Luke had access to a travel itinerary of Paul which he used as the basis for the Pauline section of Acts. It has been

---

[18] See the discussion in Cadbury, *The Making of Luke-Acts*, pp. 204–9. The difficulties are treated more fully by J. M. Creed in *The Gospel According to St. Luke* (London: Macmillan, 1930), pp. 48–50.

The Ephesus theater was, according to Acts 19, the scene of a public assembly to protest the effects that Paul and his co-workers were having on the city, and especially on the economy connected with its temple of Artemis.   *(Darryl Jones)*

proposed that those sections of Acts in which Luke shifts from the customary third-person plural to the first-person plural of the narrative indicate the author's use of a travel diary. The account begins, "They went down to Troas" (Acts 16:8); but while referring to the same group, the writer without warning changes person to include himself: *"We* sought to go on to Macedonia" in 16:10. Some have thought that Luke joined Paul at this point, especially since the "we" passages are resumed when Paul returns to Troas on a later journey (20:5).

There is no difference in literary style or in vocabulary between the "we" section and the rest of Acts, so that we can be sure the author has reworked the whole carefully to suit his purposes. But the feeling that the events are being reported by an eyewitness is surely heightened by the "we" sections. Although it is possible that Luke had access to traditions or even to sources deriving from Paul, the sense of immediacy arises from Luke's literary achievement. And whatever his sources may have been, he has shaped and adapted them with great skill to serve his particular aims.[19]

Although it has been proposed that Acts ends inconclusively because it

---

[19] Efforts to demonstrate the historical reliability of Acts as a source for our knowledge of Paul, such as that of F. F. Bruce in *Paul: Apostle of the Heart Set Free* (Grand Rapids: Eerdmans, 1977) founder on the inexplicable conflicts between Paul's and Luke's accounts of such central features as Paul's conversion and the Jerusalem consultation between Paul and the other apostles.

was written before Paul's trial was over,[20] it is more likely that it ends as it does because the Gospel has by Acts 28 achieved the goal of being freely proclaimed in Rome, the capital of the Gentile world. The author of Acts does not leave us in any uncertainty as to the ultimate fate of Paul, however; the touching story of Paul's farewell to the elders from the church at Ephesus (20:17–38) makes it clear that Paul is to die for his testimony to the faith. The language of Paul's valedictory speech uses terms and envisages situations in the Church which correspond to the post-Pauline era and which have their closest parallel in such writings as the Pastorals. This is especially noticeable in 20:28–30. Accordingly, we may infer that Luke has written the history of Paul and the beginnings of the Church at some time after the events he is describing. The changed situation in which he finds himself is reflected in the way he depicts the earlier state of affairs, but it also provides perspective on the meaning of what has occurred. If we assume, as it appears we must, that he is writing after the apostolic generation has passed, we can understand why the eschatological note, which is so dominant in Paul's Letters, is muted in Acts. What Luke has done, then, is not consciously to distort the history of Paul, but to place it in a wider setting of the overarching redemptive purpose of God, which is the main concern of his entire work.

THE ENDURING CONTRIBUTION OF LUKE

We are now in a position to evaluate what Luke has done. It is true that he has given us nearly all the information we have about the historical beginnings of the Church, even though we should like to have more details and to have them placed in a framework more suitable for modern historical inquiry. Specifically he has given us some additional tradition about Paul which we could not infer from Paul's Letters and which we cannot evaluate historically: his residence in Tarsus, his education under Gamaliel. But Luke's chief contribution is a theological one: He provided a perspective of meaning for the Church and its mission which enabled the Christian community to survive what might have been a fatal crisis in the nonfulfillment of the expectation of the *parousia*.

Paul has reckoned with a delay in the *parousia* (Phil. 1:23ff; 2 Thess. 2:3ff). Matthew had provided regulations for the Church's life (Matt. 5–7, 18), but there was no broad framework for comprehending the meaning of the Church in the long-range purpose of God. It was this need that Luke so brilliantly filled by showing that the redemptive work promised in the holy scriptures and begun by the earthly Jesus was to be carried out under the power of the Holy Spirit through the Church. The *parousia* was still to come, and the judgment that would occur then was a solemn matter for all people. Its urgency was not so great, since the groundwork of redemption was already accomplished by the one who was seated at God's right hand. The carrying forth

---

[20] According to A. Harnack, *Neue Untersuchungen zur Apostelgeschichte und zur Abfassungszeit der synoptischen Evangelien* (Leipzig: J. G. Hinrichs, 1911), pp. 63–114.

of the Gospel and the manifestation of redemptive power was the task of the Church, but God had already acted through the apostles to see that work to completion in principle, with the progress of the Gospel from Jerusalem to Rome. Even now his Spirit was at work in the Church to bring it to consummation throughout the world.

There are a number of questions Acts hints at, but does not really formulate, much less answer. We feel as we read this book that there must have been a tension between the young Church and the Roman state, and that the author is trying to speak to that problem at least indirectly. He takes care to show that every time Jesus or his later followers were brought before civil authorities, there was no charge that could be made to stick against them. The tensions between Judaism and Christianity, of which we learn from Church historians and which are reflected in the oral traditions from this period later included in the rabbinic writings, are hinted at but not directly depicted. Luke is content to lay stress on the shift of focus of the Gospel from the Jew to the Gentile. One suspects, however, that the issue of the theological and institutional relationships between Judaism and Christianity was still a live one in the time that Acts was being written.

Most clearly of all, the Church in Luke's day seems to have been struggling with the problem of changing from a free-moving evangelistic enterprise to a settled institution. It may be that Luke-Acts documents a move in the early second century to change the Church from a free association of regional groups honoring the apostle whom each major city and its surrounding territory regarded as its founder (John in Ephesus; Peter in Rome; Mark in Alexandria; James in Jerusalem) and to create a unified (in Greek, *kath' holos*) church. But it would have been impossible to have had such a geographically and culturally diverse religious community or series of communities, if someone had not earlier taken on the assignment of spreading Christianity outside Syria-Palestine. And there would have been no problems of cultural and political adjustment throughout the empire if someone had not by the mid-first century gone with the Gospel to its major cities and done so with sufficient effectiveness to attract followers as well as official suspicion and hostility. The one person who, above all others, was responsible for launching that outreach effort to the wider Roman world was Paul. It is to his conversion, career, and understanding of Jesus that we now turn.

ANNOTATED BIBLIOGRAPHY

BROWN, RAYMOND E.   *The Gospel According to John.*   2 vols. Garden City, N.Y.: Doubleday (Anchor Bible), 1966, 1972. The finest commentary on John available today with rich, detailed studies of the background, including linguistic, historical, and cultural details.

CADBURY, H.J.   *The Making of Luke–Acts.*   London: S.P.C.K., 1921, 1958. The classic study of the cultural and religious setting in which Luke and Acts were written.

EDWARDS, RICHARD A.   *The Theology of Q.*   Philadelphia: Fortress Press, 1976. A useful analysis of the Jesus tradition included in the Q source.

ELLIS, E. E. *The Gospel of Luke.* London and Camden, N.J.: Thomas Nelson & Sons, 1966. Excellent, nontechnical commentary on Luke.

FITZMYER, JOSEPH A. *The Gospel of Luke.* Vol. I. Garden City, N.Y.: Doubleday (Anchor Bible), 1981. A comprehensive, technical introduction and analysis of Luke's Gospel.

FOAKES-JACKSON, F.J. and LAKE, KIRSOPP, with CADBURY, H.J. *The Beginnings of Christianity.* 5 vols. Reprint of 1933 ed. Grand Rapids: Baker Book House, 1965–66. An unsurpassed analysis of the origins of Acts and its setting in the Roman world, which it depicts and of which it is a reflection. Especially fine are the commentary volume (IV) and the collection of essays on the background (V).

HAENCHEN, E. *The Acts of the Apostles.* Philadelphia: Westminster Press, 1971. Detailed study of the contents and early analyses of the book of Acts.

JEREMIAS, JOACHIM. *Jerusalem in the Time of Jesus.* Philadelphia: Fortress Press, 1969. Despite the title, the book is a superb survey of the social conditions in all of Palestine during the lifetime of Jesus, and it furnishes material essential to understanding the background of his life and teaching.

KEE, HOWARD CLARK. *The Community of the New Age: Studies in Mark's Gospel.* Philadelphia: Westminster Press, 1977. Detailed studies of the literary, historical, cultural, and religious background of Mark's Gospel.

———. *Jesus in History.* 2d ed. New York: Harcourt Brace Jovanovich, 1977. A survey of the sources for our knowledge of Jesus, including both biblical and nonbiblical material. Analyzes each of the Gospels and other noncanonical Jesus traditions.

KELBER, WERNER. *The Oral and the Written Gospel.* Philadelphia: Fortress Press, 1983.

KINGSBURY, JACK DEAN. *Matthew: Structure, Christology and Kingdom.* Philadelphia: Fortress Press, 1975. An excellent analysis of Matthew along the lines suggested in the subtitle.

NINEHAM, D.E. *The Gospel of Mark.* Baltimore: Penguin, 1964. The best nontechnical commentary on the Gospel of Mark.

THEISSEN, GERD. *The Sociology of Early Palestinian Christianity.* Translated by John Bowden. Philadelphia: Fortress Press, 1978. A creative analysis of the Gospel tradition from a sociological perspective, with emphasis on the Jesus movement as a charismatic phenomenon.

THROCKMORTON, B. H., ed. *Gospel Parallels.* 4th ed. Camden, N.J.: Thomas Nelson Sons, 1979. An essential tool for the careful study of the first three Gospels. By listing the Gospel material in parallel columns, this book facilitates detailed comparisons of the ways the Gospel writers have transmitted and modified the tradition.

PART III

FROM INCLUSIVE COMMUNITY TOWARD UNIFIED INSTITUTION

Introduction:

Paul
and the
Pauline Tradition

Less than a century after the Crucifixion of Jesus, Quadratus, bishop of Athens, was presenting an apology for Christianity to Emperor Hadrian, on the occasion of the latter's visit to Athens. Justin, a native of Neapolis in Palestine, was converted to the Christian faith in Ephesus after a period of time spent as an itinerant philosophical seeker, and went on to Rome to become a major apologist for the faith before Hadrian and a martyr under his successor, Antoninus Pius. On the coast of the Black Sea, the Christians were viewed by the Roman authorities as a threat to the peace, and Emperor Trajan instructed the governor to suppress the movement. How could such an apparently insignificant movement that began in Palestine within the framework of Judaism have become within a century so significant and wide-ranging a phenomenon as to demand the attention of emperors?

Unfortunately it is not possible on the basis of available sources to trace these developments in detail. The fourth-century Church historian and court advisor to Emperor Constantine, Eusebius of Caesarea, has preserved fragments of earlier writings in which are reported traditions about the journeys, activities, and fates of the followers of Jesus, but in very few cases is it possible to check the accuracy of these reports or to distinguish legend from historical recollection. We learn from various sources that Thomas went to India, that Mark went to Alexandria, that Peter went to Rome, that John lived to a great age in Ephesus, and so on. These reports are of varying historical value, but they shed no light at all on the crucial question of the stages by which the Church moved out from its Jewish matrix to become an inclusive, Gentile-dominated movement. Irenaeus and other later writers[1] report the existence of strongly Jewish sects that considered themselves to be Christians but that came to be regarded as heretical by the main body of the Church. But since Gentile Christianity rather rapidly became the leading element in the early Church, it is with its origins that we must be chiefly concerned.

In the Book of Acts there are bits of information about Christian groups in cities of Palestine other than Jerusalem—Azotus (Ashdod), Samaria, Damascus. Indeed, the conversion of Paul is consummated through a leader of the Church in Damascus, according to Acts 9, but of the founding of Christianity in that city we learn nothing at all. Acts reports that two Christians who had been driven out of Rome, Priscilla and Aquila, were in Corinth when Paul arrived there (Acts 18),[2] but offers no hint how the Gospel reached Rome. On this question we have no firm historical clue,[3] only later traditions and legends. According to Acts, the Church was already well established when Paul arrived (Acts 28).

Accordingly, we are almost wholly dependent on the Letters of Paul for our knowledge of the spread of Christianity beyond Jerusalem, both geographically and culturally. It is not a matter merely that Christian communities are to be found by the middle of the first century from Damascus to Rome, and from Thessalonica to Alexandria, since there were Jewish groups already in these cities that could have provided persons willing to recognize Jesus as the Messiah and as the fulfillment of Jewish prophetic expectations. Far more dramatic is the fact that in these widely dispersed centers of Hellenistic and Roman culture there were persons willing to stake their future, and perhaps even their lives, on an obscure prophet who had been executed a few decades earlier as a fomenter of Jewish nationalism and a claimant to Jewish royal authority. How could Jesus and his message have undergone a transformation so profound as to exercise this appeal across ethnic, regional, and cultural lines?

And even with the letters of Paul we have neither a chronological ac-

---

[1] In his *Against all Heresies;* also Epiphanius, Philostratus, and St. Augustine. Simon Magus, who appears briefly in Acts 8, was credited by some of the Church Fathers with being the founder of Gnosticism, but the Acts account is too sketchy and unreliable to decide whether he did indeed contribute to the development of Jewish-Christian speculative sects. See also Jean Daniélou, *The Theology of Jewish Christianity* (London: Darton, Longman & Todd, 1964), especially pp. 55–85.

[2] That they were Christians is implied in Acts 18, and may be inferred from 1 Corinthians 16:15, where Paul names his earliest converts in the Corinth-Athens area, but does not mention Priscilla and Aquila.

[3] See the discussion of the historical background on p. 213.

count of his career nor a systematic statement of his thought, not even on such a crucial issue as how he came to interpret Jesus as he did and why he was motivated to preach his message in such a way as to appeal to non-Jews. At first glance, Acts would seem to be our most promising resource for reconstructing the development of Paul's life and thought, since its narrative includes reports of the events that purportedly took place after Jesus's death, as well as an account of Paul's conversion and several biographical summaries attributed to Paul himself. But careful examination shows that Luke–Acts is a fine example of theological history[4] and is even a good demonstration of Hellenistic writing,[5] but it can be used only with caution as a historical document in our modern sense of the term. The author's aim is only partly to recall traditions surrounding the careers of Paul and his fellow apostles; it is much more concerned to show how the divine plan of the ages was being worked out in this period. He writes from the perspective of the generation after Paul, so that the issues which are alive in Paul's Letters are not significant for Acts; and the controversies that raged in the Pauline churches are either given in stylized form or simply passed over in silence.

Some scholars have adopted the policy of using Acts as a historical source where it is not in conflict with the Letters of Paul, but no one can be sure that a document that has proved to be historically unreliable where it can be checked against Paul's writings is somehow reliable where it cannot be checked. Accordingly, in our reconstruction of Paul, we will draw upon the information of Acts as a possible supplement to what we can infer about Paul from his own Letters.

When it comes to the background of Paul's *thought,* and the distinctive ways in which he came to adapt the Christian message for Gentile hearers, we are entirely reliant on his letters. Indeed, Acts portrays the apostles, including Paul, as preaching very much the same kinds of sermons, even though we know from Paul's writings that there were sharp disagreements among the apostles. In our study of Paul, therefore, we must distinguish sharply between Paul's Letters as our primary source and Acts as a secondary source which tells us less about the historical Paul and more about how Paul was understood in certain quarters by the end of the first century.

Thirteen of the twenty-seven books of the New Testament are written in his name and another has often been attributed to him: the Letter to the Hebrews. Careful analysis of the language and content of these writings shows, however, that the so-called Pauline writings fall into the following categories: (1) those unquestionably by Paul: Romans, 1 and 2 Corinthians, Galatians, Philippians, 1 Thessalonians, and Philemon; (2) a letter about which questions have been seriously raised, where the evidence is ambiguous: 2 Thessalonians; (3) letters which are not by Paul, but which have been developed out of his thought: Colossians and Ephesians; (4) letters which bear his name, but

[4] For other treatments of these themes, see Hans Conzelmann, *Theology of St. Luke* (New York: Harper & Row, 1961); H. Flender, *St. Luke: Theologian of Redemptive History* (Philadelphia: Fortress Press, 1961); David L. Tiede, *Prophecy and History in Luke-Acts* (Philadelphia: Fortress Press, 1980).

[5] M. Dibelius, *Studies in Acts* (New York: Scribner's, 1956); H. J. Cadbury, *The Making of Luke-Acts,* 2nd ed. (Naperville, Ill.: Allenson, 1958).

which clearly come from another time and set of circumstances in the Church: 1 and 2 Timothy and Titus (the so-called Pastoral Letters); (5) a letter which does not bear Paul's name and which evidences a wholly different thought and religious vocabulary from that of Paul: the Letter to the Hebrews. It is obvious that our major sources will be those in categories 1 and 2. The rest will be discussed in Part IV as evidence for the developments in the Church after the time of Paul.

Since we lack any chronicle of Paul's life, we are dependent on a hypothetical reconstruction of his career by inference from his Letters. And the evidence is sufficient to provide us a serviceable framework, even though it is not possible to show the development of his thought in chronological sequence. With some confidence, however, fixed points in the chronology of Paul's career can be determined. What seems to be an odd remark in passing (2 Cor. 11:32–33) provides an important clue. Paul is seeking to show that, unlike some of his detractors who like to boast of their accomplishments, his life has been characterized by human weakness. In spite of his own personal difficulties and seeming failures, God has worked through him to accomplish his purposes. In 2 Corinthians 11 he offers a specific example, without explaining its full import: King Aretas, the Roman ruler of Damascus, had apparently been trying to capture or even to kill Paul, but he had managed to escape by being lowered over the city wall in a basket.

From other historical sources it can be determined that this was Aretas IV, king of Nabatea, and supported by the Roman emperor Gaius (37–41) as a puppet ruler. Nabatea was an Arab kingdom comprising parts of what is now Jordan and Syria. The incident probably ended what Paul refers to as a three-year stay in Damascus (Gal. 1:18), which marked the period from his conversion (Gal. 1:15–17) and his initial visit to Jerusalem to confer with the apostles based there (Gal. 1:18–24). This departure from Damascus by basket, with its mixed elements of excitement and humiliation, could not have taken place later than 39 or 40, since the latter is the year of Aretas's death, and may have occurred as early as 37. If we chose the earlier date, that would imply that Paul was converted in 34, or within a year of the most likely date of Jesus's Crucifixion.

For the date of Paul's death, we have no fixed indicators. The probability is that it occurred under Nero (54–68), who in 62 restored the Roman law of *maiestas,* which made it illegal under penalty of death to speak or act in such a way as to challenge or undermine the imperial authority. If this was the charge on which Paul was tried and condemned in Rome, as seems likely, then that probably occurred in 62.[6] Within the span of years between Paul's conversion and his execution, he gives us only a few hints of chronology. In

[6] Robert Jewett has conducted an exhaustive analysis of the chronology of Paul's life, based on data from his letters, from Acts, and from nonbiblical sources. The results of that investigation are offered on pp. 96–104 in his *A Chronology of Paul's Life* (Philadelphia: Fortress Press, 1979). The theory that Paul was executed under Nero gains plausibility from the report in the *Annals* of Tacitus (55–117) of that emperor's senseless persecution of the Christians in Rome following the disastrous fire of A.D. 68. The reconstruction of Paul's life suggested here, however, would require us to suppose that Paul died at an early stage of the persecution, which would have reached its climax in the events reported by Tacitus.

Nero was emperor of the Roman Empire when the first persecutions of Christians in Rome began. *(Courtesy of the Musei Capitolini, Rome)*

Galatians 2:1 he reports that fourteen years after his initial visit to Jerusalem (which would have been about A.D. 37), he returned for a conference with the Jerusalem-based apostles, which would have taken place about A.D. 51.

These dates fit well with others which can be arrived at by combining evidence from Acts with information from Roman historical sources. Acts 18:1-3 tells us that two persons who became important associates and supporters of Paul in Corinth, and later in Ephesus (1 Cor. 16:3) and probably later still in Rome (Rom. 16:3) had come to Corinth when they were driven out of the imperial capital by an anti-Jewish decree of Emperor Claudius. Suetonius, in his *Lives of the Twelve Caesars,* tells how Claudius (41–54) settled a dispute that had arisen among the Jews living in Rome by expelling them all. Since the instigator of the disturbance is called by Suetonius "Chrestus"—almost certainly a mistaken form of Christos—the conflict among Jews seems to have been the result of the advent not of Chrestus/Christos, but of missionaries trying to convert Jews in Rome to believe in Jesus as the Messiah (Christos). The date of that decree is probably 49 or 50. That would fit well with the likely date for the proconsulship of Gallio in Achaia (the Roman province which included Corinth), 52 or 53. Those dates happen also to fit well with the note in Acts 18:11 that Paul stayed in Corinth for a year and a half. Approximate dates can also be fixed for other events in Paul's life on the basis of encounters with Roman authorities reported in Acts, such as those in Palestine which led to the transfer of his case to Rome

(Acts 22–26).[7] It is sufficient for our purposes to have in mind the general chronological framework for his career:

Conversion	34
First visit to Jerusalem	41
Mission activity in Asia Minor and Greece, followed by second journey to Jerusalem	51
Journey to Rome	59–60
Death in Rome	62

Far more important than questions of chronology, however, are the issues related to the conversion of Paul and how it came about that non-Jews were invited to share in the covenant promises originally made to Israel. Without this outreach, the Christian community might have been nothing more than a protest movement within Judaism, and like other dissenting groups that arose in this period out of the heritage of Israel—Samaritans, Essenes, baptizing sects—might have vanished or else remained as tiny eddies in a cultural backwash somewhere in the Middle East.

[7]Discussed in detail in Jewett, *Chronology.*

8

Paul,
Apostle to the Gentiles:
Galatians and Romans

However much we might like to know about Paul's life and views before he became an apostle of Jesus in that moment of revelation which he describes so vividly and yet so compactly—"God was pleased to reveal his Son to me" (Gal. 1:16)—he has provided us with only a few clues about himself in that earlier period. We must look closely at the passages from his letters in which he tells us what he was like before the revelation occurred.

A PERSECUTOR OF THE CHURCH

[PHIL. 3:6]

In one of his later letters (Philippians), Paul mentions the human qualifications about which he could boast if he chose to do so. These all have to do with his standing within the Jewish community, of which he was a part by birth and to which he was so fiercely committed. He lists his spiritual assets as a pious Jew in Philippians 3:5–6:

> Circumcised on the eighth day, of the people of Israel, of the tribe of Benjamin, a Hebrew of Hebrews, as to the law a Pharisee, as to zeal, a persecutor of the church.

The first two of these "boasts" are not at all surprising. He was treated as any male offspring of a pious Jewish family would have been, as the law of Moses required (Lev. 12:3) and as the precedent had been set by Abraham in the covenant between God and the founder of the covenant people (Gen. 17). To fail to receive circumcision was to be disqualified from participation in the covenant community (Gen. 17:14). In fulfillment of that covenant obligation, Abraham's son Isaac had been circumcised on the eighth day, so that both precept and precedent were firmly established.

Not surprisingly, therefore, Paul asserts his identity with the people Israel. But what may seem strange to the modern reader is that Paul claims to have known from which of the twelve tribes he was descended. Although Benjamin was a small tribe with a tiny territory, its members had two grounds for pride: Israel's first king, Saul, was descended from Benjamin (1 Sam. 9:1–2); and since Benjamin was the only son of Israel to have been born in the land of promise, the rabbis taught that the divine glory (*Shekinah*) dwelt within that tribe. The phrase "Hebrew of the Hebrews" could mean simply that he was born of pure Jewish stock, as contrasted with someone whose ancestors had intermarried with Gentiles, or who included a convert to Judaism from a non-Jewish race. Or it could mean that he was considered to be a thoroughly Jewish person. If the term Hebrew is used in the linguistic sense, however, it could mean that he was a native speaker of the language, even though he was obviously at home in Greek as well. Whichever may be his intention, he wants to assert the authentic Jewishness of his upbringing.

Judaism of this period was by no means of one mind as to how the laws attributed to Moses and the other prophetic and wisdom traditions of what came to be the Jewish Bible were to be interpreted. We have already noted the range of approaches to this fundamental question, and we will have occasion to sketch the range of views in a moment. But in this text Paul declares himself as interpreting the law from within the Pharisaic tradition. The only clue he offers as to what that involved is his firm insistence that he was zealous not only for the law as such, but also "for the traditions of my fathers" (Gal. 1:14). What he has in mind here is probably similar to the devotion to the "traditions of the elders" expressed by Pharisaic opponents of Jesus (Matt. 15:2). Those traditions were primarily concerned with ritual purity and the observance of the dietary laws. The task taken on by the rabbis to codify and interpret what they claimed as that oral law was not completed until about A.D. 200 and probably did not get under way until decades after Paul's death.[1] For Paul the Pharisee in the period before the destruction of the Temple, therefore, the essential thing would have been the maintenance of Jewish covenantal identity through the observance of the ethical, dietary, and Sabbath laws. It was presumably on these issues that he was so zealous for "the traditions of the fathers."

A direct consequence of his concern for the purity of the covenant people was his hostile reaction to a group of Jews who began to infiltrate the towns and villages of southern Syria, claiming simultaneously that the Messiah had come to establish the new covenant and that participation in that community was open to Jews and Gentiles alike. The Gospel tradition reports that during Jesus's itinerant ministry, his work had penetrated the cities of the Decapolis, and Damascus was the largest of that group of Hellenized cities. It was there that Paul was living at the time of his conversion. Paul mentions nothing of having sought and received authorization from the High Priest to root out the heretical movement from the Damascus synagogues, as reported by Acts 9. Nor does he describe the dramatic encounter with Christ on the road to Damascus, or Ananias's preparation by means of a dream to accept Paul/Saul into the Christian community in Damascus. All that we learn from Paul himself is that his efforts to destroy the church (Gal. 1:13; Phil. 3:6) were

---

[1] Jacob Neusner, *From Politics to Piety* (Englewood Cliffs, N.J.: Prentice-Hall, 1973) thinks it likely that it was during the reign of Herod (after 4 B.C.) that Pharisaism changed from a political movement into a fellowship concerned for the ritual purity of its members and fostering that mode of piety among other Jews. It flourished under Hillel, from A.D. 10 to 70 presumably, although all that can be said of him with certainty is that he lived prior to the destruction of the Temple in 70. On the proposition that the oral law concept is a device to lend authority retroactively to rabbinic tradition, see Jacob Neusner, "History of Mishnah's Ideas," in *Method and Meaning in Ancient Judaism,* second series, Brown Judaic Studies (Missoula, Mont.: Scholars Press, 1981), p. 51.

transformed into a lifelong zeal to preach the Gospel of Jesus Christ as widely as possible in the Gentile world in order to create as inclusive a covenant community as possible.

AS TO THE LAW, A PHARISEE
[PHIL. 3:5]

Paul's position as a Pharisee represented one option chosen by some Jews of the first century in answer to the basic question that concerned them all, except for those who became apostates. That question was one of identity: What is a Jew? Or to put it more sharply, and in terminology closer to that of the biblical tradition: How does one become a member of God's covenant people? A corollary of that is: How does one maintain status within the covenant people? We have seen how widely the answers diverged, even though the centrality of these issues was universally recognized among Jews. To summarize our more extended survey in Chapter 2, some Jews understood their obligation to be centered primarily on the Temple cult, whereby God and his people maintained a right relationship; others, like the Qumran community, despaired of maintaining covenantal identity even in the midst of a predominantly Jewish populace in Palestine, since the nation was thought to be corrupted from the priesthood on down. The only solution was withdrawal to the desert pending divine intervention and vindication of this faithful remnant, which was preserving authentic purity and correct interpretation of scripture. A third option was to view Jewish identity as political, and to regard Jewish hopes as awaiting fulfillment in the establishment of an independent Jewish state. Jewish nationalism was on the rise during the career of Paul, which would have made the Roman authorities highly suspicious of an aggressive movement that spoke of Jewish aspirations in the rhetoric of politics—king, lord, liberator—whether those terms were used in a nationalistic or an eschatological sense.

The central and universal criterion for Jewish identity, regardless of the specific point of view, was the circumcision of males. Even the Jerusalem-based Christians agreed with their Jewish heritage on this. It represented the ultimate expression of ritual purity in the Jewish tradition, as Paul himself acknowledged. Yet for Paul, following the appearance to him of the Risen Lord (Gal. 1:16), it was a violation of the significance of the new covenant to insist on circumcision as an admission requirement. We shall consider later in this chapter how Paul justified his position on this question, but it is essential to inquire whether there were factors in Paul's own background—apart from his training in the traditions of the fathers and the scriptures—which would have especially suited him to become the apostle to bear "the gospel to the uncircumcised" (Gal. 2:7–8). Paul did not believe that the course of his life had been abruptly altered in a way that destroyed all continuity between his earlier life and his subsequent vocation as a Christian. Indeed, he says explicitly that God "had set me apart before I was born." Paul's consciousness had changed, but not God's purpose for him. But the evidence concerning earlier experiences that seem to have prepared him for this apparent about-face may be grouped as (1) implicit, (2) inferential, and (3) conjectural.

Pagan Influences: Stoicism

One of the striking features of Paul's letters is the frequency and the accuracy with which he uses technical terms from the Greek philosophical tradition, especially from Stoicism. Paul not only uses the terms for specific moral and personal qualities that were held up by the Stoics as models, as we shall see, but he also perceives human nature as motivated by nature and by conscience, in a way clearly akin to Stoicism. He regards human existence as inconceivable apart from the body (though he does not regard a *physical* body as essential). This view was shared by Jews with the Stoics. He believes that human history is moving toward a consummation, just as the Stoics did. He modifies these Stoic concepts in order to adapt them to his own understanding of human nature and destiny.

In Acts, Paul is said to have come from Tarsus (Acts 9:30; 11:25; 22:3), which was the city of origin of many leading Stoic teachers in the Hellenistic and Roman periods. Paul, however, never mentions Tarsus; he speaks only of Damascus and later of Antioch as his places of residence in the Eastern Mediterranean world. But there is no necessity to assume that Paul's education and upbringing were in a pagan context for him to have had direct contact with Hellenistic philosophy.[2] Josephus, in his *Jewish Wars* (II.119–166) and his *Antiquities* (XVIII.11–25), describes the four Jewish "sects" as "schools of philosophy," and suggests specific ways in which their teachings corresponded with Hellenistic notions. He emphasizes particularly the teaching of the Pharisees about predestination, or "fate," as he calls it. In the *Jewish Wars* (III.374), Josephus describes himself as arguing against suicide with the insurrectionists at the time of the fall of Jerusalem to the Romans. Central to his argument is the promise that those "who depart this life in accordance with the Law of Nature" will, after a sojourn in heaven, "return to find in chaste bodies a new habitation." Although Josephus has obviously modified the philosophical notions on which he draws, his outlook remains true to two basic Stoic concepts: that the good life is to be lived in harmony with the law of nature, and that human existence requires a body.

An earlier contemporary of Paul, Philo of Alexandria, in his treatise *On the Creation of the World,* adopted a Stoic view of natural law, of the harmony of the cosmic order, of God's ordering of the universe in accordance with natural law. He saw a close analogy between God's role in the universe and the human role (as depicted in Gen. 1:28) as responsible for the creation: "The human mind evidently occupies a position in human beings precisely answering to that which the Great Ruler occupies in all the cosmos." This is a basic Stoic notion. Further, Philo regularly employed Stoic terms in portraying God's role as governor of the universe (leader, pilot, driver) and in specifying human virtue: righteousness, integrity, wisdom, intelligence. But Philo was by no means unique in this regard. The Wisdom of Solomon, which is included in the Alexandrian official collection of Jewish scriptures, is filled with

[2] For the wide and deep influence of Hellenistic thought and culture on Judaism, see Martin Hengel, *Judaism and Hellenism*, 2 vols., trans. John Bowden (Philadelphia: Fortress Press, 1974). Also, S. Liebermann, *Hellenism in Jewish Palestine* (New York: Jewish Theological Seminary, 1950).

the technical language of Hellenistic philosophy and uses poetic terms that were being employed by devotees of Isis. The Fourth Book of Maccabees retells the story of the bravery of the Jewish nationalists in their successful struggle against the Seleucids in the first half of the second century B.C., attributing their courage to their possessing the Stoic virtues of self-control and imperturbability. A document purporting to incorporate the last will and testament of the twelve sons of Jacob, Testaments of the Twelve Patriarchs, represents these founders of Israel as looking back over their lives with satisfaction or chagrin, depending on the degree to which they have exemplified the Stoic virtues of integrity and self-control and have lived in accordance not with the law of Moses, but with the law of nature.

Central to this basic shift in attitude toward the Jewish law was the translation of the Hebrew word *torah* (teaching, instruction) by the Greek word *nomos,* which can mean law in the judicial sense, but also principle or implicit order. Once that translation had come into common use among Greek-speaking Jews, it was inevitable that what thoughtful Greeks were saying about ethical and cosmic principles would be transferred by thoughtful Jews to their own religion. Philo even went to the point of expressing preference not for the Mosaic law, written on tables of stone, but for "the law written on the minds" of human beings, although he sees no fundamental conflict between the two. The purpose of the Sabbath as a day of rest is to free one to devote time "to the one sole object of philosophy with a view to the improvement of character and submission to the scrutiny of conscience" (*On Creation*, XLIII). He then went on to describe conscience as the soul's judge; it administers reproofs, admonitions, or threats, as the seriousness of misconduct may require. Indeed, the basic terms used by the rabbis in biblical exegesis after A.D. 70 were taken over from Greek rhetoric, and the rabbinical thought paralleled the agenda of the Hellenistic philosophers, especially the Stoics.

Whatever the circumstances may have been of his exposure to Stoic thought (whether under Jewish or pagan auspices), Paul's way of thinking was deeply influenced by such Stoic notions as the conscience, the divine spirit within, the necessity of a body for human existence, the pervasive effect of the law of nature, and the specifics of human moral qualities. Equally significant are the correspondences between Stoic views and Pauline beliefs about the working of the divine purpose in human history. These include the subordination of human choice to the divine plan for the universe, the hope for a new era in which God's purpose will triumph, the expectation of the purgation of evil, the presence of signs of the end in present history, and the ultimate achievement of peace and harmony in the creation.

Pagan Influences: Apocalyptic and Mystical

Paul has not simply borrowed these ideas from pagan Stoicism; they had infiltrated Jewish thinking in the centuries before his time in a profound way. As we have observed, the Jewish view of history as consisting of a succession of ages (most fully documented in the Book of Daniel, with its strange beasts representing successive world empires) is akin to the Greek concept of historical ages represented by Hesiod (8th century B.C.). Although the details of Jewish apocalypticism differ widely from Stoic expectations about the future, they share the common conviction about the victory of the divine purpose and the fiery judgment of the forces of evil. Paul synthesized Stoic and Jewish eschatology in his depiction of the end of the age; for example, in 1 Corinthians 15:22–28, Paul announces both the defeat of the powers of evil (in the Jewish tradition) and the subjection of the universe to God (in the Stoic tradition).

The Hellenistic philosophical tradition, especially of the Platonic variety, had a mystical element, according to which the truly wise person could see beyond the realm of the senses and specific objects to the ideal world of unchanging paradigms or models, said by Plato to be eternal reality. Philo expresses his yearning to soar beyond the sensible world to the intelligible world, which is the realm of Ideas (*On Creation*, XXIII), an experience he describes as divine intoxication, as Corybantic frenzy (after the ecstatic rites of the goddess Cybele in ancient Greece). Another type of Jewish mysticism with which Paul had clear kinship was that of contemplating the throne of God (Merkabah mysticism),[3] a privilege granted to those whose experience of suffering did not deter them from a life of obedience and devotion. They believed themselves to be taken up to the divine throne, to have become aglow with reflected radiance from the divine presence, and thereby to have received assurance that enabled them to accept suffering and hostility. Daniel reports this kind of divine vision in Daniel 10, as does Job in the apocryphal Testament of Job. Paul describes an experience of this specific type in 2 Corinthians 12, which must have occurred in the early years following his conversion and which strengthened him to endure the rejection and suffering of his mission.

ADMISSION TO GOD'S PEOPLE: PAUL'S CONVERSION

Critical analysis of the sources shows that in the period before A.D. 70, the Pharisees were primarily concerned with gaining and maintaining ritual purity, especially with regard to dietary laws and Sabbath observance. There is no reason to doubt that Paul shared these convictions. Influences were at work from two sources, however, which would provide a challenge to this notion of participation in the covenant people as resting primarily on ritual separateness. One of these factors was the emphasis in the Stoic tradition on the unity of the human race, and the refusal to accept the distinctions between Greeks and "barbarians" or between slave and free. Access to reason, or the divine mind, was universal, at least potentially, so all human beings who chose to do so might live according to nature.

Reinforcing this notion of inclusiveness would have been the prophetic

---

[3] *Merkabah* means, literally, "chariot." In the Jewish scriptures, God's dwelling in the temple (or tent) was represented by a chariot. Elijah is taken up to heaven in the chariot (2 Kings 2:11–12). Ezekiel's vision of the divine throne includes "wheels within wheels" (Ezek. 1:1–28). In *Major Trends in Jewish Mysticism* (New York: Schocken Books, 1961), Gershon Scholem presents Paul's experience of the transforming vision of the throne of God as a classic example of throne mysticism.

Damascus is believed by some historians to be the oldest continuously inhabited city in the world. A few traces of Roman times remain in the old covered markets, but most of the city presents the modern appearance pictured here. *(Courtesy of the Embassy of the Syrian Arab Republic)*

tradition of Israel, which the Pharisees acknowledged as scripture, along with the law of Moses. In that body of material there is a fundamental tension between two different views of the destiny of Israel, the covenant people. One strand emphasizes Israel's national destiny, with stress on political autonomy for the Jewish people. The other views Israel as "a light for the nations" (Isa. 49:6): through it the knowledge of God will reach the ends of the earth. The story in Acts 1 of the outpouring of the Spirit on Jews and Gentiles alike is reported by the author to have been justified by Peter on the ground that this event is a fulfillment of the prophecy of Joel 2:28–32 that God would grant his Spirit to all humanity ("all flesh"; Acts 2:16–21), with the result that "whoever called on the Lord's name would be saved," whether of Israelite origin or not. We shall see in a moment how Paul appeals to scriptural precedent for opening participation in the covenant community to non-Jews, but it is essential to recognize that Paul's point of view can be based on the Jewish tradition in which he was reared.

As we observed in our study of the Gospel tradition, Jesus was credited with opening membership into the community of the new covenant to outsiders. Not only tax collectors, but also "sinners" of doubtful or even downright unacceptable occupations or behavior were welcomed. Mark reports, and Luke amplifies on, the travels of Jesus outside Jewish territory to announce the coming of God's rule and the defeat of the powers of evil. Significant for our concern here is the importance attached to his evangelism among the cities of the Decapolis. Although it is not mentioned by name in the Gospel narratives, Damascus was the largest and most prestigious of this group of Hellenized cities.

It seems safe to conjecture, therefore, that the type of Christianity Paul encountered during his residence in Damascus was of this inclusive type. That would account for the violence of his reaction to it, since it is thoroughly human to respond forcefully to issues that are troubling us. If Paul was particularly perplexed as a Pharisaic Jew by this contradictory element in his religion—whether the essence of covenant existence required exclusive ritual purity or openness to the Gentiles, as the divinely intended recipients of the light—one can understand why initially he would have been so zealous in opposing inclusiveness and then so eager to promote it. The decisive change came in the encounter with Jesus, the one who had launched the open community of the covenant. The combination of cultural background in the universalist Stoic tradition, of religious training in Pharisaism, with its attention to the legal and the prophetic tradition, and the faithful response of non-Jews to Jesus set the pattern for the church as inclusive community. All these factors contributed to Paul's seemingly contradictory position: (1) that Jesus is the fulfillment of the law and the prophets (Rom. 3:21); and (2) that none of the ritual requirements for admission to the people Israel is binding on Christians. Fortunately, two of the surviving letters of Paul address these issues: Galatians and Romans. The former was obviously written in a mood of anger and urgency; the latter is reflective and conciliatory. But the same basic point of view is presented in both letters.

BY FAITH ALONE: GALATIANS

The single factor that transformed Paul from a zealous antagonist of the Christians' understanding of themselves as the new covenant people into an apostle of Jesus Christ and a tireless worker in behalf of that new community was his encounter with the Risen Christ. God alone receives the credit for this experience: he it was who was "pleased to reveal his Son in me" (Gal. 1:15). What was apparently a private, inner revelation was understood by Paul to constitute a special commission for him: He was to take the initiative in preaching the Gospel among the Gentiles. It seems clear that what had aroused Paul's hostility against the Christians was not merely their claim that Jesus was the Messiah promised to Israel, but that they were inviting non-Jews to share in the community that had arisen in response to that claim. It is on precisely this point, which Paul had earlier so vehemently opposed, that he is now a chief proponent. The experience of Jesus and the time of contemplation or preparation that followed it had been purely private, taking place in the Nabatean province of Arabia (present-day Jordan). His time and energies on his return to Damascus were devoted to proclaiming the faith he had once worked to destroy (Gal. 1:23). The hearers of that Gospel were Gentiles (Gal. 2:2), who were not required to meet even the minimum Jewish ritual requirements (2:3).

The two leaders of the Jerusalem church mentioned by Paul were both originally from Galilee: Peter (Kepha in Aramaic, or Cephas in its Greek form) and James, Jesus's brother. It is probably significant that neither of these two is portrayed favorably in the Gospel of Mark, which most likely was written among Greek-speaking Christians in southern Syria, where Paul was now working. James's sole appearance in the narrative (Mark 3:19, 31–35) is as part of Jesus's family who come to take him away, on the assumption that he is crazy. Peter, for all the special disclosures that have been made to him about Jesus's suffering and ultimate triumph (Mark 8:31; 9:2–8, 31; 10:33), denied knowledge of him before the authorities, fled when Jesus was seized, and failed to show up at the tomb. The weak, vacillating character of Peter as portrayed in Mark is confirmed in Paul's account in Galatians, since Peter had initially agreed that Gentiles could be admitted to the Christian community on the ground of faith alone (Gal. 2:9). Further, he had enjoyed table fellowship with uncircumcised, nonobservers of the Jewish kosher laws when he visited the Christians in Antioch (Gal. 2:12). But when challenged by spies sent from James to determine whether the Syrian Christians were observing minimal ritual requirements, Peter had backed off from his earlier standpoint and sided with the Jewish legalist Christians (2:12–13).

What Paul sees at issue here is not how long a list of admissions requirements to the church is in effect; rather, it is his conviction that no human effort or achievement qualifies anyone for participation in the new covenant community. It is this notion of qualifying for acceptance with God by one's moral or ritual performance that Paul rejects when he denounces "works of law" (Gal. 2:16). God never did set up such requirements, Paul declares, and it would be a gross error to allow anyone—even the venerated Jerusalem-based apostles, Peter and James—to impose such entrance requirements now. To permit some to insist on such prerequisites would be to divide the new community into two parts, one Jewish and the other Gentile. Or if the Jewish legal obligations were binding on all Christians, then the Church would be a messianic type of reformed Judaism. Paul knows on the basis of his own experience that the obey-in-order-to-qualify route will not work (2:17–19). To impose such requirements on non-Jewish Christians would not only be defeating for them, but it would render Christ's death meaningless. For Paul, the death of Jesus was vicarious: his death on the cross liberates all who turn to him in faith from obligations to the law they did not and could not discharge (Gal. 2:20–21; 3:13–14).

A Member of God's People

When Paul uses the phrase "I have been crucified with Christ" (Gal. 1:20), his assumption about human existence is characteristic of ancient Semitic and other non-Western thinking, but contrary to the radical individualism of our modern, post-Enlightenment culture. Perhaps no phrase sums up the outlook and values of our contemporary world more vividly than the tired cliché, "Do your own thing." Paul, along with Greeks trained in the Stoic tradition, with primitive peoples who possess a strong sense of tribal or ethnic identity, and with faithful Jews of whatever persuasion, would have asserted that the great figures of their own myth and history are the ones who provide the members of the group with a sense of identity. The individual finds his or her own identity when the story (mythical or historical) becomes "my story."[4]

The person from Israel's past who embodies the basis for human relationship with God is Abraham. From the outset, it was God's announced intention that through Abraham all the nations of the earth could come to the knowledge of God and share in his covenant (Gal. 3:6–9; Gen. 12:3; 18:18). Through Abraham's trust in God and his promise of a son to him and his barren wife Sarah, all the nations would find a share in God's blessing and might stand in right relationship to him. The proper ground for all human life is trust in the divine promise: "He who through faith is righteous shall live" (Gal. 3:11), which might be paraphrased, "Whoever is in right relationship with God by trusting Him, has found authentic life."

In the time of Moses, however, God gave his people the Law in the desert of Sinai. Does that mean that the earlier basis for the relationship to God established through Abraham has been superseded? Paul answers with an emphatic "No" (Gal. 3:15–18). Does the law of Moses, then, serve any useful purpose? It has two functions: (1) The strictness of its requirements reminds all humankind that there is no possibility of meriting God's favor by conformity to legal demands (3:22); (2) It is a useful instrument for the human stage of religious immaturity, when like a child placed under the care of a tutor, we have someone to keep us from getting completely out of line (3:23–25). The God-opposing forces of the universe pervert the religious requirements of the law, warping and enslaving human lives (4:1–3) through fear and false hopes. These "elemental spirits" promote the foolish notion that human beings can somehow ingratiate themselves with God or qualify for his favor by religious observance (4:9–10).

On the model of Abraham's response to God's promise, there is now the possibility of moving from the role of the child or slave to that of the mature son, ready to assume full privileges and responsibilities (Gal. 3:26; 4:5–7). The agent of God who has accomplished this liberation is Jesus, who came into history under the ordinary human conditions and limitations, but triumphed over them (4:4–5). The outward sign of the commitment to God through Jesus is baptism, by which public expression is given to the new identity with the people of the new covenant—"new," and yet reaching back to Abraham (3:27, 29). In a complex allegory (4:21–31), Paul shows how those who identify with Abraham can be of two types: those still bound to the law given at Sinai, or those freed by the sacrificial death in their behalf at Jerusalem.

Within the common life of the covenant people there are important responsibilities as well as resources. These are not hidden qualifications for sharing covenant existence, but ways in which the new life in Christ manifests itself. The power of that new life is the Spirit, a term for which Paul had precedent both through his biblical heritage and his exposure to Stoic philosophy.

[4] See Appendix I for a discussion of personal identity gained through myth and ritual.

Seneca, a Roman political advisor and rhetorician whose life span matched that of Paul almost exactly (A.D. 1–65), declared in one of his Moral Epistles (XLI.1) that "God is near you, he is with you, he is within you. A holy spirit indwells within us." Seneca went on to explain that for him the divine presence is linked with human reason and is operative to the extent that human beings live in accord with natural law (XLI.7), but the basic concept of an indwelling spirit as the agent of divine presence and of moral fulfillment was abroad in the Roman world for Paul to seize upon and adapt for his own purposes.

To revert to a life under Mosaic law would place the Christian outside the life sphere in Christ, beyond the power of the Spirit (Gal. 5:1–12). But to live by the power and under the control of the Spirit is to experience authentic freedom—freedom from both the law as a merit system and from the impulses of the flesh (Gal. 5:13–20). The ground of mutual relationship within the community is love. In this we see one of the few points of direct overlap between the ethics of Paul and those of Jesus in the Gospel tradition (Mark 12:28–34). When Paul goes on to spell out what moral qualities the Spirit produces in the life of Christ's people, he draws upon his background in Stoicism, or in Stoicized Judaism. The virtues the Spirit produces in the life of the Christian— with the possible exception of love and joy—are precisely what Stoics expected to be the product of a life according to the law of nature: peace, patience, gentleness, kindness, goodness, self-control (Gal. 5:23). Paul is saying, however, that the Spirit does in fact produce these qualities in the life of the liberated, obedient member of the covenant community. These "fruits" are not the consequence of human striving, but like the basic relationship to God's people, are the outcome of a life of trust. The Christian "walks by the Spirit"—or, as it might be phrased today, the Spirit creates a Christian life style. Life in the new community of faith is characterized not by a superior moral system or a reform movement, but by nothing less than "a new creation" (Gal. 6:14–15).

When and Why Paul Wrote to the Galatians

Paul's Letter to the Galatians was probably written not long after his conference in Jerusalem with the apostles based there in A.D. 51.[5] On the assumption that his first visit with the inner circle of the apostles in Jerusalem (Gal. 1:18–19) took place in 37, the fourteen-year span before the second visit (Gal. 2:1) brings us to A.D. 51. Later tradition asserted that he wrote from Ephesus, although that is by no means certain. More difficult is the question of what territory is meant by "Galatia" (Gal. 1:2). Historically, that term was used of a district in the north-central part of Asia Minor, where Celtic tribes settled in the early third century B.C. Neither in his letters elsewhere nor in Acts is there an account of a missionary journey by Paul into that region. But the fact that he could claim to have evangelized the entire northeastern quad-

---

[5]Following Robert Jewett, *A Chronology of Paul's Life* (Philadelphia: Fortress Press, 1979).

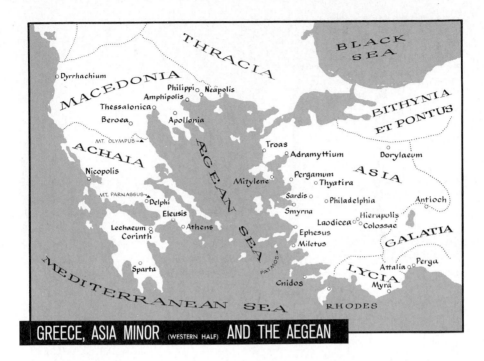

GREECE, ASIA MINOR (WESTERN HALF) AND THE AEGEAN

rant of the Mediterranean world (Rom. 15:19) reminds us that we are far from having a complete account of his activities and journeys. What seems to have happened after he had established the churches in this region is that "false brethren"[6] (Gal. 2:4) came along insisting that the true and original apostles (from which group they excluded Paul) were law-observant and that therefore all true Christians should be as well. Paul, enraged by this misunderstanding of the Gospel, dictated this letter, adding his own closing remarks in his own hand (Gal. 6:11–18).

PAUL'S LETTER TO THE ROMANS

The Letter to the Romans, different as it is from Galatians in tone, in occasion, and in literary style, is concerned with the same basic issues as is the angry, hasty Galatian letter.[7] Very likely, Paul wrote to the Roman Christian community from Corinth about three years after he had written

[6] The scholarly conjecture that the spies were promulgating a speculative, perhaps Gnostic, version of the Gospel is unwarranted and unnecessary. On this theory of the identity of Paul's opponents there, see H.D. Betz, *Galatians* (*Hermeneia Commentary*) (Philadelphia: Fortress Press, 1979), pp. 7–8.

[7] Jewett, *Chronology*, who concludes that Paul probably did not reach Jerusalem on his final visit (Rom. 15:27–28; Acts 20) until late spring of A.D. 57. From Romans 15 we know that Paul wrote to the Roman Christians in anticipation of that final act before he set sail to the West, for Rome and beyond (Rom. 15:24).

The Appian Way. The deep grooves worn by chariot wheels in the limestone blocks that form the paving of this road are clearly visible. The great highway, parts of which date back to the fourth century B.C., led from Brundisium to Rome. Paul would have travelled it as he came to the city for the first time. *(Gordon N. Converse)*

to the Galatians from Ephesus. These dates would be A.D. 53 and 56–57, respectively.[8]

Galatians was written to churches Paul had founded; Romans is addressed to a community of which he has heard and some of whose members he has come to know (Rom. 16). Galatians was written in rebuke; Romans was written as a letter of self-introduction, announcing his intention to visit the Roman Christians (Rom. 15:28–29). His tone suggests that he wants not only to instruct them, but also to ingratiate himself with them. The arguments are developed carefully, logically, and are free of attacks on opponents. Romans is clearly a letter of reconciliation, an effort at mutual understanding: "For I long to see you . . . that we may be mutually encouraged by each other's faith, yours and mine" (Rom. 1:11–12). He now sees the opportunity to accomplish the visit to them that he had so long hoped for (1:13). According to Acts, when he did reach Rome he was on his way not to Spain, but to martyrdom at the hands of the imperial authorities.

---

[8] For details of the circumstances of the writing of Galatians and Romans, see W. G. Kümmel, *Introduction to the New Testament,* trans. H. C. Kee (Nashville: Abingdon Press, 1975), pp. 293–320 and bibliography.

The Central Themes of Romans

Although the church in Rome had originally been comprised of former Jews (as Suetonius's report of the Jewish disturbance instigated by Chrestus/ Christos suggests),[9] it seems to have been predominantly Gentile by the time Paul wrote. He describes the members as being from "among the nations" (Rom. 1:5–6), and identifies his own role as "reaping some harvest among you as well as among the rest of the Gentiles" (1:13). The Christians mentioned by name in Romans 16, however, include persons of Jewish heritage, such as Prisca and Aquila. Regardless of the ratio of Jewish and Gentile backgrounds among Roman Christians, Paul's major concern throughout this, his most systematic letter, is to explain how the constituting of God's covenant people relates to both the Jewish biblical tradition and to the search for, and the knowledge of, God present among non-Jews. In short, the twin central issues are the ones we have noted earlier: How does one become a member of God's new people? And how does one maintain responsible membership?

The multiple strands of Paul's own cultural heritage are evident as he develops his arguments. Heavy weight falls on the continuity between what God is now doing through Jesus and what "he promised beforehand through his prophets in the holy scriptures" (1:2). Jesus is perceived by Paul as biologically linked with the royal line of ancient Israel (1:4). The case is made throughout the letter by appeal to scriptural quotation and precedent. As in Galatians, the most prominent single figure, apart from Jesus, is Abraham (Rom. 4). Three chapters of the letter (9–11) are devoted to the redefining of Israel and its relationship to the Church. Why should this issue be so important for churches that seem not to have been troubled by Judaizers, as the Galatians were (Gal. 2:14), and whose members were predominantly of Gentile origin? Probably two factors were of central importance: (1) The Roman Christians had been originally all or mostly Jewish, since the expulsion of "Jews" under Claudius had driven them out as well. That dimension of the Roman Christian heritage would not vanish once the Jewish Christians there became a minority; indeed, that change might have aggravated the problem of Jewish-Gentile relationships. (2) The claim by Christians of both Jewish and non-Jewish backgrounds to be the heirs to the biblical covenant promises required them to think through concretely what that meant for them ritually, conceptually, and personally.

Another issue that must have been important for Paul, as well as for the newly Gentile-dominated Roman church, was how God deals justly with Gentiles who lack the revelation of God in the law of Moses and the prophets. In responding to that challenge, Paul drew on his understanding of scripture (exploiting the possibilities of the Greek text of the Bible which he used in his evangelism among the Gentiles, and which seems to have been the version with which he was most familiar), and his training in Stoicism or in Stoic-influenced Judaism. The dynamic of his career—the Gospel—and the poten-

[9] For further discussion, see my *Jesus in History* (New York: Harcourt Brace Jovanovich, 1975), p. 46, and F. J. Foakes-Jackson and K. Lake, *The Beginnings of Christianity*, vol. 5, (New York: Macmillan, 1933; repr. Grand Rapids, Mich.: Baker Book House, 1966), pp. 81–93.

tially universal response to it—to the Jew first and also to the Greek—are set out in the introduction to the body of the letter (Rom. 1:16–17). Here Paul also draws on his knowledge of the Jewish scriptures (Hab. 2:4) in order to justify his conviction, influenced by the Stoic doctrine of the unity of the human race, that God was at work through Jesus to bring all his people into one, whether Jew or Gentile: "For salvation to *everyone* who has faith." But before Paul can set forth the universal solution to the human condition, he must depict the universal problem: humanity's alienation from its creator.

The Universal Human Condition
[ROM. 1:18–2:16]

The potential for all human beings to know God has not been denied to anyone, but it has been perverted by all. The problem is not that the truth is unavailable, but that it is suppressed (1:18). Building on Stoic tradition, Paul declares that God has disclosed to the whole race what is appropriate for humanity to know about him: Through inference from the creation and especially the natural order, God's eternal power and deity may be recognized by anyone who stops to consider. His invisible nature, which brought into being and transcends the creation itself, is apparent to human reflection. Instead of acknowledging God as creator, however, human beings have characteristically preferred to worship something they made themselves, something they can control—the created thing rather than the creator (1:22–25). Their failure to acknowledge God's sovereign power has resulted in God's turning them loose to follow their own self-serving impulses. The result is that human life is corrupted and human insights are darkened. The preoccupation of human beings with sensual gratification and their violation of the patterns of behavior and relationships established by natural law (1:26–27) are the symptoms of their universal rejection of God, not the cause of the divine estrangement. Human beings are not out of right relationship with God because they commit sins; rather, their sinful acts and attitudes are the consequence of their alienation from their creator. Not only sexual but all human relationships are warped once the basic creator-creature link has been rejected by the creatures: ". . . covetousness, malice, . . . envy, murder, strife, deceit, . . . gossip, slander." They are "insolent, haughty, boastful, inventors of evil, disobedient to parents, foolish, faithless, heartless, ruthless" (1:28–31). Their rejection of a proper relationship with God has brought the perversion of all human relationships.

Throughout this solemn, judgmental portrayal of the human condition, Paul is using both the terminology and the literary style of the Stoic tradition. The abandonment of the "natural" patterns of behavior, and the indulging in acts which are "inappropriate," is described in terms that go back to Zeno, the founder of Stoic philosophy. The same use of Stoic language is evident when Paul is painting the other side of the picture: God's "kindness" (2:4) and his operation within human hearts through the law of nature (2:14–15). At 2:15 Paul employs a term that is central to his argument, but for which there is no linguistic equivalent in Hebrew or Aramaic: "conscience." This was regarded by Stoics as an innate human capacity to discern and respond to the law of nature. Whether, therefore, the law was transmitted through the conscience (as is the case for Gentiles) or by revelation at Sinai (as is the case for Jews), all have knowledge of God's moral demands. No one has the excuse of ignorance (2:12–25). The fact that the Greek word *nomos* means "law" with as broad a range of connotations as the English word (legal code; general principle; moral demand) but was used to translate the Hebrew word *torah,* as we have seen, made it possible for Paul to weave together features from both his biblical and his Stoic background. All humanity stands condemned under law, whether the law of nature or the law of Moses.

The Seeming Advantages of Being a Jew
[ROM. 2:17–3:8]

Not only access to the law of Moses but genetic links with Israel and Abraham gave Jews, including Paul, an understandable sense of pride and privilege. For many this status carried with it a sense of responsibility toward others as well—guide to the blind, light to those in darkness, instructor of the foolish and immature. But having received divine instructions is a very different thing from following them. In fact, Israel's possession of the law had not made the nation more obedient, but had resulted in hypocritical attitudes that discredited the God of Israel in the eyes of the Gentiles, though even that was in fulfillment of prophecy (2:24; Isa. 52:5, which is relevant when quoted from the Greek version, not the Hebrew original of Isaiah).

At this point in his argument Paul articulates the most radical answer to his perennial question about how one can claim membership in God's covenant people. He denies that any external act—even circumcision, the ancient and traditional sign of covenant participation—is of itself of any value: "Real circumcision is a matter of the heart, spiritual and not literal" (2:29). In Galatians he had declared it to be unnecessary; now he asserts that it is meaningless unless matched by inward obedience, which can take place wholly apart from the ritual requirement of circumcision (2:27). The consequence for those who follow his lead will be that Jewish ritual requirements will no longer be regarded as preliminary steps toward becoming part of the new covenant community. Obedience is a matter of the heart; that is, the will, the center of decision-making.

The one advantage that Paul acknowledges the Jews to have possessed is that they were "entrusted with the oracles of God" (3:2). That is, the self-disclosure of God to Israel through the law, the prophets, and the writings has been the Jewish people's distinctive possession. The truth of those oracles, and especially of the promises they contain, is in no way undermined by Israel's failure to experience their fulfillment. Its disobedience in no way undercuts the fidelity of God or the substance of his moral demands (3:5–7). Those who charge Paul with encouraging others to act evilly in order that greater good may come from God do not understand how seriously he takes the expectations God has for the obedience of his people. The difficulty lies in the widespread notion that if people are obedient, God will accept them as his own.

Paul is convinced that only when they come to the realization that God has accepted them, no matter what their intrinsic merits or their performance record, will they be free and motivated to live obedient lives.

So long as human beings approach God on the ground of a merit system, they will be called to account by God for their moral failures. Whether Jews striving to earn favor with God by keeping the law of Moses or Gentiles seeking to obey the natural law implanted within them by their consciences, they are doomed to moral disaster. It does not lie within human nature, subject as it is to the power of sin, to live in full obedience: "All, both Jews and Greeks, are under the power of sin" (3:9). The inevitability of this plight is detailed by Paul through a mosaic of quotations from the Jewish scriptures, especially from the psalms, the wisdom literature, and the prophets (3:10–18). Anyone who seeks to achieve justification in the sight of God by moral performance will be rendered speechless by the divine condemnation: "The whole world becomes accountable to God" (3:19). The point is once more cinched by a quotation from scripture (3:20; Ps. 143:2): No human being stands justified before him when the approach to God is on the grounds of legal performance.

God's Way of Setting Matters Right
[ROM. 3:9–4:24]

The way God places men and women in right relation to himself, Paul declares, is wholly apart from any system of law. Those systems do not work, as he has sought to show in the opening part of his letter, but God's way does achieve his objectives, and it does so in a manner already sketched out in the Hebrew scriptures. All humankind has failed on its own terms and by its own efforts to measure up to the high expectations God had when he created male and female in his own image (Gen. 1:27), crowning his creation "with glory and honor" (Ps. 8:5). It is not simply that Adam and Eve disobeyed God and thereby lost "glory and honor": all human beings have been characterized by foolish self-seeking and self-serving, which for Paul is the essence of sin, and have thereby forfeited the capacity to display the divine image in and for which they were created.

God has acted not on the ground of merit, but as a gift (3:24), motivated solely by his own gracious nature. That divine action has accomplished a ransom, a liberation of humanity enslaved to sin, shackled to the folly of self-justification by a merit system. Changing the image from that of granting freedom to that of purging pollution, Paul builds on the ancient notion that a sacrifice presented to a divinity removes the sin or defilement of the worshipper and makes possible direct access to the god in spite of human failure or unworthiness. But according to Paul, it is neither the suppliant nor a priest interceding in his behalf who accomplishes this expiatory sacrifice. God himself has acted to remove the barrier of human sin. The agent through whom these intertwined benefits of freedom and access are brought about is Jesus, whose sacrificial death made both possible (3:25).

Jesus's willing offering of himself in behalf of others is a central motif in the letters of Paul. In the Hymn to Christ of Philippians 2:8, he celebrates

Jesus's obedience "unto death"; in the joyous celebration of the Resurrection of Jesus, he exults that "Death has been swallowed up in victory" (1 Cor. 15:54). Those united with Christ in baptism are baptized into his death (Rom. 6:3). Christians are reconciled to God by "the death of his Son" (Rom. 6:3). The cross on which he died is to the faithful "the power of God" (1 Cor. 1:18). By acting through the one whose obedience culminated in his death, God has revealed his basic nature: one whose very being is reconciling and forgiving, and one whose historical actions have provided the true ground of right relationship with himself. That gift of free access is not offered as a reward for meritorious performance, but as an act of grace to be relied upon by trusting in Jesus as God's agent of human redemption (3:26). Faith, or trust, is the sole ground of humanity's entering into right relationship with God (3:27–30).

This does not discredit the scriptural story of God's dealings with his people, however. Indeed, it confirms the truth of what may be read in Genesis about Abraham as the father of the covenant people, and it is supported by the psalmist (here identified as David) in his pronouncement of the blessedness of one whose relationship to God is grounded on God's grace alone (4:7; Ps. 32:1–2). Abraham's sole qualification for becoming the father of Isaac and the progenitor of the people Israel is that he believed the divine promise. He not only believed it in relation to his own offspring (Gen. 17; 22), but he also had confidence that through him the blessings of God would flow to all the nations on earth (4:18; Gen. 15:5). It is precisely this promise of God which Abraham had trusted in that is now in the process of fulfillment through the sharing in the covenant by those from many nations. Every human instinct would have told Abraham that to have such confidence about his posterity at his advanced age was nonsense. Instead, he "was fully convinced that God was able to do what he promised" (4:21). It is that principle and that promise which are still operative among those in Paul's day who place their trust in what God has done and is doing rather than in their own feeble accomplishments (4:22–24).

The New Humanity
[ROM. 5:1–11:36]

As he brings this stage of his argument to a climax, Paul turns from his earlier focus on God's act in using Jesus Christ as expiator (that is, removing human sin as a barrier) to the other phase of that divine action, raising Jesus from the dead. What Paul sees as occurring is not merely remedy but renewal. Human beings are not merely introduced into a new relationship with God, but their lives are granted the resources and potential for a transformation of human existence (4:24–25). In detailing what that involves, Paul uses a series of vivid images to depict the various facets of the new relationship in faith.

THE IMAGERY OF TRANSFORMATION. The first of these images has the double advantage of building on biblical tradition and at the same time of expressing a Stoic point of view. The Stoics stressed the essential unity of the human race. Romans 5 sets forth Paul's view of a new humanity. Although he was basically Epicurean in his philosophical outlook, the Roman poet Virgil (70–19 B.C.) shared with the Stoics the hope of the renewal and the perfection of human community on the earth under the sovereignty of a divinely endowed, beneficent ruler. His Fourth Eclogue bears witness to this:

> Now is come the last age of the song of the Cumae;[10] the great line of centuries begins anew.... Only do thou ... smile on the birth of the child, under whom the iron brood shall first cease, and a golden race spring up throughout the world.

The poet describes the renewal of the creation. The ram provides fleece and colors it without its having to be clipped and dyed. Brambles and poison plants disappear, along with voracious beasts. All will be at peace in an epoch of unprecedented prosperity. It is impossible to determine the degree to which Jewish prophecy may have influenced Virgil, but his hopes for a transformed cosmos are largely compatible with those of the biblical prophets, especially from the Persian and Hellenistic periods. Paul incorporates into his hope for human renewal the Greek aspiration for unity, especially in its Stoic form, with the result that he here traces two models of human existence: Adam, representing disobedience, estrangement, and death; and Christ, representing obedience, reconciliation, and life.[11]

The Stoic ingredients of his portrait of the new humanity are apparent in his enumeration of the qualities that characterize the new life style in Christ: suffering leads to endurance, which leads to character, and that leads to hope. The terms "character" and "endurance" are common to the Stoic tradition, but Paul has adapted them to a different eschatological view of life. Unlike the aspirations of the Hebrew prophets or those of a court poet like Virgil, hope does not lie in the future alone; rather, the new reality promised by the oracles is already a part of present experience. Paul is confident that his hope will not be disappointed, "because God's love has already been poured into our hearts through the Holy Spirit which has been given to us." The reconciliation of humankind to God has already occurred (5:6–10). The process of transformation of life which is made possible by that new relationship to God is already at work: we are being saved by his life. The stranglehold of the old humanity, with its seemingly inevitable culmination in death, has now been broken. One man's (Adam's) disobedience had set the universal pattern for estrangement and death; one man's (Christ's) obedience has opened up for all who will avail themselves of it a new pattern and possibility of reconciliation, of freedom, of life as God intended it to be (5:15–17).

[10] Cumae is the place of origin of the sibyls, oracular women who were consulted in times of personal or national decision. The phenomenon of sibyls spread to the eastern Mediterranean as well, so that there were Jewish sibylline oracles in Egypt, which in turn influenced the Roman oracles—and possibly Virgil as well.

[11] J. Christiaan Beker, in *Paul the Apostle: The Triumph of God in Life and Thought* (Philadelphia: Fortress Press, 1981) has properly drawn attention to the powerful and pervasive influence of apocalyptic expectation and outlook on the whole of Paul's life and mission. See especially the final chapter, "The Triumph of God," pp. 351–67.

THE IMAGERY OF RITUAL.   The second set of images Paul employs to describe the Christian community comes from the realm of ritual and sacrifice, though once again Paul has adapted them to his own understanding of Christian existence. In the mystery cults, a ceremonial union with the dying and rising god, Osiris, was enacted as part of the initiation, as Paul's contemporary Plutarch informs us in his treatise on the Isis-Osiris myth. But ceremonial washing as initiation was practiced by John the Baptist and Jesus in their ritual preparation of their followers for the new age, which they announced as "at hand." In describing the ceremonial union in death with Christ, Paul goes beyond the break with the old life to celebrate the beginning of a new life, made possible by God's having raised Jesus from the dead: "You also must consider yourselves dead to sin and alive to God in Christ Jesus" (6:11). That new relationship symbolized by baptism is to have direct effects on the transformation of the moral life in the new context of grace and freedom.

THE IMAGERY OF SLAVERY AND FREEDOM.   Having raised the possibility of servitude to sin, Paul shifts to another image: the slave and the free person. They have lived in involuntary servanthood under the ruthless taskmaster, sin. Now they have the possibility of voluntary servitude in a freely chosen life of grateful obedience to God (6:15-23). Another symbol of the Christian's obligations and responsibilities is marriage (7:1-6). The union of Christians with Christ in death and resurrection frees them from obligation to keep the law as completely as a literal death terminates the marital relationship. The gift of the Risen Christ, however, offers them the possibility of a new life in a new sphere of freedom in the Spirit.

A dominant theme in Paul's thought must have been God's creation of Adam and Eve. In 7:7-25 he builds on the image of the tempter who entices Adam and Eve into their fundamental acts of disobedience. Paul's radical notion here is that the law (Mosaic or natural), far from controlling sin, performs the same role as the tempter in Eden: It lures men and women to disobey by playing on their weaknesses, by bringing potential misdeeds to the level of consciousness. He does not place ultimate blame on the law, however, but sees the fatal factor to be self-serving human nature, willing and eager to accept the role of slave to sin. Taking advantage of the multiple meanings of "law," Paul describes the interior warfare among three antagonists: the divine purpose (law of God), the conscience (law of my mind), and the moral laws perverted by sin to enslave weak humanity (law of sin). Through the liberation and renewal provided by God in Christ, Paul can triumph over the tempter's law of sin and become truly obedient to conscience and the demands of God.

New Resources

Paul's focus now moves from problems and impediments to the enabling resources available to Christians (8:1-17). The new "law" or principle that makes all the others obsolete, and that works where all others fail, is the Spirit, which is the dynamic "of life in Christ Jesus." Drawing on the images used earlier, Paul declares that union with Jesus in his death and Resurrection makes possible the triumph over temptation and freedom from slavery to sin. It results in obedience with respect to what the law rightly demands of us (8:4). This new life in the Spirit is identical with a new ground of relationship to God, one so like child to parent that Paul employs the Aramaic equivalent of English terms of child-parent endearment (Daddy, Poppa): *Abba* (8:15). Paul sees himself and other Christians not standing "before Jehovah's awful throne," as an old hymn phrased it, but as sharing the profound affection and support of a loving parent.

The other resource for the Christian community is hope. For Paul this is not a vague hunch that things will turn out all right, but a deep conviction that what God has done for the human race through Jesus offers a full assurance of the divine purpose in history and of God's intention and power to bring that purpose to fruition. The trials and struggles of the Christians as they face opposition should by no means become the ground for discouragement or doubt. Rather, these sufferings are like birth pangs, necessary initial phases in the birth of the new age. The whole created order is undergoing similar struggles, but it cannot expect deliverance from these difficulties until God has completed his purpose through his covenant people. Only then will "the creation itself be set free from its bondage and obtain the glorious liberty of the children of God" (8:21). Meanwhile, the presence and power of the Spirit enables Christians to endure and to rejoice in the prospect of what lies beyond the present struggles.

Once more, Paul is synthesizing his Jewish and Stoic backgrounds, since Stoic thinkers were committed to the idea of predestination. If the universe was pervaded by the divine law, then there were no surprises. However difficult the immediate situation might seem, the true Stoic knew that the divine law was working itself out, and could accept the momentary discomfort of pain or suffering. Fate was not blind but purposive for those with the insight to recognize it. In the Jewish eschatology, especially of the apocalyptic variety as seen in Daniel and in some of the Dead Sea Scrolls, the forces of evil might seem for the moment to be in control, but that was to settle for a short view. The long perspective saw present suffering as a prelude to impending glory, when God would vindicate his own people and put down forever the powers of Satan. Paul, therefore, is not in the least disheartened by the calamities he lists: tribulation, persecution, famine, nakedness, peril, sword. These were not mere theoretical possibilities for him and other Christians, but part of the possibilities for their lives from day to day. Yet he urges the Roman community to rest confident that God is in charge, that the triumph of his purpose is sure, and that they are safely positioned in that predetermined plan of God, however harsh or hostile their present treatment may seem: "Nothing in all creation will be able to separate us from the love of God in Christ Jesus our Lord" (8:39).

THE CHURCH AS PART OF "ALL ISRAEL."   The final image in terms of which Paul depicts the Christian community is that of Israel. Obviously, participation in Israel is for Paul far more than a vivid literary image or an abstract idea: it is the ground of his own personal identity and the heritage in which he had been reared. Yet, as we see in this section of his Letter to the

Romans, it is an image he cannot simply repudiate. Nor can he accept it without major modification. Paul affirms the enduring historical benefits and privileges God has granted to Israel: the special relationship with God (sonship), the glory (the cloud of divine radiance which was thought to dwell in the Temple at Jerusalem), the covenants, the giving of the law, the proper worship of God, the prophetic promises, the traditions of the patriarchs and the chosen race that were their posterity (9:4–5). And as the climax came Jesus of Nazareth, of the seed of David (1:4) and—as Paul was persuaded—the fulfillment of Israel's messianic hopes.

Genetic links are not enough, however, as Abraham and Sarah, Isaac and Rebecca discovered. Their attempts to provide the fulfillment of God's promise by arranging on their own for a child to be born to them had failed. God alone could provide what he had promised. In his inscrutable wisdom, God chooses to accomplish his purpose through some persons, while others do not share in those plans and benefits. Paul develops his case here in unusually heavy dependence on the Jewish scriptures; indeed, this section of the letter contains more than fifty allusions to or quotations from the Jewish Bible, some of them extensive. As in his earlier argument about the faith of Abraham as the ground of his acceptance with God, Paul is not so much innovating as demonstrating an enduring, underlying principle that has been obscured. What has distorted the understanding of how God works to gather his people is the false assumption (from Paul's standpoint) that participation in the life of Israel is basically hereditary. Paul adduces evidence from the Old Testament to show that the sole ground is response in faith to the divine promise, and that many who might make the genetic claim—such as Ishmael and Esau in the Genesis stories—have been excluded. Since God is the creator and sovereign of his universe, Paul sees no ground for complaints of divine favoritism or injustice (9:14–21). God can use even the seemingly unworthy to accomplish his larger objectives.

Yet God has not abandoned ethnic Israel, Paul is persuaded (11:2). It is true that in the present time his messengers are reaping a harvest of faith among those who are "not my people" (9:25; Hos. 1:10), since Israel mistakenly assumed that conformity to legal precepts was the ground for acceptance before God (9:31–32). But throughout the history of the human race, it has been those who trust the divine promise who stand in right relationship with him, who "confess with [their] lips that Jesus is Lord and believe in [their] hearts that God raised him from the dead" who are "saved" (10:9); that is, who share in the life of his people. (In Chapter 10 we will consider what Paul meant by speaking of Jesus as "Lord").

Throughout the writings of the prophets there are explicit declarations: (1) that those who formerly did not seek God have found him, (2) that whoever turns to him in faith is accepted, (3) that his word has gone out to the ends of the earth. By a divine irony, Israel's rejection of Jesus as Messiah has provided the occasion and opportunity for the rest of the nations of the world to hear the good news. And since the ground of acceptance has always been faith alone, the Gentiles are now sharing in the life of the covenant people. That switch of focus, from Jews to Gentiles, will continue "until the full number of the Gentiles come in" (11:25), with the final result that all God's true people will share in covenant life. Why does God choose to work in this para-doxical way? Here Paul simply confesses the inability of the human mind to understand the divine reasoning (11:33–36), and ends this section of the letter with an ascription of praise to God.

New Life Within the Community
[ROM. 12]

The new covenant people is a new shrine in which the worship of God is car-ried on by spiritual rather than by physical rites, in which the "sacrifices" are the selves ("bodies") of the worshippers rather than animal substitutes (12:1). The moral dimensions of this worship include the renovation of the will and the whole decision-making process, escaping the temptation to conform to the standards of the age and thereby demonstrating publicly the will of God for his people.

Paul then outlines both the context and the content of the renewed moral life of the community. The new context is one in which the mutuality of responsibility and the diversity of gifts and functions is paramount, so that the importance of all to each is apparent. For the content, Paul draws on the wis-dom traditions of ancient Israel, on Stoic sayings, and apparently on the Jesus tradition as well (as in 12:20; Matt. 5:44; similarly in 13:8). But for Paul, Christian responsibility involves external relationships as well as functions within the community. As in the teaching of Jesus, members of God's people must decide their stance toward political powers, even though their authority is thought to be temporary, pending the fulfillment of God's rule.

Paul sees the government's role as one of maintenance of order, and as a protection for those who do not practice civil disobedience (13:3). Here again Paul combines his Jewish heritage and his Stoic training when he urges the Roman Christians to obey the civil authorities "to avoid God's wrath," but also "for the sake of conscience" (13:5). Taxes are to be paid and appropriate respect offered to the emperor. Christians are not to be social revolutionaries; the transformation of the social order is God's business in his own time. Their task is to live in obedience toward the civil authorities, in mutual acceptance toward other Christians on matters of diet and other items of personal prefer-ence. The paramount consideration is "what makes for peace and mutual up-building" (14:19). Harmony and hospitality are to characterize the relation-ships, both within the local community and toward Christians who come from elsewhere to share in the common life (15:1–21).

Immediate Plans and Long-Term Hopes
[ROM. 15:22–33]

From the vantage point of Corinth Paul asserts that his evangelizing of the northeastern quadrant of the Mediterranean world is now complete. There is no place left for the kind of pioneer activity to which he believed he had been called by God. The sole responsibility remaining to him in that part of the world was to carry through on the agreement reached with the Jerusalem leaders that, as an expression of tangible unity and support, the Gentile churches would take up and forward a collection for their Jerusalem-based fellow-convenanters. When that undertaking is completed, Paul plans to come to Rome on his way to Spain, where he can resume his pioneering work. Yet even as he brings his letter to a close, he expresses some anxiety about the treatment he may receive at the hands of "unbelievers in Judea" (15:31). This is an obvious reference to Roman and Jewish authorities in Palestine, who regard Paul as a subverter of Judaism and of the stability of the empire itself, in spite of his clearly nonpolitical stance.

His wishes and concerns were based in reality. He did come finally to Rome, probably after an interval of two years or more in prison, if the report in Acts is accurate (Acts 24:27). But he arrived as a prisoner of the Roman authorities, and seems never to have reached Spain, in spite of later legends that report his activities there. His prior personal contacts with the Roman community are detailed in Romans 16, so he was not unknown, and he did not lack previous acquaintances there. One can only surmise that, in spite of his facing martyrdom at the hands of the Romans, his prayer was answered that he might "come to you with joy and be refreshed in your company" (15:32). The ground for mutual understanding and acceptance was laid in this, Paul's most carefully organized letter.

9

Problems in Human Relations Among God's People: 1 and 2 Corinthians, 1 and 2 Thessalonians

In any social group there are sure to be problems over authority. Who is in charge? And who put him or her in charge? What are the rules by which both group and individual decisions are to be made? Who adjudicates disputes? Who decides when the limits of group tolerance have been reached and a member of the group must be expelled? When challenge to the leadership comes from within or without, how is the group to determine the legitimacy of the claims of its leadership? How are standard procedures for the group to be decided on, and how are they to be enforced? How is reconciliation to be effected when conflict or splits develop?

Those are precisely the kinds of problems that occupy most of the letters of Paul, especially his two long letters to the church at Corinth. Rather than move through these letters in the order in which Paul wrote them, it may be useful to sort out the issues according to subject. (1) Of first importance, as the prominence given to it in the letters shows, is the basic question of Paul's claim to be an apostle. (2) The perennial moral and social issues are the ones dealt with at greatest length in the Pauline correspondence: money, sex, marriage, irresponsible behavior. (3) Since Paul is working to develop a new covenant people, he seeks to deal with problems in the context of an understanding of God and his purposes in the world, with the result that the problems are addressed in theological terms. (4) Further, since he is also seeking to build an ongoing religious organization, there are many questions—organization, assignment of individual responsibilities, doctrine, liturgy, church finances—that must be handled explicitly.

CHRISTIANITY AS A CHARISMATIC MOVEMENT

The dynamics of Paul's successes and struggles involve what has been called charismatic (as against institutional) leadership. The classic study of how leadership roles develop within religious movements is that of Max Weber, a pioneer in the study of sociology of religion, and it has direct bearing on our understanding of Paul's situation. Weber's research, which encompassed both Eastern and Western religions, showed that in a society where religion has become routine through bureaucratic or patriarchal structures which seek to maintain normal, predictable patterns of religious and social behavior, the deep-seated needs of a segment of the people—especially those who feel deprived of power or significance—pave the way for the rise of what Weber called a "charismatic leader." Arising as they do in times of psychic, physical, economic, ethical, religious, or political distress, these leaders more than make up for what they lack in professional credentials by the gifts of spirit and eloquence they possess, often coupled with unnatural powers. A charismatic movement lacks an abstract code or a formal organization, as well as any fixed mode of adjudicating disputes. Its guides for life emanate from the direct appeal of one whose personal experience of heavenly grace communicates to followers. To become a follower often involves a rejection of ties to the existing external order in favor of devotion of time and energy to the work of the prophetic leader figure. This step is revolutionary, since it calls for a break with all traditional and rational norms.

Once a charismatic movement has been launched, however, it initially flourishes in a free-wheeling way. But then there begins inevitably a process of institutionalization. Those who achieve positions of power in the movement through personal gifts, wealth, or social prestige want to have their privileged positions legitimized. To achieve this, they consciously or unconsciously seek to transform their actual power into a cosmic order of divinely sanctioned rights. What began as spontaneous charismatic power becomes conserved within a structure of social domination. As that process takes place, the focus shifts from innate authority to authorized exercise of power: Who authorized whom to do what? As the first generation passes, the inevitable question is: To whom and by what process is authority within the community now to be transferred.[1]

When a religious movement like early Christianity gives rise to several charismatic leaders whose rise to power is formally similar, but whose backgrounds and experiences differ in important detail, there is bound to be friction. And as the institutionalization process moves along, the conflicts will become more severe and more difficult of solution. It is against this model of the interplay between charismatic leadership and institutionalization that one must examine the evidence in the Pauline letters of his relations with the churches he founded and with the Jerusalem-based and other contemporary leaders in the early Church.[2] As Weber has noted, the difficulties attendant on such a transition regularly include staff relationships, finances, administration, and the need to specify moral requirements and to verbalize the belief system.[3] Because the individuals involved in these conflicts operate on the basis of a set of assumptions which to each of them is self-evident, it is never possible to resolve the issues on purely rational grounds. Even though the antagonists may try to rationalize their respective positions, the unspoken and unacknowledged factors are at least as important in creating the conflict as are the ideas aired in the course of the debate. To try to reduce the conflict between Paul and his opponents to strictly theological or conceptual differences is to indulge in oversimplification of pervasive human problems.

[1] Max Weber, "Sociology of Charismatic Authority," in *From Max Weber*, trans. and ed. H. Gerth and C. Wright Mills (New York: Oxford University Press, 1946, repr. 1977), pp. 245–71.

[2] For an illuminating discussion of the tension between charismatic spontaneity and the drive toward institutionalization in primitive Christianity, see Bengt Holmberg, *Paul and Power: The Structure of Authority in the Primitive Church as Reflected in the Pauline Epistles* (Philadelphia: Fortress Press, 1978, 1980).

[3] Holmberg, *Paul and Power*, pp. 161–71.

THE SIGNS OF APOSTLESHIP: LEADERSHIP

Our English word, "apostle," is only a transliteration of the Greek word *apostolos.* No one can be certain what it meant to its first users in early Christianity, or even if it meant the same thing to all of them. On certain basic matters, of course, there was and is agreement: An apostle was someone commissioned by God, or more specifically by Jesus Christ, for a leading role in the spread of the Christian message and the development of the covenant people. The root of the term, *stol,* is related to the ordinary Greek verb meaning "send." With the prefix *apo-,* it indicates sending someone out to accomplish a task. Which was more important for those who claimed to be apostles, the nature of their commission, or the specific task for which they were appointed?

Seeing the Lord

On the importance of the first of these factors, Paul and his detractors were in basic agreement. When he raised the question "Am I not an apostle?" he promptly answered it with another rhetorical question, "Have I not seen Jesus our Lord?" (1 Cor. 9:1). The clear implication is that he is surely on a par with the other apostles since he, like them, has "seen the Lord"—meaning he has seen Jesus Christ risen from the dead. There can be no doubt that that is what he intended, since he says so specifically in his list of the post-Resurrection appearances of Jesus in this same letter (1 Cor. 15:5–7). There he reports the sequence of those appearances: first to Peter, then to the "twelve" (meaning, of course, the original circle of his followers), then to James (Jesus's brother), and finally, "as to one born out of the normal process," to Paul himself. He goes on to call himself "the least of the apostles, unfit to be called an apostle," though it is safe to guess that he would have been most unhappy for anyone else to designate him in this demeaning way. But he explains—or offers the rationalization for—his inferior status by declaring that he had been a persecutor of the Church before his conversion and commissioning as an apostle. He seeks to strengthen the view of his real equality with the other apostles by reminding his readers of his tireless efforts to spread the Gospel, the effectiveness of which he attributed to "the grace of God which is with me" (1 Cor. 15:10). We noted in Chapter 8 that the revelation of the Risen Lord to Paul was "in me" (Gal. 1:16), and hence what we would call an inner vision, rather than an external experience that might have been observed by others. Indeed, in this entire list of appearances, Paul uses a passive verb (implying Jesus "was seen by" or "became visible to" him), rather than directly asserting (as he does in 1 Cor. 9:1), "I saw." The implication seems to be that the post-Resurrection experiences were private, as the beautiful appearance stories of Luke 24 suggest. Whatever the mode of the appearance, its result was the commissioning of the apostles, including Paul.

The very fact that Paul words his defense of his apostleship in terms of having "seen" Jesus suggests that that was the ground of attack by those who sought to discredit him: He had not been a follower of Jesus, and indeed had never even seen him. The disciples' commissioning by Jesus had taken place during his earthly life, although final confirmation and full meaning came to them only after his death, in the Resurrection appearances. That conviction must have been shared by Paul and the twelve, or there would have been no point in Paul's having advanced that line of argument in 1 Corinthians 15. There was no disagreement between Paul and the other apostles on the centrality of the appearances of the Risen Lord for their apostolic commissioning; what divided them was the importance of the relationship with him during his ministry in Palestine—which the twelve had and Paul lacked. Other than describing Jesus as having lived an obedient life "unto death" (Phil. 2:8), Paul does not discuss the career of Jesus in his letters, and apart from occasional references to love of neighbor as the essence of the law (Rom. 12:9–10; 1 Cor. 13; Matt. 5:43), Paul does not make direct reference to any of the teaching of Jesus in the Gospel traditions.

Revelation and Suffering

Paul seems to have adopted three lines of defense against those who wanted to call into question his apostolic credentials. The first was to take along to Jerusalem with him, on the occasion of his formal sessions with the Jerusalem apostolic leaders, someone who apparently was highly regarded by them as an apostle: Barnabas (Gal. 2:1, 9). The second line of defense was to stress the direct revelations from God he had received. As we noted in Chapter 8, his standing as a Jew was impeccable, down through the period when he had been a leading persecutor of the church. With some reluctance, Paul mentions the "visions and revelations of the Lord" he has been privileged to experience. One of them he describes in detail: he was "caught up into Paradise," whether in bodily form or in spiritual transport he does not know, and was able to hear things too holy for him to reveal to others (2 Cor. 12:1–4). He had already indicated earlier in this same letter (3:1–18) that every Christian could have the same experience as that of Moses (Exod. 34:29–35), in which his face glowed after he had seen the glory of the Lord on the mountain where he received the tablets on which the law was written. The radiance of Moses's face had faded, however, while the faithful Christians were being transformed into the radiant image of divine glory disclosed in Jesus Christ. For Paul, these revelations were not merely moments of religious ecstasy, but stages in a continuing process of moral and spiritual transformation.

Closely related to the appeal to revelation was Paul's recounting the sufferings he had undergone. Indeed, the revelatory experience described in 2 Corinthians 12 was understood by him to be a divine confirmation of the fact that his difficulties and persecutions were not a sign of divine disfavor, but part of a process of spiritual purification. They were given to him in order to prevent him from becoming "too elated by the abundance of revelations" (12:7), and to remind him that it was by God's grace (*charis*) and not by his own native capacities that he was able to carry out his ministry in spite of the obstacles put in his path by opponents. Furthermore, the same kinds of signs and wonders that his detractors were appealing to as showing their own superiority ("these superlative apostles") were manifest in the churches under his care (2 Cor. 12:12–13). One of the charismatic gifts listed by Paul (1 Cor. 12:9–10) was the ability to heal and to perform miracles. Paul's refusal to accept financial support was contrary to the attitude of the other apostles, and is different from the instructions given by Jesus to his disciples in the synoptic tradition (Matt. 10:9–14), as we will see below when we deal with money matters. But the question remains: What was the basic point of disagreement between Paul and the other apostles?

Commission and Strategy

Paul not only based his claim to apostleship on heavenly revelations rather than earthly associations, but also understood himself to have an assignment fundamentally different from that of the Jerusalem-based apostles. Their task was to convert Jews; his was to convert Gentiles (Gal. 1:16; 2:9). Either the agreement to divide the field of evangelism was clearer in Paul's mind than in theirs, or they reneged on the original agreement. In any case, Paul had long been under attack for his allowing into his churches Gentiles who were uncircumcised and who did not obey the dietary laws. In Corinth, however, a new kind of discrediting of Paul had appeared (1 Cor. 1:10–3:21).

The *bema* at Corinth (the public rostrum), with the Acrocorinth in the background. Paul was accorded a hearing on this platform before Gallio, the Roman governor, according to Acts 18:2.   (*Courtesy of the American School of Classical Studies, Athens*)

Although Corinth was not and had never been a center of intellectual life in ancient Greece, the members of the Church there seem to have been impressed by visiting preachers whose eloquence and profundity eclipsed Paul's. The chief spellbinder seems to have been Apollos, who according to Acts 18 was a Jew from the sophisticated city of Alexandria, "an eloquent man, well versed in the scriptures." Alexandria had long been a center of learning, and Jews there had for centuries sought to develop a synthesis between the revealed religion of their scriptures and the rational views of the world developed by Greek and Hellenistic philosophers. The chief evidence for this is in the extensive writings of Philo of Alexandria, who employed allegorical methods to correlate revelation and reason, as we have noted earlier. But there are shorter anonymous works, such as The Wisdom of Solomon, which discuss such questions as creation and the origin of evil in terms of Stoic and Platonic philosophy. We have no way of determining how much pagan philosophy Apollos knew or used, but it seems highly likely that he had grown up in this atmosphere and used some of the same philosophically oriented interpretive methods to interpret the Christian Gospel. And the Corinthians found it appealing.

Paul, by contrast, refused to compete with Apollos or anyone else in terms of rhetorical skill or intellectual brilliance. His message was in direct conflict with ordinary human views of power. He is wary, lest eloquence rather than God's remedy for human weakness bring people into the Church. In support of his position he quotes scripture (1 Cor. 1:19; Isa. 29:14). Wisdom has been around for centuries, but no one has come to know God through it. Jews expect grand divine manifestations ("signs"); Gentiles want grandiose intellectual schemes. The Gospel of the crucified Jesus offends the Jews, who expect a powerful liberator; for the Gentile intellectuals it is sheer foolishness. His only defense of his strategy is to assert that "the foolishness of God is wiser than men, and the weakness of God is stronger than men" (1 Cor. 1:25). In Chapter 10 we will see that Paul has assigned to Christ the role that the more intellectually inclined Jews had granted to wisdom. We may note here that in defending his "foolish" apostolic strategy, Paul declares that God has made Christ our wisdom (1 Cor. 1:31).

Paul must take care, however, to show that his disagreements with the other apostles on questions of strategy and potential candidates for conversion do not require him to discredit them. What he deplores is the tendency of the Corinthians to choose champions, to rally around the personality of one or another of the apostles (1 Cor. 1:12). Probably to "belong to Apollos" (1 Cor. 1:12) was the watchword of those who admired his eloquence and sophistication. One can scarcely conjecture what the appeal was of those who belonged to Peter; possibly they admired his close association with Jesus, or perhaps they may have preferred his stricter stand on obeying the Jewish law. Those converted under Paul's preaching may have thought they were honoring him by claiming a special allegiance to him. And there may have been those who thought they should deny all human agency, and claim only Christ as the one to whom they belonged. From the rest of the letter, however, we can infer that Paul was most upset with those who admired wisdom in the style of Apollos (1 Cor. 3:1–6).

Personal Qualities

There were others who attacked Paul and his apostolic role on personal grounds. He quotes them in 2 Corinthians 10:10 as acknowledging the power of his letters, while describing his bodily presence as weak and his speech as contemptible. Various physical ailments have been proposed to account for his weak appearance and his speech: epilepsy, a severe stammer, facial disfigurement, bad eyesight. But his only reponse was to point to how hard he had worked and how much he had been able to accomplish in spite of his handicap, whatever it may have been. He considered himself to be a superior servant of Christ, as he recounted his labors, imprisonments, beatings, narrow escapes from death, and relentless anxieties for the churches under his care (2 Cor. 11:23–29).

This pragmatic approach to the question of his discipleship is evident as well in the explicit orders and threats he utters in his letters. In 2 Corinthians 13:5–10, for example, he tells the Corinthians to engage in serious self-examination so that he will not have to carry out that unpleasant process when he arrives for a stay with them. The content of Paul's teaching as well as that of his letters provides the norm for faith and practice in the churches (2 Thess. 2:2, 15; 3:14). The exercise of authority as apostle can be delegated, however; in Philippians 2:25–30, Epaphroditus is going to be sent by Paul to the church at Philippi, from which he had earlier brought their contribution to Paul's work (Phil. 2:25; 4:18). A more solemn deputy role was assigned to Timothy (1 Cor. 4:17): he is to set the arrogant straight before Paul's arrival.

The Shift from Charisma to Administration

What can be discerned in Paul's statements about his apostleship is that even in the process of defining that role, it is shifting from a purely charismatic function to an administrative office with credentials requiring definition. In Acts 1, one attempt at definition is presented: An apostle must be one who "accompanied us during all the time that the Lord Jesus went in and out among us, beginning from the baptism of John until the day he was taken up from us—one of these must become with us a witness to his Resurrection" (Acts 1:21–22). That, of course, would exclude Paul. Only once in the narrative of Acts does the term apostle refer to Paul (14:14), although related words, such as "commission" or "send," are used to describe God's purpose through him, as in Acts 13:2: "Set apart for me Barnabas and Saul for the work to which I have called them." In this way, according to Acts, the Holy Spirit communicates the divine will that Paul and his associates should launch a full-scale mission to the Gentiles.

Elsewhere in Acts, however, the "apostles" are the church leaders based in Jerusalem, with whom Paul checks periodically, who approve his work in advance, and with whom he is reported by Acts to have worked out a compromise on the issue of Gentile Christian responsibility toward Jewish law (Acts 15:29). It is impossible to imagine the Paul of the letters agreeing to such a concession. As we noted earlier, what is likely is that Acts was written at a time when the sharpness of Paul's principle of freedom from the law for Gentile converts had been modified, probably largely through Christians' increasing knowledge of the Jewish scriptures. This would fit well with the sociological factor of institutionalization of the Church, which on other grounds we have seen to be taking place even during Paul's lifetime. That process will be traced further in Chapter 11, where we will consider the later literature written in Paul's name at a time when definition of Church offices and doctrine had advanced markedly from Paul's own time. In those documents, apostles have become the guarantors and guardians of faith and practice.

HOW CHRISTIANS SHOULD BEHAVE: COMMUNITY PROBLEMS

In Paul's view there are three different factors to be taken into account when adjudging what is appropriate individual or group action among Christians: (1) the integrity of the covenant people, (2) the state of grace of the individual as a member of God's people, and (3) the opinion of outsiders about the Church. In specific cases, these three considerations are never fully separated, since the state of the Christian community in the public eye is as much a part of its testimony as is what its leaders and teachers say. Above all, the public image is of grave significance for the Church's long-term effectiveness.

Sex and Marriage

Not surprisingly, the largest cluster of problems concerns sex and marriage. The most serious of these is a case of incest at Corinth. To have sexual relations with one's parent was as abhorrent to the Greeks as it was to the Jews (1 Cor. 5:1). Yet a member of the church at Corinth had been living with his stepmother. Instead of being shocked, the Corinthians took it as an indication of new-found freedom in Christ. Paul insisted that this was not a private matter: the moral condition of one of the members directly affects, for better or for worse, the moral state of the community as a whole. The only appropriate response was to expel the erring member, and to do so in the name of Paul and under his authority. The analogy to which Paul appealed (1 Cor. 5:6–8) combined features of his Jewish as well as his Stoic heritage, yet he brought both together in a way that is distinctively Christian. One of the central events in preparation for Israel's exodus from Egypt was the feast of unleavened bread, which was linked with the sacrifice of the Passover lamb (Exod. 12:14–27). The old leaven was to be thrown out, as a symbol of a new beginning for the covenant people; the Passover lamb was offered to symbolize God's deliverance of his people from bondage. Paul saw both practices as fulfilled in Christ and his self-sacrifice, but he also used these symbols to point to the renewal and cleansing that ought to characterize the ongoing life of the new covenant people. That purity is not merely ritual, but moral, so the old leaven of this incestuous member must be expelled. Paul did not believe, however, that the man was beyond redemption; rather, his severance from the Church would purge him so that he might share in the eschatological deliverance. When that drastic action of expulsion was taken, Paul in his apostolic authority would be present with them "in spirit."

Paul did not hold up celibacy as the highest spiritual estate. He deplored violation of the monogamous marital relationship (1 Thess. 4:1–8), and expected members of the Church to live together in fidelity and mutual respect. This dimension of mutuality was unusual in the Roman period, since by Roman law the woman had no rights and was subject to her husband. Paul's personal preference was for avoiding marriage, since family responsibilities divert one from exclusive attention to the Lord's work (1 Cor. 7:32–33). Indeed, he saw the ability to control sexual urges as a spiritual gift (1 Cor. 7:7). Yet he believed that there was nothing inherently wrong about sexual relations, and urged those who were preoccupied with sexual desire to marry (1 Cor. 7:36), confident that there was nothing sinful about marriage (7:28). Since he was convinced that the period of time until the coming of Christ and the end of the age was so short, he hoped many would forego marriage, or if married would live as if they were not (7:25–31).

The question of divorce came up within the Christian community in a way that would be unlikely within Judaism. In addition to the familiar reasons for divorce, such as incompatibility and preference for another spouse, the Christians had such a strong sense of the new relationship into which they entered that the marital relationship with an unconverted spouse created serious, if not intolerable, tension. Should divorce be virtually automatic in such cases? Paul said no, hoping that the spiritual benefits of the believer might be transmitted to the spouse. In any case, the children should be brought up in a supportive, responsible way (1 Cor. 7:12–14). If the conflict was impossible, then divorce was to be preferred. What we see in these judgments is a mixture of Jewish law, Stoic virtue, pragmatic flexibility, and profound concern for the way human beings relate to one another.

For Paul, mutuality is not merely a mood or a feeling; rather, it has to do with the relationships within the Christian community. For anyone to have sexual relations with a prostitute is *not* a private affair. He is polluting the whole of the body of Christ, which is Paul's favorite metaphor to describe the Church and its network of interrelationships (1 Cor. 6:15–19). The "body" is far more than a figure of speech for a friendly society of human beings; it is the dwelling place of God among his people (1 Cor. 6:19). Defilement of that corporate temple of God is unthinkable.

The Role of Women

Both the Jewish and the Hellenistic cultures assumed that the only appropriate structure of society was patriarchal. Paul's attitude concerning the role of women should be assessed, therefore, not on the basis of modern concerns for equality of opportunity for the sexes, but against the background of the accepted social patterns of the first century. Two famous works of classical literature depict vividly how the larger public regarded the place of women in religious movements. In Chapter 1 we noted Euripides's tragedy, the *Bacchae*, in which is described in gruesome detail how a group of women are caught up in the wild ecstasy of the worship of Dionysus, the Greek god of wine, and discover when the orgy is over that, instead of dismembering a wild beast with their bare hands, they have destroyed the son of the woman who led the group. In the historical writings of Livy there is an account of an outbreak of secret Dionysiac worship in Rome in the second century B.C. When it became known to the authorities, the women were turned over to their husbands for punishment and restraint, lest this emotional excess spring up elsewhere. These ecstatic sects were considered to be disruptive of the social order, and women were considered to be particularly susceptible to them. But since they lacked what we would call civil rights, it was their husbands who were held legally responsible for their actions.

By contrast, Paul affirmed that women and men enjoyed reciprocal rights in the marital relationship (1 Cor. 7:1–7). Further, he expressly mentions women who were co-workers of his, who "labored side by side" with him (Phil. 4:2–3). Men's and women's names intermingle in the long list of those greeted by Paul in Romans 16, and Prisca is mentioned ahead of Aquila, her husband. At the head of that list is an officer of the Church at Cenchrae, one of the port cities serving Corinth: "Phoebe, a deaconess." For Paul, therefore, the principle enunciated in Galatians 3:28, "There is neither male nor female . . . in Christ Jesus," was not merely a slogan but a fact of life within the new community. As such, it was revolutionary in terms of the social patterns of the time.

There is another side of the situation, however. Paul's thinking was clearly influenced by the Adam and Eve story in Genesis 2. Since woman was made from man (Gen. 2:21–24), woman has a secondary rank in the order of creation (1 Cor. 11:2–9). She was created from the male and was intended to be his companion. He was created in God's image; she was formed in man's image. In what seems to the modern reader a curious turn of logic, Paul makes a play on the word "head" in this connection: "The head of every man is Christ, the head of a woman is her husband, and the head of Christ is God" (1 Cor. 11:3). From this Paul concludes that a woman should cover her head in the presence of God, while a man should not cover his head when engaged in the same pious acts. But the argument is not finished: the further conclusion is drawn that a woman should have long hair (as a kind of natural veil?), while it would be disgraceful for a man to have long hair (since that would be, in effect, a veil). The line of argument may not be persuasive to the modern student of Paul, but it is consistent with his Jewish training in the biblical story of creation and with the Hellenistic notion of the ordered nature of the universe.

Most surprising, in light of the principle of equality of the sexes, is the unequivocal declaration of Paul that all the women should keep silence in the churches (1 Cor. 14:33–35). It is possible that this restriction was in effect only in connection with the ecstatic speech of prophetic utterance, which has just been under discussion in the preceding paragraph (1 Cor. 14:20–33). Paul's prohibition is of speaking, however, not merely of prophetic speech. It appears that women in the Pauline churches were encouraged to work and to serve in a variety of capacities—which was in itself remarkable, when seen against the cultural patterns of the era—but they were not to participate orally in public worship, or at least not to address the congregation, whether to express an opinion or to ask for clarification of what others had said. As far as Paul moved in principle to give equal opportunity for women, the practices he enjoined on the Christians under his charge relegated women to a place of subservience.

Problems with Pagan Converts

Just as Paul had difficulties in sorting out how his present outlook as a Christian was to be correlated with his upbringing as a law-observant Jew, so the Gentile converts to the new faith had the continuing problem of what attitude to assume toward the pagan religions in which they had once been participants. Paul's description of the Thessalonian Christians as those who had "turned to God from idols" (1 Thess. 1:9) reminds us of their pagan origins.

EATING MEAT.   The problem of lingering ties to pagan worship was most acute and unavoidable in the matter of eating meat, since the public meat supply consisted largely of flesh of animals that had first been offered as sacrifices to the pagan gods and then made available for sale in the markets. The difficulty took two forms, depending on the attitude of the convert: For some, liberation from the worship of the pagan gods was so joyous and so complete that it strengthened their sense of freedom to know that they were eating sacrificial meat. They enjoyed giving it to others, to show how liberated they felt. For others, however, there was a greater or lesser sense that to partake of sacrificial meat involved them physically with the god from whom Christ had delivered them.

Paul was persuaded that there was no such thing as ritually unclean food—neither among worshippers of the Greek or Roman gods nor among Jews. He was completely free of a sense of obligation to keep the kosher laws of his upbringing. He insisted, however, that there was an important issue here. It was not when or even whether food was clean or unclean. It was rather the question fundamental to the communal nature of Christian covenant existence: How will my behavior affect other members of the covenant people? He warned, therefore, against indulging in any practice in such a way as to offend a weaker member of the community. But also he pleaded with his readers not to adopt an attitude of superiority because they are so liberated that ritual attitudes toward food are no longer a problem for them (Rom. 14:1–23; 1 Cor. 8:1–13). He declared, as we might paraphrase it, "If your brother or sister is being injured by what you eat, your life style is no longer characterized by love" (Rom. 14:15).

CUSTOMS AND RITES.   On a related issue, Paul reminded the Galatians (4:8–10) that they had once been subject to false gods ("beings that by nature are no gods"). He asked them how, now that they have come to know the true God through Jesus Christ, they seem to feel it necessary to subject themselves to the same kinds of religious regulations (observing holy days, sacred seasons, and years) as though those practices would ingratiate them with the God who had delivered them from such pagan obligations. Later Christianity did take over and incorporate such pagan customs as evergreen trees and wreaths (from pagan Nordic fertility rites), Easter eggs (of widespread origin, also as fertility rites), and the adoption as Christian shrines of places, springs, caves that were originally associated with pagan rites. Paul's point is that one does not earn points with God by pious observances, and Christians were foolish to carry over such practices into their new faith.

Christians as Law-Abiding Citizens and Subjects

In Chapter 8 we noted that Paul's attitude toward the state was similar to that of Jesus as reported in the synoptic Gospels: The present order is soon to pass away with the coming of God's new age, so there is nothing to be gained by working for the overthrow of the state. Rather, one should meet the basic obligations, such as paying taxes, and take advantage of the law and order the state maintains (Rom. 13; Mark 12:13-17). Two other issues involving church and state appear in 1 Corinthians. The first is whether Christians should appeal to civil courts to settle disputes among themselves (1 Cor. 6:1-8). Here Paul's answer is an emphatic no. Referring to Christians by the term taken over from apocalyptic tradition (as in Dan. 7:18, 22), "saints" or "holy ones," he reminds them that they are to share in the judgment of the world that will take place in the end, so it is wholly out of place to appeal to an institution for judicial opinion that one is soon going to share in bringing under divine judgment. Similarly, on the question as to whether slaves converted to Christian faith—and therefore sharing in a new relationship in which "neither slave nor free" (Gal. 3:28) exists—should seek legal liberation from bondage, the answer is (1 Cor. 7:20-24) that the time before the end of the age is so short that everyone should remain in his or her present social status. Freedom should not be turned down if offered (7:22), but "whoever was called in the Lord as a slave is already a freedman in the Lord." Paul's attitude is that an ultimate social revolution will take place when God brings in the new age, but for the present he is quite content to live within, and to benefit from, Roman order.[4]

As in the case of the man flaunting his freedom in the incestuous relationship (1 Cor. 5), Paul had constantly to remind the members of the community that those who had been forgiven their sins, who had been liberated from subjection to the powers of evil, and who looked forward to the status of "saints" in the new age, were expected to manifest the qualities of holiness or saintliness in the present. As he wrote to the Thessalonians: "For this is the will of God, your sanctification" (1 Thess. 4:3). The Greek words translated as "holiness" and "saints" are from the same root, so that there is a direct, verbal connection when he tells them that mutual love from the Lord ought to "establish your hearts unblamable in holiness [or better, saintliness] . . . at the coming of our Lord Jesus with all the saints" (1 Thess. 3:13).

---

[4] On threats to Roman rule, see Ramsay MacMullen's superb study, *Enemies of the Roman Order* (Cambridge, Mass.: Harvard University Press, 1966).

To be a saint is not to sit in a lonely cell, withdrawn from the world in quiet contemplation, however. It involves fidelity in the marital relationship (4:4–5), fair dealings with other Christians, minding one's own business, doing one's daily work faithfully, meriting a good reputation among outsiders (4:6–12). Paul is quite explicit when he tells the Corinthians that they are not to live "out of this world" (1 Cor. 5:10). They are to judge the behavior of those who are members of their Christian community, and if they find a person whose pattern of behavior is inappropriate for the "saints" and who is unrepentant, that member is to be expelled. Paraphrasing the law of Moses in Deuteronomy 17:2–7, Paul gives the order, "Drive out the wicked person from among you" (1 Cor. 5:13).

PAUL'S VIEW OF THIS WORLD
AND THE NEXT

Obviously these ethical questions are not resolved by Paul on purely legal grounds. He takes into account the social and cultural circumstances, and appeals to the authority of scripture as well as to Stoic virtues in resolving moral issues. Yet there is a deeper framework within which Paul's thinking operates, and which is a dominant factor in every case, as we have seen. That is the structure of theological understanding within which he views the world, God, the future, the Christian community, and his own mission and destiny. Central to Paul's view of God and the world is his understanding of Jesus as the Christ, the anointed agent of God for reconciling the world to himself (2 Cor. 5:19). That theme will be central in Chapter 10; it will be sufficient to note here that Paul appeals to the self-giving obedience of Christ as the model for Christian living (Phil. 2:1–8). But Paul is persuaded that the redemptive purpose of God through Christ has direct ethical implications for Christians as persons and in their group relationships. It is to the interplay between eschatological conviction and ethical implication that we now turn.

Parousia

Central for Paul was his confidence that the present age was nearing an end, soon to be replaced by the rule of God over his creation. That was the ground of his hope not merely for the long-range future, but for the events he thought were soon to occur. The question arose among the Thessalonians, whose faith was threatened when some of their members died without having seen the expected "coming" of Christ. The term Paul uses is *parousia*, which refers to someone being present in full exercise of power, as when an officer deputized by the emperor makes his appearance in one of the Roman provinces to settle a dispute or to demand fulfillment of an obligation. As God's deputy, Jesus would appear to establish his rule on earth. Accompanying him would be the Christians who had already died ("fallen asleep," 1 Thess. 4:14). Paul expected to be among those who were alive at the time of this event. The dead would arise first, then the living Christians would join them to serve as a welcoming committee to meet the Lord as he came to earth to set up his king-dom, which would last forever (4:16–17).

According to 2 Thessalonians 2,[5] another related problem arose in the same church. Some Christians decided that "the day of the Lord"—meaning the *parousia* of Christ—had already taken place, and they had been left be-hind. Paul balances the picture of immediate expectation he had sketched in 1 Thessalonians 4 by explaining that there were certain events which would take place before the coming of Christ (2 Thess. 2:1–11). Accordingly, they would have some warning of the end of the age. The eschatological portents in an apocalyptic world view such as is apparent here included an outbreak of violence, destruction of holy places, the unseating of legitimate authority, special oppression of the faithful community. This view is attested in Daniel 9–12, in Mark 13, and in Revelation 9–18, where the desecration of the Tem-ple in Jerusalem, the usurpation of imperial power, and the martyrdom of the saints are all described in symbolic language. We do not know what Paul conceived "the rebellion" to be, or who the "man of lawlessness" was expected to be. The power to perform these actions derived from Satan, and was part of a diabolical scheme to lure the unwary into blind allegiance to this despotic, demonic figure. Paul expressed confidence, however, that the Thessalonians would see through the dramatic sham, and would remain faithful to God and his purpose, thereby moving along in the process of "sanctification by the Spirit" (2 Thess. 2:13). They were to live during the interim before the end of the age performing their regular daily work, not "living in idleness, mere bu-sybodies" (2 Thess. 3:11).

The fullest statement we have from Paul about his expectation of the events at the close of the present age is from 1 Corinthians 15. He regarded the Resurrection not as a miraculous event in itself, but as the climax of God's re-demptive purpose. The human race was seen by Paul as having two possibili-ties: It could continue in the model of Adam, the disobedient founder of the race who doomed it to alienation and death, or by faith it could become joined to Christ, who not only announced the new humanity, but exemplified it by his obedience and especially by the triumph over death God effected in his behalf. God's having raised him from the dead—of which Paul and all the original apostles are witnesses—is what a farmer might call the "first fruits" or what a financier might call a down payment on God's promise to establish a new creation of obedient human beings. When the *parousia* takes place, Christ will gather around him all those who belong to him and the new humanity by faith (15:23). Meanwhile, however, he continues to exercise his royal power as he continues the process of bringing the disobedient powers of creation into submission to God's will (15:24).

The promise made to Adam in Genesis 1:16 and repeated in Psalm 8:6–8 that human beings would exercise control over all creation in God's name and by his authority is reinterpreted to mean that, through Jesus, God will gain dominion over all his estranged, self-willed creation (15:27). Even Christ, the agent through whom this is to be achieved, will himself be subject

---

[5] Scholars have questioned whether 2 Thessalonians was written by Paul; see discus-sion of authorship at the end of this chapter.

to God in the end, resulting in God's full sovereignty over the universe (15:28). (This Pauline theme is treated more fully in Chapter 10.)

How may human beings now share in the inaugural stages of that process? By aligning oneself with Christ by faith. In keeping with ideas of family solidarity, as opposed to our modern radical individualism, it appears that some early Christians were undergoing baptism vicariously, in the expectation that the beneficial effect through which they expressed publicly their union with Christ might be transmitted to those who had died, that they too would share in the life of the age to come. Paul did not condemn this practice, but reminded the Corinthians that it would be an empty exercise if there were no such thing as the Resurrection, just as it would be foolish for him or others to risk their lives for the sake of the Gospel if this short lifetime is all there is to human existence (15:29–32).

New Life in Christ

He then returns to the theme of the new humanity. The old humanity was and is characterized by an earthly, physical body. The new humanity lives in a "spiritual" body (15:42–44). Instead of adopting the idea of a disembodied soul or spirit as leaving the physical form at death, Paul insisted there had to be a form, or "body," if there was a person. It was essential that those who share in the new humanity have a spiritual body. Adam was the "man of dust"; Christ is "the man from heaven." He is the embodiment of what God intended humans to be, in contrast to Adam, whose disobedience brought disappointment, decay, and death (15:43–49). Death itself is "the last enemy to be destroyed" (15:26). The final act of the redemptive program of God will be the change that will occur at the *parousia*, when the perishable human nature is replaced by the imperishable. Or as Paul put it, "we shall be changed" (15:50–57). It is to that ultimate victory that Paul called the Corinthians to look as the ground of their hope and as the motivation for their steadfastness in the faith.

That does not mean, however, that present existence in the earthly body is meaningless or morally indifferent. Paul's clear preference was to be "absent from the body" and "at home with the Lord" (2 Cor. 5:6–8), but he reminded his readers that they would be accountable before God for what they did in this life. Yet the controlling force in his life was not to be fear of judgment but love of Christ, so that Paul no longer lived to serve his own selfish ends (5:14–15). All that he did by way of service he regarded as part of the work of divine reconciliation God has undertaken in Christ. That work of reconciling the world to God had been committed to Paul and the Church at large, "God making his appeal through us" (5:20). Paul could conceive of no higher calling for human beings than that of "ambassadors for Christ."

The union with Christ that Paul claimed to have experienced was not merely being united in a common task, however. We noted above that he considered the new humanity to be a new corporate reality, replacing the lamentable solidarity of Adam in sin and defeat. The outward seal of belonging to Christ was baptism, the initiation rite by which the old life passes away and the new life begins (Rom. 5). As Jesus died, was buried, and rose again, so the

Christian joined to him by this sacred rite undergoes ritual death and rebirth. The full impact of the Resurrection is yet to come—"We *shall* certainly be united with him in a resurrection like his" (Rom. 6:5)—but Christians have already been freed from enslavement to sin and death. Therefore they should no longer submit to that hostile power to which they were formerly in subjection (Rom. 6:12–22). As children of Adam, they had no choice and no escape from the power of sin and the prospect of death. As children of God in Christ, they received as a gift the new life Christ makes possible. They are to accept the gift in faith, and live by it (6:23).

Using a different image (in 2 Cor. 11:2–3), Paul described the relationship to Christ in terms of sacred marriage—which has precedent in the mystery religions of the Greco-Roman world, but also in Judaism's portrait of wisdom as God's consort. Referring not to Adam but to Eve, he reminded his readers how Adam's marital relationship brought disaster, and contrasted it with the union of the "pure bride," the faithful Church with its spouse, Jesus Christ. The false apostles against whom he was warning the Corinthians were trying to entice them to be joined to an unworthy bridegroom (11:3). The infidelity of God's people was depicted by the prophet Hosea (2:19–20) under the image of the faithless bride of Yahweh, the God of Israel. Later Christian tradition expanded on that image, as Ephesians 5:26–27[6] and Revelation 21:2 show. Although it was a symbol of universal appeal, its background in the prophetic tradition of Israel made it especially suited for clarifying the nature of covenant relationship between God and his people.

The supreme heights of religious experience recounted by Paul came in the ecstatic transport to paradise, to the "third heaven," which in Jewish tradition was the place where God dwelt. Significantly, Paul does not begin the description of this spiritual exaltation in the first person, but refers rather to "a man in Christ" (2 Cor. 12:2). The capacity to endure the sufferings through which he passed was seen by him to be "the power of Christ" resting upon him (12:9). Even in what might humanly speaking have been regarded as frustrations or failure by God to come to his aid, such as the imprisonment mentioned in Philippians 1:12, Paul saw in it an opportunity to carry forward his work of evangelism among hearers whom he could not otherwise contact: the Praetorian Guard (the elite unit of imperial troops) who kept him incarcerated. The courage of Paul in these circumstances had beneficial effects on local Christians, who were themselves emboldened to bear testimony to Christ. His view of God's sovereignty over history did not lead him to pessimism or resignation to an inescapable fate, but led him rather to rejoice at the ways in which God, through sufferings and apparent setbacks, worked to accomplish his redemptive purpose. The most important thing for Christians to do in similar circumstances, therefore, was to stand firm in the Lord (Phil. 4:1). Perhaps his greatest joy was to learn, as he had from Timothy, that the Thessalonians, who were undergoing affliction of an unspecified kind, had not abandoned the faith but had stood firm (1 Thess. 3:1–8). This outlook was not naive. It was wholly realistic about the depth

[6] For arguments that it is not a writing of Paul, but a product of later developments of Pauline thought, see Appendix IV and Chapter 11.

of human conflict and the way evil seems to triumph over good, but it could discern positive value in suffering and above all could look beyond suffering to divine reconciliation.

INSTITUTIONAL CONCERNS

The Problem of Money

One problem that pervades the known letters of Paul is the handling of money. At times the difficulty is that of Paul's financial support—either that someone is providing it or that he refuses to accept it and supports himself. But in the later letters the misunderstandings with which he must deal arose from his having agreed with the Jerusalem-based apostles to take up a collection for them, apparently as a tangible expression of their unity in spite of the different clienteles they served (Gal. 1–2).

SUPPORTING THE APOSTLES.   On the matter of financial support for Paul, it is evident that he had different policies for different communities.[7] The opening section of his letter to the Philippians, with its expression of gratitude and deep affection to them for having shared in "partnership in the gospel from the first day until now" (Phil. 1:6) could be read as pointing to feelings of commonality or mutual love, but his reference to "a good work" that they have begun suggests something more tangible is involved. The concluding lines of the letter (Phil. 4:8–19) make it obvious that what he is talking about is the generosity they have shown him since he launched his work among them. There had been an interim when that support was not forthcoming, but when Epaphroditus returned from visiting them with a gift in hand for Paul, he knew that their "concern" for him had "now at length been revived." Their "partnership" with him had indeed taken the concrete form of "giving and receiving."

In sharp contrast, Paul seems to have had continual conflict with the church at Corinth because he insisted on paying for his own upkeep, unlike the other apostles, who came there and lived off the church's generosity (1 Cor. 9:1). With bitter irony, Paul asks: "Is it only Barnabas and I who have no right to refrain from working for a living?" The argument appeals to two analogies to prove that he has the right to claim support from them. The first is an allegorized interpretation of an Old Testament rule of a kindness-to-dumb-animals type which ordered that an ox treading out grain should be allowed to eat as he trudged (Deut. 25:4). Then he refers to the practice of his day in pagan temples, where the temple functionaries received support from the worshipper for the liturgical tasks they fulfilled (1 Cor. 9:13). But he had determined to maintain his freedom from a sense of obligation to any of the Corinthians by working to support himself. Acts 18:3 tells us that his trade was that of a tentmaker, though he never mentions it in his letters. Self-

---

[7] See the discussion of financial "partnership" between Paul and the churches in J. Paul Sampley, *Pauline Partnership in Christ* (Philadelphia: Fortress Press, 1980).

support was apparently his way of avoiding any obligations that might limit him in dealing with the impetuous, cantankerous Corinthians.[8] As he puts it: "that in my preaching I may make the gospel free of charge" (1 Cor. 9:18).

THE COLLECTION FOR JERUSALEM.   Once that pattern had been established, however, it became more difficult to persuade the Corinthians that they should offer financial support for Paul's commitments in their behalf. At the end of the first of his preserved letters to them (1 Cor. 16),[9] he mentions in a straightforward way that they are to start assembling the money for the collection to be sent to Jerusalem and to choose delegates to accompany the gift and him to Palestine. He plans to spend some time with them (1 Cor. 16:7), and apparently expects to be received in a conciliatory mood.

In 2 Corinthians 12, 14–17, however, it is obvious that Paul's motives in taking up the collection have been questioned, as though he were using the notion of a collection for Jerusalem to line his own money pouch (12:16). To these charges Paul responded with a blend of tenderness and sarcasm, mixing metaphors: children should take care of their parents; he is willing to spend and be spent for their benefit; his visit will be at no cost to them. But there can be no mistaking that he expects them to be ready with their share of the collection. The original terms of that agreement between Paul and the apostles in Jerusalem were not precise, at least as Paul reports them in Galatians 2:10: "Only they would have us remember the poor." Since the other side of that agreement was the recognition of Paul's authority by the other apostles, he was not about to allow a relatively affluent congregation like that at Corinth to go back on the commitment. The fact that there were members with houses large enough to serve as meeting rooms for the entire community (1 Cor. 16:19; Rom. 16:23) and that among those sending greetings to Rome through Paul is the city treasurer of Corinth (Rom. 16:23) indicates that the church there was upwardly mobile both socially and economically.[10] It is perhaps characteristic of human nature that a wealthy congregation should be the one that was worked up over financial obligations.

Paul was concerned that the genuineness of the Corinthians' love for him and for other Christians be demonstrated concretely through their assuming responsibility for their share in the contribution for the Jerusalem

[8] Sampley thinks it was the conflicts and hostility Paul encountered in Corinth that prevented him from expanding the partnership with the Corinthians to include financial matters. *Pauline Partnership,* pp. 51–77.

[9] In 2 Corinthians 2:4, Paul refers to a letter he had written to the Corinthians "out of much affliction and anguish of heart," which does not seem to fit the mood in which 1 Corinthians seems to have been written. He must have had considerable correspondence not only with the Corinthians, but from them, as is implied in his mention of "the matters about which you wrote" (1 Cor. 7:1). See the final section of this chapter for theories about the extent and sequence of the Corinthian correspondence. It is sufficient to note here that the letters we know as 1 and 2 Corinthians were indeed written in that order.

[10] On the social stratification of the Corinthian church, see the essay by Gerd Theissen in the collection of his essays translated and edited by John H. Schuetz, in *The Social Setting of Pauline Christianity* (Philadelphia: Fortress Press, 1982); "Social Stratification in the Corinthian Community: A Contribution to the Sociology of Early Hellenistic Christianity," pp. 69–119.

church. With that end in view, he devoted a long section of his letter to detailed preparations for collecting the money and arranging for its delivery to Jerusalem (2 Cor. 8:1–9:15). His approach was shrewd. By beginning with praise for the churches in Macedonia who have contributed so generously, he put them on notice as to what others were doing; by reporting his boasting to the Macedonians about Corinthian bounty, he informed them of a reputation they now must live up to. Their generosity was placed by Paul in the context of God's "inexpressible gift" (2 Cor. 9:15), so that the primary motivation was gratitude for God's unmerited grace to them.

Important as a churchly concern was the administrative process for handling this large contribution. Paul had sent on ahead to Corinth Titus (8:6) and another unnamed deputy (8:22) who were not only to supervise the final stages of the collection, but also apparently to audit the account as well, so that neither within the Christian community nor among outsiders could there be any accusation of dishonesty or of personal gain (8:20–21). Paul then underscored the impeccable reputations both these "brothers" enjoyed. Their role was not merely as intermediaries between Paul and the Corinthians, however. They were emissaries (literally, apostles) of the churches as a whole (8:23). And the Corinthians, by meeting their obligation, would be "glorifying God" by their "obedience in acknowledging the gospel of Christ" (9:13). That is, by means of their concrete gift of money they would be following through on the obligation that Paul had assumed in behalf of the Gentile churches— which at the time of the agreement had only begun to come into existence—to provide support for "the poor" in Jerusalem (Gal. 2:10). The unity of the body of Christ, in spite of differences in ethnic and cultural backgrounds, found expression in tangible form through the collection; it did not exist merely as a vague community spirit. The institutional arrangements for deputy collectors and public audit were essential to ensure the reality and durability of that unity.

Cohesion and Conflict Within the Church

In spite of the impressive Pauline images of the Church as the bride of Christ, God's agent of reconciliation, and the new humanity, the Church remained for Paul a very human institution, with all the problems human nature characteristically shows. First among these was the problem of conflict among the members themselves. The first letter to the Corinthians, following the stylized prayers and greetings Paul drew from literary traditions of his time, adapting them to his own purposes,[11] turns directly to the dissension and quarrels within the church which have been reported to Paul. He appeals for agreement among them, for their being "united in the same mind and judgment" (1 Cor. 1:10–11).

[11] For a detailed study of the style and form of letters in early Christianity, see W. C. Doty, *Letters in Primitive Christianity* (Philadelphia: Fortress Press, 1973). Examples of letters written in the Hellenistic and early Roman world are offered in translation in H. C. Kee, *The New Testament in Context: Sources and Documents* (Englewood Cliffs, N.J.: Prentice-Hall, 1983).

The issue was far more than merely discord or disagreement, or even disorder. At stake is the basic conception of the Church as an organic unity, the body of Christ: "For just as the body is one and has many members, and all the members of the body, though many are one body, so it is with Christ. For by one Spirit we were all baptized into one body—Jews or Greeks, slaves or free—and were made to drink of the same Spirit" (1 Cor. 12:13). What was required was far more than a feeling of togetherness: There must be mutual respect, recognition of the value of the other's contribution and of the necessity for different gifts and capabilities within the Church, if it is to function as an organic unity, not just a tightly run organization.

The most complete discussion we have from Paul about the diversity of roles within the Church and their importance for the welfare of the whole body is in 1 Corinthians 12–14. There (12:27–28) he lists the major tasks: apostles, prophets, teachers (ranking in that order); then workers of miracles, healers, helpers, administrators. And last he mentions the one function that seems to have caused him the greatest annoyance, probably because its practitioners flaunted their spectacular achievement: speakers in tongues. The phenomenon of ecstatic speech is by no means limited to Christianity, or even to the ancient world.[12] Paul insisted that there must be an interpreter present and functioning (14:5), so that the ecstatic speech may not be a display of the spiritual prowess of the individual, but a means of communication and enlightenment for the entire Church.

The phenomenon of speaking in tongues is quite differently perceived by the author of Acts (2:1–13), however. On the day of Pentecost in Jerusalem, the Spirit fell upon the apostles, and all began to speak in tongues. Pious Gentiles and Jewish pilgrims who were attending the festival were astounded that the outpouring of tongues was accompanied by a miracle of simultaneous translation, with the result that "we hear, each of us, in his own native language" (2:8). Since the narrative reports that there were representatives present "from every nation under heaven" (2:5), the linguistic miracle far exceeded that of any modern ecumenical translation facility or service. Surely for the author of Acts this was a symbolic scene, as the text quoted in the sermon of Peter shows. The outpouring of the Spirit is in fulfillment of the prophecy of Joel, with the aim of making it possible for whoever wills to call on the name of the Lord and be saved (2:17–21; Joel 2:28–32). For Paul, on the other hand, ecstatic speech is not an instrument of worldwide evangelism, but a conflict-producing phenomenon within the local congregation.

For the problem of divisions Paul has two basic solutions. One is to develop orderly process within the Church, to avoid chaos or bedlam in the meetings. Each one displays his or her gift at the proper time, but in limited numbers, and with deference shown by those not called upon. Otherwise, outsiders who attend the meetings will think they are all mad (1 Cor. 14:23). The orderliness is not merely to give a dignified impression, but to contribute to edification of the community as a whole (14:26).

---

[12] A careful analysis of "tongues" and other spiritual gifts is offered by John Koenig in *Charismata: The Gifts of God for the People of God* (Philadelphia: Westminster Press, 1977).

Christian Love

Set in the middle of the discussion of diversity of charismatic gifts and the consequent conflicts within the Church is one of Paul's most beautiful and profound passages: his words about Christian love. The early Christians avoided using the Greek word *erōs*, which is the ordinary word for human love, especially sexual attraction. Instead, they occasionally use the word *philia*, and related nouns and verbs, which connotes friendly affection, as in brotherly love. But the word little used in secular Greek, *agapē*, is the characteristic Pauline term to describe God's love for humankind and the Christian's love for God and neighbor. In 1 Corinthians 13, Paul tells what love is and does, and indicates the superiority of its value over all other human qualities. Far more to be sought than charismatic gifts, such as tongues or even prophecy, more important than being able to penetrate the mysteries of the divine purpose or the ability to know the divine will, or even to possess a faith so great that it produces spectacular results, is to have love. Compared with love, all other virtues and capabilities are nothing. Even willingness to accept martyrdom is nothing, unless that commitment is in a context of love.

After depicting in vivid beauty how different love is from typical human self-seeking, self-serving egotism—which he recognized to be at the root of the competition and conflict within the Corinthian church—he went on to contrast the transitory nature of all these charismatic gifts with love that never ends. Love is the evidence of maturity, the antithesis of the childish showoffs with which the Church is plagued. Maturity is not a state Paul has reached, but a process in which he is engaged: "Now I know in part, then I shall understand fully, even as I have been fully understood" (13:12). The great reality that made possible the transformation of human nature from the ugly state Paul knew to be evident generally throughout humanity but also specifically in the Corinthian church was love. That quality is not an emotion the Christian must cultivate or work at acquiring: "God's love has been poured into our hearts through the Holy Spirit which has been given to us" (Rom. 5:5).

The Love Feast and Its Perversion

Central to both the ritual and the social unity of the Church were baptism and the common sacred meal, which Paul referred to as participation in the body and blood of Christ, or as the table of the Lord (1 Cor. 10:16, 21). The Corinthians had divided themselves into factions based on who had baptized them (1 Cor. 1:13–17). Paul deplored this division and minimized the importance of the person who performed the rite, although the rite itself was for him indispensable for those admitted to the Christian community. Recalling the experiences of Israel during the Exodus from Egypt (Exod. 13–14; 16:4–35; Num. 20:7–11), Paul saw in the imagery of delivery through water a figure of baptism, and in the miraculous water from the rock and food that fell from the sky he perceived an analogy with the cup and loaf of spiritual food in which Christians participate in the communion. The aim of those common experiences in the desert was to bind together an obedient people, who shared in the divine deliverance from slavery. Similarly, the participation in the bread and wine is the celebration of God's act of deliverance of his new people from bondage to sin and death. Yet in neither case is participation in itself a license for irresponsible behavior. The Israelites who had benefited from these divine acts of redemption slipped easily into idolatrous worship and sensual excesses. The Corinthian Christians were sliding back into pagan worship, and indulging in behavior inappropriate for Christians. Paul issued the solemn warning that sacramental participation must be matched by purity of life: "You cannot partake of the table of the Lord and the table of demons. Shall we provoke the Lord to jealousy?" (1 Cor. 10:21–22).

As fiercely independent as Paul was, there were certain issues within the life of the churches for which he appealed to tradition. In one of the few places at which we have close verbal correspondence between Paul's words and those of the Gospel tradition,[13] he recalled what he had passed on to them earlier about the details of the Last Supper, which had become the liturgical pattern for the Lord's Supper, or Eucharist (from the Greek word for giving thanks). The presentation of the material in the letter begins not with solemn language of the ritual, however, but with a dressing-down of the Corinthians for their having perverted the solemn meal into a raucous community picnic (11:20–22). Without waiting for others and with callous disdain for the poor who have little or nothing, some plunge ahead with the meals they have brought, and others are soon drunk. Obviously, the sacred supper was held in association with an actual common meal, although it was not like a church supper in which the same menu was provided for all. What was intended as an enacted expression of Christian unity became the occasion for demonstrating social, economic, and cultural differences that disgraced the Church and embarrassed the poor.

It is against this abuse of the sacred meal that Paul repeated the account of Jesus's last meal with his disciples (Mark 14:22–25; Matt. 26:26–29). It too was an actual meal, since the ceremony with the cup did not take place until "after supper" (11:25). The introductory words vary in the New Testament accounts: here we have "give thanks, broke"; in Mark, we have "took, blessed, broke, gave." But on the two essential elements there is agreement among the sources: The bread symbolizes the body or self given in their behalf; the cup symbolizes the death (blood) that ratifies the new covenant. Paul alone of our sources added the phrase "Do this in remembrance of me," which was a millennium and a half later to become the most commonly used eucharistic phrase among Protestants. Catholic and orthodox traditions took the word "is" more literally, declaring that in the act of dedication or consecration of the elements of the meal, the bread and wine *become* the body and blood of

[13] In his excellent study, *Theology and Ethics in Paul* (Nashville: Abingdon Press, 1968), Victor P. Furnish finds only eight "convincing" parallels between the ethical teachings of Paul and the Jesus tradition in the synoptic Gospels (53). The only places where Paul's choice of words ("receive . . . hand on") makes explicit his dependence on older tradition are here at 1 Corinthians 11:2ff and in 1 Corinthians 15:3ff.

Jesus, rather than merely representing them. In any case, the process of institutionalization of the sacrament is already under way in this, the oldest record we have of its beginnings.

As in the discussion of the sacraments in 1 Corinthians 10, Paul here insisted that the effects of participating in the Lord's Supper were not magical or automatic, but directly dependent on the moral condition of the participant (1 Cor. 11:27–32). To share in the meal in an unworthy or inappropriate way was not to gain grace; it was to profane the sacrament and to run the risk of divine judgment. He went so far as to say that some who have thus taken communion irresponsibly have fallen sick or even died as a consequence of God's displeasure with their behavior. Better to judge oneself in advance, and thus to experience the Lord's purifying chastisement rather than his wrath. To share in the sacraments, therefore, was for the obedient Christian a privilege, but it was also a solemn responsibility, which would bring punishment or even death to those who abused it.

Spiritual Maturity

For all his stress on the unity of the Church, Paul acknowledged that among its members were various levels of spiritual maturity. He regarded himself as in a process of maturation, the goal of which was a relationship to Christ that Paul variously described as "knowing," or "gaining," or being found in Christ (Phil. 3:8–9). It involved sharing in his suffering, resembling him in his death (as a martyr?), and the hope of sharing in his Resurrection (3:9–11). This was not perceived by Paul as an automatic process of spiritual transformation, but as a goal toward which he was striving. He did not consider himself to have achieved "perfection" (a technical term employed in the mystery cults of those who had attained the highest stages of initiation into the divine secrets).[14] The account of Apuleius's initiation into a series of higher levels of mystical knowledge is the pagan counterpart to what Paul is describing here.[15] Unlike Apuleius and the devotees of the pagan mystery gods and goddesses, however, Paul did not expect the attainment of full knowledge until the day of resurrection at the end of the age—what he called "the prize of the upward call of God in Christ Jesus" (3:14).

Meanwhile, there are levels of insight and corresponding levels of instruction that differentiate members of the Church from each other. While decrying the attempt to convert the Gospel into some kind of humanly appealing wisdom, Paul acknowledged that there is a "wisdom" which is accessible only to the mature (1 Cor. 2). It is "secret and hidden" wisdom, coming from God and dealing with the redemptive purpose of God in overcoming the hostile powers. Had they had access to this wisdom, people would not have brought about their own defeat by crucifying Jesus, since his redemptive death is their undoing. That fundamental insight cannot be attained by human wisdom, but is reserved for those under the tutelage of the Spirit: "We

[14] On the Greek term *teleios*, see p. 285.

[15] L. Apuleius, *Metamorphoses* (The Golden Ass), IX.21–30. Translation in H. C. Kee, *The New Testament in Context: Sources and Documents.* (Englewood Cliffs, N.J.: Prentice-Hall, 1983).

impart this in words not taught by human wisdom but taught by the Spirit, interpreting spiritual truths to those who possess the Spirit" (2:13). This seems closely akin to the saying in the synoptic tradition (Mark 4:11–12) according to which Jesus discloses only to the inner circle of his followers God's plan for establishing his rule on earth. Those perceptions are reserved by Jesus and by Paul for the "mature."

The specifics of moral and community responsibilities are not left by Paul to precept, but are reinforced by an appeal to imitate certain paradigms of obedience and courage. In 1 Thessalonians 2:14 he appealed to the example of the churches in Judea who had suffered much from Jews there.[16] The Thessalonians had also suffered at the hands of their countrymen, and were urged to emulate the bravery of Palestinian Christians. We noted earlier that the Macedonians and the Corinthians were presented to each other by Paul as models of generosity.

More frequently, however, Paul offered himself as the pattern the churches were to imitate. His way of life was presented to them as a paradigm for their own. The mixture of joy and suffering with which they received the Gospel initially matched Paul's outlook and personal experience (1 Thess. 1:6). Portraying himself as their spiritual father, he urged the Corinthians to accept the rejection and attendant suffering some of them were undergoing (1 Cor. 4:16). On the other hand, there were certain practices which, unfortunately, had become common among Christians and which his readers should follow Paul in avoiding. One of these is behaving in such a way as to offend others, whether Jews or Greeks (1 Cor. 10:32). Another is the self-indulgent life style many have adopted, in spite of their claim to belong to Christ (Phil. 3:17–19). They live as though they were enemies of Christ. Not only do they worship their belly, but they take pride in their shameful behavior, and occupy their minds with earthly things.

Paul then turned to a concise declaration of what should be the paramount values and goals for Christians (Phil. 3:20–21). The Christian is only temporarily a citizen of this world. The Greek root used here, *polis,* means far more than our word "city," since it connotes not only where we live, but the focus of our identity and of our sense of belonging, as well as the values and goals we share. It is with that fuller set of connotations that Augustine wrote in the early fifth century *The City of God.* Paul expected not merely a change of regime, but the transformation of himself and of all other faithful Christians when the *parousia* of Christ occurs, and when God's sovereignty is effective over the universe. Paul's setting himself up as a model was not the egocentric ethic it may seem to be. Rather, he regarded himself as having achieved all that he had and as being able to affirm the hope of complete, ultimate renewal solely because of Christ. In Chapter 10 we turn to the specific theme

[16] No direct evidence of Jews persecuting Christians has been preserved from these early decades other than the explicit charges made by Paul and others, although mutual hostility is reflected in the Gospel tradition. It is likely that the refusal of Palestinian Christians to take sides against Rome involved them in the pressures by Jews on their co-religionists to join the nationalistic Jewish movement of the 60s, as described by Josephus in his *Jewish Wars.* See further discussion in my *Community of the New Age* (Philadelphia: Westminster Press, 1977), p. 93. Reprint, Macon, GA, Mercer University Press, 1983.

of Paul's beliefs about Jesus Christ, and especially the factors that contributed to his way of formulating his views of the nature and function of Christ. Before that, however, we should consider the circumstances under which Paul came to write these letters to the Corinthians and the Thessalonians, from which we have been reconstructing some of the main themes of his thought.

Keeping in Touch with the Churches in His Charge

The four letters we know as 1 and 2 Thessalonians and 1 and 2 Corinthians were apparently all written in a space of a few years after Paul returned from the visit to Jerusalem he described in Galatians. His missionary activities had taken him across the Aegean Sea to the mainland of Greece, first to the region known as Macedonia, where Philippi and Thessalonica are located, and then to Attica, where he visited Athens (1 Thess. 3:1) and settled down for an extended period of work in Corinth. The exact chronology cannot be determined, and to try to do so by correlating the information from Acts with what can be inferred from the letters only increases the difficulties and the uncertainties. Enough can be inferred from the letters to enable us to determine the sequence and the basic circumstances for the writing of these four documents.

1 Thessalonians is probably the oldest of Paul's preserved letters. It seems to have been written only some months after Paul left the city (which in modern times is known as Salonika). Affection and concern shine through his letter, and it was the occasion, as he indicates in 3:1–5, for his having sent Timothy to learn how they were faring in his absence. The report that came back was encouraging (3:6). He recalled the parental care and solicitude that had characterized his role among them from the time he had first found refuge in their city after being driven out of the Macedonian capital, Philippi, named in honor of himself by the father of Alexander the Great (1 Thess. 2:1–2). What the ground of his concern was is not specifically stated in the letter, other than the general problem of their continuing in the faith (3:5). The one problem he addresses directly is their attitude toward the *parousia* of Christ. They are not to be troubled by the notion that members who have died will not have a share in the age to come, nor are they to become lazy and complacent because the present age is coming to an end (4:1–5:9). Rather, they are to act responsibly toward one another (5:11) and toward their leadership within the Christian community (5:12).

Preoccupation with the return of Christ continued to be a difficulty in the Thessalonian community, as 2 Thessalonians indicates. Probably not long after the first letter was written, word reached Paul that some were declaring in Paul's name—probably by means of a faked letter (2 Thess. 2:2)—that the Day of the Lord had already occurred. No, Paul reminds them: The *parousia* will be preceded by a series of events in which Satan and his agents will be vigorously active and seemingly winning the struggle against God and his people. But that will be only the prelude to the great consummation in which Christ will come to vindicate his people. The fact that Paul uses words in this letter not found elsewhere in his surviving writings has led some scholars to conclude that he did not write it. But in fact he is merely drawing on the imagery and vocabulary of apocalyptic literature to amplify and round out the picture of the end of the age he had described in his first letter to the Thessalonians.

     1 and 2 Corinthians give us the best evidence that correspondence between Paul and the churches was two-directional. In 1 Corinthians 7:1 he mentions explicitly that he is responding to a letter of inquiry he had received from the Corinthians. In 5:9 he mentions an earlier letter he had written them, though it has not survived. 1 Corinthians is the best organized of Paul's letters; 2 Corinthians is the most disorganized. In 1 Corinthians Paul lists the subjects that are of mutual concern, and treats them in sequence; 2 Corinthians must have been dictated in stages, since it contains a curious mixture of discontinuities and references back to matters dealt with earlier in the letter. Common to both are his defense of his apostleship against his detractors, and his concern that due preparations will be made for the collection to be delivered to Jerusalem. In 1 Corinthians 16 he outlined his original plans for the offering; in 2 Corinthians he indicated how the plans had shaped up in the interim (especially 2 Cor. 8–9). There had been an intermediate "painful" letter (2 Cor. 2:2–3), and a third visit to Corinth is planned (2 Cor. 12:14; 13:1). The first letter was written from Ephesus (1 Cor. 16:8). The second was written from Macedonia (2 Cor. 7:5–9:5), which he had announced in the first letter he planned to visit (1 Cor. 16:5). His overall plan, therefore, is to revisit the churches of Greece to complete the collection for Jerusalem. What none of these letters reports or anticipates is an extended imprisonment of Paul, which is presupposed by his letter to the Philippians (Phil. 1:14). It is to that letter and its bearing on the end of Paul's career—as well as how that relates to his understanding of Christ's death—that we turn in Chapter 10.

10

Jesus as Lord and as Divine Wisdom: Philippians and Colossians

Our study of Paul thus far has concentrated on his religious experience of encounter with and commissioning by the Risen Christ, on the preconditions of that conversion in his earlier life (Chapter 8), and on the consequences of these factors for his subsequent career and for the communities of the new covenant he established (Chapter 9). Central to all these developments, of course, was the figure of Jesus as the Christ, or as Paul preferred to phrase it, "Christ Jesus as Lord." As God's agent to enable the human race to participate in the covenant people, Jesus not only provided Paul with the answer to his basic questions, but more significantly, transformed the questions. We turn our attention now to the details of Paul's understanding of who Jesus Christ is, and of how Paul thought Jesus both fulfills and transforms the expectations of Israel concerning God's new covenant people. We shall see that central to Paul's perception of Jesus as the Christ and of covenant existence were his own life as a seeking, faithful Jew, reared in an environment profoundly influenced by the Jewish scriptures and the pervasive Hellenistic culture.

HOW GOD IS ESTABLISHING
HIS COVENANT COMMUNITY

As is apparent from Paul's disdain for the worldly wisdom and rhetorical pretentiousness of the admirers of Apollos at Corinth, his interest in Christ and his Church were by no means just an intellectual inquiry. At least four major questions are implicit—and at times explicit—in his surviving letters. They were no doubt important for him before his conversion. Yet a prime factor in the power of his experience of the Risen Christ was the new answers that were provided for these perennial questions.

The Holy People

We have already seen that the first of these issues was how God would achieve his purpose of establishing a holy, obedient people. Anyone reared in accord with the law of Moses, as Paul claims to have been, and who boasts of his having outstripped most of his contemporaries in his zeal for the "traditions of the fathers" (Gal. 1:14) must have taken with full seriousness the two interrelated obligations under the Mosaic law: holiness and obedience. The notion of holiness in the world of ancient Israel was far more concerned with purity than with what we might think of as personal piety. Most of the laws in the books of Moses from Exodus 19 (where the law is given to Israel ini-

270

tially) to Numbers 10, at which point the narrative of Israel's march from Sinai toward the Promised Land begins, are concerned with the purity of the offerings to Yahweh, the God of Israel, and with the purity of his people. Indeed, the three factors are closely linked: the holiness of Israel's God, his special favor in entering into covenant relation with them, and their obligation to be a ritually pure and therefore holy people. This is made explicit when, as Yahweh begins to give the law to Israel through Moses, he declares that he expects them to be "a holy nation" (Exod. 19:6). Midway through the giving of the law, the link between Yahweh's holiness and Israel's is directly asserted: "You shall be holy; for I the Lord your God am holy" (Lev. 19:2); in 20:26 it is repeated. In 22:31–33 it is elaborated, so as to combine the holiness of God, of his name, and of his people with his having brought them out of the land of Egypt.[1]

In both accounts of the giving of the law to Moses—the first from Exodus into Numbers, and the second in Deuteronomy—there is an expected stress on obedience. It is beautifully summarized in Deuteronomy 10:12: "And now, Israel, what does the Lord your God require of you, but to fear the Lord your God, to walk in all his ways, to love him, to serve the Lord with all your heart and with all your soul, and to keep the commandments and statutes of the Lord, which I command you this day." The same obligation is more briefly expressed in Deuteronomy 11:32, but this is like an echo of the commitment that Israel is reported to have made when the law was first given: "And all the people answered together and said, 'All that the Lord has spoken we will do' " (Exod. 19:6).

Paul's participation in the Pharisaic movement would have meant that he was not a pedantic legalist in his effort to obey the law, but that instead he would have sought to interpret it in a way that was relevant for himself and his contemporaries in their world. Yet from what he writes, especially in Romans, he came to see the law as an ineffective instrument for righteousness, since it lacked the power to create a holy and obedient people. In the analysis of Romans we saw how the depth of Paul's despair about the moral condition of the entire human race, "both Jews and Greeks" (Rom. 3:9), is vividly set forth in a dirgelike mosaic of quotations chiefly from the Psalms: "None is righteous, no not one; no one understands, no one seeks for God . . . the venom of asps is under their lips . . . in their paths are ruin and misery . . . there is no fear of God before their eyes" (Rom. 3:10–18). Central to Paul's conviction about the desperate plight of the human race was the failure of law—whether revealed Israelite law or natural law—to produce an obedient people: "By works of law no human being will be justified in his sight,[2] since through law comes the knowledge of sin" (Rom. 3:20). All that law does is to remind

---

[1] The words in the Hebrew Bible usually translated "holy," "hallowed," and "sanctify" (as in Lev. 22:31–33), are all from the same root, *qadosh*. The same root appears in the form of a noun in Daniel 7, where it is translated "saint," describing the obedient people of God to whom God gives the kingdom when the new age comes.

[2] Paul is here quoting from Psalm 143:2 in the Greek translation (LXX), which would have been used in the synagogues and schools he attended. He uses the quotation to support his contention that no justification before God is ever possible through any kind of act performed in obedience to law.

human beings of their failures; all it accomplishes is a heightened sense of guilt. Should Paul abandon the search, or was there some way in which God's goal for his covenant people might be achieved? How could God deal responsibly with the disobedience of his people, apart from destroying them in judgment?

The Inclusion of All in the Covenant

A second basic question was this: If all human beings were created in the image of God, as the Genesis creation stories implied, was it not God's obligation, at least potentially, to make a place among his covenant people for those who were not Israelites? From the prophets and the psalms, as well as from the books of Moses, Paul was able to furnish scriptural support for the inclusion of Gentiles in the people of God, as a careful reading of Romans 10 and 11 will show. For example, by weaving together two passages from Hosea (1:10 and 2:23), Paul offers the words of the prophet as proof that from of old it has been God's plan to include those earlier regarded as outsiders ("not my people") as members of the covenant. The second half of Romans 10 is occupied with a series of rhetorical questions about God's plan for having the good news about Christ reach the ends of the earth. And once more the case is made by means of a network of quotations from scripture (Rom. 10:14–21). Even Israel's current hostility toward the Gospel is described by Paul as a part of the divine plan for the evangelization of the whole human race, though eventually Israel will receive the message as well.

Even more fundamental than the stages by which the message, presently rejected by Jews, will reach the Gentiles, is the second pervasive theme in Paul that all human beings spring from Adam, who was created in the image of God. What is at stake in Paul's view is not only the destiny of the human race, but also the dependability of God. Are not God's wisdom and power under suspicion if his purpose in the creation of the world and of humankind has failed? When the human race is viewed with the image of Adam, all distinctions—racial, social, ethnic, religious—lose their significance. All that matters ultimately is that "sin came into the world through one man [Adam] and death through sin, and so death spread to all men because all sinned" (Rom. 5:12). This brings us to the center of Paul's understanding of Christ. There is no special remedy for Jewish sin; there is only the final remedy which creates a new human race: "one man's [Christ's] act of setting things right which leads to acquittal and life for all human beings" (Rom. 5:18). If God is to deal responsibly with the sad, cruel fact that Adam in his disobedience is the sole paradigm for the entire human race, including both Jews and Gentiles, then a solution that did no more than to make available to Jews a remedy in the form of a purely Jewish paradigm would be a mockery and a betrayal of the purpose announced in creation and expanded in the psalms: "Let us make *man* [not merely Israelites] in our image ... male and female he created them" (Gen. 1:26–27); "Thou hast made him [human beings] little less than God, and dost crown him with glory and honor" (Ps. 8:5). What has happened to this glorious image and why? What is God going to do about it?

Death and Destiny

The third theme, already hinted at in the portrayal of universal human disobedience as leading to death, is human destiny. Under the curse of Adam, humanity faces the gloomy termination of life in death. That appears to be as much a defeat for God as for humanity, since the divine image in which humans were created did not, in Paul's view, include death. In fact, God's warning to Adam and Eve in the garden of Eden had been that disobedience would result in death (Gen. 3:3). Can the God who "saw everything that he had made, and behold, it was very good" (Gen. 1:31) tolerate a universe dominated by sin in which human life terminates, seemingly inevitably, in death? For Paul, as for every other thoughtful human being, that is not a purely intellectual issue, but a deeply personal one as well.

God's Ultimate Triumph

Akin to this is the fourth theme that runs through the Pauline letters: How will God rectify what has gone wrong throughout his creation, having initially intended that humankind was to subdue the earth and to rule over it as obedient agents of God, presiding over a realm of peace and prosperity (Gen. 1:26–31)? Will God settle for "Paradise Lost"? In the Genesis stories of the creation and fall there is present a factor basic for Paul's understanding of what went wrong in the creation and of how it will be remedied. This is the role of the serpent (Gen. 3), who for centuries before the time of Paul had been identified with Satan, which means "the adversary." During Israel's exile in Mesopotamia (sixth to fifth centuries B.C.) the people were exposed to Persian religion, with its strongly dualistic ideas of a host of evil powers in conflict with the powers of good. Although the Jews did not abandon their belief in one sovereign God, they did adopt the notion of spiritual powers which had penetrated heaven itself and which were at work throughout creation, seeking to thwart God's purpose in the world.[3] For God's plan for his creation to triumph, Satan must be defeated.

Since the creation stories (as well as other Old Testament descriptions of God, such as Isaiah 6) describe God as apparently conversing with associates ("let us"), we may infer that God was portrayed in older tradition as having what any monarch would want to have in his court: a council of advisors. When dualistic ideas began to penetrate Jewish thinking, however, the members of the heavenly council came to be understood as having a potential for roles that were either helpful or hostile toward the divine purpose. Satan came to be perceived as the leader of what we might call "the disloyal opposition." For Paul and many of his Jewish contemporaries, Satan's wicked actions

[3] To see graphically how dualistic ideas were adopted by Israel during the period of national exile in Babylon one has only to read the two accounts of David's sin in conducting a census in Israel: In the account that originated before the exile, God incites him to perform the wicked act (2 Sam. 24:1); in the version of the incident written after the exile (1 Chron. 21:1), it is "Satan" (which means "the Adversary") who moves David to pry into matters that were God's affairs, not his, such as how many subjects there were in his kingdom.

were by no means limited to heavenly plots and counterplots. The Adversary intervened directly, thwarting and frustrating the activities of God's people. Paul's failure to reach the Thessalonians at the time he had planned was a result of Satan's having hindered him (1 Thess. 2:18). Satan is always seeking ways to gain control over the faithful (1 Cor. 7:5), and harrasses them in the form of bodily disabilities (2 Cor. 12:7). He will eventually be crushed (Rom. 16:20), but before then he will put on a final display of wicked power (2 Thess. 2:9). Even now he masquerades as an angel of light (2 Cor. 11:14).

The other unseen powers or messengers (angels, from Greek *angeloi*), however, are also at work in the human sphere, where their actions may be for good or evil. Paul considered the Roman civil powers to be beneficent, since they maintained law and order (Rom. 13), without hindering the progress of the Gospel. Yet the unseen powers could become instruments of evil, enslaving Christians in ways no longer clear to modern readers of Paul (Gal. 4:8–9), though they probably included the imposition of ascetic or ritual obligations Paul regarded as antithetical to the Gospel. We will see that the overcoming of these opposing powers is an essential part of Christ's redemptive role as Paul perceives it. The solutions to all these fundamental questions Paul found in his encounter with Jesus Christ as Lord.

CHRIST, THE WISDOM OF GOD

Before examining directly what that confessional phrase meant for Paul, we must consider in detail some of the assumptions Paul must have carried over from his earlier life as a pious Jew. However radical he may have considered his break with Judaism to have been, there was a large and pervasive set of assumptions that he brought over into his new faith, often with only slight modification.

A Trustworthy God

The first of these is the fidelity of God to the promises made to his people. The figure of Abraham is central for Paul, since it was God's promise to him and Abraham's trust in that divine promise that led to his becoming— against all human expectations—the progenitor of the covenant people. Trust becomes the middle term in this divine-human relationship: Abraham trusts a trustworthy God. Paul finds confirmation for his perception of God and God's mode of dealing with his people throughout the psalms and the prophets, as the scriptural quotations throughout his letters abundantly attest. He does not need to repudiate his biblical tradition; rather, he merely modifies it, building on themes and insights that were surely a part of his own rearing in Jewish tradition. The belief in divine grace is basic for Paul's view of God and his dealings with the whole of creation, from the initial acts of creation down to the accomplishment of his purpose for the cosmos.

Jewish Wisdom

A second assumption basic to Paul's view of the redemption of the creation comes from his background in Jewish wisdom tradition. We have already noted that Paul had little interest in the proverbial and philosophical aspects of Jewish wisdom. But the role of wisdom as the instrument of God's creating and ruling the universe are of fundamental importance for him, as his letters show. He does not, however, depict Jesus Christ as associated with or participating in the creation of the world, as we find in John 1, Hebrews 1:2, and Colossians 1:15. Paul is concerned not with the creation of the world by wisdom, but with its redemption through wisdom.

In addition to the different role for wisdom in the thought of Paul, there are two important features, one of which differentiates his attitude from that of Jewish philosophers like Philo or the author of The Wisdom of Solomon, and the other which shows that for him wisdom is closely linked with an apocalyptic world view. This is especially clear in 1 Corinthians, where Paul is dealing directly with the difficulties and divisions that have arisen in the church there because of champions of what he refers to scornfully as "worldly wisdom" (1 Cor. 1:26). He characterizes it as taking pride in eloquence and plausibility (1 Cor. 1:17; 2:4), but it is merely human wisdom. Through it no one comes to know God (1:21), and God's wisdom is not communicated (2:13). God will destroy human wisdom (1:19), as he had announced long ago through the prophets (cf. Isa. 29:14). True faith can never rely upon it (2:5), since God has chosen what is humanly speaking foolish in order to put the wise to shame (1:27).

In Paul's view, Jesus Christ does not merely bring superior wisdom—he *embodies* it (1 Cor. 1:24, 30): "God made him our wisdom." Unlike human wisdom, which is characterized by impotence, Christ is not only wisdom but power. The paradox is that, as one who in human eyes may appear to have been a helpless, powerless victim of the ruling authorities, his death is in fact the ground of the defeat of those powers (1 Cor. 2:8). Realizing this is not a matter of shrewd observation or clever rational conclusion, but part of the secret wisdom God has reserved for his people. That hidden wisdom is being imparted to those granted by God the maturity to receive it. Here again we have the apocalyptic notion of the mystery of God's purpose, reserved for the faithful, as in Mark 4:11–12. The typical belief among those who hold an apocalyptic world view—such as we see in Paul, in Revelation, in Mark, in Daniel, and in the Dead Sea community—is the conviction that God's wisdom is privileged information reserved for his faithful, obedient community. We shall see that this theme, as well as the role of wisdom in creating the world, are linked with Christ in the Letter to the Colossians.

Missing from the Pauline view of Christ as wisdom, however, is the notion some scholars have claimed influenced Paul's interpretation of the role of Jesus: the Gnostic theory developed in the second and subsequent centuries that the material creation is inherently evil, so that human beings seek liberation from their involvement in its inherently ungodly state. These ideas, like Paul's and those of other New Testament writers, were influenced by and built on Jewish wisdom speculation, but in Paul there is never the slightest hint that matter is evil. The word "matter" (*hulē*) appears only once in the New Testament, and never in Paul or even in any of the writings attributed to him. For Paul, the creation was originally good, the work of God himself— not, as in the Gnostic teaching, the work of a hostile power. Whatever human beings need by way of redemption, it is not liberation from a material body. What is required is understanding of and readiness for the dramatic events, already launched with the coming of Jesus, by which God will bring to consummation his purpose in and for the world.

The Coming of the New Age

That brings us to a third presupposition by which Paul operates: that the present age, dominated as it is by powers which have rebelled against God and by death as a consequence of human disobedience, is soon to come to an end and to be replaced by a new age in which God's purpose will triumph. As we have noted, there was widespread belief in the Judaism of this period that God's victory would come, though there was broad disagreement as to what form that victory would take and who the beneficiaries would be. Paul foresaw the fulfillment as the accomplishment by God of what he intended for the creation, and especially for the human race, when he first called the universe into being. As is characteristic of the apocalyptic world view, he was persuaded that the present difficulties through which he and other members of the new covenant community were passing were the birth pangs of that long-awaited new age.

CHRIST, THE PERFECT SACRIFICE

Though Paul had no connection with the priestly family (he was descended from Benjamin, he claimed; Phil. 3:5), and though we have no indication of his special interest in the ritual system that was carried on in the Jerusalem Temple, his letters are strewn with imagery drawn from the liturgical laws and assumptions carried forward from ancient Israel. In the days of Noah (Gen. 8:20), of Abraham (Gen. 17), of Moses (Exod. 24), the ratification of a covenant between God and his people required a sacrifice to be offered by the people. Its purpose was not to appease divine wrath; rather, for reasons never explained, it is simply assumed that a covenant must be accompanied by sacrifice.

Israel, however, continually violated the laws God had laid down for it under the Mosaic covenant. In order that the misdeeds and failures should not simply cause God's repudiation of the covenant relationship, precedent was established within the Mosaic law for offering sacrifices as a way of interceding with God in behalf of the disobedient people. An example of this was Moses's plea in Exodus 32:30–32, when he went "up to the Lord" in an effort to "make atonement" for the sins of the people. On that occasion, Moses suggested that he lose his own place in the covenant relationship, rather than that the covenant be lost for all the people. In the ritual regulations there were provisions for periodic ceremonies (Lev. 4) and even for a solemn annual ceremony (Lev. 16) in which the priests brought sacrifices before God as acts of intercession in behalf of the sinful nation. *How* those sacrifices accomplished reconciliation between God and his people is never explained; *that* they effected atonement is everywhere assumed. Confession and sacrifice are basic to covenant renewal.

At the same time, however, there was in Jewish tradition a conviction that more important than the ritual sacrifice was the contrition of the sinner. This is powerfully expressed in the oft-quoted Psalm 51, where the poet movingly confesses his sin and need of cleansing ("Have mercy on me, O God, according to thy steadfast love. . . . Against thee, thee only, have I sinned, and done that which is evil in thy sight," Ps. 51:1,4). But the surprising feature of the psalm is the denial that God desires any sacrifice other than that of the contrite heart: "For thou hast no delight in sacrifice. . . . The sacrifice acceptable to God is a broken spirit; a broken and contrite heart, O God, thou wilt not despise" (Ps. 51:16–17). The prophet Amos reports that God despises the sacrifices offered to him by a disobedient people, and pleads rather that justice might "roll down like waters, and righteousness like an ever-flowing stream" (Amos 5:21–24).

Paul's familiarity with these themes of human sin and divine forgiveness is evident from the quotations and allusions in his letters to Psalm 51 and to the prophet Amos.[4] Significantly, it is the Septuagint version of Amos to which Paul makes allusion in a mosaic of Old Testament passages that he quotes in 2 Corinthians 6:16–18, where he is sketching the ground of God's relationship to his people. Paul does not feel any need to explain these perceptions. They derive from his Jewish heritage and are documented in scripture. His only aim is to show how they have found their fulfillment in the sacrifice of Jesus.

Jesus's Death

This brings us, then, to the last of the assumptions on which Paul draws in his formulation of the Gospel: the significance of Jesus's death on the cross. That was a known fact—known to Christian and non-Christian alike, although it must have been a wholly minor incident in a remote Roman province and therefore known to very few persons throughout the empire.[5] But even more problematical than the obscurity of his death were two factors: Jewish messiahs were expected to triumph, not to be executed; the initial hopes of his followers for the speedy establishment of the kingdom of God were not fulfilled, or at the very least, not in their original form. Yet in the

[4] References to Amos appear in 2 Corinthians 6:18 (cf. Amos 3:13; 4:13); in Galatians 4:16 (Amos 5:10) and in Romans 12:9 (Amos 5:15). Psalm 51 is quoted in Romans 3:4 and 7:14.

[5] For a summary of extrabiblical evidence about Jesus, and especially about his death, see H. C. Kee, *Jesus in History* (2nd ed. 1977), New York: Harcourt Brace Jovanovich pp.40–54.

Gospel tradition, as well as in the quite different strand of early Christianity which seems to lie behind Paul, Jesus's death on a cross was not admitted to grudgingly or with embarrassment, but was heralded as central for understanding what God was doing through him for the redemption of the human race.

CHRIST, THE POWER OF GOD

How does this set of assumptions function for Paul to provide answers, shaped and transformed by his experience of the Risen Christ, to the four great questions with which our chapter began? The solutions to the four basic problems—the holy people, the inclusive community, death and destiny, God's ultimate triumph—Paul saw as in process of achievement through Jesus Christ and the work God was accomplishing through him. In depicting for his readers who Jesus is and what he is accomplishing, Paul employs three christological motifs. They are distinguishable from one another, but they are nearly always intertwined: Jesus as willing sacrifice; Jesus as the last Adam; Jesus as king awaiting enthronement. Each of these has a counterpart in the form of the human response to what God's grace has provided through Jesus for the benefit of his people, and ultimately for the whole creation.

The Willing Sacrifice

The overarching significance of Jesus under the first of these images is apparent in 2 Corinthians 5:19: "In Christ God was reconciling the world to himself, not counting their trespasses against them." The term for "world" he uses here in *kosmos*, which implies that not merely the entire human race, but the whole created order is in process of being reconciled to God through Christ. That is wholly appropriate, of course, since in the creation stories of Genesis on which Paul was so heavily dependent, the fall of humankind carried with it the curse upon and disorientation of creation as a whole. That situation God has already begun to reverse. In the text quoted from 2 Corinthians 5, however, the emphasis falls on forgiveness. What is involved in that act of forgiveness is spelled out more fully in adjacent verses (5:15, 21): "He died for all . . . God made him to be sin for us, him who knew no sin." The language and imagery, as well as the underlying assumptions about how reconciliation with God is effected, are powerfully operative here: Jesus is the God-provided sacrifice by which an erring, alienated race now has the possibility of a right relationship with God.

The same basic motif is central to the argument of Romans, where Paul has been making the case that neither through natural nor revealed law can human beings become obedient people, worthy of divine acceptance. That fundamental need for life as the holy, obedient covenant community can be fulfilled not by human achievement, but solely as a divine gift: "Since all have sinned and fall short of the glory of God [that is, the divine image according to which Adam was created, as in Ps. 8], they are set in right relationship by God's grace as a gift, through the redemption which is in Christ Jesus, whom

Philippi was the eastern terminus of the Via Egnatia, which led across from the Adriatic to the northern Aegean Sea. Paving stones of the ancient road are visible at this excavated point where the Via passed through the agora of Philippi. *(Darryl Jones)*

God put forward as an expiation by his blood [the seat of life according to Is-raelite anthropology, Gen. 9:6] to be received by faith." The need is entirely human; the initiative is wholly God's.

In Philippians 2, where Paul is probably quoting (or adapting) an early Christian hymn, he describes the sacrifice of Jesus from his side, as one who willingly chose to pursue a course that led to death in behalf of others. The hymn presupposes that God's redemptive agent did not come into being when Jesus was born, but like wisdom in the Jewish tradition, had a prior existence in association with God: "Though he was in the form of God, he did not count equality with God a thing to be grasped. . . ." That prior existence was will-ingly given up, however, in order to meet the basic need of the human race for reconciliation to God: "He emptied himself, taking the form of a servant, being born in the likeness of human beings. . . ." This voluntary identification with the human race is how Paul understands the incarnation—what John 1:14 calls "the Word made flesh." The only feature of the earthly life of Jesus with which this hymn, or indeed Paul himself, is concerned is the pattern of absolute obedience that characterized Jesus's career. There are no hints of the activities of Jesus reported in the Gospel tradition, and no references here to any of his teachings. The sole focus is on "Being found in human form, he humbled himself and became obedient unto death, even death on a cross."

We might have expected Paul to make reference to the servant poems of Isaiah 42–53 in order to demonstrate the biblical model for Jesus's redemptive role, but there are no allusions, not even to the suffering servant poem of Isaiah 53. Paul uses a different word for servant (*doulos*) from the one found in the Septuagint of Isaiah (*pais*). Three factors that may have helped shape the understanding of Jesus's sacrificial death as pictured so vividly here are (1) the general Old Testament conviction that atonement is effected only by sacrifice; (2) the tradition that wisdom as God's agent often meets hostility or rejection from those lacking in perception; (3) the apocalyptic belief that the faithful, who have been granted to know and share in God's redemptive purpose, must suffer before the consummation comes (as in Daniel). In Daniel, the faithful are undeterred by royal prohibitions against their observance of the dietary laws, against prayers to the God of Israel, and by the demand for universal participation in idolatrous rites. Obedience to God's will is paramount, even in the face of death. The Gospel tradition, of course, confirmed that picture of Jesus as pursuing his mission under God in the face of fierce and mounting hostility from civil and religious authorities. Paul's references to Jesus's death are compatible with the Gospel accounts, although there are no overlapping details, apart from the agreement that his death was by crucifixion.

Had his death been the end of the story of Jesus, we should not have the claims made for him either by Paul or by the Gospel writers. It was because they were all persuaded that, in response to his obedience "unto death," God had "highly exalted him and bestowed on him the name which is above every name" (Phil. 2:9) that Paul was confident God vindicates those who suffer in obedience, that he had given a new standing to those who trust in Jesus (Phil. 3:9), and that he called on Christians to adopt Jesus's "mind" or stance toward life (2:5). His advice in 2 Corinthians 5:17–20 goes beyond these theoretical claims to insist that the work of reconciling the world which God launched through Jesus has now been assigned to his new people, whom Paul styles "ambassadors for Christ," and whose major task is to beseech others to become reconciled to God through Jesus. The depth and height of his substitutionary role is to be seen in Paul's contrast: "For our sake God made him to be sin for us, though he knew no sin, so that in him we might become the righteousness of God" (2 Cor. 5:21). That is how, through Jesus, God has set his people, disobedient and estranged, in right relationship with himself.

The Last Adam

The phrase just quoted, "in him," brings us to the second image on which Paul draws in his portrayal of who Jesus is and what God has done through him: the last Adam. In 2 Corinthians 5:17, he declares that "if anyone is in Christ, there is a new creation." Paul does not believe God is patching up the old creation, characterized by disobedience, failure, and death, but that he has already launched the new creation, distinguished from the old by reconciliation, holiness, and life. In Romans 5:12–21 he sets out a series of vivid contrasts between the old humanity (typified by Adam), and the new humanity (typified by Christ). The contrasting roles of the first Adam and the last may be laid out in graphic form, based on Paul's rhetorical sketch in this passage:

Through Adam	*Through Christ*
Sin entered	God's grace abounds to many
Death spread to all	Grace leads to justification
Judgment fell	
Condemnation followed	
One man's trespass led to death's universal reign	The gift of righteousness brings a reign of life
One trespass brought condemnation for all	One act of righteousness brings acquittal and life for all
Many were made sinners	Many will be made righteous
Law entered and increased the trespass	Grace entered in spite of sin
Sin reigned in death	Grace reigns in righteousness to eternal life

In 1 Corinthians 15 Paul develops the contrast in other directions: "As in Adam all die, so also in Christ shall all be made alive" (15:22). The differences between them go back to their origins: the first man was from earth, a "man of dust" (Gen. 2:7); the second man is from heaven (15:47). The first is a living being; "the Last Adam became a life-giving spirit" (15:45). The consequence of these two kinds of humanity is that the earlier one is characterized by a life that is merely physical, subject to earthly limitations, and terminates in death. The new humanity is characterized by spirit, the agent of life and power; its model is "the man from heaven," and its prospect is the Resurrection. Paul cannot conceive of human existence apart from a body, but neither can he imagine bodily existence within the limitations of "flesh and blood" (15:50). He does not teach the immortality of the disembodied soul, but neither does he believe in the resuscitation of the physical corpse. He considers Jesus to have inaugurated a new mode of being in a form he calls the "spiritual body" (15:44), by which he means some transformation of the person that retains identity but overcomes physical limitations. That change will come only at the end of the age (15:51). Meanwhile, however, the faithful have access to a new sphere of existence and a new resource for life within that structure: life in Christ under the power of the Spirit.

As we have seen, initiation into the "body of Christ" is considered to take place in baptism. It is by the Spirit that all Christians become members of the Body of Christ, regardless of their social, ethnic, or religious heritages (1 Cor. 12:13; Gal. 3:27–28). The new unity that is found in Christ involves personal identification with what he experienced: buried with him in baptism; raised from the dead, so that "we too might walk in newness of life" (Rom. 6:4). The Resurrection includes not merely what is believed to have happened to Jesus in the past, nor is it simply what believers hope will happen to them in the future; it involves a transformation of life in the present. Having once been slaves to sin, along with the first Adam, Christians are now liberated in order to become "obedient from the heart" (Rom. 6:16–17). As in the case of the image of Jesus as the willing sacrifice, so the image of the last Adam does not remain for Paul in the realm of abstract theory, but has direct moral implications for everyday life.

Jesus as King

The third image of Jesus as king is also most fully developed in 1 Corinthians 15, though details are evident in the other letters of Paul. It was God's intention when Adam was created that he should exercise dominion over the creation in God's behalf, as the Genesis story asserts (Gen. 1:26–30) and as Psalm 8:6 confirms. Adam's self-serving defiance of God resulted in the cosmos deteriorating into chaos. Only through the faithful obedience of the last Adam will that goal be attained. Even now he is exercising kingly power on God's behalf (1 Cor. 15:25), and that process of subduing the hostile forces of the universe will continue until it has been fully accomplished and God's royal sovereignty over creation is complete. Paul sees in the prophetic anticipation of the defeat of the God-opposing powers, including death itself, the victory over death which has already been gained in his Resurrection (Isa. 25:8; Hos. 13:14). As in the case of the other two motifs, this one also has direct implications for the responsibilities of Christians: They are to bend every effort in the Lord's work, confident that they are sharing in the preparation for the coming of God's kingdom.

This assurance of the end of the age will enable the faithful to have comfort when their Christian friends and loved ones die before the *parousia* (1 Thess. 4:13–17). But he also warns them that even more severe opposition from civil and religious powers is likely to come upon them before the day of consummation (2 Thess. 2). They are able to endure misfortunes because through Jesus, God has already shown that he is in control of his universe, and that he has acted and will continue to act to assert his sovereignty. In the end even Jesus, the agent of royal authority, will voluntarily subject himself to God (1 Cor. 15:28).

In summary, what emerges in Paul's teaching about Jesus as the Christ, both who he is and what he does, is a convergence of the basic questions we indicated earlier as articulating Paul's view of what is essential about God, his creation, and humanity's place within it. In seeking answers, his thought was inevitably influenced by the presuppositions that his training as a Jew and his experience within the Hellenistic world provided him. But it was the religious encounter with Christ that transformed both Paul and his questions, and provided him with answers. He came to see that God through Jesus was creating a new covenant people, composed of Jews and Gentiles, people from every social, cultural, and economic level. Their participation was grounded on the divine promise and their trust in that promise. The holiness the old covenant people failed to achieve was made possible in the new community through the power of the Spirit, which God provided for and which resided within the faithful. The agent through whom this new humanity was taking shape was the last Adam, whose self-giving life of obedience, ending in a cruel death, provided the ground for divine forgiveness and the sacrificial ratification of the new covenant. The Christians celebrated this in the Eucharist, "the new covenant in my blood" (1 Cor. 11:23). God's having raised him from the dead gave assurance that the original purpose announced to the first Adam would be accomplished through the last Adam's victory over all that opposes God.

FROM PAUL TO PAULINE TRADITION: THE COLOSSIAN LETTER

Thus far in our analysis of Paul, we have made only occasional references to the Letter to the Colossians, merely raising the question whether it is authentic or pseudepigraphic. For details of such specific questions as whether or not the letter may fit into the career of Paul or into his pattern of thought and its relationship to Ephesians, see Appendix IV.

Fundamental in the Colossian letter is redemption, which is understood as the forgiveness of sins (1:14). The cross is portrayed as the instrument of peace, through which all mankind and all the creation have been reconciled to God (1:20). The effect of this reconciling act has been to transform former alienated, wicked enemies of God into his holy, obedient children (1:21–22). Not surprisingly, the author likes to refer to Christians as "saints" (1:2, 12, 26; 3:12); in the closely related brief Letter to the Ephesians, the author uses the term no less than twelve times.[6] Paul preferred to speak of human beings apart from Christ as enslaved to sin, although on occasion he referred to submission to religious regulations as subjection to the God-opposing powers (Gal. 4:3–10). In Colossians, this image is made more concrete (2:13–15). In forgiving sins, God took the publicly posted bond or official notice of our guilt under the law and canceled it by transferring it—in a way that is profoundly ironic—to the scene of the public execution of a condemned malefactor, the cross of Christ. The one who seemingly died in defeat was actually the victor over the very powers that brought about his death.

In Colossians 1:12–18 we hear of the establishment of God's kingdom in language reminiscent of 1 Corinthians 15, where Paul describes the ongoing but soon to be completed process of the defeat of the hostile powers and the establishment of God's rule. Here in Colossians, however, past tenses dominate: the saints *have been delivered* from the dominion of darkness; he *"has transferred* us" to the kingdom. Again in 2:15, the principalities *have been disarmed;* he has publicly triumphed over them. In 1 Corinthians 15 the appeal is to rejoice in what has begun; to await in hope the consummation of God's rule. In Colossians the weight falls on what has already been accomplished, though there remains the expectation of Christ's future manifestation (3:4). The term used elsewhere by Paul for the coming of Christ, *parousia,* does not appear in Colossians, although the event is still awaited.

Insight into what God purposes for the creation is called a mystery (1:24–28) in Colossians, as in the other Pauline letters. In 1 Corinthians 15:51–54 the mystery is eschatological: the resurrection of the dead and the

---

[6] To put the frequency of use of this term in perspective, it should be noted that it appears only about 25 times in all the undisputed Pauline letters.

triumph over the evil powers is soon to occur. That connotation of mystery is consistent in Paul's letters, since whenever he uses the term there is always a reference to a divine plan that still awaits fulfillment, but that God has disclosed to the faithful (1 Cor. 2:1, 7; 4:1; 13:2; 14:2) through the Christian prophets, including Paul himself. The plan for the creation of the new covenant people, which will include both Gentiles and Israel (Rom. 11:25; 16:25) is likewise for Paul a mystery. In Colossians, however, the mystery concerns what already is in existence and operative: the inner presence of Christ among his people. The "hope of glory" is still in effect, but the indwelling of Christ is a present reality and the essential "mystery."

Mystery is used in Colossians 2:3 with another connotation, in which knowledge of Christ is itself the "mystery," since "in him are hid all the treasures of wisdom and knowledge." Yet the author is even more emphatic than we might expect of Paul in insisting that there is a sharp distinction between this divine wisdom and human wisdom, which is characterized by "beguiling speech." He goes on to dismiss false wisdom as "philosophy"—a word not found elsewhere in the New Testament—as empty deceit, exploited by the arrogant spiritual powers (2:8). The true wisdom, which is available in Christ, is to be the ground of their instruction within the community, enriched by corporate worship (3:16).

The Cosmic Christ

Although neither the first nor the last Adam appears in Colossians, there is great importance attached to Jesus's role as the paradigm and pioneer of the new humanity. Employing a term used in Romans 8:30, where Paul pictures Jesus as "the firstborn" (*prototokos*), the primary model on the basis of which God has purposed and brought into being the new covenant people, Colossians widens its significance. In 1:18, we have the word used with connotations very close to those in Romans, but in 1:15, Christ is "the first-born *of all creation.*" The role of wisdom in the Jewish tradition as the agent for the creation of the universe is now explicitly assigned to Christ. Everything was created through him, whether seen or unseen. Not only is he prior to and the agent of creation of all things, but also he is the one by which the universe *coheres.* Here the term is a technical philosophical word, used by Plato and Aristotle to describe the rational coherence of the creation. Although the author mocks philosophy, as we have seen, he is familiar with it in a form compatible with an intellectual synthesis of Hellenistic philosophy and Jewish wisdom tradition, and he now exploits it for his portrayal of Jesus as the Christ.

In this same passage (Col. 1:17), Christ is also described in a metaphor drawn from Paul's other letters as the "head of the body." To this we may compare 1 Corinthians 12:12–29, where the theme of the diversity of functions of members within the "body of Christ" is elaborately developed. The figure of the head is used in a vivid way in 1 Corinthians 11:2–3 to depict the hierarchy of authority in the universe, beginning with God, then Christ, then the husband, then the woman. In Colossians 1:18 and 2:10, however, Christ is seen as head of the Church, but also as head of all powers and authorities. The image of the Church as body has disappeared, although in Ephesians the relationship of Christ and Church as head and body will be repeated along lines similar to Colossians (Eph. 1:22–23). But in Ephesians it is largely eclipsed by the image of the Church as an organic structure, a temple that grows (Eph. 2:19–22). In Colossians 2:19, the head is Christ, with which the body is organically linked and from which it receives nourishment. Paul's vivid metaphor of head and body has taken on elaborate allegorical features in these later letters.

In imagery that more closely resembles that of the first and last Adams, Colossians describes the new and old "human" (3:9–11). The author does not use the abstract term nature, which is found in many translations, but the much more concrete *anthropos* (human being, man) in depicting what happens when anyone shifts the model for existence from disobedient, impotent Adam to the transforming power of Christ. A process of renewal is launched, with the aim of achieving the divine image in which God created humans. This theme parallels that of 2 Corinthians 3:17–18, where the ongoing vision of the Lord changes the beholder into his image, a theme found elsewhere in Paul (Rom. 6:12–19; Phil. 3:12–15). In Christ all the traditional human distinctions vanish, as all become transformed "in Christ" (Col. 3:11).

Christ's Household

As is the case throughout Paul's letters, this process of renewal is not a matter of inward spiritual change alone. Rather, it manifests itself directly and observably in the transformation of the life of the individual, in relationships with others, and in participation in the life of the community. The characterization of the Church as "the elect, holy people" (Col. 3:12) is in complete harmony with the perceptions of Paul as we see them in the other letters, in every one of which Paul addresses the Christians as "saints" or "holy" or comments on the process of their sanctification. He also frequently reminds them that they are "the elect"—which is the ground for responsibility, not for sloth or empty self-congratulation. It is not surprising that these themes appear in both Colossians and Ephesians as well.

Similarly, the virtues the Colossians are enjoined to manifest are given in common ethical terms also found in the other Pauline letters: compassion, kindness, lowliness, meekness, forbearance, patience, forgiveness. Love is given the highest priority in Colossians (3:14) as it is elsewhere in Paul, especially in 1 Corinthians 13. On the other hand, the term the author uses here to characterize love, "the bond of perfection" (*teleiotēs*), is not found elsewhere in Paul, and appears only in Hebrews 6:1. In Hellenistic philosophy, and in the wisdom tradition, it is a common term for moral perfection. Paul speaks several times of being perfect, but usually in contexts that disclaim perfection (for example, Phil. 3:12). He expects perfection only in the new age. Otherwise, he uses the adjective *teleios* to mean mature, ready to receive more complete revelation (as in 1 Cor. 2:6). Other terms of Hellenistic religion which the writer of Colossians refers to in a critical way are the "worship" of angels and the "initiation" into divine secrets through visions (2:18). The first term is rare in the New Testament; the second occurs only here, which may mean that the practices alluded to and roundly denounced have just begun to affect the Christian communities at the time the letter was written.

Another technical term used in passing in Colossians (2:17) occurs following a criticism of those who are trying to force Christians into some form of fasting or special dietary practices or of observance of holy days. The writer does not scoff at those practices or abstinences, but remarks that they "are only a shadow of what is to come." The word "shadow" standing in contrast with "what is coming" sounds thoroughly Pauline at first, since he often speaks of the events that are to take place in the new age as "what is about to come" (Rom. 5:14; 8:18, 38). There Paul is merely contrasting present and future, as 1 Thessalonians 3:4 and 1 Corinthians 3:22 show. The use of the word "shadow" in the Colossians context, however, is related to Platonic thought, with its distinction between the earthly phenomena, which are only shadow copies of reality, and the heavenly eternal ideas or archetypes. That is surely what the "shadow" connotes in Hebrews 10:1 and 13:14, and it carries the same meaning in Colossians.

This brings us to one other feature of Colossians that has no counterpart in the letters of Paul: the lists of responsibilities for various members of the Christian households in 3:18–4:1. In 1 Corinthians and in Romans Paul offers specific suggestions for slaves, wives, and husbands, but this compact list of ethical rules for six different classes of persons has no parallel in the other Pauline letters, and is found elsewhere in the New Testament only in Ephesians 5:22–6:9, where the list is somewhat longer. That style of ethical checklist—especially for the range of persons who would be represented in what we might call a middle-class household—is a familiar feature of popular Stoic philosophy of this period. Does its use here indicate a difference in the social level of the Christians in Colossae? Is it a sign of upward mobility? Or have the social changes implied by this list taken place after Paul's day?

It seems that in Colossians the process of institutionalization, which will come to fuller flower in Ephesians and the Pastorals, has already made considerable progress. The socially conservative attitude of Paul was predicated on his conviction that the end of the age was soon to come, so there was no need to change such basic institutions as slavery or the family. In Colossians, on the other hand, there is a high value placed on stability and order, as well as on public image (4:5). The mind of the Christian is to be occupied with "things above," yet for Paul the aspiration was not up to heaven, but forward to the new age. The eschatological dynamic of the Pauline community has almost wholly vanished.

We may conclude, therefore, that this letter comes from someone devoted to Paul, knowledgeable about his life, including his last years, but eager to reinterpret his views for a situation within the Church that has shifted, or is in process of shifting, from that of Paul's day. The burning issue is not Gnosticism, as some scholars have suggested. There is nothing distinctively Gnostic about what the writer affirms or what he is combating, though he does oppose certain ascetic rules or esoteric claims, on neither of which second-century Gnosticism had a monopoly. What has happened is that the Church is having to come to terms with an ongoing existence, rather than expecting the end of the age in the immediate future. Socially, culturally, organizationally, it must *learn to cope with those continuing needs if it is to survive. The author of Colossians found the basis for making these changes* in the Pauline tradition in which he had been trained. Others of his or subsequent generations were to use the Pauline tradition—including the letter to the Colossians—to effect that transition.

ANNOTATED BIBLIOGRAPHY

BARRETT, C. K.   *From the First Adam to the Last.* London: A. & C. Black, 1962.   A perceptive study of the theme of Christ as the center of the new humanity in the thought of Paul.

BORNKAMM, GÜNTHER.   *Paul.*   New York: Harper and Row, 1971.   The best analysis of Paul's life and thought against the background of his Jewish and Hellenistic heritages.

DUNN, JAMES D. G.   *Unity and Diversity Within the New Testament.* Philadelphia: Westminster Press, 1977.   An excellent, detailed exploration of the ways in which Jesus's significance was understood within the various groups that constituted the Church in the first century of its existence.

FURNISH, VICTOR PAUL.   *Theology and Ethics in Paul.* Nashville: Abingdon Press, 1968.   A careful examination of the influences that shaped Paul's understanding of Jesus and how they affected his views on ethics.

HENGEL, MARTIN.   *Judaism and Hellenism.* 2 vols. Philadelphia: Fortress Press, 1974.   A comprehensive and in depth analysis of the ways in which Judaism responded to the challenge of Greek thought and society.

HOLMBERG, B.   *Paul and Power.* Philadelphia: Fortress Press, 1980.   A brilliant study of the social dynamics within the churches of Paul, and of his relationship to the other apostolic leaders.

MEEKS, WAYNE.   *The First Urban Christians.*   New Haven: Yale University Press, 1983.

NOCK, A. D.   *Conversion: The Old and New in Religion from Alexander the Great to Augustine of Hippo.* Oxford: Oxford University Press (1933), 1961.   The classic study of religions in the Hellenistic and Roman epoch as background for the rise of Christianity.

THEISSEN, GERD.   *The Social Setting of Pauline Christianity.* Philadelphia: Fortress Press, 1982.   A superb collection of essays which analyze the social roles and tensions within the church at Corinth.

Important commentaries on Paul's letters include C. K. Barrett, *Romans* (New York: Harper, 1957), E. Kaesemann, *Romans* (Grand Rapids: Eerdmans, 1980), and H. D. Betz, *Galatians* (Philadelphia: Fortress Press, 1980).

PART IV

THE COMMUNITY ORGANIZES FOR SURVIVAL AND STABILITY

Introduction:

The Passing of the Apostles and the End of Jewish Christianity

In the last quarter of the first century, a series of events in the Roman Empire, within Judaism, and in the Christian Church profoundly affected the Christian community with respect to both its internal life and its relationships with the wider Roman world. Some of these developments were part of the inevitable changes that occur within any religious movement as it shifts from the initial phase of enthusiasm and improvisation to the stage of preparation for an enduring institution.

The most important single event in the history of the later first-century Church was the fall of Jerusalem. That outcome of the Jewish nationalistic revolt brought an end to the Temple and to the functioning of the priesthood. That priesthood not only had its reason for being in the Temple cult, but also depended for its income on the revenues from the sacrifices and offerings presented there. As we have noted, the Essenes were apparently destroyed by the Roman troops as they passed through the Jordan Valley. The survival and subsequent prospering of the Pharisees we will consider in

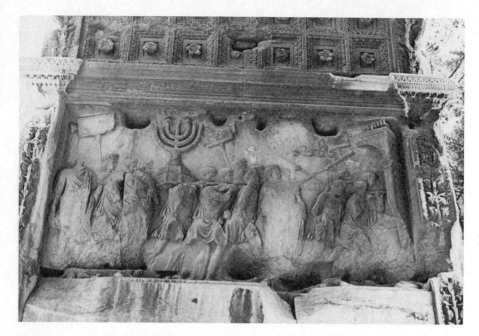

The Arch of Titus in Rome contains this bas-relief. The structure was erected to celebrate Titus's triumph over the Jews. The victors are carrying off from the Temple of Jerusalem the seven-branched lamp-stand, the sacred trumpets, and the table where the sacred bread was kept.   (*Gordon N. Converse*)

detail in a moment. But why was the fall of Jerusalem so significant for the Christians?

There are at least two reasons for the enormous importance of this event. The first is that, in connection with the Roman armies' approach to and siege of Jerusalem, the Jewish Christians based there fled from the city, effectively disappearing from the stage of history, as we have noted above. We also observed that the Christians interpreted this event as a sign of divine judgment on Israel, which had rejected the one they considered to be God's final messenger to his covenant people (Chapter 4). But when that event passed and the new age did not arrive, the Christians had to rethink what God's purpose for them and for the future of the world might be.

Related to this need for reassessment of the destiny of the Church was the passing of the first generation of leaders, the apostles. In Paul's letters and in Acts great importance was attached to the apostles. So great was the authority linked with their having been commissioned by Christ for their work that their deaths raised serious questions as to how authority was to be understood and how it was to operate in the post-apostolic Church. It is important to see the range of ways in which the apostolic figures were remembered in the Church, and the variety of ways in which their authority was perceived.

The Roman Forum and the Arch of Septimius Severus from the Palatine Hill. The plain, squarish building across the Forum is the Curia, where the Senate convened. At the lower right are the steps and column bases of the Basilica Julia, one of the colonnaded porticos used for transacting business in ancient Rome. Behind the arch appears the flat roof of a small church that was built over the ruins of the Mamertine Prison, where, according to tradition, Peter and Paul were imprisoned. *(Courtesy of Trans-World Airlines)*

The Martyrion was a simple shrine erected over the probable burial place of Peter. The remains of this shrine, which date back to the beginning of the second century, were discovered directly below the high altar of St. Peter's Church in Rome. The fact that the shrine is in the midst of the pagan tombs tends to confirm its authenticity, since it is unlikely that Christians would have invented a burial place for Peter on unholy ground. The martyrdom of Peter is reported to have occurred in the reign of Nero in the gardens between the Vatican hills.

We have already mentioned the fate of James, Jesus's brother, in our analysis of Acts. Linked with him is Jude who, in the letter that bears his name, is depicted as calling himself "Jude, the brother of James." About Jude we know nothing else, although there was a person of this name among the brothers of Jesus (Mark 6:3; Matt. 13:55). He would have been dead at the time of Domitian, when his grandsons were investigated by the future emperor as being descendants of David and therefore possible pretenders to the Jewish throne.[1]

As to the fate of James and John, the sons of Zebedee (Mark 1:19; 10:35), we have very little to go on. James was the first victim of Herod Agrippa (Acts 12:2); later tradition supports the suggestion that his brother John died with him in A.D. 44. Irenaeus in the late second century speaks of the residence in Ephesus of the venerable John," a disciple of the Lord," for which report he is probably relying on the earlier witness of Papias. Papias's own account seems to have differentiated between John the Elder (to whom Irenaeus probably is referring) and John the son of Zebedee. It is possible that the John of Ephesus (John the Elder) was one who had become a follower of Jesus during his lifetime, and who had subsequently become a leader of the Church in the vicinity of Ephesus following his migration there from Palestine. The remark by Bishop Polycrates of Ephesus (mid-second century) that John of Ephesus was a priest would fit with this conjecture. Significantly, in these early references, John of Ephesus is described as a "disciple," not as an "apostle." Thus, the tradition that connects the Johannine Gospel and Letters (and the Revela-

---

[1] Eusebius, *Ecclesiastical History*, III.20.6. For more on Jude, see Chapter 13.

Obelisk in St. Peter's Square, brought to Rome from Egypt by the emperor Caligula. The obelisk was placed by Nero in the pleasure gardens that he built between the low hills of the Vatican. (*Alinari/Editorial Photocolor Archives*)

tion) with John of Ephesus does not claim that these works were written by the apostle John, the son of Zebedee, who probably was long dead by this time.

The Acts of the Apostles report the departure of Peter from Jerusalem at the time of the persecution under Herod Agrippa, but give us no information as to where he went (Acts 12:17). He reappears briefly in Acts 15 at the time of the so-called Jerusalem council, though he is called "Symeon" on that occasion (Acts 15:14). There is strong support for the theory that he spent much time on extended missionary journeys. Later Church tradition claims that Peter went to Rome and that he became the first bishop of the church there. There is considerable plausibility in the report that he was martyred in Rome under Nero (A.D. 64) in the same year that Paul was executed. Since Peter was not a Roman citizen, he could have been crucified, as tradition reports he was. The site of his execution and burial is thought to have been in the gardens of Nero, which lay across the Tiber from the main part of Rome. It is in this area that archeologists have uncovered a pagan cemetery, in the midst of which is a memorial thought to have been erected in honor of Peter by early Roman Christians. Over this spot was built the Church of St. Peter in the time of

Old St. Peter's in Rome: interior view, early fourth century, as shown in this Renaissance fresco in S. Martino ai Monti, Rome. One of the largest and most famous of the basilicas built by Constantine after Christianity became the official religion of the empire, it was demolished to make way for the present enormous Renaissance structure, St. Peter's.   (*Fototeca di Architettura e Topografia dell'Italia Antica*)

Constantine, which was replaced in the sixth century by the great Basilica of St. Peter.[2]

We have only traces or pious legends about the fate of some other apostles. Thomas is said to have gone to India, where the Mar Thoma Church preserves his name. Andrew, the brother of Peter, may have preached in northern Greece and Scythia. He is reported to have been crucified in Patras, Greece. The most significant monument of all that the Jerusalem apostles left was their living witness to Jesus, the Risen Christ, and to the power of the Spirit by which the Church believed God was guiding it in the changing situations it confronted as the first Christian century ended.

[2] For a full discussion, see Daniel W. O'Connor, *Peter in Rome: The Literary, Liturgical and Archeological Evidence* (New York: Columbia University Press, 1969). A comprehensive investigation of the Peter question is O. Cullmann, *Peter: Disciple, Apostle, Martyr*, rev. ed. (Philadelphia: Westminster Press, 1963).

The field of leadership was left to other Christian groups—especially those in the Pauline tradition—who viewed the continuities between the old covenant and the new in ways very different from the perspective and convictions of the Jerusalem apostles, as we see them reflected in the letters of Paul. We will examine in the following chapters the other options open to Christians around the turn of the second century.

Perhaps even more important for the subsequent development of Christianity was the fact that the fall of Jerusalem was not accompanied by the *parousia* of Jesus. Although Paul did not link his expectation of the coming of Christ to the fall of the city, the passing of his generation without that cosmic event taking place demanded a rethinking of the divine timetable for the establishment of God's rule. According to Mark 9:1 and 13:30, as well as Paul's remark in 1 Thessalonians 4:15, neither Jesus nor Paul expected a delay of more than a few decades beyond the rise of the Resurrection faith and the return of Christ in triumph to accomplish God's plan for the renewal of the creation. When the Temple fell and the generation passed, how was the Church to maintain the credibility of its faith? As we have seen to be the case in the Letter to the Colossians, the later New Testament writers do not evade this problem, but deal with it in a variety of ways.[3] We will trace in the next two chapters some of the ways in which the failure of expectations was handled in the New Testament period.

As careful studies of the makeup of the early Christian communities have shown,[4] from the beginning the Gospel attracted leading members of society in Gentile cities. Prisca and Aquila (1 Cor. 16:17) had a house large enough to serve as the meeting place for the Ephesian congregation, and the means to travel around the Mediterranean, probably in connection with their business (Acts 18:1–3). It is probably not merely understatement that leads Paul to note that among the Corinthian Christians were "not many wise . . . not many powerful, not many of noble birth" (1 Cor. 1:26). He suggests, rather, that although they were in the minority, there were persons from these categories of social and intellectual achievement among the converts in that city. The "partnership in the gospel" for which he commends the Philippian Christians is their sizable financial contribution to his work (Phil. 1:3–5). The wise and wealthy seem to have been in the minority, however, with the result that the Christian communities could develop during the first generation without coming to the attention of the authorities, unless specific charges were brought against members by their opponents, as is the case in the many court scenes presented in the Book of Acts. The persecution of Christians in Rome by Nero in A.D. 64 seems to have been unprecedented and not duplicated by

[3] The problem raised by the failure of expectations of the arrival of a savior figure or of the end of the age has arisen throughout history. Recently it has been studied sociologically, as in the analysis of "disconfirmation" of millennial hopes in *When Prophecy Fails,* by Leon Festinger and others (St. Paul: University of Minnesota Press, 1956).

[4] Gerd Theissen, *The Social Setting of Pauline Christianity: Essays on Corinth,* ed. and trans. by John H. Schuetz (Philadelphia: Fortress Press, 1982). "Legitimation and Subsistence," pp. 27–54. The author shows the social and economic tensions discernible in Paul's letters to the Corinthians and in the personal references to Corinthian Christians at the end of his letter to the Romans.

him or his successors until well into the second century. As we have observed, a major factor in the early tolerance of Christians is that they were almost certainly regarded officially by Rome as a Jewish sect, and therefore enjoyed the degree of respect and acceptance tendered the Jews down to the time of the nationalist revolt.

The Pharisees' successful attempt to organize Judaism as a whole with Roman official sanction has been described earlier. At their base in Yavneh, or Jamnia, that effort at consolidation of Jewish scriptures and practices was carried forward in the 90s. The outcome was the designation of the official Jewish canon of scripture (which excluded not only Christian writings, but some that were being used by Christians, such as The Wisdom of Solomon) and the clear designation of Christians as outside the Jewish pale. From that time on, therefore, the Christians were visible, as well as vulnerable, to Roman opposition.

A dramatic instance of what that could mean occurred in the reign of Domitian (A.D. 81–96). When he decreed that he should be addressed as *Dominus et Deus* (Lord and God), thereby arrogating to himself the divine honors which the Senate had previously reserved for deceased emperors only, the refusal of Christians to comply by taking part in religious ceremonies honoring the state gods and the incumbent ruler subjected them to criminal charges on civil (*crimen laesae majestatis*) and religious grounds. The report that Domitian ordered the exile of his niece, Flavia Domitilla, and the execution of her husband, the consul Flavius Clemens, probably indicates that they fell afoul of his charge of "godlessness." This interpretation receives confirmation from the fact that an ancient Christian cemetery in Rome has been found to have been a gift of Flavia Domitilla, strongly suggesting that she was indeed a Christian. If this is the case, we have the astonishing situation that in about sixty years Christianity had travelled from a proverbially provincial village in Palestine, Nazareth, to the imperial household itself. The negative result of that unprecedented transition was that from the time of Domitian on, the Christian community had to adopt a clear policy toward the Roman state, including the emperor cult. In Chapter 12 we will see some of the ways in which that issue was handled.

Another consequence of the geographical spread, as well as of the social and cultural diversity of the response to the Gospel, was that the churches themselves were very different from one another, and that there were marked differences within the membership of a single community as well. The attitudes toward the pagan state ranged from the tranquil acceptance of suffering evident in Hebrews and 1 Peter to the bitter denunciation of Rome—in cryptic apocalyptic language—as demonic in origin and doomed to destruction in Revelation. The divisive issue of wealth and poverty in this period is evident in Hebrews and James. The intellectual range of those included as members of the churches is apparent in the use of technical philosophical terms in Hebrews, of popular literary styles in Acts, of widespread ethical language and rhetoric in James, and of the distinctive terminology of Hellenistic religions in 1 Peter. Except for Revelation, where the stance is that of Christ against contemporary culture, the later books of the New Testament demonstrate how, in

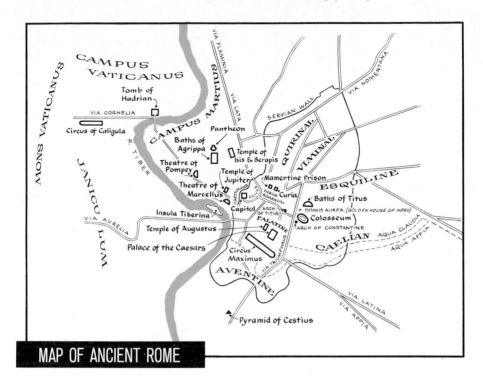

MAP OF ANCIENT ROME

the name of Christ, Greco-Roman culture was transformed and exploited by the various facets of the Christian community.

Yet it was just this diversity within the early Church that led to two kinds of difficulties: (1) How was structural, organizational, and administrative unity to be achieved in order to keep the Christian community from becoming a scattered group of diverse sects spread across the Roman territories and beyond? (2) Was it possible to achieve some kind of conceptual unity, some common base for faith and practice, through which the Church could present a solid front to the Roman world? Under Paul, faith was primarily trust in the divine promises, awaiting speedy fulfillment. Already in Colossians, as we have seen, faith is on the way to becoming a body of truth to be affirmed as a norm for participation in the life of the Church. For Paul, the issues of challenge to his authority had to do with immoral behavior, with unwarranted speculation about the nature of Christ, and with wrong notions about the end of the age. In the post-70 period, eschatological expectation had waned or been altered; speculation about the nature of Christ had proliferated; ethical issues were being addressed increasingly in terms deriving from Hellenistic philosophy, rather than from direct religious experience, as in Paul's letters.

Similar changes are evident in the definition of Church leadership. In Paul's letters, the titles of the leaders are largely functional: An apostle is someone commissioned for a specific task in the development of the Christian community; the deacon or deaconess has responsibility for ongoing needs in the life of the local congregation. In the writings that build on the Pauline tradition—Ephesians, 1 and 2 Timothy, and Titus—these roles have been sharply defined and arranged in a hierarchical structure. As Max Weber's sociological studies showed long ago, there was a shift from charismatic to institutional leadership in the later part of the first century.[5] A basic aspect of this change is the concern to demonstrate continuity with the founding generation and to lend authority to subsequent developments within the Christian community by appealing to Jesus and the apostles as the agents and spokesmen of the divine will. The popularity of the legends about the apostles reminds us of the mounting desire to establish norms of faith and practice by appeal to the authority of an apostle. Is it not surprising, therefore, that the later books of the New Testament were written in the name of, or were linked to, leading figures of the apostolic age. These later New Testament writings, accordingly, manifest a range of ways in which the dialectic is handled: How to maintain links with the original tradition while adapting it and demonstrating its relevance to a situation fundamentally altered politically, socially, and culturally.

[5] Max Weber, *On Charisma and Institution Building*, ed. S. N. Eisenstadt (Chicago: University of Chicago Press, 1968).

II

Establishing Authority and Achieving Unity: Letter to the Ephesians and the Pastorals

The oldest manuscript containing the text of the letters attributed to Paul, which dates from about the year 200,[1] gives no indication of the place to which the work we know as the Letter to the Ephesians was addressed. The same vagueness about the destination of this writing is evident in other very old, highly reliable manuscripts as well.[2] Most modern translations identify the recipients as merely "the saints who are also faithful in Christ Jesus" (Eph. 1:1b). Is this a letter addressed to a specific group and concerned with a specific local issue? Related questions about this letter that arise are these: If this was not written for a particular situation, why was it written at all? And why did the writer address his readers in the name of Paul, and do so in what has the outward form of a Pauline letter? The answers to these questions will contribute toward our understanding the dynamics of change, within the late first-century Church as well as in its relationship to its environment.

A TREATISE IN THE FORM OF A LETTER:
EPHESIANS

A thoughtful reading of Ephesians by someone who has read Paul's letters shows that the first three chapters of the writing are an elaborate set of introductory remarks, similar to those simpler greeting formulas that open his authentic letters. The last three chapters correspond to his characteristic concluding ethical observations and appeals. In other words, the letter has a lengthy introduction and an extended conclusion, but nothing corresponding to the main, middle part of a specific Pauline communication to one of the churches under his charge. Paul regularly reminds his readers that he mentions them in his prayers (1 Thess. 1:2; Phil. 1:3; Rom. 1:9). In Ephesians, the writer declares in 1:15 "for this reason," repeats the statement in 3:1, but only in 3:14 does he explain that it is "for this reason" that he is praying for his readers. The bare form of Paul's writing style survives, but it has been adapted to serve as the framework for a discourse on a number of subjects. Only in 6:21 is there a reference to a specific person, and—what is of signifi-

[1] So-called P[46], which together with P[45] (divided between the libraries of the University of Michigan and the John Rylands in Manchester, England) comprise the oldest consecutive manuscript evidence for the Gospels, Acts, and the Pauline writings. See on this W. G. Kümmel, *Introduction to the New Testament*, trans. by H. C. Kee (Nashville: Abingdon Press, 1975), p. 518.

[2] For a full discussion of evidence and issues, see Kümmel, *Introduction to the New Testament*, pp. 353–56.

Ephesus today: the ruins. In Paul's day, Ephesus was one of the great cities of the eastern Mediterranean, but the silting up of its harbor rendered it useless as a port and caused it to be abandoned. (*Darryl Jones*)

cance for the question of the origins of the Letter to the Ephesians—that mention seems to have been taken over from Colossians 4:7–8. A careful reading of Ephesians shows that nearly half of this letter has direct parallels in Colossians. Furthermore, words used in Colossians (and in the undisputed Pauline letters) have been transformed in Ephesians to convey different meanings. As we observed in Chapter 10, for example, *mysterion* ("mystery") in Colossians 1:21 means the Gospel, which Paul can preach because God has disclosed it to him (cf. 1 Cor. 2:7). But in Ephesians 1:9 and 3:3–6, the "mystery" is that Gentiles share with Jews in the new "body," which is the Church. It is clear from Ephesians as a whole that the writer's central interest is in the composition, structure, and unity of the Church.

The Central Issue: Apostolic Authority

In Paul's own account of his conversion and commissioning as apostle (Gal. 1:16–17), the claims are that God took the initiative in selecting Paul for his role, that his transformation took place by means of an inner revelation of Jesus to him, and that the goal of his assignment was to preach Christ among the Gentiles. He takes care to point out that, in accepting his commission as apostle to the Gentiles, he had no conference with and no stamp of approval from the other apostles. In Colossians, the term "apostle" is never used; rather, Paul is spoken of as the "minister of God" (Col. 1:23, 25), using the word *diakonos* in its fundamental sense of "one who serves others." In Ephesians 2:20, however, the apostles have a very different function: they are the structural foundation on which the Church, God's new temple in the Lord, has been erected. Its constituent elements have been joined together, and—changing the metaphor—the new building is in process of growth. We shall see that in the Pastorals, the apostolic office develops in authoritative terms. In 1 Corinthians 3:5–14, Paul uses the images and metaphors of building, growth, and foundation. There, however, the only foundation is Jesus Christ. He and the other leaders are no more than workmen through whose skillful labor the Gospel has been preached and the new community has begun to grow. The outcome will be known only when "the Day" (the new age) comes (1 Cor. 3:13). For Ephesians, however, the mix of organic and architectural imagery depicts an enduring establishment, in which Christians are to deport themselves as good citizens. The image of the building that is growing is further developed in Ephesians 4, where the goal of the process is seen as twofold: (1) the attainment of the unity of faith, and (2) the achievement of maturity and full organizational integration of the new structure.

The basic guarantee of the integrity of the Church as structured community is the apostle. We have already noted that central to the divinely revealed mystery was the inclusion of Gentiles along with Jews in the one body of the faithful. That disclosure was made only to "the holy apostles and prophets" (Eph. 3:5). God's grace was given to "Paul" specifically to enable him to serve as the instrument of this revelation (3:3) and the agent by which the new community would be realized (3:8). Surprisingly, the author of Ephesians asserts that this truth has been disclosed through the Church to the spiritual powers as well as to all earthly human beings (3:8–10). The person crucial to the launching of this project of cosmic redemption is Paul (3:2), even though he modestly refers to himself as "the least of all the saints" (3:8). Yet he is the sole apostolic figure through whom this reconciling plan was disclosed and launched (3:8–9). It is not surprising, therefore, that it is in Paul's name (Eph. 1:1) that this grand scheme is reported and the structuring of the Church is called for. Before turning to an analysis of that scheme and its background, we must consider how the strategy of appeal to apostolic authority may have arisen.

Ephesians: The School of Paul

The Letter to the Ephesians seems clearly to have been prepared as a recasting and adaptation of the Letter to the Colossians,[3] which is itself a reworking of themes and terminology found in the undisputed Pauline letters, as we have noted. It is easy to understand why an early Christian, eager to promote and then to consolidate the outreach of the Church to Gentiles, would want to claim Paul as a supporter. But is it legitimate, or even moral, to

[3] Ibid., pp. 358–62.

claim Paul as the author of writings that actually date from a period after his death? In the modern world, such an enterprise would be both illegal and deceitful. In the ancient world, however, producing pseudonymous writings was a widespread and acceptable undertaking.

In both Greek and Jewish cultures, the development of philosophical thought and of religious tradition was typically carried on through a school honoring the name of a great figure of the past, as we noted in Part I. Plato carried forward his appropriation and development of the philosophy of Socrates in the Academy, the public park where his pupils and his successors gathered for more than a century; Aristotle, who broke with Plato on both substantive and methodological grounds, founded his own school in another public area of Athens known as the Lyceum. Later in the fourth century Epicurus established a philosophical school in Athens, as Pythagoras had done at Crotona in southern Italy a century and a half before Plato's Academy. So the pattern of preserving and appropriating the wisdom of a venerated teacher, and doing so in his name, was firmly established in the Greek world.

In the Jewish world, the Old Testament writings themselves represent the development of ancient traditions. Although the whole of the Pentateuch (the first five books of the Bible) was attributed to Moses, these writings received their present form no earlier than the sixth century B.C., when the Jews in Babylonian exile reworked their traditions and codified their moral and cultic regulations. Similarly, the writings of the prophets, such as Isaiah and Zechariah, were added to by later prophets, both to honor and to bring up to date the venerated older oracles. Solomon is given credit for much of Jewish wisdom tradition, even though some of it—such as The Wisdom of Solomon—uses the language and technical terminology of the Hellenistic culture, and hence is at least six or seven hundred years younger than Solomon. Apocalypses were written in the names of venerated figures from Israel's past such as Ezra (2, 3, 4 Ezra) and Enoch (1, 2, 3 Enoch).

Central to the Pharisaic method of interpreting and even reshaping the law to fit their own circumstances was their belief that, in addition to the written law given to Moses on Mt. Sinai, God had given an oral law by which the written was to be understood and supplemented. It was almost certainly Rabbi Hillel who transformed Pharisaism from an activist group into a pious sect and who was regarded by later generations as the central authority on the oral law.[4] Although the historical information about him is fuzzy and fragmentary, he probably lived from about 50 B.C. to A.D. 10. His major impact on Judaism, however, is evident in the centuries following his death, when his way of interpreting the law and the authority that clung to his name were both catalyst and organizing center for the rabbinic movement that has been the essence of Judaism ever since the end of the first century. Although we have no sure evidence of a School of Hillel comparable to the Academy or the Lyceum, the aura attached to his name was the major formative influence in the subsequent shaping of Judaism.

Similarly, we can see in the development of a major strand of early Christianity around the name of Paul and the authority attached thereto a

[4] J. Neusner, *From Politics to Piety*, p. 41, states that Hillel was "everywhere claimed as the major authority—after Moses and Ezra—for the Oral Torah."

"school" tradition roughly analogous to that linked with Hillel. Later in this chapter we will see how increasing emphasis was placed on the authority of the apostle, with Paul given credit for instituting that powerful role. But already in Ephesians the function of the apostle to establish and guarantee both structural and doctrinal unity is evident. That task is made explicit in Ephesians 4:1–16. This passage begins with a call for mutuality and cohesion within the Christian community, with the implication that this enhances the public image of the Church: "Eager to maintain the unity of the Spirit in the bond of peace." But the focus shifts instantly from the sense of cooperation and togetherness to a formulaic listing of the ground of that unity within the one body: "one Lord, one faith, one baptism" (4:5).

For Paul, there was no question that there was one God and one Lord (Jesus), as 1 Corinthians 8:4–6 shows. Similarly, there is only one Spirit, by which all were baptized into Christ (1 Cor. 12:12–13). But for Paul faith is always trust in God's promise, as it was to Abraham (Rom. 4), never affirming a set of beliefs or doctrines. Yet in Ephesians 4:13–14, the "unity of the faith" is contrasted with its antithesis: "every wind of doctrine . . . the cunning of men . . . deceitful wiles." Faith is directly linked with knowledge (4:13), and the apostle is the judge and guarantor of both. The affective, personal connotations of faith as trust have been replaced by the objective, formulated belief in doctrine. In any age that esteems good feelings more highly than true concepts, such a change will be viewed with regret. Yet it is doubtful if the Church could have survived or could have attracted a more intellectual clientele without precision in the formulation of its beliefs.

Central to the achievement of unity of faith is an authoritative leader: the apostle. The author of Ephesians (in 4:8) derives the warrant for the establishment of this authoritative office from the Jewish scriptures, which the Christians had, of course, appropriated as their own. In the Septuagint of Psalm 68:18, the psalmist describes the coming of Yahweh from Sinai to take up residence in the Jerusalem sanctuary. Yet for the author of Ephesians, God did not receive gifts, but bestowed them on men. The Greek word used here, *dōmata,* is from a completely different root than the word Paul uses in 1 Corinthians 12 and elsewhere for the special enablement that God provides through the Spirit for the diverse responsibilities within the church: *charisma.* The latter is for Paul a divinely given aid to fulfill a task. For Ephesians, "the holy apostles" are given or assigned to an office within a hierarchy, which places apostles at the top (Eph. 4:11). Once more, the modern romantic spirit may prefer the informality and improvisatory quality of a charismatic gift, but the organizational and administrative structure implied in the developing authority of the apostolic office would have been essential for the survival of the Church.

The Church as Guardian of the Truth

Closely related to the authority of the apostle, and his role as safeguard of developing tradition, is the emerging sense that there is a fixed body of truth about Jesus (Eph. 4:21, "as the truth is in Jesus") which is to be preserved and passed on. The "gospel of salvation" is equated with "the word of truth" (Eph. 1:13). Elsewhere it is characterized as a divine plan, kept from human and angelic knowledge in past ages, but now disclosed as "the manifold wisdom of God" (Eph. 3:10)—that is, the "unity of the faith and of the knowledge of the Son of God" (4:13). Paul never used that sort of language in relation to faith, but for those who stood in the Pauline tradition in the later first century, apostolic authority and doctrinal soundness had come to be regarded as essential for the welfare of the increasingly institutionalized community.

More was changed than the vocabulary of faith, however. For Paul, faith and hope are intimately linked: God's rule has been inaugurated or launched; it has yet to be consummated (1 Cor. 15:25). Christ must continue to exercise kingly power until God has subjected all the creation under him. For Ephesians, however, everything in creation has already been put "under his feet" (1:21–22), and his followers have already been "blessed . . . with every spiritual blessing in the heavenly places" (1:3). They have already been "raised up with him" and seated with him in heavenly places (2:6). Even though on occasion the author uses the more traditional language of the future hope ("this age . . . the age to come," 1:22), the composite picture in Ephesians is of a cosmic plan (3:9) that has already been effectively carried out through God's exaltation of Jesus.

Similar to the development of this view of cosmic achievement is the subtle way in which the author transforms some of Paul's basic ideas. In Galatians 4:4 Paul asserts that God sent Christ to redeem his people "in the fulness of time"; that is, at the appropriate point in the working of the divine scheme. Ephesians uses a similar phrase at one point (1:10), although under discussion there is a cosmic rather than a chronological plan. But elsewhere the author links the term to "the fulness of God" (1:23; 3:19) or of Christ (4:13). Paul shared with his Jewish contemporaries—especially those reared in the Hellenistic culture, as he was—the belief that God was the only ultimate power in the universe—but by no means was he the only spiritual power at work. There were forces he called "rulers," "authorities," and "powers." It is these which Paul told the Corinthians would soon be brought under divine control, at the end of the age, when Christ's reign achieves its full and final effect (1 Cor. 15:24–25). Using the identical terms, Ephesians 1:21 reports that Christ is already triumphant over those powers. Christians still face opposition from these spiritual powers (Eph. 6:12), but the victory is accomplished and believers are already seated with Christ in the celestial realms (Eph. 2:6).

In Ephesians (and Colossians), the term used by Paul, "fulness" (in Greek, *plērōma*) is used with very different connotations than in his undisputed letters. The connotations the term carries in these post-Pauline Christian documents recall the speculation, noted earlier in our discussion of John, about wisdom as the instrument of God and the revelation of his purpose for the world, especially as wisdom is portrayed in The Wisdom of Solomon, written in Greek in the first century B.C.[5] The Pauline school has apparently taken

---

[5] The technical term *plērōma* (fulness) is not used in The Wisdom of Solomon, nor in other Jewish wisdom literature, with the complex of meanings found in Ephesians; only in Hellenistic-Jewish wisdom literature are all these functions brought together in a single revelatory figure, as they are in Ephesians.

over a hymn addressed to wisdom and modified it in order to make it portray Christ as the one through whom creation was achieved and reconciliation of the universe to God accomplished. What is distinctively different from the wisdom tradition, however, is the climactic line: "For in him all the fulness was pleased to dwell" (Col. 1:19). This is the equivalent of Paul's "God sent forth his son" (Gal. 4:4) or John's "the Word was made flesh" (John 1:14). The wisdom tradition is transformed, therefore, in light of the universal Christian belief in God's incarnation in Jesus.

That basic conviction is significantly modified in Ephesians. The "fulness" has become identified as a kind of spiritual sphere in which God is fully known. Building on Paul's notion of the Church as a corporate organism, in which "body" is a vivid metaphor for mutual dependence and shared responsibility (as in 1 Cor. 12:13–26), the Church is for the author of Ephesians a mystical place, also referred to as "the heavenlies" (1:3, 20), where Christ reveals to his own people the full nature and purpose of God (1:23; 4:13). In this sphere one can experience "the love of Christ, which surpasses knowledge" and "be filled with all the fulness of God" (3:19). Neither the spatial gap between earth and heaven is removed, nor the temporal gap between this age and the age to come; but in Ephesians, the "fulness" of God's being and his redemptive plan are accessible to the spiritual experience of the believer. That transforming experience takes place within the human being (3:16), and results in the acquisition of a transformed human nature (4:23–24).

The Christians striving for a synthesis of doctrinal unity and mystical participation in the divine were not the only ones drawing on the traditions of Jewish wisdom speculation. The links between that speculation and Greek intellectual tradition are pointed up in the designation of the false teaching in Colossians 2:8 as "philosophy and vain deceit." In 1 Timothy 6:20 it will be characterized as "what is falsely called 'knowledge,'" for which the Greek word is *gnosis.* Not surprisingly, it is the Gnostics, with their claim to true *gnosis,* who combine Jewish wisdom tradition with Christian ideas,[6] weaving them together with strands from Greek philosophy and Iranian cosmology to create the diverse, complex school of thought known to historians as Gnosticism. Significantly, the earliest evidence for Gnosticism denies that the good God has created the world. Basilides some time before A.D. 150 was appealing to the religion of the Persians to show that there are two eternal principles, good and evil, and that the latter is responsible for the pain and evil of the material world.[7] Similarly, Marcion of Sinope in the same period made a distinction between the bad god of creation and the God of love.[8]

The Gnostic system of Valentine (between 135 and 170) separated the ultimate god of the universe from the creation by an elaborate series of intermediary beings, known as the *plērōma,* comprised of fifteen pairs of "aions." The first pair, Depth and Silence, produce Mind and Truth, which then gen-

---

[6] See Pheme Perkins' superb introduction to the Gnostic documents, *The Gnostic Dialogues: The Early Church and the Crisis of Gnosticism* (New York: Paulist Press, 1980), pp. 15–18.

[7] From Basilides's *Thirteenth Tractate,* quoted in the *Acta Archelai* 55, from J. C. Ayer, *A Source Book for Ancient Church History* (New York: Scribner's, 1913), pp. 83–84.

[8] Quoted in Tertullian, *Against Marcion* 1.

erate Word and Life, from which come Man and Church. (Each of these is conveniently a union of masculine and feminine terms in Greek.)[9] Both the role of wisdom in creation and the meaning of *plērōma*, which were adapted by the later Pauline tradition to explain the significance of Christ, have now been utterly transformed by the Gnostics into a system that denied the goodness of the creation and denigrated bodily existence. Attributed to Valentine, but also found in the apocryphal Gospel tradition of the second century,[10] is the declaration assigned to Jesus that human sexuality should be obliterated: "When you trample on the robe of shame, and when the two shall be one, and the male with the female, and there is neither male nor female." There is no hint in Colossians or Ephesians that such dualistic views were being combated by the authors, much less that these writings were influenced by what later emerge as Gnostic notions. Yet the locating of redemption within the spiritual realm, "the heavenlies," and the decline of expectation of the renewal of the creation by God's direct action in the immediate future, opened the way for this transmutation of Jewish wisdom teaching and the older Christian eschatological tradition.

Obedient Living in an Alien World

By the middle of the second century, persons claiming to have the true interpretation of the Christian tradition were denying the goodness of the creation and assigning responsibility for this evil world to a power other than the good God. There is no hint of this dualistic view in Colossians or Ephesians, but the shift of the locus of Christian experience from the struggles of the present age (as in Paul and the Jesus tradition) to a spiritual sphere could be—and was—adapted readily by Gnostic dualists. We will see that conceptual conflict shaping up even more clearly in the Pastoral Epistles, covered later in this chapter.

In both Colossians and Ephesians, however, the exact reverse of withdrawal from or denigration of the present world is apparent. One of the major results of sharing in "the fulness" is the development of a Christian citizenship or life style. Once again, the term for Christian citizenship or political loyalty, *politeuma*, is found in Paul's letters: in Philippians 3:20, for example, where he reminds his readers that their ultimate allegiance and real ruler is Jesus Christ, who is now in heaven but who will return to establish his rule in the earth. His most nearly systematic letter, Romans, includes detailed moral instructions to Christians (Rom. 13–15), among them orders to obey the emperor and pay taxes to the Romans (13:1–7). Yet all this advice is placed in a framework of expectation of the end of the age, and the consequent replace-

---

[9] Summarized in Henry Chadwick, *Alexandrine Christianity* (Philadelphia: Westminster Press, 1954), p. 31.

[10] Quoted from Chadwick, *Alexandrine Christianity,* Clement of Alexandria, "On Marriage," xiii.92. A variant form of this saying from the Gospel of Thomas promises entrance into the kingdom when one becomes "as a little child"—that is, when one's sexual identity is overcome. See on this saying my *Jesus in History,* 2d ed. (New York: Harcourt Brace Jovanovich, 1977), pp. 277–78.

ment of the earthly power by the rule of God: "You know what hour it is . . . salvation is nearer than when we first believed; the night is far gone, the day is at hand" (13:11–12). In Colossians, on the other hand, the framework for the moral appeal is a combination of the rule of Christ within the hearts of the faithful (Col. 3:15) and conducting oneself wisely toward outsiders (4:5). The specific instructions to members of the Christian households—to wives, husbands, children, slaves—are closely patterned after similar lists in the popular philosophies of the day.[11]

In Ephesians, however, a much more elaborate structure is presented as the ground of moral responsibility. Christians are members of a third race, distinct from Jews or Gentiles (Eph. 4:17). They share in a new humanity, which achieves what the old humanity failed to gain: "the likeness of God, in true righteousness and holiness" (4:23). Relationships within that new community are neither spontaneous nor informal. Elaborating on the household lists of Colossians is a clearly defined order of obligations in Ephesians, a hierarchical structure. In it Christ is at the head, with men and then women ranked in descending order of authority; below are the children, and finally the slaves (5:21–6:9). There is to be a mutuality of affection and concern, but rank is to be respected. Through baptism and instruction in the scriptures ("the washing of water with the word," 5:26), Christ is purifying the Church to make it a worthy consort. Christians are to use their time wisely not because the end is at hand, but "because the days are evil" (5:16). The life of the Church is not an interim existence, awaiting the new age, but an ongoing process in which social and institutional stability are combined with moral renewal, with the announced goal of a more nearly perfect Church. The aim, which blends morality and mysticism, is vividly summarized in Ephesians 4:15–16.

> Speaking the truth in love, we are to grow up in every way into him who is the head, even Christ, from whom the whole body, joined and knit by every joint with which it is supplied, when each part is working properly, makes bodily growth and upbuilds itself in love.

An essential contribution to the sense of mutuality of the Church is its worship. Paul quotes what is widely assumed to be an early Christian hymn in Philippians 2, in which the incarnation, the obedience unto death, and the exaltation of Jesus are celebrated (Phil. 2:6–11). Similarly, Colossians 1:15–20 is a Christ hymn, in which the divinely given role of Jesus in the creation and redemption of the universe is portrayed. Earlier, we noted hymns included by Luke in his stories of the birth and childhood of Jesus (Luke 1–2). Ephesians makes explicit that common life in the Spirit manifests itself through "addressing one another in psalms and hymns and spiritual songs, singing and making melody to the Lord with all your heart" (Eph. 5:19). Thanks, in the name of the Lord Jesus Christ, are to be given to God "for everything" (5:20). Stability, contentment, and respectability are to characterize the Church as the author of Ephesians represents it.

---

[11] An excellent summary of these household lists is that of Eduard Lohse, in *Colossians and Ephesians, A Commentary* (Philadelphia: Fortress Press, 1971), pp. 154–63.

THE APOSTLE AS AGENT OF AUTHORITY: THE PASTORALS

Further development of the Pauline tradition is documented in the three let-ters known as 1 Timothy, 2 Timothy, and Titus, all purportedly addressed to younger associates of Paul. Scholars have long treated the three as a distinct group of writings, designating them the Pastoral Epistles. The common strat-egy of these short writings is to portray Paul as he neared the end of his apos-tolic career, offering warnings and advice to those who will carry on after him. This device of pseudonymity does not conceal the fact, however, that the au-thor is addressing the situation of his own time, probably the early second century. His conceptual goal is succinctly set out in 1 Timothy 1:5: "The aim of our charge [to our successors] is love that issues from a pure heart and a good conscience and sincere faith."

The basic problem confronted in the Pastorals is the mix of bad doctrine and immoral behavior fostered by the opposition and threatening to under-mine the integrity of the Christian community. It was these interrelated issues of faith and practice that were to trouble the Church internally in the second and subsequent centuries. (The concurrent problem of the Church's stance to-ward the Roman culture, and especially the Roman state, will occupy us in Chapter 12). How did the writer of the Pastorals perceive the difficulties, and how did he propose dealing with them?

Right Belief and Right Behavior

Central to the well-being of God's people is sound doctrine; from it there is to be no deviation (1 Tim. 1:3). Those who were regarded as "swerving" from these norms were involved in "vain discussion," including "myths and endless genealogies" (1:4–6). Apparently the reference here is to the growth of speculation about emanations from the divine and a hierarchy of celestial beings of the kind later elaborated by Valentine and other Gnostics. A similar denunciation of the false teachers is uttered in 1 Timothy 4:6–8, where the myths are denounced as "silly," and in 2 Timothy 4:3–4, where those who find these speculations appealing are said to be afflicted with "itching ears." The primary task of the successor of the apostle is to "give instruction in sound doctrine," which requires him both to "hold firm to the sure word as taught" and "to confute those who contradict it" (Titus 1:9).

The direct link between sound doctrine and good conscience that per-meates the Pastorals shows that this segment of early Christianity is per-suaded that faulty theology gives rise to immoral behavior. This is vividly set forth when, following a list of various forms of wickedness—including murder of one's parents, sodomy, kidnapping—the writer adds: "and whatever else is contrary to sound doctrine" (1 Tim. 1:10). Those who fail to join correct faith and sound doctrine make "shipwreck of their faith" (1 Tim. 1:19). The "un-holy, inhuman, implacable slanderers and profligates" of 2 Timothy 3:3 are at the same time those of "counterfeit faith" who "oppose the truth" (3:8). The proponents of false doctrines are possessed of corrupt minds and consciences (Titus 1:15). The one dimension of the author's announced aim that is missing is love. Lashing out at those whose theology is unsound, he declares: "They profess to know God, but they deny him by their deeds; they are detestable, disobedient, unfit for any good deed" (Titus 1:16). After the heretic has been admonished "once or twice," if he fails to return to the true faith, "have nothing more to do with him" (Titus 3:10).

Conversely, those persons who are models of good deeds, manifesting "integrity and gravity," showing "entire and true fidelity," are those who "adorn the doctrine of God our Savior" (Titus 2:9–10). As for their faith, they have been responsible stewards of the treasure that has been entrusted to them. "The glorious gospel of the blessed God" was first committed to Paul (1 Tim. 1:11); he has now transferred that trust to Timothy (1 Tim. 6:20). Or, as it is stated in 2 Timothy 1:11–14, Paul had been commissioned as preacher, apostle, and teacher; he has entrusted Timothy with the truth, which he is to guard, and with the "pattern of sound words," which he is to follow. Similarly, that sacred trust is to be passed on to others, who will in turn share it with those who succeed them (2 Tim. 2:2). It will be preserved until the Day of Judgment (2 Tim. 1:12). Although the imagery of the Spirit is still used, the work of the Spirit is seen as preservation, stability, normative doctrine, rather than as the spontaneity and charismatic endowment for urgent tasks in view of the imminent end of the age, as in Paul's own letters.

True Piety

Before turning our attention to what "sound faith" includes, we must consider what kind of moral life a "good conscience" would produce. The role of apostolic leadership inevitably involves suffering (2 Tim. 1:11) and conflict (1 Tim. 1:18). Timothy is instructed to "fight the good fight of faith" (1 Tim. 6:12). The purpose of enduring suffering is the achievement of self-discipline. In a series of vivid metaphors—including a soldier, an athlete, and a farmer—"Paul" tells Timothy how struggle, competition, and hard work are essential for producing desirable results. There will be persecutions from the civil authorities, as Paul has himself experienced (2 Tim. 3:11–12), but what is called for is patient endurance, in confidence that God will care for his own, and will reward fidelity on the Day of Judgment (2 Tim. 4:8). Yet what is to be striven for is not conflict, but peace (2 Tim. 2:22), and a life in conformity to the law (1 Tim. 1:8).

Conceived in this way, the Christian life is a religion or a system of piety (in Greek, *eusebeia*), a term never used by Paul, but common in Hellenistic philosophy and religions. The discipline of the Christian is aimed at the attainment of piety (1 Tim. 4:7), which will be characterized by proper speech and conduct and purity of heart (1 Tim. 4:12; 2 Tim. 2:22). The development of true religion begins with baptism, which is described as "the washing of regeneration" (Titus 3:5), and is then fostered by a Christian upbringing (2 Tim. 3:15). Indeed, Timothy is a member of the third generation of Christians in which maternal instruction has fostered his "sincere faith" (2 Tim. 1:5).

Essential to the Christian nurture, through family instruction and public reading, are the scriptures (2 Tim. 3:16; 1 Tim. 4:13). It is impossible to tell whether that term refers only to the Jewish Bible the Christians had adopted as their own, or whether—as we can infer from other early second-century Christian writings and from 2 Peter 3:15–16—the Christians were already assembling what was to become the collection of sacred writings that we know as the New Testament (see Epilogue). The corporate worship life of this Christian community is presupposed by the hymn quoted in 1 Timothy 3:16, which is preceded by the liturgical words, "Great, indeed, we confess, is the mystery of our religion." Confession is the common public declaration in a context of worship of the ground of the community's faith. Not surprisingly, the confessions were to become not merely the ground and norm of inclusion within the Church, but the basis of controversy and schism among Christians, since by inference and even by design, the confessions defined those who were to be excluded as well as those who were orthodox.

The distinguishing mark of the true Christian was the life of responsible Christian citizenship. That responsibility was to be evident both within what is significantly called "the household of God" (1 Tim. 3:15) and toward the culture at large. Thus, slaves are to obey their masters "so that the name of God and of the teaching [Christian instruction] may not be defamed" (1 Tim. 6:1). Christians are to be models of good deeds and self-control (Titus 2:6–7), renouncing irreligion and living lives of sobriety and uprightness (2:12). The public image of the pious Christian is effectively summarized in Titus 3:1–2: ". . . be submissive to rulers and authorities, obedient, ready for any honest work . . . speak evil of no one, avoid quarreling, be gentle, show perfect courtesy toward all."

Yet one of the false practices the author sees as flowing from false doctrine is that of asceticism. The heretics are requiring of their followers abstinence from marriage and from certain foods (1 Tim. 4:2), as well as from wine (1 Tim. 5:23). The author regards this attitude as contrary to the correct view of creation, which affirms that everything comes from God and is to be accepted gratefully, including sexual and gustatory experiences. Although physical exercise (in Greek, *gymnasia*) is of some value, it does not play the central function in the achievement of spirituality assigned to it by the ascetics, and is in any case inferior in importance to true piety (1 Tim. 4:7–8). For the community represented by the Pastorals, there is no denigration of bodily, physical existence. The creation and its essential goodness are affirmed; the Christian is asked to use responsibly the resources God has given.

A Creed in Process of Formulation

But what is the "sincere faith" that is correlated with the "good conscience"? It is a doctrine wholly compatible with the conviction that "everything created by God is good" (1 Tim. 4:4)—namely, that "the blessed and only Sovereign, the King of kings and the Lord of lords" (1 Tim. 6:15) has already in Jesus Christ caused salvation to appear within the human realm (Titus 2:11). His work of redemption of the human race is completed:

He was manifested in the flesh,
vindicated in the Spirit,
seen by angels,
preached among the nations,
believed on in the world,
taken up into glory.

—1 TIM. 3:16

In describing how God has disclosed and accomplished his saving purpose for the world, the author uses the technical term of Hellenistic religions, *epiphany* (in Greek *epiphaneia*), which means "the self-disclosure of a divinity." Paul prefers rather to refer[12] to Jesus's expected appearance to his people at the end of the age as *parousia,* a word not found in Colossians, Ephesians, or the Pastorals. More than a verbal distinction is involved. For Paul, Jesus has been with God since the Resurrection and will return to earth to signify the accomplishment of divine sovereignty over creation, the establishment of the kingdom of God, the age to come. For the Pastorals, however, the rule of God has already been disclosed—and here the verb root is identical with that of the noun, *epiphaneia:* "The grace of God has appeared for the salvation of all men" (Titus 2:11); "When the lovingkindness and goodness of God our Savior appeared, he saved us" (Titus 3:4–5). The kingdom looked forward to in the Pastorals is in heaven (2 Tim. 4:18). The only future role of Christ still awaited by the Church is that of judge (2 Tim. 4:1, 8). Eternal life was promised ages ago, but now "at the proper time" has been "manifested through the preaching" with which Paul and his successors have been entrusted.

One doctrinal point on which we might expect clarity from the writer of the Pastorals is the relationship of Jesus to God. At times he seems to make a sharp distinction: "God the Father and Jesus Christ our Lord" (1 Tim. 1:2); "there is one God, and one mediator between God and men, the man Christ Jesus" (1 Tim. 2:5). Elsewhere, however, both God and Jesus are identified as "savior": God, in 1 Timothy 2:3, 4:10; Titus 2:10, 3:4; Christ in Titus 1:4, 3:6. One can only conclude that the sharp distinctions between God and Christ that were to be developed in the later creeds of the Church had not yet been formulated. But the interchangeable titles of Jesus and God already imply that the former is being perceived in more than merely human terms.

Office and Rank in the Church

Much more precise are the definition of role and the enunciation of qualifications for the various levels of officials in the churches. 1 Timothy 3:1–13 consists of a list of requisites and responsibilities for those designated as bishops and deacons. The managerial function of the bishop is pointed to in 3:5, where the need to organize and administer his own household is compared with his tasks along similar lines in the Church.

[12] Some scholars deduce from the fact that *epiphaneia* occurs only in 2 Thessalonians among the letters we are attributing to Paul the conclusion that Paul did not write this work. For a discussion of the authenticity of the letter, see Kümmel, *Introduction to the New Testament* (Nashville: Abingdon Press, 1975), pp. 264–69.

Also taken into account is the changing role of women in the churches. It is likely that the "women" mentioned in 3:11 are deaconesses. From the relatively frequent mention of women in the personal greetings addressed by Paul to and from the churches in Rome (Rom. 16) and Corinth (1 Cor. 16), we should infer that women from the outset had leadership roles in the churches founded by him. Although in general the place for women leaders seems to have diminished in the later second century and subsequently, their standing appears to have been a significant factor in the churches of the Pastorals. The widows of 1 Timothy 5 may be women on a welfare plan, or they may be older women, free of family responsibilities, who devoted themselves to the work of the Church, something like the nuns of a later period.

The elders (1 Tim. 5:17–22) have the office of rulers within the Church, and are to receive financial support from the churches over which they preside. The elders, and presumably the other officers as well, are to be selected by a deliberate process, and then commissioned by a ceremony of laying on of hands. Thus Timothy received his trust of the Gospel and his assignment within the Church, as well as the power of God to carry out his tasks, "through the laying on of my hands" (2 Tim. 1:3).

The only mention of bishop in the authentic letters of Paul is in Philippians 1:1, where the term occurs in the plural. That is, there are bishops in Philippi at the initial stage, rather than a single presiding bishop. The Greek word *episkopos* means simply "overseer," and it is not surprising that there would be a group of overseers in a local church. In the Pastorals, the plural of the title is used, though with no indication as to whether there was more than one bishop in any given place. There is no hint, however, of a single bishop in a city or territory with central authority over the Church there.

In the early Christian writings outside the New Testament, however, there are indications of the development of what Church historians have called "the monarchic episcopacy." Perhaps the earliest of these is in the writing of Clement of Rome (A.D. 96–97), in which he asserts that "the detestable and unholy sedition" which has been created in the church at Corinth by "a few headstrong and self-willed persons" has brought dishonor to a community famed for the respect in which its elders were held, the "modest and seemly thoughts" of the young, and the discretion of its households (sec. 1).[13] More than the reputation of the Corinthian Christians is at stake, however: The schism there is in conflict with the cosmic order established by God throughout his creation (sec. 20; 33). What Clement calls for is a recognition of the diversity that should characterize the body of Christ, including both the powerful and the members of more modest capacities (sec. 37). Most important, however, is the necessity to submit to the authority of the bishops throughout the Church, since they have been appointed by the apostles and carry forward the authority invested by Christ in the apostles (sec. 42). Once commissioned, the bishops are not to be deposed, since they stand as successors to the apostles (sec. 44).

In the early second century Ignatius, bishop of Antioch in Syria, was taken in custody and escorted to Rome, where he was to be martyred under

[13] Clement, *Epistle to the Corinthians*, trans. J. B. Lightfoot (1891, reprinted Grand Rapids: Baker Book House, 1965).

the emperor Trajan (A.D. 98–117). Linking the mind of Christ to the mind of God, and the mind of the bishop to the mind of Christ (Ignatius, Eph. 3), Ignatius instructs the Ephesian Christians to be attuned to the mind of the bishop, in order to produce a chorus of harmony and concord, singing in unison a hymn of praise to God through Christ (Ignatius, Eph. 4). Setting aside the musical imagery, his warning is direct: "Be careful not to resist the bishop, that by our submission we may give ourselves to God" (Ignatius, Eph. 5). Stated more strongly, he declares: "We ought to regard the bishop as the Lord Himself" (Eph. 6). Elsewhere he asserts that the bishop presides in God's place (Ignatius, Magn. 6), and that Christians should "do nothing apart from the bishop" (Ignatius, Phil. 7). Or again, "He who pays the bishop honor has been honored by God, but he who acts without the bishop's knowledge is in the devil's service" (Ignatius, Smyrna 9). The gathering of the Church, the practice of baptism, and the celebration of the Eucharist are invalid unless approved by the bishop or by one to whom he has delegated responsibility (Ignatius, Smyrna 8). Through him, the presbyters and deacons carry out their responsibilities; but the bishop is the deputy of Christ. Though his authority derives from God through Christ, it is absolute in the churches over which he presides.

GUIDEBOOKS FOR COMMUNITY LIFE: THE TWO WAYS

Other documents preserved from the late first or early second century show that the institution of episcopal authority was not universal in the Church of this period. Two closely related writings—in that they share a central section which outlines the "two ways" of life open to Christians—are the Epistle of Barnabas and the so-called Didache (from the Greek word for "teaching" or "instruction"). As in the letters of Paul, bishops and deacons are appointed locally to assume certain responsibilities necessary for the life of the community as a whole (Did. 15:1–2). The important role represented by these writings themselves is that of the instructor, whose explanation of the scriptures and of the Jesus tradition provides the basis for the moral and liturgical life of the Christian communities. Both writings were originally composed in Greek, as evidenced by their common use of the Septuagint for Old Testament quotations, and by their frequently making points in the argument that turn on a Greek original. Neither writer claims to be an innovator, nor does he stress his own authority. Rather, each is handing on tradition, much as Paul claims in 1 Corinthians 11:23ff to be passing on to others what he received "from the Lord." Since this passage is one of the very few in Paul where there is any direct overlap between his letters and the material found in the Gospels (cf. Mark 14:22–25 and parallels), it is important to note that he is not talking about what he received by revelation, but what came to him—probably by oral tradition—as recalled by the disciples of Jesus, and traced back by them to the original Last Supper. We have no clues as to a possible chain of tradition in the case of either Barnabas or Didache. Although the earliest manuscript of each (dating from the fourth century) assigns one writing to Barnabas (apparently meaning the companion of Paul mentioned in his letters and in Acts) and calls the other The Teaching of the Twelve Apostles, both are anonymous works. Both give clear evidence of having grown and developed in the course of use within the Church, so it is pointless and probably impossible to date them, either in their present form or in terms of the materials they incorporate.[14] The single historical clue in either is the reference in Barnabas to the Jerusalem temple standing in ruins, which points to a post-70 A.D. date (Barn. 16:4). The fact that the emperor Hadrian built a Temple of Zeus on the site about 135 may require us to assume that Barnabas wrote between these two dates. But what is evident in both these writings is the evolution of standards and guidebooks for Christian worship and moral practice, building on older tradition, including the New Testament writings.

These two documents—Barnabas and Didache—by their mixture of overlap and dissimilarities show how differently the Christian tradition developed in the period during which the later New Testament books were being written. Common to Barnabas and Didache is the extended treatment of moral obligation in terms of "the Way of Life" and "the Way of Death" (Barn. 18–21; Did. 1–6).[15] The details shared by the two versions of this material are nearly all stated in the imperative—"do" or "do not"—and derive mostly from the Old Testament. Some, however, such as the appeal to a conscience, show the influence of Hellenistic moral concepts and terminology. In their catalogues of vices, both versions include sorcery and magic. But they also emphasize failure to meet the needs of the poor and the downtrodden (Did. 5:1–2; Barn. 20:1–2). Both emphasize love of neighbor, apparently quoting Leviticus 19:18.

Barnabas places the whole of his body of instructions in the setting of what he calls "the perfect *gnosis*" (1:5). Yet even if one possesses *gnosis*, should he follow the Way of Darkness, he shall perish (5:4). That *gnosis* includes wisdom concerning not only present events, but knowledge of the past and of "what is about to happen." Barnabas has little to say about the events of the future, except for the Day of Judgment, when all humanity will be accountable to God for their deeds, whether good or evil. The Church is the true heir of the covenant promises to ancient Israel, which has now been abandoned by God (4:8) and replaced by the Church as the new people of God. The sufferings of Christ were both foretold and foreshadowed in the Old Testament. One of Barnabas's insights, of which he is exceedingly proud, is his observation that the number of those circumcised by Abraham (Gen. 14:14), which is 318, is a symbolic number pointing to the Crucifixion of Jesus. Taking advantage of the numerical value assigned to Greek letters, Barnabas observes

[14] Robert A. Kraft has coined the appropriate term "evolved literature" for the type of writing that evolves as it is used, in his excellent introduction, translation, and notes, *The Apostolic Fathers: A Translation and Commentary,* Vol. 3, *The Didache and Barnabas* (New York: Thomas Nelson, 1965), pp. 1–3.

[15] Some scholars have seen in the opening of the Dead Sea Manual of Discipline or Scroll of the Rule (2:18–4:25) an analogy or even a prototype of the two ways. But the Qumran moral exhortations are more abstract than the specific, direct moral injunctions of the two ways. Both build on the contrast of light and darkness (that is, life and death), but the distinction is too commonplace to warrant an assumption of dependence of the Christian two ways on the Qumran sect.

that 18 equals JE (that is, Jesus), while 300 equals tau (T), which represents the cross. The author comments: "No one has learned from me a more trust-worthy lesson!" (Barn. 9:9). The temple is the heart of the Christian in which God dwells (6:14; 16:1–10). Circumcision is the transformation of the ears and the heart, so that the divine wisdom can be grasped (9:1–10:12). The Sabbath is the symbol of the completion of God's work in the creation (15:1–9). The highest values for Barnabas are enunciated at the end of his writing, where he promises the faithful "wisdom, insight, understanding, gnosis, endurance" (21:5).

In Didache, however, both the framework in which the two ways are set out and the details unique to this writing are different from Barnabas. The climactic emphasis of this work is on the need to be ready for the final period, which will bring to a close the present age and usher in the age to come (Did. 16:1–8). The community will pass through testing and be fractured from within by apostasy prior to the last judgment, when all human beings will be called to account. This aspect of the document cannot be regarded as the vestige of a fading eschatological belief, but constitutes rather an urgent expectation and motivation for a group living at the end of the present epoch. Far more evidence is present in Didache than in Barnabas that the Jesus tradition—especially the promises and warnings of the so-called Sermon on the Mount—is part of the living, authoritative basis of this community. At times the author transmits the Gospel tradition in a form closer to Matthew; at other times he shows the influence of Luke's version of the material. This is possibly an indication that this source is being preserved by oral memory, rather than by reliance on the written Gospels, even though the latter were known in widening circles in the second century.[16]

Yet even though Didache expects the end of the age, the writer gives detailed instructions about the life of the Church, both liturgically and administratively. There are specific guidelines about the sacraments of baptism and the Eucharist, about fasting and prayer (Did. 8–9), and about practices not explained to the reader but presumably comprehensible to them: "unction" and "sacrifice" (Did. 10:8; 14:1–3). An extended section treats the rules for hospitality and support for the itinerant apostles, prophets, and evangelists who spend time with a local church. The local roles of prophecy and instruction are to be carried out by bishops and deacons locally appointed, as we noted above. In the details of the moral appeal, the impact of the synoptic apocalypse in the form known to us from Matthew 24–25 is especially powerful. It is surely not an accident but a significant indicator of kinship that the basic prayer set forth by Didache is the Lord's Prayer—in its Matthean version, with the addition of the ascription of praise to God now in common use, though not in Matthew ("For power and glory are yours forever").

In the letter of Polycarp, bishop of Smyrna,[17] written to the Philippians during the reign of Hadrian (117–138), there is an appeal to "the wisdom of the blessed and glorious Paul" (sec. 3). The form of the ethical instruction in

---

[16] See Helmut Koester, *Synoptische Überlieferungen bei den apostolischen Vätern* (Synoptic Traditions in the Apostolic Fathers) (Berlin: Akademie Verlag, 1957).

[17] Modern Izmir, on the west coast of Turkey, north of the site of Ephesus.

the letter is that of the household lists, with guidelines for wives, widows, deacons, younger men, and elders (presbyters). His writing is filled with quotes from scripture, which include the letters of Paul and the writings attributed to John.[18] There are direct quotations from the Gospels as well, however (sec. 2), so that the tendency to look to either Jesus or Paul as the source of tradition seems to be fading. Whether this trend is the cause or the result of the emergence of a Christian canon of scripture in this period is impossible to say; perhaps both processes were mutually supporting. Significantly, both for Polycarp personally and for the Church in this period, the linking of the Jesus and Pauline traditions leads to the formulation of a policy toward the persecutions that were beginning to mount in intensity, and that by the middle of the second century were to bring Polycarp himself to a martyr's death. Some twenty years before that event, he wrote in this letter: "Pray also for kings and powers and princes, and for them that persecute you and hate you, and for the enemies of the cross, that your fruit may be manifest among all men, and that you may be perfect in Him" (sec. 12). Here he is adapting the words of Jesus from the Sermon on the Mount (Matt. 5:43–44), as well as Paul's instructions to the Roman church about the attitude toward the state (Rom. 13:1), but with the addition of a direct allusion to 1 Timothy 2:1–2, where prayer for the rulers is enjoined.

What we see developing in the first part of the second century is the consolidation of the Church organizationally and conceptually. The earlier differences among the leaders were the results of personal links with Jesus or Paul, and were widened by local cultural influences on the way in which the Christian Gospel was heard and received. Those particular factors have now begun to fade. The eschatological hope is no longer the occasion for improvisation, but remains rather a reminder of ultimate responsibility to God and the eventual day of reckoning. Rooting out schismatics and encouraging behavior among Christians that is conducive to harmony and responsibility within the Church and a good public image are primary concerns. But the price of organizational efficiency and social appeal is vulnerability. The movement that uses the title "Lord," "sovereign," "king" in its liturgy and awaits a coming kingdom cannot avoid suspicion and hostility on the part of an imperial power that is itself struggling to achieve universal sovereignty. How that inescapable problem was dealt with in various segments of the early Christian community is the focus of the next chapter.

---

[18] Section 7 quotes 2 John 7 concerning the need to acknowledge that Jesus came "in the flesh;" that is, not as a spiritual phantasm.

12

Encounter
With the Roman World:
James, Hebrews,
1 Peter, Revelation

In a profound sense, all of Christianity arose from encounters with the Roman world. The central figure was crucified as a violator of Roman law under Pontius Pilate. Ancient tradition reported that his birth occurred in Bethlehem as the result of a decree of Caesar Augustus. The movement as a whole, however, had spread with only occasional notice by or conflict with the Roman authorities. Its leaders and writers had imbibed Greco-Roman culture almost unconsciously, except for a few like the writer of Luke-Acts, who exploited his knowledge of the culture for propaganda goals. By the end of the first century, however, the Church was forced by circumstances to adopt a conscious policy toward the Roman state and its predominant culture. It is some of these responses, and the range of their differences, that can be traced in the later New Testament writings. In this chapter we will deal with external pressures; in the next chapter, our major concern will be the pressures that arose from within.

The differing responses to Rome correlated directly with the estimate of the state and the prevailing culture that each segment of the Christian movement developed. The reactions varied from subtle syntheses to violent hostility, with distinguishable gradations in between. Unqualified opposition to Rome is apparent in the Revelation to John. Radical modification of the older apocalyptic world view, adapting it to prevailing conceptual currents, may be seen in the Letter to the Hebrews. More eclectic in the use of contemporary culture and more ambivalent in the stance toward the state are, respectively, James and 1 Peter. Each of these writings embodies an attitude that continued to influence Christianity in subsequent centuries. Each adopts a different world view and defines the Christian community in its own distinctive way. We begin with the more conciliatory writings, James and 1 Peter, and then move to a work that is more aggressive in its synthesis of Christian faith and pagan thought, Hebrews. Finally we look at one that is equally aggressive in its denunciation of the Roman state, Revelation.

PEACEABLE WISDOM

[JAMES 3:17]

Only the opening lines of James resemble a letter. There the writer identifies himself imprecisely—James, a servant of God and of the Lord Jesus Christ (1:1)—while his addressees are even more vaguely designated: "the twelve tribes in the Dispersion." The body of the writing is a discourse, not a letter, and leans heavily on the diatribe style of Hellenistic philosophy. This style is well exemplified in a letter attributed to Socrates, but probably written in the

The Colosseum in Rome. Built by Vespasian and Titus as an arena for great public spectacles, it seated more than 50,000 people. In the later years of the empire, many Christians were slain here by Roman gladiators and wild animals.   (*Courtesy of Lufthansa Airlines*)

early second century A.D.[1] In it the author asks questions of the reader, and then furnishes the answers. The tone is provocative, with vivid illustrations drawn from everyday life, such as the analogy between persons using cosmetics to cover up their true complexion and concealing their moral condition by performing showy good deeds. The writer composes questions and objections his opponents will raise and answers them. One of the major issues treated in these so-called philosophical letters is the problem of wealth and personal possessions, and the immoral effect of riches on the possessor. "Socrates" proclaims his freedom from that sinister power, as a consequence of his refusal to accept pay for his services. Both the style of James and the major recurrent issue discussed in this "letter," written in the name of a worthy Christian of an earlier era, of wealth and poverty, are akin to the style and strategy of the Cynic diatribes.

[1] Text and translation of these letters attributed to Socrates in *The Cynic Letters,* ed. Abraham Malherbe (Missoula, Mont.: Scholars Press, 1977), esp. No. 6, pp. 232–39.

The Old Testament Heritage

James, the announced writer of this epistle, cannot have been the brother of Jesus, who was leader of the Jerusalem church according to Paul (Gal. 1:15) and Acts (15:13). The aspects of the Jewish law which according to Paul remained of fundamental importance for James and his Jerusalem-based group were circumcision and ritual purity in relation to dietary laws (Gal. 2:12). These matters are not so much as hinted at in the Letter of James. Furthermore, the language of the document is smooth, literate Greek, and the biblical text used throughout is the Septuagint, neither of which one would expect from a Semitic-speaking ex-Galilean villager. As the opening lines assert, and as the body of the epistle confirms, Israel as such is no longer a significant factor for the writer. The people of God is the Church (5:14).

So completely has the author claimed the heritage of the Old Testament for his Christian readers that he draws his illustrations from that source, rather than from the Jesus tradition. It is Abraham (2:21–24), Rahab the harlot (2:25), Job (5:11), and Elijah (5:17) who are the shining examples of faith and perseverance for James. The suffering of Jesus is never mentioned, nor are his Crucifixion and Resurrection. Indeed, except in the formulaic introductions of 1:1 and 2:1, the name of Jesus is never used. Throughout the letter it is difficult to know whether "Lord" is a reference to God or to Christ. Although the author uses the same word for trial or testing (in Greek, *peirasmos*) that occurs in the Gospel tradition, the temptation is not described as the work of Satan or the Devil (as in Mark 1:13; Matt. 4:1), but as originating within the individual and stimulated by personal desire. There seems even to be a rejection of the idea implied in the Lord's Prayer, "lead us not into temptation" (Matt. 6:13) when James declares that God tempts no one (1:13). The devil can still harass Christians, but if resisted will flee (4:7). In James there is little of the framework of conflict between good and evil, between the agents of God and those of Satan, which are basic for the Gospels and Paul. God is more distant, and evil arises from within human desire.

The importance of the law is basic to James's view of true religion: "He who looks into the perfect law, the law of liberty, and perseveres, being no hearer that forgets but a doer that acts, he shall be blessed in his doing" (1:25). Elsewhere there are references to the "law of liberty" (2:12) and to the "royal law" (2:8). Warnings are issued against those who speak evil against the law or judge it (4:11–12). Yet surprisingly little of the Jewish law is actually quoted or alluded to. The commandments against adultery and murder are quoted in brief form (2:11; Exod. 20:13–14; Deut. 5:17–18), but they are mentioned only to show that one cannot obey part of the law and ignore or violate another part. The most positive attitude evident toward any specific precept is the quotation from Leviticus 19:18 (James 2:8): "You shall love your neighbor as yourself." This is, of course, a central feature of the teaching of Jesus, as reported in the synoptic tradition (Mark 12:28–34; Matt. 22:34–40; Luke 10:25–28), where Jesus replies to the inquiry about the greatest commandment by combining love of God and love of neighbor. But James does not, even implicitly, refer to Jesus's response; he merely quotes in abbreviated form the precept from Leviticus.

The Cultural Context

As for the structure of the Church implied in James, only elders are mentioned (5:14). They are to be called in to perform a ceremony of anointing, with the aim of cure for the sick. Neither bishops nor deacons appear in the writing; there is no mention of baptism or the Eucharist. The central figure in the Church, at least in the opinion of James, is the teacher. His sudden shift into the first person plural (3:1)—"we who teach"—makes it clear that he is one who bears that solemn responsibility. It requires bridling of the tongue, which has a potential for affecting the whole course of a human life (3:3–5).

In the course of his discussion of the great influence of the tongue, James uses a series of comparisons that are also to be found in popular Hellenistic philosophies of the period: the bit and the horse, the ship and the rudder, fire raging out of control, the expected produce of springs and fruit-bearing trees (3:3–12). In the midst of this list of metaphors, however, James mentions the "wheel of life" (3:6), a notion that has no counterpart in Jewish imagery, but derives rather from the notion, found among the speculative philosophies of the Orphics and Pythagoreans, of metempsychosis, according to which the human soul moves at death to another body and continues thereby the "wheel of life."[2] Similarly, terms that had currency in ancient astronomy are used loosely in 1:17, where it is asserted that with the Father of Lights "there is no variation nor shadow cast by change."[3] The point is that, although changes in the heavenly bodies are evident through shadows—eclipses and the solstices—there is no change in the God who controls them and all of human life as well. In 1:21, the phrase "implanted word" recalls the Stoic image of divine reason as a seed (*logos spermatikos*) permeating and vivifying the world and human understanding of it. Barnabas uses the same term to describe the gift of the Spirit (Barn. 1:2; 9:9) by which the divinely given instruction enables the faithful to achieve true knowledge. Here, then, is a writer who is in touch with contemporary culture, who knows its language and appreciates its concerns and insights. He endeavors to express his understanding of Christian faith and responsibility in such a way as to make contact with that culture, to exploit it and adapt it to his own purposes, so that while his readers remain faithful to their Christian heritage, they may affirm their beliefs with rationality and self-respect.

Steadfastness and Wisdom

The central interest of James is laid down in the opening lines of the work, with the exhortation to strive for (1) steadfastness, which can lead one to perfection and (2) wisdom, which God gives generously to those who ask for it (1:2–5). The chief characteristic of one who gains such wisdom will be integrity. Its opposite is the instability and lack of direction of the double-minded

[2] Discussed by Sophie Laws in *The Epistle of James* (San Francisco: Harper & Row, 1981), p. 151. Laws notes that the idea is also found in Plato.

[3] See also Laws, *James*, pp. 73–74.

person (1:7–8), who will receive nothing from God. The highest goal of human aspiration is "perfection and integrity" (1:4). In describing how it may be achieved, James shows remarkable kinship to the popular Stoic philosophers of his day.

In the famous Hymn to Zeus by Cleanthes, the third-century Stoic philosopher and successor of Zeno as head of that school, there is a celebration of (1) the universal divine plan for the creation, (2) humankind's kinship with the god through reason (*logos*), and (3) the true happiness of those who live in accord with universal law (*nomos*). Seneca, philosopher and counselor to emperors (4 B.C.–A.D. 65), transformed the viewpoint of Cleanthes's hymn by acclaiming the god as father of the human race. The divine presence within human lives he identified as soul and reason (using *ratio*, the Latin equivalent of *logos*). The human's highest good is attained if he or she lives in accord with this principle, akin to and bestowed by the god. Like Paul, James would agree with Seneca (Epist. xli.1): that "God is near you, he is with you, he is within you. . . . A holy spirit dwells within us." This divine presence within human beings, which he equated with soul and reason, is moving them toward perfection (Epist. xli.7): "Reason is nothing else than a portion of the divine spirit set in a human body" (Epist. lxvi.12). Human beings can achieve the highest good if they have fulfilled the good for which they were designed by the god at birth (Epist. xli.8).

For James, the gifts men and women possess come down from the Father of Lights, who "of his own will brought us forth by the word [*logos*] of truth that we should be a kind of first fruits of his creatures" (1:18). The central gift is wisdom. Coming "from above," it "is first pure, then peaceable, gentle, open to reason, full of mercy and good fruits, without uncertainty or insincerity" (3:17). What it produces is peace and righteousness (3:18). Similarly for Seneca, the virtues that are produced in the life lived according to divine reason are wisdom, justice, a noble steadfastness, and a calm stance toward life (Epist. xxiii.7). According to James, it is the testing of one's faith that develops steadfastness. Such testing is not sent by God, but arises from wrong motivations and evil desires that emerge within the person (1:2–3, 13–15). Seneca declared that the forces which seem to be harmful are actually working for the preservation of the world and are part of the divine scheme for bringing to fulfillment the order of the universe. Human beings should develop their own resources so that what seems evil can be overcome. By the power of reason, pain and wrong can be brought under control, and they will arm one to triumph over the greatest hardship (Epist. lxxiv.20). Although Seneca had no concept of the future return of a savior figure, as did James (5:8), he taught that there is a divinely determined plan for the universe, which will move through conflict and even cosmic conflagration to the fulfillment of that purpose.[4]

---

[4] F. H. Sandbach, *The Stoics* (London: Chatto and Windus, 1975), notes the belief in the eschatological fire, which remained part of Stoic orthodoxy down to the time of Marcus Aurelius (late second century A.D.). The themes of the ultimate fire and the divine plan are discussed by Seneca in his "Questions about Nature" (3:27) and "On Providence," respectively.

The Integrity of Belief and Behavior

Both Epictetus (50–120?) and Seneca considered human virtue to be attainable only in a social framework, not as an individual accomplishment. For Epictetus a cardinal virtue was *pistis* (usually translated in James and throughout the New Testament as "faith"), which for him meant "reliability, loyalty, helpfulness." In his *Discourses* (I.13–4–5), the desired effect of this virtue is the emergence of an orderly society—in short, a brotherhood. Using the mode of rhetorical questions that we discover in James as well, Epictetus writes: "Will you not endure your brother, who has the god (Zeus) as his forefather, who is as it were born of the same seed as you and begotten like you from above?" One must always keep one's eyes fixed on the divine law, and thereby deal justly with one's brothers and sisters. Similarly, James speaks of the "royal law" of love of neighbor (2:8), which is also the perfect law of liberty (1:25). His argument against special favors for the rich (2:1–7), against showing partiality (2:9), against failure to aid the needy (2:14–17), against pride (4:6,10), against complaints against others (5:9)—all turn on the power of love of neighbor. For Seneca the unity of human common life is achieved, in spite of the diversity of persons in social status and power, by the indwelling spirit, which he equates with reason (Epist. lxvi.33–34).

James claims to be quoting scripture when he asks the rhetorical question: "Do you suppose it is in vain that the scripture says, 'He yearns jealously over the spirit which he has made to dwell in us'?" (4:5). There is no such passage of Jewish scripture in any surviving canon or in any other writing that contains these words. But they come very close to the point of view found throughout the writings of James's contemporaries, Seneca and Epictetus. This is not to claim that he is quoting from them, or from any other non-Jewish or non-Christian source. Rather, James has so thoroughly adopted from popular philosophy and then adapted for his own purposes the concept of the divine spirit as the indwelling agent that frees men and women from enslavement to the material world and enables them to live in peace and harmony that he can simply identify his source as possessing authority equal to that of the traditional sacred writings. James is not criticizing contemporary culture, nor is he carelessly conforming to it. Rather, he is seeking to transform it, in order to make it useful in the service of the Christian community of which he is a part and for which he bears a deep sense of responsibility. His strategy was to set a pattern for other Christian teachers and apologists in the early second and subsequent centuries.

The integrity for which he calls is discernible in various ways in his brief epistle. We have observed some of the details of his effort to blend faith and culture. He is deeply committed to the unity of the Christian community as well. But most important of all for him is the integrity of belief and behavior. His discussion of faith and works, while using the Pauline debate in Romans 3–4 and Galatians 1–3 as its literary starting point, has actually moved far from the issue central in Paul's lifetime: whether Christians had to become Jews (by circumcision and obedience to ritual law) before they could be acknowledged as members of the community. Law is for James the universal rule of human moral obligation, to be discerned in the Old Testament, but in broadly human ethical principles as well. It is the integration of faith and practice that, in James's view, will achieve the unity of God's people and their conformity to the divine purpose.

SEEKING A HEAVENLY HOMELAND
[HEB. 11:14]

The writing known as *The Letter to the Hebrews* is both a masterpiece and an enigma. The oldest copy of this document[5] identifies it as "To the Hebrews," in a manner like Paul's letters to the Romans, the Corinthians, and the rest. Yet this work is not a letter. It includes a few lines of a personal nature (Heb. 13:22–24), but they follow the formal conclusion to the document, and have no point of contact with the main body. The opening section of Hebrews has none of the characteristic features of letters from this or any other period, and throughout there are no suggestions of a specific occasion for the writing.

Indeed, the personal remarks made in passing imply that this communication was meant to be presented orally. The medium used by the author, as evidenced by the terms he uses, has to do with speaking and hearing, not writing and reading (2:5; 5:11; 6:9; 8:1; 9:5; 11:32). The use of alliteration, and the author's excellent Greek, combined with the skillful way in which he underscores recurrent themes and leads from explanation to exhortation and back again, would make an effective vehicle of oral communication. What seems likely, therefore, is that what was originally written for oral presentation has been addressed to a wider audience by means of material appended to the work in the form we now have it.

Purpose and Sources

If we assume that this document was not originally a letter, what are we to conclude about its being addressed "to the Hebrews"? Was it sent to Jews? Or at least to Jewish Christians? There are more than a hundred quotations from or clear allusions to the Jewish scriptures. Major parts of the argument of the work as a whole turn on the author's interpretation of such texts as Psalms 2, 8, 110 and Jeremiah 31, as we will note below. Many of the moral appeals in Hebrews 12 and 13 depend directly on parts of the Jewish Bible, both the law and the prophets. A major feature of the work (Heb. 11) consists of a summary of details from the history of ancient Israel. The dominant theme of the book as a whole is the true worship of God through the authentic high priest. Was it written as a kind of reform move within Judaism? Clearly not, since the argument seeks to prove the obsolescence of the Jewish system, and explicitly excludes from participation in Christian worship the Jewish priests: "We have an altar from which those who serve the tent [i.e., the Jewish sanc-

---

[5] P[46], the early manuscript of the New Testament mentioned in Chapter 11, note 1, includes Hebrews with the Pauline letters.

tuary] have no right to eat" (Heb. 13:10). Significantly, that shrine is always referred to as "the Tent" rather than "the Temple," which suggests that the author is contrasting the Jewish *system* of cultic approach to God with the one he regards as the "true tent," which opens access to the very throne of God in heaven (Heb. 8:2). Whether the Temple in Jerusalem was standing or not is unimportant for the writer.[6] His contention is that the priestly pattern outlined in the scriptures has now been superseded. What is of central importance is the contrast between the perfect sanctuary in heaven and the imperfect "copy and shadow" on earth, as depicted in scripture (8:5).

At many crucial points, the argument of the author turns on the text of scripture as it appears in the Septuagint, as distinct from what is in the Hebrew Bible. For example, the effort to show that Christ is superior to the angels culminates at 2:7 in an argument from scripture: "Thou didst make him for a little while lower than the angels," quoted from Psalms 8:5 in the Septuagint. The point is obvious: God placed Jesus, during his incarnation, at a lower status than the angels, and then exalted him to his role of glory and universal sovereignty. The Hebrew original, however, says: "Thou hast made him little less than God." Both the contrast between Jesus and the angels and his temporary humiliation are absent from the Semitic source, but both can be documented in the Greek translation used by the author of Hebrews. Similarly, in Hebrews 1:3 there is an allusion to two attributes of wisdom, as presented in The Wisdom of Solomon 7:25, so that it is now Christ who is "the reflection of the divine glory" and "bears the impress of the divine nature." That writing is part of the Septuagint, and therefore in the Bible of the early Church, but it had no Hebrew original and was therefore excluded from the canon of scripture adopted by Jewish leaders in Palestine in the last decade of the first century.

The world view evident in Hebrews is that of a group which sees itself as the true heirs to the biblical tradition, the true members of the new covenant community (8:6–13). Yet the concept of a sacrificial system and of a priestly intermediary who offers access to God is by no means dismissed along with the "obsolete" covenant of Israel (8:13). The dominant theme of the entire work is that God has provided through Christ a new access to his presence and has opened the way for a newly defined people to attain that access. Far more is involved in the contrast than a simple old-new way. To discern this fundamental difference, we must examine portions of Hebrews in detail.

A Synthesis of Biblical History and Greek Metaphysics

One of the results of increasing emphasis among later prophets and Jewish wisdom-teachers on the transcendence of God, with its stress on his remoteness and his otherness from human beings, was the growth of concepts of intermediary beings to bridge the gap between God and his universe. This is

[6] Some interpreters of Hebrews have assumed that the writer's mention of the cult sacrifices implies that the Temple was still standing and functioning when he wrote, which would place the date of the document before A.D. 70.

apparent in wisdom speculation, as we have noted, in the assignment to wisdom of the role of God's chief assistant in the actual creation of the world (Prov. 8:22–31; Wisd. of Sol. 7:15–8:1). Other kinds of speculation built on the ancient notion of God as surrounded by angelic beings (Isa. 6:2–6; Ezek. 1:4–2:1) to assign them roles in carrying out his work. In Psalm 91:11–13, the angels guard the faithful. In Daniel 10:13 and 12:1, Michael appears as helper to Daniel and the faithful community. In Jude 9 and Revelation 12:7, he leads the opposition to the hosts of evil. Similarly, Gabriel has a role as interpreter of the divine messages in Daniel 8:16 and 9:21, and in Luke 1:19, 26, where he helps the mothers of John the Baptist and of Jesus understand that the wanted but long-delayed pregnancies are part of the divine plan of redemption.

It appears that those who wanted to discredit Jesus or misguided members of the Christian community were assigning him a place among these angelic aides of God. The author of Hebrews seizes on this notion as the point of departure for his setting forth the uniqueness of Jesus in God's plan. An important factor in Jewish conviction about the binding nature of the Mosaic law was the tradition that when it was given on Sinai, angels were present to convey it to humans and to confirm its divine origin (2:2).[7] Our author begins with that assumption to demonstrate the superiority of Jesus not only to the angels, but also to the ritual access to God it established.

Hebrews opens with a statement about how God communicates to the human race (1:1–2). Although he does not use the technical term *logos,* as in the opening of the Gospel of John, the author uses verbs that match the creative speaking of God in Genesis 1, "And God said. . . ." Earlier he spoke through the prophets; now he has spoken in a son. But the son was fulfilling his role—which corresponds to that of wisdom in the Jewish tradition—in the process of creation from the beginning, since he radiates the divine glory and bears the divine impress, and especially since it is his word that now upholds the universe (1:3). The final task assigned to him in God's plan is purification for sins. Having completed that, through his incarnation and death, he has been exalted to the highest place of honor in the universe: seated at God's right hand. Here the author has already alluded to a text that will be central to the whole of his document, Psalm 110. That text in Jewish tradition was a royal psalm; that is, a hymn or ritual used in connection with or in celebration of the enthronement of Israel's king. Since the psalm combines in one person the roles of king and priest, however, it cannot come from the time of the Davidic rulers, when the descendants of Levi were the hereditary priests. Rather, it must date from early in the Maccabean epoch (165–40 B.C.), when the rulers combined the functions of kings and priests. We will see how important that factor is for the author of Hebrews.

The significance of Christ is traced out by a string of quotations from scripture: he is God's Son (Ps. 2:7; 2 Sam. 7:14); he is worshipped by the angels (Deut. 32:43 in Septuagint); he is addressed as God and assigned a royal throne (Ps. 45:6–7); he is the anointed of God (Messiah); he is called Lord (Ps.

---

[7] Elsewhere in the New Testament the apparently widespread belief that angels, or heavenly messengers, were present at the giving of the law on Sinai is documented: Galatians 3:19; Acts 7:53.

102:25–27 in Septuagint). Most important, however, is the claim that he is not subject to time or change—he is an eternal being. He is now seated at God's right hand awaiting achievement of full sovereignty (Ps. 110:1). By contrast, angels are merely those who serve (Heb. 1:14). That "little while" of suffering and death in the incarnation was necessary if he was to have full identity with weak, erring humanity. But now that it is past, he is already seated at the right hand of God (2:3–4). Now he has been "crowned with glory and honor" (2:7; cf. Ps. 8:4–6). In tragedy and triumph, he is the pioneer and perfecter of human salvation (2:10).

The use of these two terms—in Greek, *archēgos* and *teleiotēs*—and their repetition at the crucial concluding section of the work (12:2) provide a clue to the framework of meaning in which Jesus is understood by the author of Hebrews. That inference is confirmed by scores of details as well as by the cumulative argument of the book. Jesus is here represented as the originator and the consummator of the divine purpose for the universe. The first of these terms is used by Plato[8] to designate the force that brings into existence the entire universe, the personification of that which puts first principles into action and thus brings into being the visible, tangible world. In the Platonic system, reality consists of eternal master-images or models in the heavens. All earthly phenomena are merely copies of the heavenly realities, transient and subject to decay. Their existence is continually repeated as new copies replace the old, so that their multiplicity contrasts with the unchanging archetype from which they derive. The beginning (in Greek, *archē*) of this process is assigned to the *archēgos*. The completion (in Greek, *teleiosis*) of the process would result in the replacement of the transitory world and the triumph of the eternal world of heavenly realities. Is it possible that the author of the Hebrews has this sophisticated philosophical system in mind?

That this is indeed the case is stated in unequivocal terms in 8:1–13. So that the hearer or reader will not miss the force of the argument, the passage is introduced by the notice: "Now the point in what we are saying is this. . . ." He then states that the sacrifice of Jesus (which is once for all, 7:27) as "the priest forever" (5:6; 6:20; 7:21) was presented before the throne of God in the "true" sanctuary (8:2). But the author then goes on to explain that the inadequacy of the earthly sacrificial system derives from the fact that it is merely "a copy and shadow of the heavenly sanctuary" (8:5). That point is made in scripture, when God told Moses: "See that you make everything according to the pattern which was shown you on the mountain" (8:5). That passage, quoted from Exodus 25:40 in the Septuagint, uses the term *typos*, which in the Platonic system is the technical word for the celestial archetypes.[9] Similarly, the terms found in 8:5, "copy" and "shadow," are used by Platonists to designate the transitory earthly copies of the eternal models. The old cultic system, with its repetitive offerings and fallible priests—of which the annual Yom Kippur, Day of Atonement, is the enduring expression—was a reminder that the ultimate divine provision for human redemption had not yet been disclosed (9:1–10). The experiences of the present are not meaningless, however,

[8] *Timaeus* 21E.
[9] Plato, *Republic* 379a.

since they point symbolically to the new order (9:10) in which the divine purpose will be accomplished or perfected.[10]

That goal has now been attained: "But when Christ appeared as a high priest of the good things that have come, then through the greater and more perfect tent [not made with hands—that is, not of this creation] he entered once for all into the Holy Place, taking not the blood of bulls and goats but his own blood, thus securing eternal redemption" (9:11–12). The same claim is repeated in slightly different words in 9:24 and in 10:12–14, where we are reminded that, having completed the eternal[11] sacrifice, Christ is now seated at God's right hand.

The only human response appropriate to this divine action is faith, the ability to look beyond present transitory existence to the divine reality. Technical philosophical terms are used in 11:1, where *hypostasis* (usually translated as "assurance") means "substance, reality, exact representation," and *elenchos* ("conviction") means "proof of ultimate realities." In this life, that archetypal reality remains unseen and hoped for. Yet faith asserts its being, because Christ has already entered and opened the way. The stories of the men and women of faith in the experiences of the old covenant community (Israel) have positive value, since they show in each case how faith can look beyond space and time to the divine promise of the heavenly reality (Heb. 11). Faith enabled them to survive tragedy and abuse, since they "endured as seeing him who is invisible" (11:27). It was not until God's ultimate word was spoken (Heb. 1:1–2), the once-for-all sacrifice presented in the heavenly sanctuary (9:24), and the eternal access to the divine presence opened (10:19–20) that the constitution of the new and true people of God was complete (11:39–40).

Guidance, norms, and models for earthly existence are now provided for the faithful through Jesus, "the originator and accomplisher of our faith" (12:2). What is called for is perseverance, the ability to see trials and difficulties in eternal perspective, "so that you may not grow weary or fainthearted" (12:3). There is no need to rehearse the basic doctrines of the Church—though he does list them (6:1–2), including repentance and faith, baptism and laying on of hands, the Resurrection and judgment. Those who defect from the faith have no possibility of restoration to the community (6:4–8). The details of the moral obligations within the community derive from the scriptures, but are influenced by Stoicism as well, as evidenced by the recurrent term "conscience" (9:9, 14; 10:2, 22). Also akin to the Stoic world view are the repeated references to the Day of Judgment (4:7; 9:27; 10:27).

Only vestiges of the earlier belief in the *parousia* of Jesus at the end of the age survive in Hebrews. In 9:28 there is the promise that the High Priest will become visible to his people once more, although he goes on to declare that already "by a single offering he has perfected for all time those who are sanctified" (10:14). Temporal existence is for the writer a situation of discipline

---

[10] Here too is a technical term for an enduring order, as contrasted with a transient condition. Plato, *Laws* 1, p. 642.

[11] From the time of Homer on, the term translated in the Revised Standard Version of the Bible as "for all time" (as in Heb. 10:12) means "forever" or "eternally," as contrasted with the merely temporal.

(12:7), yet through faith the members of the community already share in "the city of the living God, the heavenly Jerusalem" with its "innumerable angels in festal gathering ... the assembly of the first-born who are enrolled in heaven." There the faithful are already in the presence of "a judge who is God of all, and ... Jesus, the mediator of a new covenant. . . ." (12:22–24). Meanwhile, the members are to exhibit basic human concerns: brotherly love, hospitality to strangers, marital fidelity, avoidance of love of money, support for Church leaders.[12] They are to avoid "strange teachings," to participate in the food of the altar, to be prepared for persecution, to make financial contributions, and to offer continual praise to God (13:1–17).

Who Wrote Hebrews?

There is no way to determine by whom, for whom, from where, or to where this document was prepared. The closing lines, with the personal remarks, mention "those who come from Italy," which could mean that local members of Italian origin send greetings back to Rome. That inference receives meager support from the fact that a leadership designation used in 13:7, 17 is also attested from Rome in Clement's Letter to the Corinthians (1 Clem. 1), and from the occurrence in Clement's letter of the oldest surviving quotation from Hebrews (1 Clem. 36:2–5; Heb. 1:1–14). The vocabulary and viewpoint are basically different from that of Paul. The closest kinship in style and mode of biblical interpretation is with the works of the Jewish philosopher and biblical interpreter Philo of Alexandria, with his symbolic method of exegesis and mixture of Platonic and Stoic orientation. Some scholars have conjectured that the one early Christian leader whom we know to have come from Alexandria, Apollos, wrote this work (Acts 18:24–28).

That is not an impossibility, but we have no information about his writings or his ecclesiastical role. Recent studies of extrabiblical Jewish sources have made it clear that Jews in Palestine as well as in other cities around the Mediterranean were writing in Greek, and that they were seeking to restate their religious convictions in terms of the prevailing intellectual and ethical modes of their day. The Testaments of the Twelve Patriarchs, for example, though it deals with the messianic hopes of Israel,[13] in its discussion of responsibility to "the law" uses distinctive ethical terms derived from Stoicism (self-control, imperturbability, integrity, and the law of nature) without any reference to the specific commandments of the Mosaic code. It is basically Jewish in its concerns; it is thoroughly Hellenistic in its language and intellectual outlook. Similarly, the so-called 4 Maccabees retells the story of the Macca-

---

[12] The leaders are not given the title of bishop, elder, or deacon, as in the Pauline tradition. The term used here, *hēgoumenoi,* is also found in 1 Clement.

[13] Although there are fragmentary documents from Qumran that purport to be the last will and testament of some of the sons of Jacob, their language is Semitic, and their content does not overlap with the Testaments of the Twelve Patriarchs. For details of the ethical stance of the Testaments of the Twelve Patriarchs, see my introduction and translation in *The Pseudepigrapha,* ed. J. H. Charlesworth, vol. 2 (Garden City, N.Y.: Doubleday, 1984).

bean victory over the Seleucids in terms of Stoic virtues. The use of Hellenistic philosophy in the interpretation of Jewish scripture and history was not invented by the author of Hebrews or by any other Christian; it had a long and rich development within Judaism before and during the time of Jesus.[14]

The importance of Hebrews for the subsequent life of Christianity can scarcely be overestimated. Here the precedent was established to synthesize faith and culture, to take over claims of pagan origin and to exploit them for fresh interpretation of Christian tradition. It was in the work of Clement and Origen of Alexandria—the so-called Christian Platonists—in the late second and early third centuries that this intellectual strategy developed. It enabled Christianity to engage and to persuade those with scholastic interests. At the same time, it opened the door for the importation into Christian thinking of ideas that the main body of the Church later came to denounce as heresy. Tertullian discerned this danger in the late second century as he watched the rise of Gnosticism, and he warned that Athens (the symbol of pagan academic values) and Jerusalem had nothing to do with each other. These factors will occupy us in the next chapter. Hebrews stands as a monument to one segment of the Christian community that was convinced God's sovereignty over the creation extended beyond feelings or personal piety to the intellectual dimensions of human existence, so that faith should not reject culture, but seek to transform it.

A PEACEFUL PEOPLE
PREPARES FOR SUFFERING
[1 PET. 4:12]

1 Peter calls on Christians to be prepared always "to offer a reasoned defense [in Greek, *apologia*] to any one who calls you to account" for your faith (3:15). There can be no mistake that the author expects members of the Christian community to take on those who oppose them on rational or political grounds. The challenge and solemn warnings laid down in this short letter are attributed to Peter the apostle (1:1), although the concluding remarks imply that it was written by or at least dictated to Silvanus (5:12). Someone of that name is mentioned as an associate of the apostles in Acts 15–18, and is linked with Paul in several of his letters (2 Cor. 1:19; 1 Thess. 1:1; 2 Thess. 1:1). Is it likely that Peter, who vacillated on the issue of accepting Gentiles into the Christian fellowship (Gal. 2:11–14), would now be so eager to engage them, and to do so at an intellectual level? When the text is read in the original, it is apparent that it was written in sophisticated, highly literate Greek, with the biblical quotations from the Septuagint. Once again, we have in 1 Peter, therefore, a writing that appeals to apostolic tradition and claims apostolic authority, but that is written by a later generation and addressed to circumstances for both the Church and its environment that are different from those during the lifetime of the apostles.

[14] A masterful, fully documented study of the relationship of Judaism to Hellenism is Martin Hengel's *Judaism and Hellenism*, 2 vols. (Philadelphia: Fortress Press, 1974).

Writer and Purpose

The letter is an encyclical, written for circulation among the churches of northern Asia Minor (1:1). Of those mentioned, only Galatia was visited by Paul.[15] Acts 16:6–7 reports that Paul was divinely hindered from going into this territory, but offers no clue to the reason why. It is possible that, since Paul's declared "ambition [was] to preach the gospel, not where Christ has already been named" (Rom. 15:20), he could not enter these Black Sea regions because Peter had already gone there. Whether that was the case or not, Peter was the apostle whose name and associated image of "the Rock" carried special authority there, as 2:4–8 shows.

One of the few Roman historical texts that mention Christians comes from this region of the empire. In the correspondence between Pliny the Younger (A.D. 62–113) and Emperor Trajan (98–117) while Pliny was governor of Bithynia, there is a discussion about handling the Christians, whose movement was spreading so rapidly in his district that attendance at the official shrines was dropping off drastically.[16] Does this evidence require us to assume so late a date for 1 Peter? Probably not. The problem Pliny faces is not new in his time; it is rather that he is new to it and to the region. The conflict between the empire and the Church can be documented in Roman historians back to the time of Nero,[17] but it seems to have been localized in Rome itself and to have faded with Nero's death. Domitian, as we have noted, apparently found Christian converts within the imperial household and reacted violently to stamp out the movement, which he rightly saw as a threat to the promotion of divine honors to himself as emperor. The persecution of Christians in Asia Minor, which seems to have been the immediate occasion for 1 Peter (4:12–16), could have begun any time after A.D. 95. But that would be long after Peter had died.

The Apocalyptic View

While the theme of the trials the Christian faces permeates the letter from beginning (1:6) to end (5:9–10), much more space in the document is devoted to quite different themes: the respectability of the Christian community and its stability as an organization. The latter should contribute to the former. Building on the traditional Jewish image of the covenant people as pilgrims, exiles, or in dispersion (1:1; 2:11), the writer stresses the transience of the present life, as did James. Yet the underlying assumption about the imper-

[15] Some scholars think Paul never visited the northern part of the province of Galatia, adjacent to those provinces listed in 1 Peter, which border the Black Sea. But Paul's heated letter to the Galatians is interested in issues, rather than political geography.

[16] Pliny, *Letters* 10.94. Text and commentary, ed. A. N. Sherwin-White, *Fifty Letters of Pliny* (New York: Oxford University Press, 1967).

[17] Tacitus, in his *Annals* 15:44, describes the horrors committed by Nero against the Christians in Rome, whom he made scapegoats for his own mad arson in setting fire to the city. They were slaughtered, burned, crucified, and torn to pieces by wild animals to amuse the crowds in the circus.

manence of life is not at all that of Hebrews, with its contrast between the phenomenal and the ideal worlds. Rather, 1 Peter's world view is still largely shaped by the earlier apocalyptic outlook, even though the outward circumstances and inner state of the community are significantly different from those in the time of Paul or of Mark. Though he portrays the Church as structured and stable, and pleads for its members to deport themselves as law-abiding Roman subjects (2:13, 17), the writer of Peter is convinced that the present age will soon end (4:7), and that the great event awaiting the Christians is "the revelation [in Greek, *apokalypsis*] of Jesus Christ" triumphant over his and God's enemies (1:7). Yet for the author of 1 Peter, of greater importance is how Christians "live for the rest of the time" until the end comes (4:2).

Strong indications of the kinship between the world view of 1 Peter and the apocalyptic outlook of Paul come from the importance attached by both to the Resurrection of Christ (1 Pet. 1:3, 21; 3:18, 21)—an event never mentioned by the author of Hebrews. Still more revealing is the way that the Old Testament tradition is understood in 1 Peter, in contrast to the Platonic model found in Hebrews. In 1 Peter 3:18–4:6 the experience of Christ includes not only death and being "made alive in the spirit," but also a visit to the imprisoned disobedient spirits languishing, presumably, in the underworld. The connection with Noah (3:20) shows that the author is taking over a tradition based on the curious account in Genesis 6, which tells how the cross-breeding of angels and women resulted in the corruption of the human race and moved God to judge the world, destroying all its inhabitants except the eight saved in Noah's ark (Gen. 7). That story was elaborated in Jewish apocalyptic circles, as is evident from 1 Enoch, which devotes nearly twenty chapters (6–22) to the account of Enoch's earnest but fruitless intercession for them with God. By the time of 1 Enoch (second century B.C.), the fallen angels (disobedient spirits) have names and special roles. The author of 1 Peter has adapted this tradition to show that even the pagan rulers should have a chance to hear the Gospel, since Christ (like Enoch) preached to the wicked angels. The connection between the destiny of the fallen angels and that of earthly rulers is also made explicit in a later section of Enoch, known as the Similitudes (67:12) and dating from the first century A.D..

Other typical features of the apocalyptic world view are evident in 1 Peter: the future judgment (2:12; 4:5); the presence and the scheming of the Devil (5:8–9); the interpretation of present suffering as prelude to impending vindication (4:12; 5:12). Those of the flock who remain faithful during the present time of testing will obtain "the unfading crown of glory" when at the end of the age the chief shepherd is manifested (5:4). Then God will fully and finally restore and establish his people (5:10).

How the Community Is to Live

Meanwhile, however, how is the community to live? 1 Peter addresses that question in broad symbolic terms as well as in precise, pragmatic instructions. Using a series of vivid metaphors, the author portrays God's new people (2:4–10). Prior to that section, he has used imagery shared with the Greco-

Roman mystery cults, which speak of initiation into the cult group as new birth. Unlike the mystery religions, however, for whose devotees the moment of mystical transport and the experience of spiritual renewal were ends in themselves, for 1 Peter the Christian is "born anew" (1:3) into a new hope, for a new age of fulfillment in the future. The ground of that hope is the Resurrection of Christ. Its present base is the divine promise, "the word of the Lord which abides forever" (1:25), and the corporate strength of the new community of faith in which the faithful are called to grow toward spiritual maturity (2:1–3).

The interlocking imagery begins with an allusion to Christ as the rock, a living foundation for the community of faith, and a stone on which the unbelieving stumble (alluding to Ps. 118:22 and Isa. 8:14–15). But the members of the community are also "living stones" (2:5), who together constitute "a spiritual house." This could imply a common dwelling place, or as is more likely, a household—that is, a structured society of the faithful. The function of this new religious society is that of a holy (2:5) or royal (2:9) priesthood, which offers spiritual sacrifices to God through Jesus Christ. In contrast to Hebrews, where Christ as High Priest is the central figure, for the author of 1 Peter there is a corporate priesthood, in which all have access to God and perform the appropriate acts of devotion.

The distinction between this new covenant people and the old covenant community of Israel is sharpened in 2:9–10, where it is the Christians who are the elect race and the holy nation. They have no historic or ethnic claim on God. But God has chosen to illumine them and to shower his grace upon them, so that they "now are God's people." So completely have the members of this new community taken over the tradition of Israel for themselves that they can even refer to outsiders as "Gentiles" (2:11). Although there is not a hint of ritual or dietary purity for this community, it has appropriated for itself the blend of divine demand and declaration that established Israel as the covenant people: "You shall be holy, for I am holy" (Lev. 11:44–45; 1 Pet. 1:16).

In spite of this special status as God's chosen people and regardless of the promise of the end of the present order, the community is called to respectability, not rebellion. It is precisely as "aliens and exiles" that they are to "maintain good conduct among the Gentiles" (2:12). They are to obey their earthly rulers, from local governors to the emperor. Indeed, they are instructed to honor Caesar (2:17). Here is obvious kinship with the point of view of Paul (Rom. 13), for whom civil disobedience was incompatible with Christian responsibility. The writer is intensely realistic, however. He knows there will be conflicts that will result in persecution, but insists that the conflict must arise because the Christian has done what is right and not because of violation of the Roman law. He hopes that non-Christians will be impressed by the virtuous lives of Christians (2:12), even to the point of being astounded when the faithful refuse to take part in the self-indulgent sensuality of the contemporary culture (4:3–5). Stated succinctly, "It is better to suffer for doing right, if that should be God's will, than for doing wrong" (3:17). For this style of life, Christ is the supreme example (2:21); he did not revile his tormentors or threaten them, trusting rather in the judge of the universe.

The oldest bapistry (reconstruction) ever found was in a tiny chapel at Dura Europos, on the Euphrates River in northeastern Syria. The walls of the chapel, which was destroyed in A.D. 258, were covered with paintings of biblical scenes, traces of which are still visible. The person to be baptized stood in the shallow pool and had water poured over his head.   (*Yale University Art Gallery, Dura Europos Collection*)

Internally, there is to be "unity of spirit,[18] sympathy, love of the brethren, a tender heart and a humble mind" (3:8). The concrete evidence of that mutuality is to be seen in the submissive behavior of servants (2:18–25) and of wives to their husbands (3:1–6), and in the consideration husbands show for members of "the weaker sex" (3:7). Women are warned against ostentatious dress (3:3–5), which suggests that there were wealthy women in the community who were vulnerable on this charge. The implication of the letter that the social stratification of this community included the rich is congruent with the literary evidence that its author was a literate person who expected his readers to be attracted to and persuaded by his rather elegant style.

The sole reference to sacramental usage in the community is the link between Noah's ark and baptism, with the former as the symbolic equivalent of the latter. The claim is explicit: "Baptism . . . now saves you" (3:21). The notion of ritual salvation is immediately qualified, however, by the references to purity of conscience and the redemptive role of Jesus Christ, by whose Resurrection the powers of evil are already overcome. In spite of the symbolic reference in this mention of baptism, it offers evidence of the tendency to regard the sacraments no longer as merely symbols of divine action, but as efficacious instruments.

[18] Apart from mention of the Spirit in the trinitarian formula at the opening of the letter ("God the Father . . . Spirit . . . Jesus Christ," 1:2), the Spirit plays no role in 1 Peter.

The only ecclesiastical role mentioned by 1 Peter is that of the elders. The younger members are called upon to respect them (5:5), and they are to exercise authority within the community with constraint and compassion, to set an example for the flock (5:1–3). Apparently the elders received some kind of compensation for their work, although they are warned against exploiting their role for personal gain. The writer identifies himself as a "fellow elder," rather than as an apostle or a bishop. Deacons are never mentioned in the letter, and the only one to receive the title of bishop is Christ (2:25).[19] Although, as in Hebrews and in Paul, Jesus has been exalted at God's right hand, he is not (as in Hebrews) a celestial archetype, but a human example of suffering and obedience. As he conducted himself before the authorities, so the members of the faithful community are to be prepared to offer their defense, but to do so "with gentleness and reverence" (3:15).

CHRIST OR CAESAR:
THE REVELATION TO JOHN

In the confrontation with an increasingly hostile state, not every segment of the Christian community was willing to adopt the attitude of tranquil courage enjoined in 1 Peter. Radically different in viewpoint, and radical in its assessment of the Christian situation, is the Revelation to John. Outwardly 1 Peter and Revelation appear to have marked features in common. Both expect the end of the age to occur soon (1 Pet. 4:7; Rev. 1:3). Both regard the community with the image of a corporate priesthood (1 Pet. 2·9; Rev. 1:6). For 1 Peter, the central issue is suffering as a Christian (4:16); in Revelation, it is "on account of the testimony of Jesus" that John the seer is on Patmos, either in exile or in prison. Both expect vindication by God at "the revelation of Jesus Christ" (1 Pet. 1:7; Rev. 19:11–16). Yet the world views embodied in these two documents are significantly different. The crisis growing out of the imperial insistence on divine honors in the reign of Domitian (A.D. 81–96) elicited different responses among Christians. That of Revelation is the most dramatic and the most radical.

A Unique Apocalypse

In order to assess the strategy of this work, we must examine its literary origins and aims. Both the first word of this text, *apokalypsis,* and its overall use of visions and vivid imagery prove its kinship with Jewish apocalyptic writings. Daniel and the visions of Ezekiel have deeply and directly influenced the writer, as shown by his portraits of world empires with the image of grotesque beasts (Rev. 17; Dan. 7) and his description of God's new dwelling place among his people (Rev. 21:2–4; Ezek. 43). The use of symbolic numbers and the predictions of conditions prior to the end that last for a predetermined number of days (Dan. 12:11–12; Rev. 11:3; 12:6) are also features characteris-

---

[19] Modern translations prefer to render *episkopos* in this passage by a nontechnical term, such as "guardian," "keeper," or "overseer," rather than as "bishop."

tic of apocalyptic writing. More important than the literary elements, however, is the framework of fundamental conflict between the power of God and
that of his adversary (Satan) in terms of which the struggle of God's people is
understood by apocalyptists. There is mention of the Devil and of the need to
resist him in 1 Peter, as well as of Christ's engaging the hostile powers after his
death and prior to his exaltation. But these become dominant elements in the
outlook of Revelation.

Equally important for the apocalyptic outlook in general, and for Revelation in particular, is the way in which the community for whom the writing
was produced regarded itself, both internally and in relation to the power
structures of its contemporary world. As studies in the anthropological[20] and
sociological[21] fields have shown, members of groups that hold an apocalyptic
world view customarily sense themselves to be only on the fringe of the wider
social, political, and cultural forces. Though they may appear insignificant to
society from the perspective of outsiders, they believe that God has given them
privileged information about his present and future purposes. They are called
upon to accept opposition, suffering, or even death, but they look forward to
God's vindication of them in the near future. Mark and the Q tradition, as
well as Paul, represent this point of view within the New Testament, in spite
of differences in details.

As can be discerned from the book of Daniel, the divine revelation is not
offered to the elect community in the form of a blueprint of the future or a
carefully outlined scenario. Rather, the knowledge of the end of the age is
communicated in elaborate cryptic images, dramatic and compelling in their
intensity, but conveying nothing to those who lack insight into the mystery.
An important aspect of apocalyptic belief is that those who claim to be the
heirs of the religious tradition have betrayed it, either by indifference or by
direct violation. Both the apostates and the worldly powers have become the
instruments of Satan; but God will triumph over them in his time and by his
own agents.

Although most of these features are evident in Revelation, there are
some important differences between the Revelation of John and most other
apocalypses. Those produced within Judaism are regularly pseudonymous. In
them, the writer has adopted the role of a figure from the past, such as Ezra or
Daniel (from the days of the exile of Israel in Babylon) or Enoch (from antediluvian times) or one of the prophets. Revelation, on the other hand, seems to
have been written by someone actually named John, who speaks to his readers
out of a shared set of circumstances. His apocalypse begins where he sees the
Christian community to be now—that is, in his own time—rather than
adopting the literary fiction of moving back into an earlier epoch. John ex-

[20] For example, K. O. L. Burridge's study of millennarian sects, in *New Heaven, New Earth: A Study of Millennarian Activities* (New York: Schocken Books, 1969).

[21] Norman Cohn, *The Pursuit of the Millennium,* 2nd ed. (New York: Harper & Row, 1961); Bryan Wilson, *Magic and the Millennium* (New York: Harper & Row, 1973). For an extended discussion, see John G. Gager, *Kingdom and Community: The Social World of Early Christianity* (Englewood Cliffs, N.J.: Prentice-Hall, 1975); and additional bibliography in H. C. Kee, *Christian Origins in Sociological Perspective* (Philadelphia: Westminster Press, 1980), pp. 174–77.

pects his apocalypse to be read aloud (1:3). Unlike Daniel (12:4), his work is not to be sealed up (22:10), but is to be referred to continually by the community (22:6, 9), heard and heeded (22:18). The close identification between the seer and his addressees is explicit: "I John, your brother, . . . share with you in Jesus the tribulation and the kingdom[22] and the patient endurance" (1:9). There is no hint as to the identity of "John," other than his common name. He does not claim to be an apostle or a follower of Jesus. His language is reasonably fluent Greek, with quotations from the Septuagint, but with traces of Semitic idiom as well. He is best designated simply as "John the seer."

The apocalypse, apart from the letterlike introduction (1:1–11) and conclusion (22:6–21), is divided into two major sections: the vision of "one like a son of man," who instructs John to deliver messages to the seven churches of Asia Minor (1:12–3:22); and a series of visions, oracles, prayers, and hymns (4:1–22:5). The literary structure of the main section of Revelation is complex. Clearly marked out are three clusters of sevens: seven seals; seven trumpets; seven angels with seven plagues. But interrupting the sequence of each of these are interludes and apparent shifts of focus or subject. Some scholars have tried to account for this by supposing that an original document has been carelessly edited, or that two separate documents were rather crudely joined. But from reading other apocalypses, one should learn not to expect simple logical or chronological narrative sequence. Obviously, the ultimate interest is the eschatological outcome: the defeat of the powers of evil and the establishment of God's rule. But the strategy of this type of writing is to move back and forth between hopes of deliverance for the faithful and warnings of catastrophe for the disobedient or indifferent. One of the more appealing proposals for an outline of the apocalypse is the following:

OUTLINE*

A. Prologue and epistolary frame 1:1–8	Title 1:1–83
	Greeting 1:4–6
	Motto 1:7–8
B. The Community under judgment 1:9–3:22	Author and situation 1:9–10
	Inaugural vision 1:11–20
	(1) Censure and encouragement 2:1–3:22 (seven messages)
C. God's and Christ's reign 4:1–9:21; 11:14–19	Heavenly court 4:1–5:14
	(2) Seven seals 6:1–8:1
	(3) Seven trumpets 8:2–9:21; 11:14–19

(Arabic numbers designate seven series)

* From *Invitation to the Book of Revelation* by Elisabeth Schüssler Fiorenza. Commentary copyright © 1981 by Elisabeth Schüssler Fiorenza. Reprinted by permission of Doubleday & Company, Inc.

[22] As may be inferred from Revelation 1:6, "kingdom" is one of the terms John uses for the community itself, since he is convinced that God's sovereign rule is already operative in the truly obedient Church.

D. The Community and its oppressors 10:1–11:13; 12:1–15:4	Prophetic commissioning 10:1–11:13 Enemies of the community 12:1–14:5 Eschatological harvest and liberation 14:6–20; 15:2–4
C'. Judgment of Babylon/ Rome 15:1,5–19:10	(4) Seven bowls 15:1,5–16:21 Rome and its power 17:1–18 Judgment of Rome 18:1–19:10
B'. Final judgment and salvation 19:11–22:9	Parousia and judgment 19:11–20:15 The new world of God 21:1–8 The new city of God 21:9–22:9
A'. Epilogue and epistolary frame	Revelatory sayings 22:10–17 Epistolary conclusion 22:18–21

This analysis of the structure of the Revelation resembles the menorah, or traditional Jewish seven-branched lampstand, with pairings of (1) the epistolary beginning and end, of (2) the sections dealing with judgment, of (3) the contrast between God's promised reign and the reign of Satan. The central portion depicts the faithful community and its present testing.

The Risk of Martyrdom

The letters to the seven churches (Rev. 3–4) reflect local circumstances of the late first century in all probability, but the allusions or images can no longer be determined in most instances. What is commended in nearly every one of the seven churches is the fidelity of the members in the face of threatened persecution. The ground of that threat is not explicitly stated, but the best clue is provided by the description of Pergamum as "where Satan's throne is" or "where Satan dwells"—that is, where the chief center of the imperial cult is located (2:13). From the time of Augustus (30 B.C.–A.D. 14), the

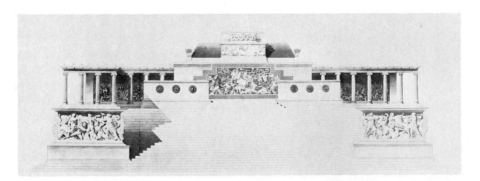

The Great Altar of Zeus at Pergamum: a reconstruction. With its grand proportions and its magnificent sculpture, this was one of the wonders of the ancient world. The allusion to Satan's throne in the letter to the church at Pergamum (Rev. 2:13) may have been a reference to this colossal architectural monument.

The Stoa of Attalos has been reconstructed at the foot of the Acropolis. The original was built as a public portico by Attalos II, King of Pergamum, and the marble for the reconstruction was taken from the same quarry that he used in the middle of the second century B.C. *(Courtesy of the American School of Classical Studies, Athens)*

cities of Asia Minor vied with one another for the favor of the Roman rulers by fostering the cult of Rome and the divinized emperor. The divinity of the king had been an accepted politico-religious concept in the eastern Mediterranean since ancient times, but it had been promoted by the successors of Alexander the Great. Now the fundamental issue for the Christians of the area, many of whom were from the wealthy merchant classes, was whether they should participate in the ceremonies of divine honors to the emperor. To do so, even in a perfunctory way, would contribute to social acceptance and freedom from governmental hostility. To refuse to do so might mean death. Should Christians go along with what they knew to be an empty show in order to survive? On this issue John could not allow any compromise.

The other problems John addresses in his allusive, symbolic style in the letters to the churches are more difficult to specify. At Ephesus there seem to have been those who, in his view, falsely claimed apostolic authority for themselves (2:2). In Smyrna, some were calling themselves "Jews" but were actually of "the synagogue of Satan" (2:9)—which may be a cryptic way of saying that some professing members of the covenant community were betraying that alliance by taking part in the imperial cult. A similar accusation is brought against the church of Philadelphia in 3:9. In Thyatira, the church is tolerating a new Jezebel (2:20), namesake of the queen who promoted the worship of Baal, the heathen god, in the days of the prophet Elijah (1 Kings 16:31); she is a false prophetess, encouraging idolatry and the eating of food offered to idols. The latter problem appeared early in the churches under Paul's care, as 1 Corinthians 8 shows. Apparently social conformity among the affluent Christians of Asia Minor led many to participate in sacred meals which they probably regarded as in essence foolish nonsense, but as nonetheless useful for public relations. At Sardis, only a few have not "soiled their garments" (3:4), which may be yet another reference to taking part in the cult of the emperor. John has nothing commendatory to say to the Laodiceans, who are too complacent and self-congratulatory in their economc security to perceive their true condition of poverty before God (3:17–18).

It is not likely that John expected to persuade all the members of all the seven churches about the truth of his revelation. Rather, in each case he singles out those faithful ones who will withstand the pressures to conform, who will risk martyrdom, and who will therefore, as he phrases it, be "one who conquers." Only these will share in the eschatological blessings: to eat of the tree of life (2:7), to be unhurt by the "second death" following the Last Judgment (2:11), to share the hidden manna and the new name God will give to his own (2:17; cf. Isa. 62:2), to be robed in white and have one's name in the Book of Life (3:5), to be a pillar in God's new temple (3:12), to sit at the throne with Christ and the Father (3:21). But what assurance can anyone have that such reward and vindication lie beyond the impending struggle to the death? The answer is given in the apocalyptic visions.

Visions of the End

The dominant themes that pervade these visions, in spite of changes in the symbolic representations, are these: the royal redeemer figure; the faithful community; the satanic majesty, together with the imperial idol; God as sovereign over his creation. The opening vision (4:1–5:14) is of the throne of God surrounded by heavenly attendants, like that of an Oriental monarch. The picture builds on representations of God's throne in Isaiah 6 and Ezekiel 1, even to the thrice-holy ascription of praise to the One who sits on the throne. The hymnic passages, here and throughout Revelation, have led some to assume that the writer is incorporating existing liturgical elements into the work. That is possible, but the hymns may be John's own creative response to the visions granted him. The first liturgical poem is addressed to God as creator ("Worthy art thou, O Lord . . . for thou didst create all things," 4:11). The second is sung to Christ as the obedient Lamb led to the slaughter ("Worthy art thou . . . for thou wast slain and by thy blood didst ransom for God those from every . . . people and nation to be a kingdom and priests to our God," 5:9–10). What is clear is that the visions are offered in the context of a worshipping community, rather than to a group gloating over the prospect of the defeat of enemies.

The scroll, on which is inscribed the divinely predetermined course of history, is fastened with seven seals (6:1–17; 8:1). As each is opened, another facet of the future is disclosed. The familiar four horsemen revealed successively by the first four seals symbolize military might (white horse), warfare and slaughter (red horse), famine (black horse), and pestilence (pale or green horse). The fifth seal releases the prayer of the martyrs for deliverance, but the response tells them only that the divinely fixed number of the martyrs is not yet complete (6:11). The sixth seal unleashes all manner of seismic, cosmic, military, and political catastrophes, as the certainty of divine judgment mounts. An interlude of reassurance describes two groups preserved by God from the effects of universal judgment: (1) the faithful, true Israel, the present people of God; (2) those from earlier times and from all nations who have trusted in the Lamb, God's agent of human redemption (7:1–17). Their deliverance from suffering is poignantly described in a hymnic passage that ends with the promise, "God will wipe away every tear from their eyes."

The opening of the seventh seal makes way for the seven trumpet-sounding angels. Again the series of revelations linked with the trumpets (8:2–11:19) is interrupted by an idyllic passage reassuring the faithful of God's care and the certainty of his plan (10:1–11:13). The trumpets herald new disasters not only in the realm of nature, but in the kingdom of the evil spirits who, symbolized by locusts—like horses, but with the sting of scorpions—harass the human race. The invasion of troops from beyond the Euphrates probably is a reference to the coming of Parthian armies, a constant source of anxiety to the Roman rulers and a threat to their control of the Middle East. The comfort to the faithful is a vivid reminder that God is in control and that he will soon bring to happy completion his plan for his own world and his own people (10:1–11). Even though the Jerusalem sanctuary lies in ruins and under pagan occupation (11:1–3), and even though God's prophetic messengers are killed,[23] God assures the community that he will purge the wicked who now control life on earth and reward his faithful servants (11:1–18).

Before and following the third set of sevens—angels with plagues (15:1–21)—there are other groups of visions. The woman and her child sought out for destruction by the dragon (12:1–17) symbolize the covenant people and the satanic opposition the Christians are encountering. The multiple horns and heads recall the visions of Daniel 7, and like Daniel's grotesque beast, they represent the satanically supported pagan imperial power. God will preserve his people from their enemies, however, in spite of the unrelenting warfare against those "who keep the commandments of God and bear testimony to Jesus" (12:17).

In the second vision, the imperial beast appears again, but this time he serves as a kind of public relations agent for the dragon, who gives him authority and enables him to recover from what seemed to be a mortal wound

[23] The notion of God's chosen witnesses on earth, with power to control natural events, goes back to Moses (Exod. 7:17) and Elijah (2 Kings 1:10). But in Zechariah 3:1–4:14 there are two witnesses, Zerubbabel and Joshua, who announce in Jerusalem the purgation by God of his people and the establishment of his rule over "the whole earth."

(13:3–4). This may be a diabolical imitation of the role of Jesus (as word of God, as crucified and risen), and at the same time an historical allusion to the crisis for the imperial establishment when Nero died. With his death the Julio-Claudian line of emperors passed away, followed by a vacuum of leadership, eventually filled by the establishment of the Flavian dynasty under Vespasian.[24] The second beast "out of the earth" rounds out a kind of pseudo-trinity, extending further the authority and influence of the dragon, luring people to worship the dragon (13:11–12), including the performance of miracles to attract popular support (13:13–14). The demand for universal submission to "the beast" points to the imperial decree that all subjects participate in the divine honors to Caesar. It was Domitian who first ordered that he be addressed as *Dominus et Deus;* that is, as "lord and god." Failure to conform was punishable by death. Probably by assigning numerical value to the letters of the emperor's name (plus his title), the mysterious sum of 666 was arrived at—here to serve as a cryptic signal for the idolatrous imperial cult.

Countering these visions of threat and destruction are those of assurance in Revelation 14. There the Lamb and the 144,000 of the elect sing praise to God, while three angels herald the arrival of the hour of judgment (14:6–7), the fall of Rome (Babylon, 14:8), and the punishment of the wicked (14:9–11). Building on the prophetic image of the harvests of grain and grapes as the symbols of the divine day of reckoning (Joel 3:13; Isa. 5:1–70), John pictures the coming to fruition of God's plans for both judgment and redemption (14:13–20). Similarly, in Revelation 17 there is a vivid portrayal of Rome as a harlot, "drunk with the blood of the saints and the martyrs of Jesus" (17:6), losing control over the nations of the earth which she has dominated (17:15–18). A literarily superb lamentation follows in Revelation 18, recounting the greatness of Rome in spite of her wickedness, and announcing the destruction and ultimate desolation and silence that is her divinely decreed destiny:

> Alas! Alas! thou great city,
> Thou mighty city Babylon!
> In one hour has thy judgment come.

The living sounds of music, of crafts, of grinding, of festivities for bride and bridegroom, will be heard in her no more (18:10, 22–23).

The third set of sevens, the angels and plagues (Rev. 15–16), recall the divine warnings that fell on Egypt prior to the exodus of Israel (Exod. 7–12): sores, water turned into blood, frogs, hail. Interspersed among these dire predictions are the hymns of praise to God for his power and justice in overcoming evil and vindicating the faithful (15:3–4; 16:5–7). From Revelation 19 to the end of the book the themes of praise dominate, the original from which all later Hallelujah choruses derive (19:1–3, 6–8). The revelations include that of Christ as Word of God, triumphant judge and ruler at the marriage supper (19:9–16) celebrating the union of Christ and his people; the gruesome supper

---

[24] After Nero's death, there were four Caesars in a single year (A.D. 68–69), with the Senate declaring finally for Vespasian, whose heirs continued in power for nearly thirty years, to be replaced in turn by the Antonine dynasty.

of the vultures feeding on the corpses of the wicked (19:17–21); the doom of Satan (20:1–3) and the triumph of Jesus and his faithful community (20:4–6), followed by a last, spasmodic and futile effort by the evil powers and then the Last Judgment (20:7–15).

The concluding images of Revelation portray the New Jerusalem, in which God and his people dwell together in eternal peace. It is significant that John chooses a political, social figure—the city—to depict the culmination of God's creative purpose for the universe and for humanity. There is no individualistic, private redemption, according to John. There is instead a new society, in which mutuality and common participation in the divine will characterize the goal of human existence. The beauties of the city are presented in a series of vivid metaphors. It is a city designed in heaven, but established on earth (21:10). It needs no temple in which the divine glory is concealed, as was the case with the ancient Temple in Jerusalem: all within it are illumined by the divine glory (21:23). Here God, the Lamb, and "his servants" are bound together in perfect and eternal community: "They need no light of lamp or sun, for the Lord God will be their light, and they shall reign forever and ever" (22:5).

13

Establishing Norms for Faith and Ethics: Letters of John, Jude, 2 Peter

In addition to the tensions experienced by the Christian community at the turn of the second century arising from cultural and political forces, there were internal conflicts as well. These arose from disagreements on a wide range of basic issues. How and by whom were limits to be drawn as to what those calling themselves Christians might believe? Who should set the rules for Christian behavior, and who would enforce them? What was to be done with those judged to be unacceptable on grounds of faith or practice? Which of the various leadership models handed down by those who claimed to be successors of the apostles was the right one? Or should Christians be guided solely by the Spirit, without rules or creeds? In view of the variety of answers to these and related questions, should one work for compromise and consensus, or should one fight for what one was convinced was the truth?[1]

That wing of the early Christian movement linked with the Gospel and letters of John seems to have set out with a first-century ideal of complete equality like that which characterizes late twentieth-century communes or *kibbutzim.* Yet that seeming freedom from authority carries with it a basic peril: if "the spirit (or wind) blows where it will" and that is the way "it is with everyone who is born of the spirit" (John 3:8), then how can anyone know what the Spirit is doing? Or how can anyone deny that another person's action or notion is not a manifestation of the Spirit? Is it possible to insist on freedom in the Spirit without inviting moral and doctrinal chaos? Apparently persons claiming the guidance of the Spirit began to think and act in ways which were different from the more ordered, authority-oriented segments of Christianity in the Pauline and Petrine traditions but which also seemed strange and questionable within the Johannine group. By what criteria could they be judged? Who are the true followers of Jesus?

[1] For all the great learning it displays, Walter Bauer's classic statement, *Orthodoxy and Heresy in Earliest Christianity,* trans. R. A. Kraft et al. (Philadelphia: Fortress Press, 1971) adopts a simplistic position: that orthodoxy and centralized episcopal authority were third- and fourth-century developments which the Church Fathers read back into the earlier period. Certainly the ecclesiastical and doctrinal authority structures were not in existence in the first century, but it is historically important to see how the components of later credal and ecclesiastical authority took shape. Some scholars who have worked on the Gnostic library have contrived a curious reverse version of Bauer's thesis, which assumes that the really primitive faith and practice of the early Church were closer to Gnostic ideas and ethics than to the orthodoxy that ultimately triumphed. But that assumption rests on personal preferences rather than historical documentation. For a consideration of the differences among early Christian authority models, see Appendix V.

WE ARE ONE IN THE SPIRIT: 1 JOHN

This possibility of division within a group lacking specific doctrinal or ethical norms, avowedly bound together by love and the Spirit alone, became an actuality by around the year 100. The Letters of John are a response to this crisis.[2] Not only the nature of the challenge, but also the outlook of those who presented the challenge, were to have far-reaching consequences for Christianity in subsequent centuries. Ironically, it was the champions of freedom, love, and spiritual unity who dissolved the cohesion of the community. It would be a mistake, however, to think that the members of the dissenting wing were merely stupid or perverse. In one sense they were more consistently faithful to the values just listed than was the writer of 1 John. The dissenters were convinced they were the ones who took most seriously the love of God and the freedom in the Spirit. By what logic could they have developed their point of view out of the Johannine tradition?

The portrayal of Jesus in the Gospel of John asserts his humanity ("the Word became flesh and dwelt among us," 1:14). But the human side of Jesus is qualified by John: his miracles disclose his divine glory (2:11); the food and drink of which he partakes are always treated as spiritual realities (4:10; 6:33); Jesus refers to himself by the sacred name of God in the Jewish tradition (in its standard Greek translation): I AM (8:58). He possesses knowledge of the future, was in existence before time, has immediate access to God, indeed is one with God (10:30). For anyone who knew the Johannine tradition and treated it selectively, it would be possible to infer that Jesus's earthly career was no more than a symbolic shadow of his timeless divine substance. His suffering and death are represented by John as triumph rather than as tragedy (10:17–18; 18:6), and at its accomplishment Jesus announces, "It is finished." His Crucifixion is his exaltation (12:32–33). From this outlook one *could* conclude that the Crucifixion is not a historic event at all, but a visible symbol of divine redemption.

Similarly, one could understand the Christian life to be characterized by the present experience of eternal life (3:13–21; 5:24; 11:26; 14:7–10), rather than as lived in expectation of a fulfillment in the near future, such as we find in Paul and in the synoptic tradition. Intimacy of relationship with God (8:31–34) freed one from any sense of impending judgment or besetting sin (3:18; 5:24). The sole moral responsibility was to manifest love toward those who were members of the favored community to whom God had revealed the truth and imparted his purpose (13:34–35; 15:12). There was no need for concern about the return of Christ, since his presence was already being fully and powerfully experienced in the community through the Paraclete, the Spirit whom he sent (14:16), and who teaches everything (14:26), including what the community needs to know about Jesus (15:25–26). Although there are features of John's Gospel that balance these views, or that put them in another per-

---

[2] In this assessment of 1 John, I am dependent on the detailed analysis and reconstruction offered by Raymond E. Brown in *The Community of the Beloved Disciple* (New York: Paulist Press, 1979), pp. 103–44.

spective, a selective use of the tradition could sketch this picture of Jesus. From the Letters of John, it would appear that this understanding did, in fact, develop.

THE PROBLEM OF JESUS'S HUMANITY
[1 JOHN 4:2]

Before looking at the evidence from the Johannine letters, however, it is important to note that these features of the early Christian tradition were taken up by various groups, who combined them with a radical concept of being that resulted in a total distinction between the realm of spirit and the realm of matter.[3] Since the early Christians took as their starting point the biblical view of God and the world, they affirmed that God had created the world and that his creation was "very good" (Gen. 1:31). By the middle of the second century, however, the biblical tradition—both Jewish and Christian scriptures—was being reinterpreted along dualistic lines. The creator-God of the Jewish tradition was denounced as evil and assigned responsibility for the material world, with all its evils and sorrows. What we are confronted with here is not an organized religious movement, or even a consistent system of ideas, but a way of trying to deal with the problem of evil on the assumption that knowledge (in Greek, *gnosis*) brings salvation to those who possess it. If one knows the truth about the universe, so as to be able to perceive the nature and the stragegies of the powers of darkness, and especially to understand the ultimate deity, characterized by goodness and light, one could then be confident of achieving release from the material world, of overcoming evil, and of ascending to the realm of light.

Contributing to the rise of this way of thinking were (1) Jewish speculation about personified wisdom as God's agent in fashioning the universe; (2) Persian influence on Judaism during the exile in Babyon, which led to an emphasis on the transcendence of God and his nonhuman otherness,[4] as well as (3) the notion of the existence of good angels and wicked demons who participated in the cosmic struggle of good and evil, working, respectively, to foster or frustrate the divine purpose. Contributing to the development of full-blown Gnosticism, as known from the second- and third-century writings of both Gnostics and anti-Gnostics,[5] was mystical philosophical speculation in the

[3] *Hylē*, the word used by the philosophers for "matter, tangible stuff," is also used with the meaning "firewood" (as in our expression "combustible matter"). The word appears only once in the New Testament (James 3:5), where it means "firewood."

[4] Compare, for example, the pre-exilic prophet of Israel, Isaiah's vision of God (Isa. 6), and its straightforward claim, "I saw the Lord sitting on a throne," with Ezekiel's circumlocutious account of his vision in Ezekiel 1:4–26, where he describes "the likeness of four living creatures" over whose heads "there was the likeness of a throne and seated above the likeness of the throne was the likeness, as it were, of a human form" (God). We have noted earlier how the pre-exilic account of David's prideful act in taking a census is instigated by God according to 2 Samuel 24:1, but by Satan according to the post-exilic account of 1 Chronicles 21:1.

[5] So long as our knowledge of Gnostic thought was limited to attacks on the Gnostics by Christian writers of the second and third centuries (Irenaeus, Tertullian, Clement of Alexandria), it was easy to assume that the movement was older than the second century and that it had existed independently of the rise of Christianity. The Christians were dis-

later Platonic tradition, which portrayed the ultimate goal of human existence as union with the divine spirit. This view was given full expression in the third century by Plotinus. Astrology, the influence of which on Judaism of this period is obvious from the inclusion of the signs of the zodiac on synagogue mosaic pavements,[6] contributed the notion that human life is determined by the heavenly powers. By the late second century, Jesus was being portrayed as a wholly divine, spiritual being who willingly descended into the earthly realm in order to release from enslavement to the material world the chosen recipients of divine knowledge.

The antecedents of Gnosticism were unmistakably Jewish. Later, similar speculation took place in circles that were neither Jewish nor Christian but influenced by both, as is the case with the Mandaeans, a baptizing Gnostic sect that still exists in Iraq and Iran.[7] Its redeemer figure is of heavenly origin and comes to earth to bring divine knowledge. Yet the catalyst that precipitated the Gnostic systems—if we can honor them with that designation—as we observe [can document] them in their oldest forms was not pagan myth or Jewish speculation. It was Jesus as he is pictured by the New Testament writers. The potential for the Gnostic exploitation of Jesus may be discerned in depictions of him as superhuman, preexistent, and offering release from the earthly realm. When John's Gospel is read along the speculative, spiritualizing lines we have traced above, it may be readily accommodated to Gnostic interpretation. Not in the least surprising is the fact that John was the Gnostics' favorite Gospel, as their extensive reworking of it in newly-discovered Gnostic documents has confirmed.[8] In the Dialogue of the Savior, for exam-

---

torting as they reported the spread of Gnosticism. The discovery of a Gnostic library in 1945, now published completely in English translation [*The Nag Hammadi Library*, ed. J. M. Robinson (New York: Harper & Row, 1977)], has greatly enriched our knowledge of the movement, but it has also confirmed the general accuracy of the Church Fathers' accounts while providing no evidence that the movement took definite shape before the middle of the second century. See on this Pheme Perkins, *The Gnostic Dialogue: The Early Church and the Crisis of Gnosticism* (New York: Paulist Press, 1980), especially the opening chapter, "Gnosticism in Its Context."

[6] In flagrant violation of later Jewish strictures against any kind of representational art, the floral, animal, and human figures of the zodiac are reproduced in the mosaic pavements (which date from the second and subsequent centuries) of synagogues. Some include representations of the deity as well, pictured as the sun charioteer, Helios.

[7] The mythological portraits of the Mandaean texts, which date from the sixth century A.D. and later, were used by such scholars as R. Bultmann to construct a hypothetical pre-Christian Gnostic redeemer figure. Bultmann traced this notion back to earlier baptizing sects, on the assumption that it had served as a model for the portrayal of Jesus in the Gospel of John. Careful analysis of the Mandaean texts by Carsten Colpe and others has shown that this hypothesis is untenable. Further, the study of texts that originated demonstrably with first-century sects which probably practiced baptism—namely, the Dead Sea community at Qumran—give no hint of a Gnostic redeemer figure or of the denigration of the material world essential to Gnosticism.

[8] Elaine Pagel's monograph, *The Johannine Gospel in Gnostic Exegesis* (Nashville: Abingdon Press, 1973), demonstrates this in detail, although she thinks the Gnostic viewpoint was the original, which was discredited and displaced by later, male-dominated ecclesiastical orthodoxy. This viewpoint was given a popular statement in her *The Gnostic Gospels* (New York: Random House, 1979). Pheme Perkins draws attention to the pervasive influence of John on the form and content of the Gnostic writings in *The Gnostic Dialogue*.

ple, the literary form resembles that of Jesus's farewell discourses in John 14–17, and the account of creation is a detailed expansion of the Logos as agent of creation in John 1:1–3. The Apocryphon of James, however, includes an extended refutation of Jesus's promise in John 14:3 that he will come again: the Gnostic teaching is that the soul will be released to escape from this evil world. What is clear is that the Gospel of John provides fertile soil for this kind of speculation and expansion. The Letters of John point to an early stage in this process, which "John" regarded with deep concern.

What Divides God's People

The first of the Letters of John is a pastoral encyclical, apparently addressed to a group of churches out of a general concern, rather than to a single church on a specific occasion. The concerns implied and expressed in John center on two matters: the moral state of the community and the reaction to a split within the group. In 2 John, that schism continues to exist, with practical consequences that are apparent in 3 John.

John's strategy in dealing with these issues is not to meet them head on, but to place them in a larger context in terms of which they can be addressed. The letter shifts back and forth between the two major problems: in 1:1–2:17 and 3:1–24, the focus is on morals and morale; in 2:18–28 and 3:1–24, the subject is the norms for discerning the truth. The letter opens with lines which, in both form and content, recall the opening of the Gospel of John: "That which was from the beginning . . . concerning the word (*logos*) of life" (1 John 1:1–3). A different point is made here than in the prologue of John, however. Instead of showing the role of the Word of God in creation, "beginning" (*archē*) here is used to stress the continuity between what God was doing in sending Jesus into the world and what he is doing now through those, like John, who stand in that chain of tradition. Anticipating his attack on the views of those who have withdrawn from the community, John emphasizes that the Word is a visible, audible, tangible reality, not merely an idea or a spirit. Similarly, the basic moral obligation of Christians—the commandment to love one another (2:7–11)—has been in force "from the beginning" as well. For John truth is not innovation but recovery of, and fidelity to, tradition.

The breakdown in the unity of the community is implied without being directly described in 1:5–7. The essential qualities of the children of God are that they "walk in the light" and that they thereby "have fellowship with each other." By implication, defectors do neither. Or more precisely, their withdrawal from the fellowship attests to the fact that they do not walk in the light of God. Ironically, those who have thus turned from light to darkness deny that they sin, or even that sin has any effect on them. John's response is that they are fooling no one but themselves (1:8), and that they are making God out to be a liar, since he has accepted the sacrifice of Christ as the expiation for human sins (1:7; 2:2). Essential to maintaining proper moral status within the community is the regular confession of sin, which is heard by God and results in continual cleansing and renewal. Those who deny the need for this divine remedy for the human condition, proud of their religious condition though they may be, are actually walking in the dark.

A characteristic feature of this letter is a series of striking contrasts between God's true children and the children of darkness—or of the devil (3:8). For example, love is not regarded by John as just an emotion or an attitude, but as a way of acting. To claim to be in the light is incompatible with hating one's brother or sister in the faith (2:9). Only the one who loves his brother abides in the light; the one who hates his brother remains in darkness and has no notion of where he is going (2:10–11). Or again, in 3:4–10, the one who is mystically united with Christ, or who is born of God, does not characteristically commit sin; while the lives of the children of the Devil, as shown by their hatred of their brethren, are dominated by sin. For the children of light, the model is Christ. For the children of darkness, it is Cain, who is here said to be "of the evil one," since it was by yielding to the serpent's temptation that Adam and Eve had sexual intercourse and Cain was born (Gen. 4:1). Cain's most notable deed was the murder of his brother (Gen. 4:8–16), and it is this stance toward life that is typical of the unloving separatists. Once more, John reminds his readers that the love commandment is fundamental. In sharp contrast is the image of Christ, who lays down his life for others (3:16), an act of vicarious sacrifice we should be willing to perform as well. Instead, the group that has withdrawn talks much about love, but its adherents will not even share their worldly goods with a needy brother or sister (3:17).

In 2:12–14 John gives a series of moral exhortations that bear some resemblance to the household lists used in the later Pauline tradition (Col. 3; Eph. 5; 1 Tim. 5; Titus 2). Unlike the latter material, which includes specific instructions, John's list consists merely of a series of affirmations. The children are reminded that their sins are forgiven; the young men are congratulated on having overcome the evil one and on their strength through the divine word within them. In a phrase that goes back to the opening lines of the letter, the Fathers' knowledge of God is traced back to "the beginning"—yet another reminder that the community stands in continuity with tradition. The closest John comes to specific moral statements, apart from the repeated commandment of love, takes the form of a warning about "the world" (2:15–17). He declares that those human urges which serve only self-gratification or which do no more than inflate the ego ("the pride of life") are characteristic of the present world order (Greek *cosmos*), which is not subject to the divine will and is merely transitory. The choice, therefore, is between fleeting, seemingly self-serving impulses and commitment to the eternal will of God. Even in this passage, however, John is more concerned with moral stance and attitude than with specific rules and regulations.

The two passages that link moral performance with future judgment are 2:28–29 and 4:17. In neither text are the criteria for judgment or vindication spelled out, but John reminds his readers that Christ will appear in the future, and he uses the traditional term *parousia* to refer to his coming. That some will then be ashamed is a gentle warning that irresponsible acts now will be called to account on the day of judgment. Elsewhere, however, John emphasizes what is already occurring in the fulfillment of the divine redemptive purpose in the world: "The darkness is passing away and the true light is already shining" (2:8).

Not only is the eschatological fulfillment portrayed as already in process; the eschatological conflict is likewise presently taking place. "Children, it is the last hour; and as you have heard that many antichrists are coming, so now many antichrists have come; therefore we know that it is the last hour" (2:18). With this passage, another major theme is introduced: the split within the community. Both the reason for the break and the way in which John explains how a break could occur within God's family are illuminating, as well as important for seeing the developing self-understanding of this segment of the Church. John declares that the withdrawal of the dissenters is no more than a visible manifestation of what had been true from the beginning: "They went out from us, but they were not of us." Had they really belonged, they would not have left. Their departure merely makes obvious what might otherwise have been unrecognized—the seceders were not true children of God to begin with.

How to Identify the True Children of Light

How is one to differentiate between true and false claimants to be children of God? We have already seen that the true are distinguished by the consistency with which they obey the command of love, but now doctrinal criteria are introduced. Decisive for identifying the "liars" is their denial that Jesus is the Christ. To deny the Son is to deny the Father; to confess the Son is to confess the Father. Here John is using the terms "confess" and "deny" in a technical sense, meaning credal affirmation or rejection, a usage that goes back to Paul (Rom. 10:9–10), but which here requires even greater precision and specificity.

The details of the normative confession about Jesus are provided by John in 4:2. It is no longer adequate to assume that the Church can live by an open-ended freedom in the Spirit. Now the conflicting spirits abroad in the Church must be tested; they must be shown to conform to a standard. That standard is the confession "that Jesus Christ has come in the flesh." Having invited its adherents to conclude that Jesus was a purely spiritual being, unhampered by human limitations, the Johannine tradition must now insist unequivocally that Jesus came into the world in fully human form. The attractiveness for second-century Christians of representing Jesus as not really human is apparent in the apocryphal Gospel of Peter, which suggests that on the cross he felt no pain (4:10) and did not actually die, but was "taken up" to God (4:19).[9] Against such notions John insists that it is Jesus's "blood" that cleanses from sin (1:7), that he gave his *life* for his own people (3:16), that the divine purpose through Jesus is marked by "water and blood" (5:6); that is, by his baptism and his death.

It is only those who affirm that Jesus was truly human who are true children of God (4:2–4). It is not sufficient to claim to have the Spirit. There is a triple confirmation of belonging to God's people: the Spirit, plus the experi-

---

[9] The entire trial, Crucifixion, and Resurrection stories from the Gospel of Peter are given in translation in *New Testament Apocrypha*, ed. E. Hennecke, W. Schneemelcher, R. McL. Wilson, vol. 1 (Philadelphia: Westminster Press, 1963), pp. 183–87.

ence of baptism, plus the reality of Jesus's death (5:6–7). When that threefold witness is heard and affirmed, then the one who believes this God-given testimony concerning his son has eternal life (5:12). The power of the tradition is supported by the witness of the Spirit, which may be what is referred to metaphorically in the "anointing" which instructs the believer mentioned in 2:27. In any case, the sole external guarantee is the confession of Jesus as the incarnation of the Word of God: "that Jesus Christ has come in the flesh" (4:2).

Those who share the tradition, the confession, and the anointing of the Spirit are united in a community of love. Indeed, John says simply that God is love, so that "he who abides in love abides in God, and God abides in him" (4:16). Yet that divine love is not merely a universal attribute of God; it has been specifically, even concretely, manifested in a historic person, culminating in his death: "In this is love . . . that he loved us and sent his Son to be the expiation for our sins" (4:10). The assurance that members of God's people experience does not rest on feelings or superior information, but on God's trustworthiness, even when doubts arise (3:19–21). Gratitude for that confidence manifests itself in obedience to his commandments (3:22). That attitude of trust in God's reliability is the basis for prayer to God, including petitions in behalf of erring members of the community (5:13–17).

Yet believers in the true word must reckon with unrelenting hostility from "the world," which now includes the former members of the community who have withdrawn (3:1; 4:5). In the community of love there is no place for fear, however hostile the world may be (4:17–18). By standing firm in their confession of Jesus and in their commitment to mutual love as a way of life they can overcome not only fear, but the world itself (5:5). The world is triumphed over in the life of faith, but it does not disappear: "The whole world is in the power of the evil one." The assurance lies in the conviction "We know that we are of God" (5:19), and that in spite of weakness and failure, "we have an Intercessor with the Father, Jesus Christ the righteous" (2:1). Neither qualifications for membership in the community nor standards for doctrine or moral behavior are spelled out in detail. The essence of faith is much more divine-human relationship than content of belief. The same is true of moral obligations for John, at least in the first letter.

In 2 John, however, we can observe the growing necessity to draw the line even more sharply between truth and error in matters of faith. In the opening lines stress is laid on truth and those who *know* it. This is later declared to rest on right doctrine, which must be not only affirmed but also held to steadfastly (v. 9). Those who swerve from correct doctrine are not to be offered hospitality (v. 10), since to entertain one who believes error is to share in his false doctrine. The error is the same as in 1 John, as represented by "the deceivers who have gone out into the world . . . who will not acknowledge the coming of Jesus Christ in the flesh." But the response to and the treatment of them is harsher here, even though the old commandment, "from the beginning," is still affirmed (v. 5).

In 3 John there is a similar emphasis on truth, which apparently includes both belief and behavior (vv. 1–4). The issue of hospitality toward itinerant preachers or teachers is raised, first to commend those who have received messengers of the truth, and then to denounce one Diotrophes, who has apparently refused hospitality to those sent by John. We have no way to guess why Diotrophes refused to acknowledge John's authority, or what the substance was of the evil words he used in "prating against" John. Worst of all, Diotrophes not only repudiated John and his emissaries, but also prevented others in the Church from receiving them.

Whatever the specific issue may have been between them, John and Diotrophes have incompatible views on how authority is exercised within the Church. Was Diotrophes a self-appointed leader? Was he the champion of some other apostolic figure or of a more rigidly structured concept of Church order? Or was he a champion of local autonomy for churches? We have no basis for answering these kinds of questions, which loomed so large in subsequent Church history. But we can be sure that from at least the time of the Letters of John these problems could not be evaded.

ROOTING OUT ERROR: JUDE

The little book of Jude lays claim to hereditary authority,* as is evident from the author's self-identification as "brother of James," the brother of Jesus who was head of the Jerusalem apostles in the days of Paul. He is not himself an apostle, but appeals to their "predictions" as the ground of his warning that the Church is now living in the last days. The fact that the direct quotation he offers in v. 18 is not found in any surviving text, but sounds rather like a free allusion to the Pastorals (1 Tim. 4 and 2 Tim. 3 both mention "the last times"), suggests (1) that the apostolic tradition is being preserved and transmitted in oral as well as written form, and (2) that the writer is living at least a generation after the apostles have disappeared. Nevertheless, their apostolic teachings are an important part of the authority on which Jude rests his case.

The Perverters of God's Truth

Before we consider the other bases to which Jude appeals, we must examine what the case is that he seeks to make. Absolutely fundamental to Jude's understanding of Christianity is that its truth is eternally embodied in "the faith which was once for all delivered to the saints" (v. 3). His epistle is a fierce attack on those who threaten or pervert this citadel of truth. The problem is not with outsiders, but with traitors and subverters within the Church, or as he phrases it, "those who have sneaked in." He has no questions about who they are or what fate awaits them. His only concern is to warn the naive and gullible within the community so that they will not be taken in by these secret agents of Satan.

Jude seems to be addressing a counterargument to those who insist that membership in the people of God is perpetual and irreversible. He adduces, therefore, a string of precedents to show that God has always brought condemnation on those who, though greatly favored by his grace, proved to be

---

* See Appendix V on Authority Models in the Early Church.

unfaithful or disobedient. This was the case with the doubters and dissidents among the Israelites in the days of the Exodus (Num. 21); it happened when the wicked angels violated the divine decrees and cohabited with human beings (Gen. 6); it occurred when the cities of the plain tolerated sexual deviance (Gen. 19). Those in divine favor came under divine judgment. The point is obvious: The same fate awaits those who now enjoy special status within the covenant community, but whose thought and acts are contrary to God's will.

What is it that these perverters of God's truth have done to merit the doom that awaits them? They indulge in sensual fantasies (v. 8); but even worse, they "reject authority and revile the glorious ones." These last phrases are often interpreted as references to angelic or heavenly powers, but the illustration that follows—the dispute between the archangel Michael and the Devil over the body of Moses—seems to point rather to the importance of following divinely established procedure. In this case, the false brothers have defied authority within the Church, insulted its divinely exalted leaders, and made blasphemous pronouncements and diabolical judgments.

Jude denounces them in bitter language combining a supply of biblical stories of villainy with a string of mixed metaphors. The apostates' denunciation of the Church's leaders exposes their own lack of understanding and proves that their motivation is at the irrational level of animal instincts (v. 10). Their behavior models are Cain, who murdered his brother (Gen. 4); Korah, the arrogant leader of a faction in Israel that refused to accept the priestly dominance of Aaron and his tribe (Num. 16); Balaam, the pagan soothsayer, who prostituted his supernatural gift (Num. 22–24). Though these wicked persons take part in the sacramental feasts of the Christian community, they defile them (v. 12). Jude then offers a string of images of these pseudo-Christians, all of which portray objects which fail to fulfill their proper ends: clouds without water; trees without fruit; waves that produce only polluted foam; stars that do not guide, but end in darkness. A final string of epithets in v. 16 rounds out Jude's estimate of these people: "grumblers, malcontents, passion-driven, loud-mouths, sycophants."

By contrast, the faithful community is to build itself up in "the most holy faith" (v. 20). In the process of his appeal Jude brings together a trinitarian formula, in contrast to 1 John, for example, which speaks simply of father and son. Jude mentions (1) praying in the Holy Spirit, (2) the love of God and (3) the mercy of "our Lord Jesus Christ" (vv. 20–21). The final lines of the letter constitute an impressive liturgical formula ascribing to God and Christ the honor due them.

The Widening Definition of Scripture

What is striking about the Letter of Jude—in addition to the bitter tone in which he denounces the defectors from the true faith—is that the author treats as normative for Christians not only what they came to call the Old Testament, but also writings that stand outside what came to be acknowledged as the canon of scripture. In vv. 14–15 is a quotation from "Enoch"

taken from a document known to modern scholars as 1 Enoch.[10] It is an apocalyptic writing that purports to include predictions by the antediluvian
Enoch (Gen. 5:18–24), whose place of special favor with God is indicated by
two factors: (1) he was the seventh (the sacred number) from Adam, and (2)
he did not die, but was taken up directly to God ("God took him"). His authority for Jude is obviously very great, since it is the quotation from his apocalypse that makes the final thrust in Jude's argument concerning the impending judgment. The fact that fragments of the Enoch literature have been
found among the Dead Sea writings at Qumran show that these were highly
prized among Jews of Palestine in the first century, and more particularly that
they were regarded by the Dead Sea sect as authoritative. The curious detail
in v. 9 about the contention between Michael and the Devil over the body of
Moses is identified by the Fathers of the Church, Clement of Alexandria and
Origen, as deriving from the Assumption of Moses, another apocalyptic writing preserved only in fragments in various translations. Possibly an allusion to
this writing appears in the Dead Sea writing called the Scroll of the War Rule,
in which instructions are given for preparing to fight the final eschatological
war against the powers of darkness (1 QM 17:7). The passage in Jude 9 builds
also on a portion of Zechariah 3 in which a contest between Yahweh and his
adversary Satan over the penitent Joshua culminates in Yahweh's rebuke of
Satan. The same passage, with its account of Joshua's being cleansed from his
filthy garment and rescued from the fire of judgment (Zech. 3:2, 5) is echoed
in Jude 23, where it serves as a description of the purified converts to the true
faith.

For Jude, the eschatological expectation is alive and central to his outlook. There is no mention of the *parousia,* however; rather, it is the prospect of
the believer being presented before God in purity (v. 24). The major issue for
Jude is the perverters of the faith and the need for ridding the Church of these
enemies of the truth. Processes for expulsion are not indicated; the criteria for
identifying the false claimants are the main concern of the writer. His warnings did not go unheeded; they were seized upon, intensified, and addressed to
a different readership by a subsequent writer who claimed the authority of the
apostle Peter.

TRUE RELIGION:
PARTICIPATION IN THE DIVINE NATURE
[2 PETER]

The desire of the writer of 2 Peter to be identified with that original apostle is
apparent not only in the opening lines of the book, but also in his claim to
have participated in the transfiguration experience reported in the synoptic

[10] To distinguish it from other writings attributed to Enoch, who appears briefly and
disappears enigmatically ("he was not, for God took him," Gen. 5:24). Scholars distinguish
the following: 1 Enoch (preserved in Ethiopic and recognized as canonical by the Abyssin-
ian Church); 2 Enoch (The Secrets of Enoch); 3 Enoch (preserved in a late Hebrew version). The central section of 1 Enoch, chapters 37–71, known as the Parables (or Similitudes) of Enoch, was probably written in the first century A.D.

Gospels (Mark 9:2–8; Matt. 17:1–8; Luke 9:28–36). Yet a thoughtful reading
of this brief work makes it obvious that, rather than having been written in
the first generation, 2 Peter is perhaps the latest of all the New Testament
books, and the one that gives the clearest evidence of the existence of other
New Testament writings. The most powerful evidence is the author's reference to the letters of Paul as "scripture" (3:15–16), a point to which we will
return. But the literary dependence of this work on Jude is also evident, especially when Jude 4–16 is read in conjunction with 2 Peter 2:1–8. There are
even unmistakable verbal shifts, as when *spilades* (Jude 12, which can mean
either "reefs" or "blemishes") is replaced by *spiloi*, which means simply "blot"
or "blemish."[11] Detailed comparison of the two shows far more than literary
relationships, however: it discloses that 2 Peter is using the same basic material as Jude, but adapting it and expanding it in order to make it appropriate
to what is culturally a very different readership. Both the author of 2 Peter
and his readers are steeped in popular Hellenistic philosophy—its terminology, its problems, and its aspirations. The author seeks to express his faith in a
way that will appeal to the Hellenistic mind and at the same time provide answers to perennial problems.

Knowledge, Not Faith

From the beginning to the end of 2 Peter, the stress is on knowledge (1:2,
3, 8; 2:20; 3:18). It is knowledge rather than faith that brings one into right
relationship with God. Life is intimately linked with religiosity (in Greek, *eusebeia*, usually and misleadingly translated as "godliness"). The goal of this
kind of life is the union of knowledge with virtue, with the end in view to become—in a phrase found widely in popular Hellenistic religion but nowhere
else in the New Testament—"partakers of the divine nature." Aristotle had
scoffed at such a notion, but it is affirmed in the mystical Hermetic writings
and in the one surviving ancient account of initiation into a mystery cult in
the *Metamorphoses* of Apuleius.[12] A. D. Nock's classic study *Conversion*[13] shows
how great was the appeal of these cults, which promised direct relationship
with the gods. 2 Peter here makes the Christian version of that claim. But further, he uses the technical language of the Eleusinian mysteries, both when he
describes those who lack mystical insight into divine truth (1:9, where the inadequate translation is "shortsighted") and when he uses the term for initiate
in his claim to have been an eyewitness of the divine glory in the transfiguration (in Greek, *epoptēs*, 1:16).

Further evidence of his familiarity with contemporary Hellenistic culture appears in his description of what happens when mystical illumination
occurs. To one who has dwelt in darkness there is the dawning of day, the ris-

[11] This and similar details of literary relationship are laid out by Tord Fornberg in
An Early Church in a Pluralistic Society, trans. Jean Gray (Lund: C. W. K. Gleerup, 1977), pp.
49–54.
[12] The relevant excerpts from Apuleius's *Metamorphoses* may be found in *The New
Testament in Context: Sources and Documents* (Englewood Cliffs, N.J.: Prentice-Hall, 1983).
[13] Arthur Darby Nock, *Conversion* (Oxford, Eng.: Oxford University Press, 1933).

ing of the morning star within the heart (1:19). Here the term *phōsphorus,* which is found nowhere else in the New Testament, is one that in Hellenistic literature is used of Artemis, the goddess of fertility. The role of celestial illuminator is likewise fulfilled by Isis in the mystic initiation of Apuleius referred to above, which depicts the dawning of light of divine knowledge on one who has passed through darkness. That imagery and that sort of piety have clearly influenced "Peter's" account of his own mystic illumination. Similarly, his version of the banishment of the wicked to the underworld uses the technical term *tartaroun* (2:4), found nowhere else in the New Testament but used in Greek mythology concerning Zeus's banishing of the Titans. Equally significant as an indicator of the cultural background of 2 Peter is the absence of the detailed allusions to the apocalyptic writings (Enoch, Assumption of Moses) that were central to the argument in Jude.

Also showing clear signs of Hellenistic influence is the ethical summary in 1:5–7. The chainlike pattern of virtues is characteristic of the Hellenistic diatribe, as we observed in our study of James. And the specific moral qualities enumerated there are quintessentially Stoic. Perhaps only the final link in the ethical chain—love—shows any distinctively Christian feature. Except for that last quality, which some Stoics might have found sentimental, no morally concerned pagan could take issue with this scheme for achieving virtue.

Is There a Just God?

What is different from Hellenistic philosophy in 2 Peter, however, is the promise of the kingdom (1:12). Yet even here, modifications have taken place. The kingdom is no longer a future to be awaited, but an eternal reality into which one may enter now. The *parousia* (1:16) is not a term for the future coming of Christ, but a way of describing his advent and power. But this brings us to the central question addressed in 2 Peter: Why does God delay judging the wicked and vindicating the righteous? Many interpreters have assumed that the primary problem is the familiar one of the delay of the *parousia,* and that issue is explicitly raised, quoting scoffers, in 3:3–4. What is distinctive about 2 Peter is the fact that the author places this issue in the larger context—one which was familiar and troubling to thoughtful pagans who never heard of Jesus—of *theodicy.*[14] If there is a just God, why do the righteous suffer and the unjust continue unchallenged? That is precisely the point of the claim made for God in 2:9: "The Lord knows how to rescue the godly from trial, and keep the unrighteous under punishment."

The pagan philosopher Epicurus (341–270 B.C.) had dismissed the notion of divine providence on the grounds that the universe consists of chance atoms, that the concept of providence is incompatible with human freedom and responsibility, that nature and history move by the chance swerving of atoms, and that injustice does indeed triumph, so that providence is nowhere evident. About the same time that 2 Peter was written, the pagan religious

---

[14] This analysis of the theodicy theme in 2 Peter is dependent on a study by Jerome H. Neyrey, "The Fore and Background of the Polemic in 2 Peter," *Journal of Biblical Literature* 99 (1980), 407–31. Plutarch's essay on theodicy is in his *De sera numinis vindicta.*

philosopher Plutarch (A.D. 46–120) argued that the seeming delay in divine justice is actually evidence of divine mercy, since it provides a more extended period for men and women to recognize the error of their ways and repent. It is significant that Plutarch uses precisely the same Greek terms as the author of 2 Peter for the delay, for repentance, and for the divine long-suffering. Arguments similar to those of 2 Peter are to be found in Jewish documents of this general period, both the work of Philo of Alexandria and the interpretive paraphrases of scripture called the *targumim*.[15] 2 Peter's contrast between our time and God's time (3:8) is based on Psalm 90:4, and is used by Jewish writers as the basis for similar arguments, as in Wisdom of Sirach 18:10–12. The final picture of the new heaven and new earth in 3:10 paraphrases references to the closing chapters of Isaiah (65:17 or 66:22), but the details preceding that promise of renewal—the dissolution of the heavens and the earth by fire—are a familiar feature in Greek philosophy from Zeno and Plato forward. The author of 2 Peter has skillfully synthesized features of traditional Jewish-Christian eschatology with popular secular philosophy of his day.

The Distinguishing Marks of the Unworthy

The moral charges brought against opponents in 2 Peter are much like those in Jude: carousers, with eyes full of adultery, greedy, profiting from wrongdoing, like Balaam (2:13–16). But the basic accusation is that they "have forsaken the right way" (2:15), they "live in error" (2:18) and entice others to follow their living by "licentious passions of the flesh. They promise freedom to unsteady souls, but are themselves enslaved to corruption" (2:14, 19). Worse still, these people—unlike the seceders in 1 John—were once true participants in the community: They had "escaped the defilements of the world through the knowledge of our Lord and Savior Jesus Christ" (2:20) and had "known the way of righteousness" (2:21). Now, however, they are once again caught up in the world and have abandoned the holy commandments. Perhaps in bitter reference to their having once partaken of the sacred food of the Eucharist and shared in the purifying waters of baptism, the author describes them by a revolting analogy from Proverbs 26:11 (a dog eating its own vomit) and another proverbial saying about a newly washed sow wallowing in the filth of her sty.

No criteria for dismissing the apostates are offered in 2 Peter, in spite of the vivid description of their moral and doctrinal condition. The major intended readership for this letter is the faithful, who are encouraged to wait for the day of eschatological vindication and judgment, however long it may be delayed (3:14). As an added inducement to recognize the fact that delay is actually a sign of divine forebearance (3:15), the author refers to the letters of Paul, who wrote on this subject.

Why should Peter defer to Paul? If the bitter attack on Peter in Galatians is an accurate reflection of the personal relations between these apostles,

---

[15] For example, in Philo of Alexandria, "On Providence," II.6; "Allegory of the Laws," III.105–106; "Questions in Genesis," II.13. Other references in Neyrey, "The Fore and Background," n. 24.

it would seem an unlikely development that someone in the Petrine tradition would recommend the Pauline letters to his constituents. The author's opinion that the letters, even though they are to be accounted as scripture (3:16), are difficult to understand was shared by one of the early Church's finest biblical scholars, Origen of Alexandria, who remarked in his Commentary on Romans: "It is not easy to understand what [Paul] is trying to say, since his incompetence to express himself makes him write one thing when thinking another, or the wording, because it is difficult to understand, allows of various interpretations."[16] The writer of 2 Peter warns against faulty interpretations, presumably by those whom he has just read out of the Church, and he pleads with his readers not to allow themselves to be "carried away" (3:17). The culprits are the "false teachers" who have risen up in the Church (2:1).

FROM PAULINE TO PETRINE

It is the internal pressure, fostered by those given to freewheeling interpretation of both scripture and tradition, that is causing the Church to close ranks against what is coming to be regarded as a common enemy. To counter the schisms, the central affirmations are being identified and articulated, as we saw in 1 John. The popular errors and the common forms of misbehavior are being defined, with the aim of drawing a sharp line of division between tolerated and intolerable manners of life. The principle of Paul urging acceptance of members in spite of conceptual and cultural differences, as articulated in 1 Corinthians 3, is a thing of the past. There is no longer, as there was with Paul (1 Cor. 4:5), a willingness to wait until the Lord comes to pronounce judgment on the validity of another's position or viewpoint. The basic guidelines by which decisions are to be made are (1) scripture—including the New Testament, now beginning to take shape, as well as older Jewish writings excluded by Jews from their canon (for example, Enoch, Assumption of Moses, Wisdom of Solomon); and (2) the authority handed down through the apostles.

Already within the book of Acts, there was a conscious effort to assert the ultimate authority of the apostolic circle of twelve and to refer basic issues to them for adjudication, as in the apostolic council in Acts 15. Pauline, Johannine, and Petrine traditions or schools had developed, as the later New Testament writings show. Each of them defined Christ and his covenant community in different ways. But given the dual pressures of the early second century—sociopolitical pressures from without, and doctrinal and ethical pressures from within—the various segments of the Christian community began to coalesce. Undoubtedly, the beginnings of the aggressive, dramatic Gnostic movement helped to spur unity in the face of what was regarded as a common threat to the integrity of the basic Christian belief in the incarnation of God in the man, Jesus of Nazareth, however it might be formulated.

Given the precedent taken over from Judaism for regarding the scriptures as normative, Christians must have sensed the possibility of a conver-

---

[16] Quoted by Fornberg, *Early Church*, p. 22, n. 10.

gence of apostolic and biblical authority. Before there could be anything like a normative interpretation of scripture and tradition, however, there had to be a common mind as to what comprised scripture. The pressure to come to this decision was heightened by the rapid proliferation of writings in the second century claiming to be apostolic and authoritative, and by Judaism's definition of its canon in the last decade of the first century. It is this Christian process of selection and the criteria by which the choices were made that will occupy us in the Epilogue.

ANNOTATED BIBLIOGRAPHY

BROWN, RAYMOND E. *Community of the Beloved Disciple.* New York: Paulist Press, 1979. A suggestive study of the Letters of John that traces the development of the Johannine sector of the early Church.

DIBELIUS, M., and CONZELMANN, HANS. *The Pastoral Epistles.* Philadelphia: Fortress Press, 1972. This revision of an older work traces the development of Pauline thought and Church life down to the generation after his death.

ELLIOTT, JOHN H. *1 Peter—A Home for the Homeless: A Sociological Exegesis.* Philadelphia: Fortress Press, 1981. A superb analysis of an early Christian community using sociological, cultural, and linguistic resources.

LAWS, SOPHIE. *The Epistle of James.* New York: Harper & Row, 1980. An illuminating study of this Epistle in light of the linguistic and conceptual patterns of the Hellenistic world.

MITTON, C. L. *The Epistle to the Ephesians.* Oxford, Eng.: Oxford University Press, 1951. An older but still useful analysis of the relation of this Epistle to the genuine Pauline Letters.

SCHÜSSLER FIORENZA, ELISABETH. *Invitation to the Book of Revelation.* Garden City, N.Y.: Doubleday (Image Books), 1981. An engaging, penetrating introduction to this perennially fascinating book.

Epilogue:

The New Testament Becomes Normative

Paul J. Achtemeier

The term "New Testament canon" refers to the collection of writings regarded by the Christian community as normative for its life and thought. Such a process of identifying writings that are to serve as standards for a given community is not unique to the Christian community; it could take place even in a nonreligious group. A "canon" is necessary any time a group seeks to maintain its identity, or to establish rules by which certain beliefs or behavior can be judged. For example, during the Hellenistic period the Alexandrian grammarians concerned for the purity and preservation of the Greek language drew up a "canon" of those authors whose use of the Greek language was considered standard, or normative. Similarly, the moral philosophers of the same period sought to establish rules or "canons" for the correct use of free will, or for genuine moral behavior.[1]

---

[1] E. Hennecke, W. Schneemelcher, *New Testament Apocrypha,* trans. R. McL. Wilson, vol. 1 (Philadelphia: Westminster Press, 1963), p. 63. This volume contains a good summary of material related to the process by which some books were accepted as canonical while others were rejected; see pp. 19–59.

It is in that sense that we speak of the "canon" with reference to the writings we know as the New Testament: They represent the standard or norm of belief and practice for the Christian community. The canon is simply an expression of the authority acknowledged by, and functioning within, that community. But why were certain writings singled out to perform this function? Why did various changes occur in the process of collecting that normative literature? What criteria were applied in that rather lengthy and complex process of selection?

Forces long present within the primitive Christian community made some form of canon virtually inevitable. Certain external pressures on that community, however, also contributed to the content and shape of the final canon, and we must examine those factors as well. The forming and finally the "closing" of the canon were simply an outgrowth of the process by which traditions produced by, and preserved within, that community were collected, reworked, and combined into the books that finally comprised the canon. In a sense, the canon is the end of the process begun when first Israel and then the primitive Christian community sought to preserve for future generations accounts of events that were foundational for their respective communities. Such foundation events—the Exodus of Israel from Egypt, the captivity in Babylon, the Resurrection of Jesus—were remembered, and finally written, organized, and preserved in the canon. We turn now to examine the internal and external forces at work within the primitive Christian community that caused it to give to the New Testament canon the shape it has.

INTERNAL FORCES
AFFECTING THE SHAPE OF THE CANON

The early community understood itself to be commissioned by its Risen Lord to spread the good news of the imminent incursion of God's rule into the world. Jesus himself had sent his followers to announce such news (Mark 3:14 and parallels, for the twelve; Luke 10:1–12, for the seventy), as indeed he had announced he would when he called his first followers (see Mark 1:16–20 and par.; the phrase "fishers of men" implies such missionary activity). The Gospel of Matthew closes with the Risen Christ commissioning his closest followers to undertake a worldwide mission of witness to what Jesus had said and who he was.

The Christian community understood itself as charged with proclaiming the good news about Jesus and what his career meant for the relationship between God and the human race. Such a sense of responsibility required the followers to witness to events surrounding the Lord. That assignment is reflected in the two basic types of writing included in the canon: the Gospels (which focus on Jesus as the subject) and the Epistles (which show the progress of the mission). While this division did not in fact appear for more than a century after the Christian community was formed, the very nature of the Christian experience is reflected in it, and perhaps made such a shape inevitable for the canon.

If a worldwide mission was to be undertaken, it would require activity by more than simply the twelve closest followers of Jesus. Others would have to be, and were, involved in such outreach, as the New Testament book of Acts makes clear. The danger then arose that such wider missionary proclamation would dilute or distort the information about Jesus that made up the content of that early preaching. Preachers who were not reliably acquainted with the traditions about Jesus (an example of that can be found in Acts 18:24–26) would undertake the missionary task, and would then have to be corrected by people better acquainted with those traditions. Yet even such reliable people would be in too short supply as the movement began to grow and spread. Some more reliable method needed to be found to preserve the integrity of the Christian proclamation throughout the missionary movement.

Two types of literature grew up to meet such needs. One type consisted of reliable accounts of the career and teachings of Jesus. These were drawn up to be used as handbooks by preachers, as well as for missionary purposes, such as the conversion of those who read them. Such collections of traditions about Jesus were eventually refined into the Gospels as we know them in the New Testament. A second type of literature produced to exercise oversight over the faith of mission communities was the pastoral letter, designed to meet and correct problems that arose when no reliable missionary could be present (Galatians is such a letter). In that way, the authority of the apostle could be exercised over a wider geographical area and within a larger time frame than the physical presence of the missionary made possible. In short, the carrying out of the mission of the community resulted in two kinds of literature that corresponded to the inherent structure of the Christian faith (Lord = followers; Gospels = Epistles).

Another factor, in addition to the shape of the Christian faith, that influenced the primitive community in both writing and collecting its literature into what eventually became a canon is that the Christian community understood itself as an outgrowth, indeed as the fulfillment, of Judaism. Jesus was understood to be the fulfillment of both the law (Pentateuch) and the prophets (see Matt. 5:17). So interpreted in light of the Christian faith, the writings of the Jewish community continued to be used well into the second century as primary sources for the missionary activity of the primitive community.[2] Indeed, in virtually every instance in the New Testament writings where there is a reference to scripture, the material quoted comes from those writings taken over from the Jewish community—i.e., from what Christians called the Old Testament.[3]

This appropriation of the authoritative writings of the Jewish community demonstrated the value of written documents for the life of a community of faith, and in that way hastened the production of a specifically Christian body of literature. The reference in 2 Peter 3:15–16 to the letters of the apostle

---

[2] To see how the Christian community made use of the Jewish scriptures in the second century, one may read Justin Martyr, *Dialogue with Trypho.*

[3] These writings are of course the "Old" Testament only for the Christian community, which sees a new covenant (testament = covenant) between God and humanity established in Jesus. The first (old) covenant is supplemented by a second (new) covenant. For the Jewish community, the Bible contains the scriptures produced by that community, and hence are hardly to be called "old."

Paul as "scripture" shows that this process of identifying authoritative writings had begun at an early stage in the development of a body of Christian literature.

The successful attempt to define a Jewish canon did not occur until the end of the first century (at Yavneh, about A.D. 90; see p. 56), perhaps in response to the appropriation by the Christian community of the Jewish scriptures. Indeed, the need to differentiate each community from the other may well have mutually influenced the process of the formation of a normative collection of literature. The emergence of the Jewish canon within Judaism exerted a significant influence in the direction of the formation of a similar body of authoritative literature indigenous to the Christian faith.

A third factor at work within the Christian community that led it to produce a body of authoritative literature was simply the passage of time. The primitive community expected the return of Jesus within a very short time (see Mark 9:1; Rom. 13:11b–12a). In that kind of situation, although the production of literature for internal use was important, including those very writings which inform us that Christians expected Jesus's speedy return, the need to vest authority in such literature was not so important. After all, the community was still small enough so that an authoritative person (e.g., an apostle) could be called upon to resolve disputes. If an apostle could not be there in person, he could at least send a letter in which he answered the various questions that arose (an example is 1 Corinthians). As time passed, however, and the community grew larger, such an appeal became more difficult. Even more, as the years passed the first generation of apostles and others who had known Jesus personally began to die out. It became apparent near the end of the first century that Jesus might not return before the last of the original witnesses had died, and thus the community would continue beyond the time when it was possible to appeal to a member of that generation in person.

The only recourse was to comb the writings of the apostles to find hints about how problems were to be resolved. That in its turn meant that certain writings now had to carry the importance which once the eyewitnesses themselves had carried. Instead of receiving solutions to problems directly from the apostles themselves, the community now had to resolve such problems by interpreting the apostolic traditions.

But where was true apostolic tradition to be found? After all, anyone could claim apostolic authority for a position or for an interpretation of apostolic tradition, and it could no longer be verified by direct appeal to that apostle. A writer of the early fourth century, Eusebius, describes the crisis which the death of the first generation precipitated: "But when the sacred band of the Apostles and the generation of those to whom it had been vouchsafed to hear with their own ears the divine wisdom had reached the several ends of their lives, then the federation of godless error took its beginning through the deceit of false teachers who, seeing that none of the Apostles still remained, barefacedly tried to replace the preaching of the truth by the counter-proclamation of 'knowledge falsely so-called.' "[4]

---

[4] Quoted from his *Ecclesiastical History,* iii, xxii, 8. The quotation is from the Loeb Classical Library edition, vol. 1, trans. K. Lake.

In this rather ornate way, Eusebius points to the problem that arose for the early community as a result of the passage of time and the death of those who had witnessed the career of Jesus. These factors gave added impetus to the community to begin to collect a body of authoritative writings—i.e., to form a canon. At the same time that these factors were at work within the primitive Christian community, external pressures were requiring it to speed up the process of canon formation. These outside forces invested what otherwise might have been a leisurely process with life and death urgency.

EXTERNAL FORCES
AFFECTING THE SHAPE OF THE CANON

The earliest of those external forces which had a significant effect on the formation of a canon by the Christian community was exerted by a man named Marcion, who originally stood within the Church. The son of a wealthy shipbuilder, Marcion came to Rome from Sinope (in Pontus, present-day Turkey), became a member of the church there, and supported it generously. About the year 144, however, it became evident that his understanding of the Christian faith was radically different from that of the Roman Christian community, and Marcion withdrew to form his own church. Believing all material creation to be evil, the work of a vengeful god who was ignorant of the higher God of love, Marcion held that the redemption Christ brought sprang from the desire of the higher God to redeem from the evils of this world those who would accept Christ. Since the vengeful God is the one to whom the Jewish scriptures point, in Marcion's view Christ did not come to fulfill, but to abolish the law and the prophets. For Marcion, the Jewish scriptures had only negative significance; it was from such a religion that Christ had come to redeem humanity.

Because Marcion could therefore not call upon the writings of the Old Testament as an authoritative body of literature, as did the Christian community at that time, he substituted for those writings the letters of the apostle Paul, which Marcion found to be in opposition to the Jewish law, and the Gospel of Luke, which he found "Pauline" in its theology. In order to conform those documents more closely to his point of view, Marcion apparently purged from the letters of Paul any passages that spoke in a positive way about the Jewish faith, its law, and its prophets. Similarly, he excised from Luke material that showed Old Testament influence—for example, the first two chapters of the Gospel.[5]

Marcion seems to have been the first one who formed a specifically Christian collection of authoritative literature. Ironically, he used that literature to support religious views the Christians in Rome and elsewhere felt compelled to reject. The Christian community thus faced a problem: In re-

---

[5] Although Marcion thus displayed some characteristics that were later part of the full-blown Gnostic systems, it is questionable whether Marcion himself is to be considered a Gnostic. For further information about the role of Marcion in the formation of the canon, see J. Knox, *Marcion and the New Testament* (Chicago: University of Chicago Press, 1942); E. C. Blackman, *Marcion and His Influence* (London: S.P.C.K., 1978).

jecting Marcion and his views, could it afford to reject the literature he used to support such views—i.e., the letters of Paul and the Gospel of Luke? If not, how could that literature be reclaimed? Marcion thus forced the Christian community to hasten the process of deciding what literature was indispensable and what was not.

Instead of rejecting the literature Marcion had appropriated, the community retained both the letters of Paul and the Gospel of Luke, thus confirming in their literature a structure (Gospel, apostle) which, as we saw above, was inherent in the Christian faith (Lord, followers). The community further affirmed that there were also other Gospels of equal authority to that of Luke, and other Epistles of equal authority to those of Paul. From other early Christian writings it is obvious that by the time Marcion appeared in Rome, all the literature contained in our present Christian canon (the New Testament) had been written, along with a good deal of other Christian writings. The Christian community therefore did not have to create what came to be regarded as canonical literature in order to combat Marcion. Rather, it simply reaffirmed that its basis of authority was broader than one Gospel and one apostle, and it reaffirmed the authority of the writings of the Jewish community of faith as well (the Old Testament).

If Marcion hastened the process of canonical formation, however, he did not bring it to a close. Much debate about the canon still lay ahead for the Christian community. But Marcion made it inevitable that the discussion was to be carried on in more haste than might otherwise have been the case.

A second external factor that played a significant role in the way the Christian community understood its own canonical literature was the movement centering around Montanus. Montanus appeared in Phrygia (also in present-day Turkey) about the middle of the second century and announced that with his appearance, the final stage of Christian revelation, the time of the Paraclete (Holy Spirit; see John 14:16, 26; 15:26) was at hand. He affirmed that the climax of the ages was therefore imminent, and that the New Jerusalem (see Rev. 21:2) was about to appear. He also called for a more rigorous ethical life and forbade all attempts to escape the persecutions that were being visited on the Christian communities. Accompanied by two "prophetesses" (Maxmilla and Priscilla), Montanus traveled widely, announcing the new age of the Spirit and the end of the world. In many ways, Montanus and his followers appeared to be a renewal of the apocalyptic fervor of the earlier Christian communities. The Montanist movement produced a large body of literature (now unfortunately lost), and won many converts, among them the Church Father Tertullian.

Because Montanus claimed powers promised in a writing that was widely accepted as authoritative (the Gospel of John) and seemed to renew the early fervor of the Christian movement, he represented a significant alternative to the other Christian communities, which were becoming increasingly institutionalized. How was his influence to be countered? The Christians could not deny that the Holy Spirit had been promised to them, but they could, and did, deny Montanus's claim that the Spirit spoke as authoritatively through him as it had through the apostles of Christ. But to do that, the Christian community had to affirm that the apostolic period set the standards for the understanding of any further communications from the Spirit. Since the followers of Montanus also produced a body of literature, the Christian communities that opposed him had to affirm that only those writings which drew directly on apostolic traditions were authoritative, and were therefore the norm for the faith of the community.

Marcion had made it imperative for the Christian community to collect a body of normative Christian literature; Montanus made it imperative to affirm that only those writings that could call on true apostolic authority could be included in the body of normative literature. If Marcion hastened the idea of a canon, Montanus hastened the idea of a closed canon, one to which no further books could be added. It is also worth noting that because Montanus represented an apocalyptic outlook and called on the Gospel of John to support his claims to be the Paraclete, in some areas the Revelation of John and the Gospel of John sank in esteem. For a century or more, some segments of the Christian community no longer accorded them the authoritative status they had once enjoyed.

The second and third centuries saw other movements that purported to represent truer expressions of the Christian faith than that of the more "orthodox" communities, and each of them appears to have produced its own body of literature. The most prominent among these are the Gnostic movements, which in one form or another announced a secret knowledge that would enable the initiate to transfer from the evil realm of matter to the superior realm of the spirit. Several "gospels" were produced by these movements (Gospel of Truth, Gospel of Philip, Gospel of Thomas), each purporting to contain the secret and thus true teachings of Jesus. Although they produced no new apostolic Epistles, through allegorical interpretation they did appropriate Paul as a witness to their beliefs.[6]

It was in the context of such varied claims to the truth of the Christian faith that the "orthodox" communities argued as to which writings could be regarded as authoritative, and hence which belonged to a canon. It alone would provide the norm by which true Christian faith was to be measured. We have seen some of the reasons why a canon was necessary, reasons both internal and external to the Christian community. In the actual process of sifting books as it proceeded in the first two or three centuries after the birth of Christ, by which criteria were some chosen and others rejected?

DEVELOPMENT OF THE CHRISTIAN CANON

The process of canon formation was not limited simply to deciding whether or not the twenty-seven books now included in the New Testament belonged there. That assumption would be false on two counts. Only late in the process of canon formation were the present twenty-seven books agreed upon; earlier writers tended to limit the number to twenty or twenty-two. We must not imagine a process in which, for example, all twenty-seven books were lying on a table in a conference room, with Church authorities discussing them, one by

[6] For a good discussion of the way this was done, see E. H. Pagels, *The Gnostic Paul* (Philadelphia: Fortress Press, 1975).

one, to determine whether or not to include them. As we will see, such a "conference" never did take place. Rather, one must take into account the large amount of literature circulating within the Christian community by the second century. The canonical process involved the determination of which writings from that mass of literature produced in the first century should even be considered as candidates for authoritative status. Nor did the flow of literature cease with the close of the first century. Gospels and epistles continued to be produced until well into the second century, so the Christian communities had to be engaged in a continuing process of deciding which books were to be held as normative for faith and practice, and which were not.

Gospels such as the Gospel of Truth and the Gospel of Philip produced by the Gnostic movements were never serious candidates for canonical recognition, but other gospels (the Gospel of the Hebrews, the Gospel of Peter) were known from early times and were quoted by some early Christian writers. In addition to a larger number of gospels, there were many epistles, again of early origin and quoted by early Christian writers (the Epistle of Barnabas; the correspondence between Jesus and Abgar) about which decisions had to be made. There was still other literature, such as the Teaching of the Twelve Disciples (Didache), the Shepherd of Hermas, a variety of Acts of individual apostles (Thomas, Matthew, Peter, Paul and Thecla), as well as numerous apocalyptic writings in addition to the Revelation of John (Apocalypse of Peter, of Paul, of Thomas, of Stephen). All these and more were circulating, and some communities found one or more of them useful for instruction or reading in worship services. That meant those writings also had claims to authoritative status that had to be weighed and evaluated.

Alongside such written material, oral traditions about Jesus continued to circulate, some similar to, but some also quite different from, the traditions contained in the Four Gospels we have in the New Testament.[7] An early second-century Christian, Papias, is reported to have said he preferred oral to written sources of information about Jesus: "For I did not suppose that information from books would help me so much as the word of a living and surviving voice."[8] Justin Martyr, writing later in the second century, knew and included in his writings a number of such sayings of Jesus which are not in the Four Gospels, showing how persistently such sayings survived. Justin evidently thought they had equal authority with the words of Jesus contained in the written Gospels. But if writings could be produced in the names of various apostles, it would be even easier to produce unwritten sayings of Jesus. Apart from a written source, how could the authenticity of such sayings be validated? Is quotation of them in a reliable source (such as Justin) enough? The Christian community had to decide what to do about the authority of these oral sources as well.

Given the mass of literature being produced and circulated on into the second century and beyond, it is surprising how quickly unanimity was reached on a core of writings that were acknowledged to be authoritative. The

[7] For a collection of sayings attributed to Jesus which are not contained in the four canonical Gospels, see J. Jeremias, *Unknown Sayings of Jesus*, trans. R. H. Fuller (London: S.P.C.K., 1957).

[8] Reported in Eusebius, III, xxxix, 4.

writings of the Apostolic Fathers—Christians from the generation after that of the apostles—quote from sayings of Jesus. From these writings it is evident that the four canonical Gospels not only pretty well exhausted the reliable traditions about sayings of Jesus, but also that all four were already well known in widely scattered Christian communities. A consensus had therefore emerged by the end of the first century that the Gospels of Matthew, Mark, Luke, and John were primary sources for, and authoritative expressions of, the Christian faith. The remaining question was whether one or more of the other gospels (the Gospel of Peter, the Gospel of the Hebrews) should be added to those four.

An early consensus seems also to have arisen concerning the letters of Paul as authoritative documents of the Christian faith. In late first- and early second-century Christian writings, there was no unanimity on how many letters Paul had written. Some thought Paul had written Hebrews; others did not. Marcion knew a letter of Paul to the Laodiceans (see Col. 4:16) which others doubted Paul had written. Most of the letters of Paul now included in the New Testament, however, were already known and widely regarded as authoritative by the first decades of the second century. Other letters from the three "pillars" of the community—Peter, James (Jesus's brother, not the James who was the brother of John), and John, so identified by Paul in Galatians 2:9—were also known and widely used, although there was no unanimity as to how many from each author ought to be accorded authority. In addition to these Gospels and letters, other writings were highly regarded, such as the Acts of the Apostles, the Shepherd of Hermas, the Revelation of John and of Peter, the Gospel of Peter, and the Epistle of Barnabas. How should it be decided which to include in the canon?

THE PROCESS OF CANONICAL SELECTION

The recognition that some form of written authority was necessary in order to maintain the purity of the faith by a community was one thing; agreeing on what those written authorities ought to be was another. We have already seen that the scripture of the Christian community from the outset was the Old Testament, in most cases in its Greek translation (the Septuagint). Paul quoted from many of its books in his letters; Jesus is remembered to have used it as authoritative. And the Gospel writers also made use of it in their interpretations of Jesus's mission, understanding him to have fulfilled the promises about the Messiah contained in the Jewish scriptures.

An early Christian writer, Justin Martyr, wrote an Apology around the year 160 in which, describing Christian worship practices, he referred to public reading from the "memoirs of the apostles" and the "writings of the prophets" (Apology 1 67 3). The latter very likely referred to the prophetic books in the Jewish scriptures, while the reference to the "memoirs" clearly means our Gospels. In another writing Justin introduces a quotation from Matthew 16:4 by calling it a "memoir" (Dialogue with Trypho 107, 1). In this instance of Christian community worship practice, therefore, the Gospels, at least, were held to be of equal value with the Jewish scriptures.

A papyrus fragment of a noncanonical Gospel, akin to the synoptic Gospels, but with traces of influence from the Gospel of John. It seems to be a mixture of oral tradition and imperfectly remembered traces of the canonical Gospels. It is written on papyrus, a reed often used in antiquity as a writing material. The coarse fibers are visible in this picture.   (*British Museum*)

Another writer of about the same time, Irenaeus, a bishop of Lyon in France, not only knew of the Four Gospels, but justified that number by comparing it to the four points on the compass or the four winds, in that way limiting the Gospels to four and grounding the number in creation itself.[9] Irenaeus also held in high regard the letters of Paul, 1 Peter, and 1 John. In addition, he named as "scripture" the Shepherd of Hermas and the Wisdom of Solomon.[10] He did not name in that way 2 John, 3 John, 2 Peter or Philemon, and did not seem to value either James or the Epistle to the Hebrews very highly. He apparently saw no reason to question the worth of the Revelation of John.[11] It is clear, therefore, that by the last quarter of the second century a collection of specifically Christian writings was beginning to emerge as authoritative, to be used alongside the Jewish scriptures.

Acknowledgment of the Four Gospels was not, however, universal at this time. The Gospel of John, perhaps because of the use made of it by Montanus and some Gnostics, was suspect in some areas of the Christian community. As late as the early third century, a bishop of Rome, Hippolytus, felt it necessary to defend the validity of that Gospel against attacks on it by a certain Gaius.

[9] See his major writing *Adversus Haereses* (Against Heresies) III, xi 8. This work was written about 180.

[10] He is quoted to this effect in Eusebius, V viii 1–8.

[11] Eusebius, V viii 5–6.

Another early Christian, Tatian, a disciple of Justin Martyr, combined all Four Gospels into one running narrative called the "Diatessaron." Although such a harmony of the Four Gospels was rejected by most of the early Christian community, its existence shows clearly enough that while the Four Gospels were held in high regard, they had not yet achieved canonical status, if by "canonical" we mean writings held to be normative in the present form, and not to be tampered with.[12]

The wide range of writings considered authoritative by some parts at least of the early Christian community is indicated by the writings of Clement of Alexandria, who died about 215. In his work *Hypotyposeis* (Reflections) he wrote brief explanations not only of our Four Gospels, the letters of Paul including Hebrews,[13] and the "Catholic Epistles" (James, 1, 2 Peter, 1, 2, 3 John, and Jude), but also of the Epistle of Barnabas and the Apocalypse of Peter. In another writing, *Stromateis* (Miscellanies), he also cites as authoritative the Epistle of Clement (a different Clement), The Wisdom of Solomon, and The Wisdom of Sirach.[14]

A good summary of the views of the early community about which books were considered authoritative and which were not is found in a list called the Canon Muratorianus, named after Muratori, a librarian in Milan who discovered and published the list in 1740. It seems to come from sometime in the later second or early third century,[15] and appears to have been translated from Greek (our only text is in Latin). Although the beginning is lost, it includes as authoritative the Gospels of Luke and John (the lost beginning very likely names Matthew and Mark), the Acts of the Apostles, thirteen letters of Paul (Hebrews is omitted), Jude, 1 and 2 John, The Wisdom of Solomon, the Revelation of John, and the Revelation of Peter, although it is conceded that this last is not universally recognized. The list rejects the letters of Paul to the Laodiceans and one to the Alexandrians, which were apparently also circulating, along with the Gnostic gospels and the writings of Marcion and Montanus. The Shepherd of Hermas is also mentioned as useful, but not to be read publicly in the churches. We do not know how widely held were the views contained in the Canon Muratorianus, but the list does show that what we today know as "canon" had not yet emerged, since some books

[12] This meaning of "canonical" has not always been carefully observed by scholars who write on the subject of canon in the early Christian community. The best treatment of this subject is that of H. F. von Campenhausen, *The Formation of the Christian Bible*, trans. J. A. Baker (Philadelphia: Fortress Press, 1972), who is careful not to confuse "authoritative" with "canonical."

[13] The Epistles of Paul are Romans, 1, 2 Corinthians, Galatians, Ephesians, Philippians, Colossians, 1, 2 Thessalonians, 1, 2, 3 Timothy, Titus, Philemon, and sometimes Hebrews. Early Christians varied in their opinion on whether the Pauline collection included twelve letters (omitting Philemon and Hebrews), thirteen (omitting Hebrews), or all fourteen.

[14] Eusebius tells us this about Clement's works which have been almost completely lost (VI xiii 4–9, xiv 1–3).

[15] Although a date in the second century is usually assumed for the Canon Muratorianus, some scholars have argued that it belongs to a later period. On this point, see A. C. Sundberg, Jr., "Canon Muratori: A Fourth Century List," *Harvard Theological Review* 66 (1973), pp. 1–41.

now in the New Testament were missing (Hebrews, 3 John, James), and some others were still present (The Wisdom of Solomon).

It was with Origen (182–251), who designated as the "New Testament" the collection of Christian scripture, that what we know by that term began to emerge, even though his list was shorter than ours. Origen acknowledged as scripture (and probably by now as "canonical" as well) the Four Gospels and Acts, fourteen letters of Paul (including Hebrews, even though Origen did not think Paul wrote it), 1 Peter, 1 John, and the Revelation of John. Absent are 2, 3 John (Origen knew them but doubted their genuineness), 2 Peter (also known but doubted), James, and Jude. It is noteworthy that Origen introduced three categories of Christian writings. In addition to those surely to be regarded as canonical and those to be rejected, Origen included a third category: those about which opinions differed. The third category is the interesting one for our purposes, since the books we have in our New Testament which Origen omitted from the first category he included in the third category, along with the Shepherd of Hermas.

Eusebius, writing in the early fourth century and our source for much information about the first three centuries of the Christian community, still retains this threefold classification. As genuine, Eusebius reckoned the Four Gospels, Acts, fourteen letters of Paul, 1 John, and 1 Peter. Disputed books included James, Jude, 2 Peter, and 2 and 3 John. Strangely, he included the Revelation of John in both the recognized and disputed categories, thereby showing that division of opinion about that book persisted. Otherwise, the books named in the "genuine" and "disputed" categories exhaust what we have in the New Testament. By Eusebius's time, the Shepherd of Hermas, the Epistle of Barnabas, the Apocalypse of Peter, and The Wisdom of Solomon have all disappeared from serious contention as canonical Christian scripture. It is clear from this outcome that the canonical process was more a paring down than an expansion and that acceptance on an early list did not mean acceptance by a later generation.

It was not until the year 367 that a list of Christian scriptures as we know them in the New Testament finally appeared. In his thirty-ninth festal letter, published in 367, Athanasius, then bishop of Alexandria, listed twenty-seven books as the "springs of salvation" and as included in "the canon." The books from Origen's and Eusebius's "disputed" lists have now been included, and those in the "rejected" category are also specifically rejected by Athanasius: The Wisdom of Solomon, Shepherd of Hermas, Wisdom of Sirach, the Teaching of the Apostles (Didache), and some others. They do not belong in the canon despite their age or the value set on them in some places. They can be used with profit as "reading matter" but not as canonical, as the rule of Christian doctrine and action.[16] Such language by Athanasius makes it clear enough that the idea of a Christian canon has now fully emerged. Even then, however, it was not universally accepted, and would not be by Christians from Syria until early in the seventh century.

---

[16] The text of the relevant portions of Athanasius's letter can be found in Hennecke and Schneemelcher, vol. 1, pp. 59–60. The text of the Canon Muratorianus can also be found there, pp. 43–45.

The initiative for determining which books were to be recognized as authoritative, and hence as "canonical," and which were not, did not rest with some ecumenical council or other authoritative body. The process of selection grew out of the life of the Christian community, as that community used those books and found some of them more valuable than others. The canon therefore grew up out of the community, from the "grass roots," as it were, rather than having been imposed "from above" by some authoritative person or council. Those books about which there was some perplexity, such as the Revelation of John, continue to be the source of debate among Christian readers even to the present time. Those books about which there was some doubt—2, 3 John, Jude, 2 Peter—are the books that tend to have less attention paid to them right down to the present. In that way, an informal selection process of the canonical New Testament continues to be reflected in the faith of contemporary Christians.

CRITERIA OF CANON SELECTION

Because the canon represents a collective decision reached by the Christian community at large over a period of centuries, we will not find a document in which the criteria for canonicity are given in detail. Only hints were dropped by second- and third-century authors when they discussed why they thought some books were authoritative for the Christian community and some were not. Even after a given criterion was accepted, problems could arise when someone attempted to apply that criterion. If authorship by an apostle, for example, were a criterion, the decision still needed to be made about whether or not an apostle wrote a certain book. The Revelation of John was attributed to the disciple John, but also to the Gnostic Cerinthus. The Epistle of James was attributed variously to James the brother of Jesus or to James the son of Zebedee, the brother of John. Whether or not Paul wrote Hebrews was also, as we saw, open to debate.

What were the criteria? (1) Some authors implied that their reason for attributing authority to a given writing was that it was highly valued by a number of Christian communities. (2) Others mentioned that some writing was cited in another early writing as a reason to take the book seriously. In addition to the criterion of (3) apostolic authorship is that of (4) apostolic tradition: Does the writing in question represent the kind of Christian teaching associated with the apostles? Since such apostolic tradition was regarded as the rule of faith (Latin *regula fidei*), another way to phrase the last criterion would be this: (5) Does the writing display the *regula fidei* acknowledged in the Christian community? Our task now is to examine each of these criteria, to see how it was applied and which were the relatively more important.

Use of a Writing by the Community

The public reading of Christian writings, as well as portions of the Old Testament, was a regular part of the worship of the primitive community. Justin Martyr mentioned readings from the apostolic memoirs and from the prophets, and Dionysius, a bishop of Corinth in the second century, wrote to Soter, Bishop of Rome: "Today we observed the holy day of the Lord, and read out your letter, which we shall continue to read from time to time for our admonition, as we do that which was formerly sent to us through Clement."[17] That was not a unique occurrence. Eusebius, writing of that same epistle we know as 1 Clement (sent by Clement from Rome to the churches in Corinth near the end of the first century), remarked that "We have ascertained that this letter was publicly read in the common assembly in many churches, both in the days of old and in our own time."[18] About another writing, the Shepherd of Hermas, Eusebius notes that "it has been used in public in churches,"[19] and about the letters of James and Jude: "We know that these letters have been used publicly with the rest [of the Catholic Epistles] in most churches."[20]

That such public reading of Christian literature goes back to the earliest times of the Christian community we can infer from some of the literature produced at that time. In the letter to the community at Colossae, the author, writing in the name of Paul, exhorts the recipients to read the letter publicly, and then to exchange it for a letter written to the community at Laodicea (Col. 4:16). There is every likelihood that the other letters of Paul were also intended to be read publicly to the community, most likely within a setting of worship or of instruction.

It is clear that in reading Christian literature publicly in contexts of worship and catechetical instruction, Christian communities valued what they found useful for such purposes. Public reading elevated such material to candidacy for inclusion in the canon. Even more powerful was the negative factor: Unless a writing was used publicly in worship by some community, it could not be taken seriously as a normative statement of the faith. Public use alone was not enough to confer normative (or canonical) status on such a writing; the quotations from Eusebius show that. Two of the writings he mentioned as having been used in public worship were finally included in the canon (James, Jude) and two were not (1 Clement, Shepherd of Hermas). The most such use alone could do was place the writing in the middle category of Christian literature (between canonical and rejection): "those books which are disputed yet nevertheless are used openly by many in most churches."[21]

Quotation in Ancient Authorities

Two factors are at work in the matter of quotation of one ancient (early Christian) writing by another, somewhat later author. On the one hand, it was a part of the intellectual environment of the Hellenistic world to revere what was ancient and to question what was new. For that reason Eusebius, in

---

[17] Quoted in Eusebius, IV xxiii 11.
[18] III xvi 1.
[19] III iii 7.
[20] II xxiii 25.
[21] Eusebius, III xxxi 6.

writing about the value and trustworthiness of the Christian faith, was careful to make the point that what Jesus taught was not new, but in fact had origins far older than Jesus himself. Eusebius wrote: "Thus we have demonstrated that the practice of piety handed down by the teaching of Christ is not new or strange, but, if one must speak truthfully, is primitive, unique and true."[22] In that kind of cultural and intellectual milieu, to prove a thing ancient and traditional is very close to proving it true. Thus writings which contain truth must be of an early origin. To find that an item of Christian literature quoted in the very early years of the primitive Christian community was ancient would be desirable, if not absolutely necessary, in order for that literature to be taken seriously as a candidate for normative expression of faith.

On the other hand, by the late second and early third centuries, many Gospels, Epistles, and Acts of various apostles were appearing on the scene, all clamoring for recognition, and in many instances, expressing the particular understandings of some special Christian group. If it could be shown that a writing was quoted early on, it would thereby be removed from suspicion of recent falsification. The problem was still present in the late fourth century when Athanasius, in his thirty-ninth festal letter (367) notes that those who fabricated such documents "generously assign to them an early date of composition in order that they may be able to draw upon them as supposedly ancient writings."[23] Similarly, when Eusebius notes that Polycarp in a letter to Philippi quotes 1 Peter, or that Dionysius refers to 1 Clement in his letter to Soter in Rome, Eusebius is showing that 1 Peter and 1 Clement are not recent compositions.[24] In the same vein, the absence of early quotation of the Epistles of James and Jude caused a number of Christian communities to reject those epistles as authoritative, much less normative, Christian writings.[25]

Important as such quotation in early authorities might have been, however, mention alone was not sufficient to guarantee inclusion in the Christian canon. As in the case of public use, quotation by ancient authorities lent authority to a given writing, enabling it to be used by the community, but still only placing it in candidacy for canonical inclusion.

Apostolic Origin

The major consideration for final inclusion in the canon emerges with some clarity from precisely those writings of the second through the fourth centuries which we have been considering. That criterion was whether or not the writing could sustain for itself the claim to apostolic origin. Yet how that "apostolic origin" was understood, and how it was demonstrated, present a complex picture.

[22] I iv 15; see also the whole of I iv for the discussion that led to the conclusion we have quoted.

[23] The text of the relevant portions of this letterr may be found in Hennecke and Schneemelcher, pp. 59–60.

[24] IV xiv 8; IV xxiii 11.

[25] Eusebius, II xxiii 25.

The most obvious way to demonstrate apostolic origin for a writing would be to claim that it was written by an apostle. For that reason, there was a good deal of discussion within the early Christian community about whether or not a given writing could legitimately claim to have been written by an apostle. The Gospels of Matthew and John, for example, were accepted as having been written by the two apostles who bore those names, and Mark and Luke were held to reflect the preaching of Peter and Paul, respectively (for Mark, see 1 Peter 5:13; for Luke, 1 Clem. 4:4). Those who rejected the Revelation of John did so, with some regularity, by denying that its author could have been the same person as the apostle who wrote the Gospel of John, thus effectively denying to Revelation apostolic authorship.

Yet the picture is complicated by the fact that some accepted the Revelation of John who also remained unconvinced that the apostle John had written it. Dionysius, a bishop of Alexandria in the mid-third century, in discussing the authorship of the Revelation of John, wrote: "That [the author] then, was certainly named John and that the book is by one John, I will not gainsay. . . . But I should not readily agree that he was the apostle, the son of Zebedee, the brother of James, whose are the Gospel entitled According to John and the Catholic Epistles."[26] That same Dionysius carried out what even by modern standards must be called a sophisticated analysis of the language, style, and content of the Johannine literature and came to conclusions virtually identical with those currently held by critical scholarship (Rev., 2 and 3 John were written by an author different from the one who wrote the Gospel and 1 John).[27]

It would be simple to conclude that, since those who collected the canon did so on the basis of beliefs about the apostolic authorship of the New Testament books we can no longer share, the modern Christian need no longer take seriously their decisions. In fact, apostolic authorship, while valued, was not the sole or even the major factor in determining the apostolic origin of the material! It was not authorship but content that was the determining factor. The reason is clear enough: Most later forgeries were also written in the names of the apostles, thus rendering the mere claim to apostolic authorship invalid as a primary consideration. Eusebius, discussing the various forgeries that bear apostolic names, points specifically to the fact that in such forgeries, "the type of phraseology differs from the apostolic style, and the opinion and tendency of their contents is widely dissonant from true orthodoxy."[28] Similarly, Serapion, bishop of Antioch in the late second century, was asked by some members of his community if the Gospel of Peter could be used as authoritative for the Christian community. Serapion answered in the affirmative, on the basis of reputed authorship. When, however, he read the "gospel," he withdrew his approval, since the content was not such as to uphold its claim to apostolic

---

[26] Quoted in Eusebius, VII xxiv 7. In a similar disregard for authorship, Eusebius quoted Origen, who accepted as normative the Epistle to the Hebrews, as saying about its author: "But who wrote the epistle, in truth God knows," the implication being that Origen himself certainly did not (Eusebius, VI xxv 14).

[27] See Eusebius, VII xxv 19–27.

[28] III xxv 6–7.

origin.[29] Clearly enough, it was the content of a given writing which, in the final analysis, determined whether or not it would be included in the canon.

What all this demonstrates is that before the limits of the canon (the collection) of authoritative writings were determined, a criterion was already in operation which enabled early Christians to differentiate those writings which were to be accorded normative status from those which were not, regardless of claims about authorship. That criterion came to bear the name *regula fidei,* or "rule of faith." Perplexing as it may seem, however, during a major portion of the period of canon formation, that rule of faith had itself received no fixed formulation. Such fixed formulations were to begin only with the confession adopted at the Council of Nicea in 325. Nor was there a major expression of that rule of faith apart from the writings eventually included in the canon.[30] Therefore, if the community selected the books to be included in the canon, those books themselves contained the criterion the community applied in their selection. It was, to be sure, as circular a reasoning process as it appears, but as nearly as we can determine, that is the way the canon was formed. Growing out of the common faith of the Christian community, certain writings were judged by the community, over many decades and through intimate use, to be pure and hence authoritative expressions of that common faith.

The process of canonical selection was therefore virtually identical to the process by which, for example, those traditions of the sayings and acts of Jesus were selected that were finally included in the Four Gospels. The Gospels do not purport to be exhaustive records of everything known about what Jesus said and did. John 20:30 and 21:25 make that abundantly clear, as do the frequent summaries of Jesus's activity contained in the synoptic Gospels. It was the experience of the community which, so it appears, led to some traditions being included in the Gospels and others omitted. In the same way, it was the common experience of the community with a wide variety of early Christian literature that it studied and proclaimed and read in its worship which led that community over the course of two or three centuries to decide which individual writings from that literature represented the normative expression of that rule of faith, the *regula fidei.*

One can say, therefore, that the formation of the canon was the product of the common life of the Christian community during its first three centuries of existence. It is not the case that some synod or council of bishops decided which books should be normative, and thereafter required Christians to accept them. Rather, the books finally included in the canon were so designated because over the centuries Christians had come to use them in their worship and instruction, and to revere them for the power they displayed in engendering, enriching, and correcting Christian faith. The canon thus represents the collective experience and understanding of the Christian community during the formative centuries of its existence.

---

[29] See Eusebius, VI xii 2–6.

[30] D. Luehrmann makes that point in a convincing way in his article "Gal. 2 und die katholischen Briefe," in *Zeitschrift fuer die neutestamentliche Wissenschaft,* 72 (1981), pp. 65–87.

FURTHER DEVELOPMENTS IN THE CANON

Although the canon itself reflects the common understanding of the faith during the first four centuries, it has never actually been "closed," even though on occasion some juridical body has formally declared that from that point on, no books were to be added or taken away from the canon. This openness is shown by some further developments in the Christian community in the course of the centuries.

If it is true that the canon reflects the common experience of the community of faith with certain pieces of Christian literature, then when the common experience and understanding of the community undergo some kind of significant, even radical, challenge, the perception of the canon ought also to change, even to the point of some efforts to alter it. Such a course of events is precisely what did occur at the time of the Reformation, when a significant divergence appeared in the way large groups of Christians understood their faith. A brief look at the way that divergence affected the understanding of the canon will show clearly the relationship between the canon as the normative expression of the faith, and the way the community understood its faith.

In order to understand the changes in what was perceived to be canonical that occurred at the time of the Reformation in the sixteenth century, we must return to the period of the beginnings of the Christian community. When the first-century Christian community moved from its origins in Palestine among Aramaic-speaking people out into the Hellenistic world where Greek was the universal tongue, the Septuagint translation of the Old Testament was widely used among non-Palestinian Jews and quickly became the common Christian version of the scriptures. It included some fourteen additional writings, along with a lengthened version of the Book of Esther, which had not been found in the Hebrew version of the collection of writings. Because the Septuagint had become the canonical form of the Old Testament for the Christian community, those fourteen writings were also regarded by it as canonical. When in the western Mediterranean Latin displaced Greek as the language of the community, the Latin Old Testament (the Vulgate) also included those fourteen writings, in addition to the thirty-nine writings which had appeared in the Hebrew Old Testament. The Christians, therefore, had a broader base for the scriptures in a normative sense than the Palestinian Jewish community that had produced the central core of the scriptures.

By the sixteenth century, a central issue for the Christian community was the way scriptures were to be used in the life and thought of the community. That struggle included dispute about what constituted canon as well. The supporters of the Reformation came to the conclusion that the Apocrypha (those fourteen books from the Septuagint not contained in the Hebrew scriptures) were of inferior quality to the remaining thirty-nine books in the Old Testament, and in the course of time eliminated them from their canon. Protestant Bibles in the seventeenth and eighteenth centuries were printed without the Apocrypha. Eventually a series of confessions (written statements of the basic Christian creed) confirmed this reduced canon from the Protestant side. The statements by the Roman Catholic community at the Council of Trent, however, continued to maintain the longer canon, which included the Apocrypha. That division of opinion has continued to the present day. In those events we can see clearly the relationship of canon to the way the Christian community understands its faith: When a basic shift occurs in that understanding, a shift occurs in what is regarded as normative literature—i.e., the canon.

In the Reformation, the followers of the German theologian Martin Luther (Lutherans) and the followers of the French theologian John Calvin (Reformed) disclosed how questions of faith and canon are linked by not only excluding the Apocrypha from their Old Testament, but also by disagreeing as to the value of certain New Testament writings.

Luther, in his translation of the Bible into German, rearranged the New Testament books, putting at the very end, and after a blank space in the list, Hebrews, James, Jude, and Revelation. Some years later, in a commentary on the Lutheran *Confessio Virtembergica* of 1551, a Lutheran theologian disputed the right of the Church to hold Hebrews, James, 2 Peter, and Revelation as canonical. They were valuable, he said, for edification, but were not normative statements of the Christian faith.[31] In the end such judgments did not prevail, and the followers of Luther did in fact accept as canonical the twenty-seven books of the New Testament which both the Reformed and the Roman Catholics had continued to hold.

Such disagreements between Protestants and Roman Catholics about what constitutes the canon of the Old Testament, and between the Reformed and Lutherans on what constitutes the canon of the New Testament, throw two points into sharp relief. The first point is that when the community of faith experiences direct challenges to the customary way it has understood the faith, those challenges will have repercussions in the understanding of the canon. The intimate relationship between the canon and the understanding of the faith is thus clearly demonstrated. The second point relates to the question of whether or not the canon is "closed"—i.e., unalterable. Because the canon is so closely linked to the community's understanding of its faith, it is clear that one cannot speak in fact of a closed canon. That has not meant, of course, that every individual Christian is free to add to or subtract from a personal canon, and hold it to be as authoritative for the faith as a canon based on the collective experience and understanding of the community. But it does mean that because of the close relationship between canon and community, the possibility always exists that significant changes in the experience and understanding of the community of faith at some future time will affect what that community holds to be canonical. Past experience, in which the New Testament canon emerged unchanged and the Old Testament virtually unchanged from the events surrounding the Reformation, indicates that such changes in the canon are not likely to be radical. But the Reformation does indicate that, so long as the community of faith is a living entity, the canon will not be unalterably "closed."

[31] See Luehrmann, "Gal. 2," pp. 73–75.

SUMMARY

We have seen how internal and external forces working on the primitive community of faith caused it to select, from among the variety of literature produced by the community in its first two hundred years, a limited number of writings in which it recognized normative authority for its life of faith. We have traced the process of shaping the canon over several centuries, concluding that the decision about which books were to be regarded as normative (canonical) was made primarily on the basis of their content. We have noted disagreements about the normative value of certain books of the New Testament. Some writings, enjoying early favor, were later excluded; other writings, regarded as of questionable value at first, later succeeded in demonstrating their normative value. In all this we recognize the close relationship between the shape of the canon and the community's understanding and experience of its own faith. That process continued even to the time of the Reformation and beyond. The fact that the impetus for the Reformation grew out of an understanding of the faith drawn from the Bible, and which led adherents of that understanding to challenge the community to alter its view of itself based on its own Bible, shows that because the canon grew out of the experience and understanding of the community, it retains the power to challenge that community in its understanding of the faith. Within the Roman Catholic tradition in recent decades—following the Second Vatican Council—the resurgence of scholarly and lay interest in the Bible has powerfully contributed to a changing understanding of Christian faith.

Thus the Bible has continued to function as both an expression of, and a challenge to, the way the community of faith understands itself and expresses that faith. That is to say, the Bible continues to function as canon, reflecting the apostolic origins of the community of faith and challenging that community to remain faithful to the witness of those apostolic origins, as reflected in its scriptures.

Appendixes

I. WHO AM I? WHO ARE WE?
THE IMPORTANCE OF LIFE-WORLD
FOR HISTORICAL METHOD

Looking at religion as a universal human phenomenon, Hans J. Mol—in a book significantly titled *Identity and the Sacred*[1]—has shown that a basic pattern of search and response may be perceived not only in explicitly religious movements, but also in social movements that invite human beings of whatever cultural background to find meaning and purpose through commitment to an enterprise that transcends their individual needs. As widely different as the specific values and aims might be, this generalization is applicable to movements ranging from Communist cadres to Buddhist communes, from devotees of yoga to charismatics. Mol discerns four facets of this process of gaining identity by what he calls "sacralization": (1) objectification, (2) commitment, (3) myth, (4) ritual. We must look at these factors individually and then consider their composite significance for our study of the New Testament.

By objectification is meant the construction or the unconscious acceptance of a view of the world and of the place of human beings within it. How did the world come to be? by accident? by design? by some cosmic mistake? Answers proposed for those questions will directly affect how one seeks to come to terms with life—by seeking to obey the sovereign of the universe, or by trying to change the world, or at least that portion of it, that affects my life. Whether one seeks peace, security, justice, or simply to make the best of a hopeless situation is the direct consequence of the world view one takes over from family or social context, or to which a conscious commitment is made.

That brings us to Mol's second factor: commitment. Whether the world view—or life-world, as sociologists of knowledge[2] have called it—is simply taken

---

[1] New York: Free Press, 1976. The approach and method of Mol's work as it bears on the study of early Christianity is developed in H. C. Kee, *Christian Origins in Sociological Perspective* (Philadelphia: Westminster Press, 1980).

[2] Peter, Berger, *The Sacred Canopy:* Elements of a Sociological Theory of Religion (Garden City, N.Y.: Doubleday, 1969). Peter Berger and Thomas Luckmann, *The Social*

over from one's environment by passive, nonreflective acceptance, or whether it is chosen by that dramatiç break with the past that might be called conversion,[3] it involves a commitment. Implicitly or explicitly there is the declaration: "This is what I take for granted about the world in which I live, and this is how I expect to live my life within that world."

Linked with the life-world and with commitment to it is the story about how things came to be as they are. To call it "myth" as sociologists and anthropologists do is not to dismiss such a story as mere fantasy or childish nonsense. Myth is a narrative, often poetic, way of describing the origins and purpose of the world and of life—especially of human life—within it. A myth is a kind of hypothesis about existence, just as theories of organic evolution or of the origins of the solar system are hypotheses, since they all treat of events for which there was no human observer and for which there are no records contemporary with the events other than the present results. What differentiates myth from scientific hypothesis, however, is that it does not claim to be an objective theory, but that its story becomes "my story," or better, "our story." As the myth is recounted, it becomes the basis for celebration of the origins of our world and of our heritage within it. Or if it sets forth an essentially negative view of the world, it advises us how to be delivered from evil. But in either case, we find out who we are by identifying with the story reported in the myth.

The fourth facet of the process of religious identity is ritual. By some action either public or within the purview of others of similar persuasion, the individual performs or shares in a sacred act by which his identification with those of similar conviction is demonstrated or experienced. This could be said of a puberty rite among primitive tribes, of the Nazis gathered for ceremonies evidencing their devotion to Hitler in the Nürnberg Stadium, of a vigil by Tibetan monks, or of the celebration of the Christian Eucharist. In each instance, and in thousands of others, the focal point is the bodily action or vocal affirmation (or a combination of the two) by which a person enacts identity with a committed group, thereby uniting the person with a group in values, beliefs, and purpose.

II. A CLASSIFICATION SYSTEM FOR ORAL FORMS IN THE SYNOPTIC GOSPELS

The basic assumption of form criticism is that traces of the oral forms remain embedded in our written Gospels. Various systems have been proposed for classification of these oral forms using literary terminology taken over from the Late Classical world. The following proposal for classification seeks to use terms that are descriptively accurate but that use more nearly standard English. The material incorporated into the Gospels is of two main types: sayings tradition and narrative tradition. The various categories are given below, with examples for each:

Sayings Tradition

The *aphorisms* are brief, often provocative sayings. In form they embody a contrast, distinguishing what people usually expect from life and what Jesus declares about God's way with his people.

The *parables* are extended metaphors, by which an event or a relationship in one realm of human experience is contrasted with an event in the kingdom of God

---

Construction of Reality (Garden City, N.Y.: Doubleday, 1966). Alfred Schutz and Thomas Luckmann, *The Structures of the Life-World* (Evanston, Ill.: Northwestern University Press, 1973).

[3] A. D. Nock, *Conversion* (Oxford, Eng.: Oxford University Press, 1933).

or in God's preparation of his people for his coming kingdom.

The *sayings clusters* are assembled around a key word or idea, as indicated in the topical list; the other clusters are characterized by recurrent form, as in the pronouncements by Jesus of who is blessed in the kingdom of God or who suffers as a consequence of exclusion from the kingdom.

1. *Aphorisms*

    Mark 4:9, Matt. 13:43; Luke 4:8; 14:35. "He who has ears to hear, let him hear." This maxim is also found in the noncanonical Gospel of Thomas, 24.

    Mark 4:22; Luke 8:17; variant in Matt. 10:26; Luke 12:2. "For there is nothing hid except to be revealed, nor is anything secret, except to come to light."

    Mark 4:25; Matt. 13:12; 25:29; Luke 8:18; 19:26. "For to him who has will more be given; and from him who has not, even what he has will be taken away."

    Mark 8:34; Matt. 16:24; Luke 9:23; variant form in Matt. 10:38; Luke 14:27. "If anyone would come after me, let him deny himself and take up his cross daily and follow me."

    Mark 8:35; Matt. 16:25; Luke 9:24; variant in Luke 17:33. "For whoever would save his life will lose it; and whoever loses his life for my sake and the gospel's will save it."

    Mark 9:25; variants in Mark 10:43–44; Matt. 20:26–27; Luke 22:26. "If any of you would be first, he must be last of all and servant of all."

    Mark 10:15; variants in Matt. 18:3; Luke 18:17, and Gospel of Thomas 37, 46. "Whoever does not receive the kingdom of God like a child shall not enter it."

    Mark 10:31; Matt. 19:30; 20:16; Luke 13:30. "Many that are first will be last, and the last first."

2. *Parables*

    Mark 4:3–8   The Parable of the Sower
    Mark 4:26–29   The Parable of the Secretly Growing Seed
    Mark 4:30–32   The Parable of the Mustard Seed
    Matt. 13:33   The Parable of the Leaven
    Matt. 13:47–50   The Parable of the Net
    Matt. 18:12–13   The Parable of the Lost Sheep
    Luke 10:29–37   The Parable of the Good Samaritan
    Luke 14:15–23   The Parable of the Great Supper (cf. Matt 22:1–10)

3. *Sayings Clusters*

    a.   *Topical groupings*

    Matt. 5:13; Luke 14:34–35 (salt)
    Matt. 5:14–16; Luke 11:33; Mark 4:21 (light)
    Matt. 5:17–20 (law)
    Mark 13:33–37 (watchfulness)
    Mark 2:18–20 (fasting)
    Mark 2:21–22 (old and new)
    Matt. 10:26–31; Luke 12:2–7 (freedom from fear)
    Matt. 10:37–38; Luke 14:26–27 (discipleship)
    Matt. 11:7–19; Luke 7:24–35 and 16:16 (John the Baptist)
    Matt. 5:33–37 (oaths)
    Matt. 5:38–42 (cf. Luke 6:29–30) (retaliation)
    Luke 6:27–28, 32–26; Matt. 5:43–48 (love of enemies)
    Matt. 6:25–34; Luke 12:22–31 (anxiety)
    Matt. 7:1–5; Luke 6:37–38, 41–42 (judging)
    Matt. 19:1–12; Mark 10:1–12 (cf. Matt. 5:32) (marriage and divorce)
    Mark 4:10–12; 4:21–25 (hidden and revealed)
    Mark 6:8–11; Matt. 10:9–14; Luke 10:4–11 (advice to disciples)

b.   *Formal groupings*
       Matt. 5:3–12; Luke 6:20–23 (beatitudes)
       Luke 6:24–26 (woes)
(The parables of the kingdom in Mark 4 (Matt. 13) and the woes against the Pharisees in Mark 12:38–40 (Matt. 23:1–36) exhibit a definite formal pattern and were
probably preserved in the tradition in cluster form.)

Narrative Tradition

The terminology used for classifying the narrative tradition deserves some explanation.

Anecdote is used in the usual sense of a brief narrative, usually biographical,
that reveals some unusual feature of the person described. The stories are not only
short but also lack biographical or chronological links with what is otherwise known
of the person who is the subject of the anecdote.

Aphoristic narratives are brief accounts that culminate in a proverbial or pithy
saying. The stories were probably not created as a vehicle for the saying, but they
point up an issue to which the saying is a response.

Wonder stories are told to demonstrate the extraordinary powers of Jesus. They
are often longer and provide more vivid detail than aphorisms or anecdotes, including development of the situation along dramatic lines. On grounds other than form,
the wonder stories of the synoptic tradition show the influence of the non-Christian
miracle-story tradition, for example in the inclusion of thaumaturgic detail in the
narratives of healing or exorcism (Mark 5:41; 7:34).

Legends are narratives intended to create a supernatural aura around the central figure. The specific aim of a legend may be biographical or cultic. If biographical, it serves to amplify, illuminate, or enrich the significance of Jesus for the
Church, often closely correlating detail of the narrative with Old Testament predictions. If the aim is cultic, the narrative provides the background and therefore
the authorization for the place of Jesus in the worship life of the Christian community. Thus baptism, the Eucharist, and the christological interpretation of Scripture
are all grounded in the ministry of Jesus by means of the cultic legends.

The *Passion narrative* is included here as a separate category of narrative, although with considerable reservation. There is good reason to question the older
notion that the Passion story received a more nearly fixed form earlier than did the
rest of the Gospel tradition and that it served as the nucleus around which the rest
of the tradition was later arranged. The Passion story itself does not appear to have
been so unified as was once supposed by form critics, since Luke and Matthew felt
free to introduce new material and to alter the substance of Mark's account. Indeed,
some scholars think Luke had an independent Passion narrative that he accommodated at some points to Mark's. John certainly had an independent tradition for his
Passion story. But in at least one "gospel"—Q—there seems to have been no Passion
account at all. The probability is that as the Passion became dominant in the
Church's thinking, the Passion narrative was developed and expanded, partly on
the basis of tradition units and partly on the basis of Christian reading of the Old
Testament.

1.   *Anecdotes*
       Mark 1:23–26; Luke 4:33–35
       Mark 1:29–31
       Mark 2:1–4, 11–12
       Mark 1:16–20 (cf. Luke 5:1–11)

Mark 1:40–44
Luke 7:18–23; Matt. 11:2–6
Luke 19:1–10

2. *Aphoristic Narratives*
Mark 2:23–28
Mark 3:1–5
Mark 10:17–22
Mark 10:13–16

3. *Wonder Stories*
Mark 5:1–20
Mark 5:21–43
Mark 9:14–27
Mark 10:46–52
Luke 7:11–17

4. *Legends*
   a. *Biographical Legends*
      Matt. 1:18–25 (Birth of Jesus)
      Luke 2:1–20 (Birth of Jesus)
      Luke 2:21–40 (Presentation in the Temple)
      Mark 1:12–13; Matt. 4:1–11 (Temptation)
      Mark 6:45–52 (Walking on the water)
      Mark 9:2–8 (Transfiguration)
      Mark 10:35–45 (Baptism of suffering)
      Mark 14:12–26 (Preparation for the Passover)
      Mark 14:32–43 (cf. Luke 22:43–44) (Prayer in Gethsemane)
      Matt. 27:62–66 (Guard at the Tomb)
      Matt. 28:2–4, 11–15 (Wonders accompanying the Resurrection)
      Luke 4:16–30 (Sermon and rejection in Nazareth)
      Luke 5:1–11 (Miraculous catch of fish)
   b. *Cult Legends*
      Mark 1:9–11 (cf. Matt. 3:14–15) (Baptism of Jesus)
      Mark 6:30–44; Mark 8:1–10; John 6:1–13 (Eucharist)
      Mark 14:22–25 (Lord's Supper)
      Luke 24:13–35 (Christ's presence in word and sacrament)

5. *Passion Narrative*
Mark 14:1–16:8; Matt. 26:1–28:10
Luke 21:1–24:11
John 18:1–20:29

III.   THE Q SOURCE: A FORMAL ANALYSIS

Defining Q as non-Markan material common to Matthew and Luke, and adopting the Lukan version of Q as our base, we come to the following results: (The designations in the left column are for this set of formal categories for characterizing the Q material:

Narratives	Na
Parables	Pa
Oracles	Or

Beatitudes	Be
Prophetic pronouncements	PP
Wisdom words	WW
Exhortations	Ex

Some of the material could fit under more than one of these categories, but these arrangements may be useful.

PP	3:7–9, 16b–17	John's eschatological preaching
Na	4:2b–12	Jesus's struggle with Satan
Be	6:20–23	Beatitudes: the poor, the hungry, the hated
WW	6:27–36	Promised reward for love and forgiveness
WW	6:37–42	Rewards of discipleship
Pa	6:43–46	Parables of moral productivity
Pa	6:47–49	Discipleship must survive testing: parable of the house with and without foundation
Na	7:2–3, 6–10	Healing of the centurion's slave
PP	7:18–23	Response to John the Baptist's question
PP	7:24–35	John's place in God's plan
PP	9:57–58 (–62?)	Leave behind home and family
PP	10:2–12	Disciples commissioned to extend Jesus's work
Or	10:13–15	Doom on unrepentant cities
PP	10:16	Disciples share in Jesus's rejection
PP	10:21–22	God's gift of wisdom to his own
Be	10:23–24	Beatitude: those to whom wisdom is granted
Ex	11:2–4	Prayer for the coming of God's kingdom
WW	11:9–13	God answers the prayers of his own
PP	11:14–20	Jesus's defeat of demons as a sign of the kingdom
Or	11:24–26	The return of the unclean spirit
PP	11:29b–32	The sign of Jonah and the one greater than Jonah: Jesus as prophet and wise man
Pa	11:33–36	Parabolic words of light and darkness
Or	11:39–40, 42–43	Woes to the Pharisees
Or	11:46–48, 52	Woes to the lawyers
PP	11:49–51	Wisdom predicts the martyrdom of prophets and apostles
PP	12:2–3	What is hidden will be revealed
Or	12:4–5	Do not fear martyrdom
Pa	12:6–7	Parable of God's care
PP	12:8–10	Confirmation of confession/denial of Son of Man
PP	12:11–12	God's support of the persecuted
Pa	12:22–31	Freedom from anxiety about earthly needs
Pa	12:33–34	Freedom from possessions
Pa	12:39–40	Parable of preparedness: the returning householder
Pa	12:42–46	Parable of the faithful steward
PP	12:51–53	Jesus as the agent of crises
Pa	12:54–56	Signs of the impending end of the age
Pa	12:57–59	Parable of preparedness for the judgment
Pa	13:20–21	Parable of the leaven
WW	13:24	Difficulty in entering the kingdom
Pa	13:25–29	Parable of exclusion from the kingdom
PP	13:34–35	The rejection of the prophets and the vindication of God's agent

Pa	14:16–23	Parable of the eschatological banquet
PP	14:26–27	Jesus shatters domestic ties, summons disciples to bear the cross
Pa	15:4–7	The joyous shepherd
WW	16:13	Inevitable choice between masters
PP	16:16	The end of the old era and the new age proclaimed
WW	16:17	Confidence in God's promise
Ex	17:3–4	Forgiveness within the community
Ex	17:5–6	Faith within the community
Or	17:23–37	Sudden judgment to fall
Pa	19:12–13, 15–26	Parable of the returning nobleman and rewards for fidelity
PP	22:28–30	The promise to the faithful of sharing in the rule of God

IV.   LITERARY RELATIONSHIPS AMONG THE "PRISON EPISTLES"

There are in the New Testament four letters that are claimed to have been written by Paul during imprisonment, including two that are probably not actually by Paul: Philippians, Colossians, Ephesians, and Philemon (Phil. 1:7, 13; Col. 4:3, 10, 18; Eph. 3:1; 4:1; 6:30; Philem. 1, 10, 13, 23).

2 Corinthians 11:13, with its long list of the difficulties, punishments, and tribulations through which Paul passed in the course of his apostolic work, mentions the multiple imprisonments, although that proves nothing as to how many prisons he wrote extant letters from. If the Colossian letter were to be regarded as authentic, one could infer from the writer's confidence that "the gospel is bearing fruit in the whole world" (Col. 1:6) that it is being written from prison in the world capital, Rome. Even more emphatic is the claim that the Gospel has been "preached to every creature under heaven" (Col. 1:23). But since Paul had written the Romans that he intended to go on to Spain, where the Gospel had not yet been heard, it seems more likely that this claim in Colossians represents a later (after Paul) stage in the growth of the Church.

Mention of Onesimus in Colossians 4:9 implies a historical link between the writer of this letter and that of the personal Letter to Philemon, where (v. 10) the runaway slave by that name is mentioned. It is possible, however, that the author of Colossians has built on the tradition from Philemon to tie in his work with the career of Paul. The nearest place to Colossae where there would have been a unit of the Praetorian Guard and members of the imperial establishment would have been Ephesus, though we have no direct report of Paul's having been imprisoned there. As the closest big city to Colossae, it is plausible to conjecture that Paul in fact met Onesimus in prison there. On the other hand, Acts 23–26 details a lengthy period of Paul's imprisonment in Caesarea, which was the center of Roman administration for Palestine. Onesimus could have wandered that far from Asia Minor, and Paul could have written both Philemon and Philippians from there. His hope for a return visit (Phil. 1:26) makes more sense from there than from Rome, and the imperial establishment mentioned in Philippians 1:13 and 4:22 would have been fully represented there. Further, his associates, whom he mentions in Philippians (especially Epaphroditus, whose recovery from a near-fatal illness was the immediate occasion for Paul's writing the letter, 2:25–30) is more likely to have been with Paul in Palestine as part of the delegation from the contributing Gentile churches than with him in Rome. Also, the more recent was the collection from the churches of Greece and Asia Minor, the more understandable is Paul's frequent mention of the generosity of the Philippian church (Phil. 1:5; 4:10, 18).

What seems likely, therefore, is that in Philippians and Philemon we have authentic letters of Paul, written from prison in Ephesus, or more likely from Caesarea. In all probability Colossians, but certainly Ephesians, repesent the later stage in the development of a Pauline tradition that preserves his memory and adapts his views in a later generation of the Church's life following the martyrdom he clearly anticipated in Philippians 1:19–26. Although writing under the assumed name of a historical person seems to our culture to be deceitful, even illegal, the practice was widespread in the ancient world. It was in this tradition that Paul was honored by his disciples or by others who, having chosen the Pauline view of Christianity, undertook to convey it and interpret in their own situation.

As for the literary relationship of Colossians to Ephesians, it seems that the closest kinship lies in the distinctive ethical terms and idioms: "redeem the time," "receive the inheritance," "speech seasoned with salt," which are found only here and in the parallel passages in Ephesians. Indeed, the entire structure of Ephesians corresponds with that of Colossians, except that personal greetings and instructions (as in Col. 4:7–17) are missing from Ephesians. What are we to conclude about Colossians and its place in the body of Pauline writings?

First, we can be sure that the writer was closely linked with Paul. The details of the greetings and instructions in Colossians 4 correspond remarkably well with similar references in the uncontested Pauline letters. The circumstances of Paul's imprisonment alluded to in Colossians match well with what we read in the other letters, and can easily be incorporated into a reconstruction of his career. There is an overall compatibility between what is known about Paul's journeys and missionary methods from the other letters and what is implied here. On this kind of evidence, therefore, it is impossible to make an airtight case against Paul's having written this letter.

The second line of inquiry—the linguistic and stylistic data—offers more problems for those who want to claim Colossians for Paul. There are more than a dozen words or phrases that are found only in this letter in the entire New Testament. There are at least eight expressions that appear only in Colossians and Ephesians (or Hebrews, the New Testament "letter" most pervasively influenced by Hellenistic culture). The most likely explanation for these concrete phenomena is that a writer other than Paul prepared this document in Paul's name.

This hypothesis receives confirmation if we take into account two other kinds of evidence. There is the negative evidence that the problems with which Paul deals in his undisputed letters are uniformly absent from Colossians: rivalry for leadership, the delay of the *parousia*, exploitation of charismatic gifts, circumcision, the contribution for Jerusalem, justification by faith. The positive evidence is partly conceptual and partly sociological. While Paul elsewhere limits wisdom to eschatological knowledge of God's purpose for the creation, wisdom in Colossians is drawing on intellectual traditions from Greek philosophy (1:17), even while denouncing it (2:8). It uses a unique term, "the word of Christ" (3:16), to indicate what the subject matter is to be for the Church "in all wisdom." Most striking, however, is the insistence throughout that the Christian has already been seated with Christ, the hostile powers have already overcome, believers have already been raised with Christ. The doctrine of Christ's appearing is still affirmed (3:4), but it serves no clear function, conceptually or ethically. The conclusion? Philippians and Philemon are surely by Paul, while Colossians and especially Ephesians seem to reflect a later epoch of the Church than the time of Paul.

V. AUTHORITY MODELS
IN THE EARLY CHURCH

There are at least three different ways in which the role of the authority figure is defined within the New Testament, and at least two importantly different ways in which authority functions. Not only the major historical figures who appear on the pages of the New Testament but also the later figures—whether anonymous or bearing pseudonyms of earlier leaders—must be analyzed in light of these categories if we are to comprehend the crisis of authority that sounds throughout the later New Testament books. None of the apostolic figures is a pure example of any single one of the types to be discussed, but it may be useful to distinguish these characteristics in order to become more aware of the dynamics in the struggles over ecclesial, doctrinal, and ethical authority that were apparent in the Christian communities of the decades before and after the year 100.

We have had occasion to refer several times to the basic and earliest type of leadership in the Christian tradition: the *charismatic*. Now we must consider it in greater detail. Max Weber's classic analysis of charismatic authority portrays those who possess it as natural leaders who arise in times of psychic, physical, economic, ethical, or political distress. They lack special training and are nonprofessionals. Their proposals stand in sharp contrast to the permanence and routine of bureaucratic or patriarchal structures, which have been fashioned to meet calculable and recurrent needs. Charisma lacks any abstract code and any formal means of adjudication. Its principles emanate concretely from the highly personal experience of heavenly grace and from the personal power of the leader, which derives from the gods. It rejects ties to external order, transvalues everything, calls for a break with traditional norms, and settles disputes by prophetic revelation or oracle.[1]

With the passing of the charismatic leader, the content of the discipline he demanded of his followers becomes rationalized, just as the movement he launched becomes institutionalized. The transformation of charisma into divinely sanctioned routine occurs when strata of the group, "privileged through existing political, social or economic orders, want to have their social and economic positions legitimized, and their factual powers transformed into a cosmos of acquired rights." In its altered state, what began as charisma is made to serve the acquisition and handing on of sovereign power.[2] That exercise of power may be characterized as *delegated* authority. When the transmission of authority is based on family ties, however, it represents *hereditary* authority.

The function of authority varies with the circumstances as well. Where the highest value is attached to the charismatic, supernaturally derived insights of the founder figure, the authority is experienced as the work of the spirit. The relationship with the leader is in the realm of the affections rather than in conformity to rules. Similarly, moral obligations are described in terms of human relationships rather than external ethical codes. Freedom in the spirit is the highest value, as contrasted with measuring up to standards. At the other end of the spectrum in the conception of charismatically derived authority is the valuing of clarification, codification, definition. The charismatic view of authority makes for a symbolic, affective, relational network that binds the community together. The institutional view leads to well-defined criteria for admission, for maintenance of membership, and for exclusion. Both ways of viewing the function of authority are evident in the New

[1] Max Weber, on "The Sociology of Charismatic Authority," in *From Max Weber: Essays in Sociology,* trans. and ed. H. H. Gerth and C. Wright Mills (New York: Oxford University Press, 1977), pp. 245–48.

[2] Max Weber, "Charismatic Authority," pp. 254–64.

Testament, and the consequences of these two perspectives are most clearly to be seen in the later books. Let us consider how the official and the functional models of authority are represented in the New Testament. As Weber observed concerning his "ideal types," we should not expect to find pure examples, but rather employ the models as a way of discerning similarities and distinctive features among the figures under scrutiny.[3]

Surveyed in relation to this typology, both Jesus and Paul, as represented in the various New Testament writings, match with various types. As portrayed in the Q tradition and in Mark, Jesus is a *charismatic* leader, empowered by God to call to repentance a new covenant people, to manifest power over the forces of evil, to pronounce forgiveness and acceptance to those regarded as outcasts by the official religion. His followers also match the charismatic model as they are portrayed in Mark and Q. They set out with no financial support, leaving behind families and means of livelihood, devoid of credentials except the persuasiveness of their message and the power of the spirit.

Although his cultural background and theological outlook are significantly different from what Mark and Q attribute to Jesus and the disciples, Paul too is a typical charismatic, operating as an apostle with only minimal and seemingly grudging support from the twelve, who very early must have become institutionalized in Jerusalem. His claim to authority derived from a one-time religious experience: the encounter with the Risen Lord (1 Cor. 9:1; 15:8), which he considered to have placed him on an equal footing with the other apostles. Acts 1:21–22 attributes to the Jerusalem apostles a significantly different and more elaborate set of qualifications for the apostolic office that Paul could not possibly have met: the official witnesses of the Resurrection were to be selected from those "who accompanied us during all the time that the Lord Jesus went in and out among us, beginning from the baptism of John until the day when he was taken up from us. . . ." In Luke 24:48, the risen Jesus reminds the disciples that they are "witnesses of these things," and promises to send them the Spirit so that they might be "clothed with power from on high" (24:49).

Delegated authority is presented in the Gospels in Mark 6:7–13 and parallels.[4] It is presented there as the basis for the commissioning of the disciples, with emphasis on the continuity between Jesus and his followers: "He who hears you hears me, and he who rejects you rejects me, and he who rejects me rejects him who sent me" (Luke 10:16). It appears in a more specific and personal form in Matthew 16:16–18, where Peter's confession that Jesus is "the Christ, the Son of the living God" evokes the punning response that as a consequence of this divine revelation to Peter (in Greek, *petros*) and his acknowledgment of it, he is to be the rock (in Greek *petra*) on which Christ will build his Church. This in turn is linked with his receiving the keys of the kingdom, which consist of authority to bind and loose—that is, to establish the norms for Christian behavior and the grounds of forgiveness, a promise repeated in an explicitly judicial context in Matthew 18:15–18. It is stated in Matthew 18:18 that there will be divine confirmation ("in heaven") of judicial decisions rendered by Christ's chosen deputies on earth.

Though Paul places his commissioning as an apostle on a par with that of

---

[3] Max Weber, *The Methodology of the Social Sciences,* trans. E. A. Shils and H. A. Finch (New York: Free Press, 1949), p. 93. "The ideal type . . . is a conceptual construct which is neither a historical reality nor the 'true' reality [in the sense of a Platonic ideal or paradigm] . . . It has significance as a purely *limiting* concept with which the real situation or action is compared and surveyed for the explication of certain of its significant components."

[4] Matt. 10:1–14; Luke 9:1–6, as well as the sending of the twelve in Luke 10:1–16.

Peter (Gal. 2:7–8), claiming that both Jesus and God the Father made him an apostle, the ground of his call to that office was an inner revelation: "God was pleased to reveal his Son in me" (Gal. 1:16). There was no public declaration, as in Peter's case (according to Matthew), but rather a private authorization the others could only acknowledge ("when they saw that I had been entrusted with the gospel to the uncircumcised," Gal. 2:7). His bitterly sarcastic repsonse to those who called his apostolic authority into question ("I think I am not in the least inferior to these superlative apostles!") and his extended recital of the sufferings that prove him to be qualified (in 2 Cor. 11) show that his role was fundamentally challenged by those whose Jewish credentials and whose links with Christ were allegedly superior to his. His argument then moves on (in 2 Cor. 12) to report—not surprisingly—another revelation: He was "caught up to the third heaven" and "heard things which cannot be told" (12:3). His case for apostolic commissioning therefore rests ultimately on direct divine authorization, with nothing transmitted by the earthly Jesus or his followers ("those who were of repute added nothing to me," Gal. 2:6).

In the Gospel of John, the beloved disciple has responsibility delegated to him on a basis very different from that of Peter in Matthew or of the apostles in Acts 1–2, where their original associations with Jesus are confirmed by the outpouring of the Spirit in the miraculous public event on Pentecost in Jerusalem. By the early second century, John, a follower of Jesus,[5] was understood to be the author of the Gospel that now bears his name. By the end of that century, he was declared by Irenaeus to be John, the son of Zebedee, though it is inconceivable that a Galilean fisherman could have written a document in such deceptively simple Greek, filled with subtle symbolic usage and phrases of double meaning. Even those who want to trace the Gospel and letters of John back ultimately to the son of Zebedee,[6] must acknowledge that the Gospel as we have it is the product of various editings and redactions.[7] More plausible is the proposal that the Johannine writings (excluding Revelation) were produced in a kind of Johannine School that traced its origins, or at least held up as its model, the figure of John. The important question for us is this: What sort of role model was linked with John?

On the negative side, John is critical of Peter, who abandoned Jesus in his hour of difficulty (16:23), while John remained true to the end (19:26–27). On the positive side, John's special relationship with Jesus at the Last Supper ("lying close to the breast of Jesus," 13:23) is confirmed at the foot of the cross, when Jesus proclaims John to be Mary's son (19:26–27). John's special position is noted in 18:15, where we learn that he was known to the High Priest and had access to his court, while Peter was excluded. In the post-Resurrection scenes, it is John who reached the empty tomb first (20:4–8) and who had to explain to Peter that the one who met the disciples by the lake was Jesus (21:7). John's special relationship with Jesus is one of affection, devotion, and insight, and that quality is to characterize all God's

[5] An unnamed disciple, who is mentioned as having become a disciple of Jesus (John 1:37–42) is apparently the same person who is later referred to as "the disciple whom Jesus loved," who figures prominently in events from the Last Supper (13:23–26) through the Crucifixion scene (19:25–27) and especially the post-Resurrection stories (20:2–10; 21:7, 20–23, 24).

[6] Such as Raymond E. Brown in his monumental two-volume commentary, *The Gospel according to John,* 29 and 29A in the Anchor Bible (Garden City, N.Y.: Doubleday (vol. 1) 1966 and (vol. 2) 1970), p. xcii.

[7] Brown, *John I–XII,* xxxiv–xxxix, where five stages are traced, beginning with tradition preached and taught by John the son of Zebedee, which he later organized into two successive editions of his Gospel, and which was subsequently edited in final form by one of his disciples.

people. Only in John's Gospel do we read that, while Jesus is with the Father (14:12), his presence with his followers will continue through the Paraclete, or helper (14:26). His task is to teach them, to bring to remembrance what he said to them. The Paraclete is also known as the Spirit of Truth (15:26) who "will guide them into all truth" (16:13).

The blend of love and truth is most vividly expressed in John 17, where Jesus prays that, as he departs from this world, those whom God gave him (17:6) may be joined in Godlike unity ("That they may be one, even as we are one," 17:11), that they may be sanctified through the truth (17:17), and that the knowledge of God will flourish within the community, so that "the love with which thou hast loved me may be in them and I in them" (17:26). Here we are far removed from authoritative rules, judicial pronouncements, chain of command. What we may see in the Johannine model is a very different concept of authority from that of the Pastorals, the later monarchic episcopacy, or the authoritative decision-making of Matthew 18. Here authority is the power of love, of mystical unity, of fidelity in transmission of the tradition of devotion to Christ and the spiritual discernment of his teachings. The Johannine images are not architectural (house, foundation) but organic (flock, vine).

Here, then, are the two different functional models of authority in the New Testament: (1) as decision-making, defining rules, specifying authentic and inauthentic perceptions of tradition, designating worthy persons for other authority roles within the structure; (2) as spiritual insight, discerning hidden depths of meaning within the tradition, sensitive to symbolic values, prizing most highly affectionate relationships. Clearly, Peter came to represent the first model, while John embodies the second.

By the end of the first century, the dangers inherent in all these ways of dealing with authority in the Christian community had become evident. The critical circumstances were in part internal, in part external. From without were the mounting determination of the imperial establishment to force Christians to participate in the emperor cult, and the movement from within imperially sanctioned Judaism to define Jewish life and thought in such a way as to exclude Christians. From within were the subtle pressures to social conformity, as more and more converts to Christianity were drawn from the middle and upper classes. The desire to gain social acceptance without sacrificing distinctive Christian convictions is attested somewhat later (about 150) in the apologetic Epistle to Diognetus. The writer asserts that

> Christians are not distinguished from the rest of mankind either in locality or in speech or in customs. They follow the native customs in dress and food and other arrangements of life, but their citizenship or commonwealth is in heaven,[8] so that they live as sojourners and strangers, as in a foreign land. They obey the established laws, and surpass the laws in their own lives. They love all men, yet they are persecuted by all. They are evil spoken of, and yet they are vindicated [i.e., by God]. Doing good, they are punished as evil-doers. What the soul is to the body, the Christians are to the world. As the flesh wars against the soul, so the world wars against the Christians, yet Christians love the world

---

[8] Used first by Paul in Philippians 3:20, but best known from St. Augustine's classic work, *The City of God*, which was written between 412 and 426.

and do it no wrong. As the soul dwells in a perishable body, so Christians dwell in a transitory world, looking for imperishability which is in the heavens.[9]

It is this basic outlook we have already seen in 1 Peter. A diametrically opposed view is evident in Revelation, with its denunciation of the empire as demonic and doomed. A third option is to live in quiet detachment from the world, concerned with the unity and inner purity of the community itself. It is this third stance that was adopted by the author of the Letters of John. For its ineffectiveness in dealing with the problem of authority, see the discussion of the Johannine letters.

ANNOTATED BIBLIOGRAPHY

On the history of the canon:

ACKROYD,P. R. and EVANS, C. F., eds. *The Cambridge History of the Bible: From Beginnings to Jerome.* Cambridge: Cambridge University Press, 1970.

CAMPENHAUSEN, HANS F. VON. *The Formation of the Christian Bible.* Philadelphia: Fortress Press, 1972.

On sociological method in the study of religion, and especially in the historical study of early Christianity:

KEE, HOWARD CLARK. *Christian Origins in Sociological Perspective.* Philadelphia: Westminster Press, 1980.

MOL, HANS J. *Identity and the Sacred.* New York: Free Press, 1977. The finest introduction to the identity theory of religion, which shows that individuals find identity through a group with shared values, assumptions, history, and practices.

BERGER, PETER. *The Sacred Canopy.* Garden City, N.Y.: Doubleday, 1967.

BERGER, PETER and LUCKMANN, THOMAS. *The Social Construction of Reality.* Garden City, N.Y.: Doubleday, 1967.

[9] Epistle to Diognetus, 5–6.

ROMAN EMPERORS	PROCURATORS OF JUDEA	CHRISTIAN WRITINGS

Augustus, 30 B.C.

B.C. 1

A.D. 1

10 ——

Tiberius, A.D. 14

20 ——

30 ——

Gaius Caligula, A.D. 37

Claudius, A.D. 41

40 ——

50 ——

Nero, A.D. 54

60 ——

Galba, A.D. 68
Otho, A.D. 69
Vitellius, A.D. 69
Vespasian, A.D. 69

70 ——

80 —— Titus, A.D. 79
Domitian, A.D. 81

90 ——

Nerva, A.D. 96
Trajan, A.D. 98

100 ——

110 ——

Hadrian A.D. 117-135

120 ——

130 ——

Coponius, A.D. 6-9
Ambibulus, A.D. 9-12
Annius Rufinus, A.D. 12-15
Valerius Gratus, A.D. 15-26
Pontius Pilate, A.D. 26-36
Marcellus, A.D. 36-37
Marullus, A.D. 37-41
Cuspius Fadus, A.D. 44-46
Tiberius Alexander, A.D. 46-48
Ventidius Cumanus, A.D. 48-52
M. Antonius Felix, A.D. 52-60?

Porcius Festus, A.D. 60-62?
Albinus, A.D. 62-64?
Gessius Florus, A.D. 64-66

1, 2 Thessalonians, A.D. 50-52
Galatians, A.D. 53-54
1 Corinthians, A.D. 54-55
2 Corinthians, A.D. 55-56
Romans, A.D. 56-57
Captivity Epistles, A.D. 58-60

Gospel of Mark, A.D. 68-70
Ephesians, A.D. 75-100
Gospel of Matthew, A.D. 85-100
Gospel of Luke-Acts, A.D. 85-100
1 Peter, A.D. 90-95
Hebrews, A.D. 90-95
Revelation, A.D. 90-95
James, A.D. 90-100
1 Clement, A.D. 95
Didache, A.D. 100-130
Pastoral Epistles, A.D. 100-130
Shepherd of Hermas, A.D. 100-140
Epistles of Ignatius, A.D. 110-117
Jude, A.D. 110-130
2 Peter, A.D. 130-150

Gospel of John A.D. 90-100
Epistles of John A.D. 90-110

IMPORTANT EVENTS IN EARLY CHURCH

IMPORTANT EVENTS IN JEWISH HISTORY

EARLY CHURCH	JEWISH HISTORY	Timeline
	Maccabean Revolt, 167 B.C.	
	Dead Sea Sect at Qumran, 105 B.C.(?)-A.D. 66	
	Pompey takes Jerusalem, 63 B.C.	
Birth of Jesus, 6-4 B.C.?	Herod the Great (King of Judea), 37 B.C.-4 B.C.	
	Herod Antipas (Tetrarch of Galilee), 4 B.C.-A.D. 39	1 B.C.
	Archelaus (Ethnarch of Judea), 4 B.C.-A.D. 6	1 A.D.
	Philip (Tetrarch of Iturea), 4 B.C.-A.D. 34	— 10
	High Priest Caiaphas, A.D. 18-36	
Preaching of John the Baptist, A.D. 27-29?		— 20
Ministry of Jesus, A.D. 29-33?		— 30
Crucifixion, A.D. 30-33?		
Conversion of Paul, A.D. 33-35?		
Peter imprisoned by Herod Agrippa, A.D. 41-44?	Theudas' revolt, A.D. 40?	— 40
Execution of James, son of Zebedee, A.D. 44	Herod Agrippa I (King of Judea), A.D. 41-44	
Paul in southern Galatia, A.D. 47-49?	Jews banished from Rome by Claudius, A.D. 41-49	
Paul in Corinth, A.D. 50-51		— 50
Paul in Ephesus, A.D. 52-54		
Paul arrested in Jerusalem, A.D. 56		
Paul in Rome, A.D. 60—		
Death of James, brother of Jesus, A.D. 62		— 60
	War with Rome, A.D. 66-73	
	Jerusalem and Temple destroyed, A.D. 70	— 70
		— 80
	Council of Jamnia, A.D. 90?	— 90
		— 100
		— 110
Martyrdom of Ignatius, A.D. 117?		
		— 120
		— 130

Index

Aaron, 49
Abraham, 225, 233, 274
Acts of the Apostles, 4; center of, 197–98; Church's mission in, 191–92, 195–98; conclusion of, 203–4; Jesus in, 199–200; literary preface of, 178; Paul's life in, 177, 209–14; preaching in, 198–201; progress of Gospel in, 193–94; sermon summaries of, 199; as synthesis of catholic Christianity, 195; viewpoint of, 73–74
Adam, 235, 255, 272, 273, 280–82
"Adversary," 273, 274, 340, 360
Aelia Capitolina, 119
Aelius Aristides, 30
Agape, 262
Albinus, 41
Alexander Janneus, 38, 57
Alexander the Great, 16–18
Alexandra (wife of Alexander Jannaeus), 38, 53
Alexandria, 18, 34, 130
Andrew (Apostle), 168, 296
Angelology, 62–63, 103, 124, 134, 142, 274, 330, 336, 352, 358–59
Anna, 184
Annas, 118
Anointed of Yahweh, 114
Anothen, 151
Antichrists, 356
Anti-Gnostics, 352, 352n–353n
Antioch, 195
Antiochus the Great, 20
Antiochus III, 36
Antiochus IV Epiphanes, 36–37, 117
Antipater, 38
Antiquities (Josephus), 219
Apocalypse, 99, 104, 112, 116, 124, 335–36, 339–42; birthpang imagery, 112, 276
Apocalypse of Peter, 377, 378
Apocalyptic literature, 45, 220–21, 221n; features of, 339–40
Apocrypha, 65, 384
Apocryphon of James, 354
Apokalypsis, 339
Apollos, 247, 333
Apology (Justin Martyr), 375
Apostates, 363–64
Apostles, 191, 248–49, 299–300; authority of, 300–304; death of, 112n, 117, 294–96; defined, 244; journeys of, 210; support of, 258–59
Apostleship, signs of, 244–49
Aquila, 229, 251, 297
Archēgos, 331
Archelaus, 40
Archimedes, 18
Areopagus, 197; sermon on, 179
Aristotle, 17, 305, 361
Artemis, 362
Ascension, 183
Asklepiads, 29–30
Asklepios, 29
Astrology, 24–25
Athanasius (bishop of Alexandria), 378, 381
Attis, cult of, 28
Augustus Caesar, 7–8, 16–21, 38, 40, 102, 342

Babylonian Exile, 42, 273n; return from, 35–36
Bacchae (Euripides), 27, 250–51

Baptism, 102–3, 281, 312, 357, 363; in Essene community, 62; of Jesus, 102–3, 187; and mission of disciples, 146; and Noah's Ark, 338; in Paul's Letters, 256–57, 262–63
Barnabas, 122, 171, 195, 245
Barnabas, Epistle of, 316, 317, 325
Basilides, 308
Bath gol, 102
Beatitudes, 131n, 136, 140, 189
Belial, 62–63
Bethlehem, 9
Binding and loosing, 143
Bishops, 314, 315, 339
Body of Christ, 250, 261, 281
Bread of Life, 165–66

Cadbury, H.J., 200
Caesarea, 130
Cain, 355, 359
Calvin, John, 385
Canon, Jewish, 370
Canon, New Testament, 10, 367–86; criteria of selection, 379–84; development of, 373–75; forces shaping, 368–73; number of books in, 373–75; openness of, 384–85; process of selection, 375–79; Protestant, 384–85; Roman Catholic, 385
Canon Muratorianus, 377–78
Celibacy, 250
Charis, 245
Charismatic leadership, 242–43
Christ. *See also* Jesus; as bishop, 339; return of, 351, 355; as rock, 337; sacrifice of, 354; as wisdom of God, 274–76; as Word of God, 346
Christianity, early: as charismatic movement, 242–44; diversity in, 298–99; early converts to, 6; emperor worship and, 343, 346; expulsion from, 250, 312; factions within, 262–63, 350, 351; flight of, 119–21; historical circumstances of, 117; hostility toward, 126–27, 191, 357; leadership in, 297, 299–300; locations of, 130, 210; makeup of, 297; persecutions of, 195
Christian life, 169–70, 336–39; holiness, 270–72; hospitality, 357–58; love, 262, 285, 351, 354; moral responsibilities of, 309–10, 313, 337–38, 351, 354–56; mutuality of, 338; spiritual maturity, 264–66, 337; wives to husbands, 338; women, 250–51, 315, 338
Christians: as body of Christ, 250, 261, 281; as bride of Christ, 257; as children of light, 354, 355, 356–58; as Christ's household, 285–87; as God's people, 337; as holy, royal priesthood, 337; as living stones, 337; as new flock, 167–69; as partakers of divine nature, 361; and state, 253–54; steadfastness of, 357
Chronicles, 47
Church: authority in, 350n; *charisma* in, 306; as guardian of truth, 306–9; inclusiveness of, 164, 167–69; as kingdom, 341n; leadership, 143, 297, 299–300; as locus of worship, 163; membership in, 358–59; mission of, 188–98; as mystical place, 308; offices in, 314–16, 339; structure of, 325; unity of, 170–71, 351–52
Curcumcision, 218, 231
City of God, The (Augustine), 265
Claudius, 34, 178
Cleanthes, 326